A Researcher's
Guide to
SOURCES on SOVIET
SOCIAL HISTORY
in the 1930s

A Researcher's Guide to SOURCES on SOVIET SOCIAL HISTORY in the 1930s

Edited by
Sheila Fitzpatrick and Lynne Viola

M. E. Sharpe, Inc.
Armonk, New York
London, England

Library of Congress Cataloging-in-Publication Data

A Researcher's guide to sources on Soviet social history in the 1930s
  / edited by Sheila Fitzpatrick and Lynne Viola.
     p.   cm.
  Includes bibliographical references.
  ISBN 0-87332-497-8
  1. Soviet Union—Social conditions—1917- —Historiography
—Bibliography. 2. Soviet Union—Social conditions—1917-
—Sources—Bibliography. 3. Soviet Union—Social conditions—1917-
—Archival resources. 4. Social Union—Social conditions—1917-
—Library resources. I. Fitzpatrick, Sheila. II. Viola, Lynne.

Z7165.S65R47   1989
[HN523]
016.306′0947′09043—dc20

       89-10673
       CIP

Printed in the United States of America

∞

MV   10 9 8 7 6 5 4 3 2 1

Contents

Appendices

Preface

Introductory Notes for Researchers

LYNNE VIOLA

Istochnikovedenie, or the study of sources, is a highly developed discipline in the Soviet Union. The literature on this topic is vast, and specialists are drawn from among historians as well as from archivists, bibliographers, and librarians. The study of sources in western Slavic studies, especially history, is, in comparison, rather weakly developed. Its practitioners are mainly limited to professional librarians and bibliographers. Historians seldom discuss sources in forums separate from historical writing and reviews. Yet sources are the very lifeblood of the historian's enterprise. Description and analysis of sources should be an integral part of the profession. This is especially so in the case of the study of Soviet history, an area in which nonspecialists routinely underestimate or dismiss the source base. While it cannot be denied that research in Soviet history—and particularly in the social history of the Stalin period—is a difficult undertaking, there is an abundance of different types of sources available to Western scholars. Precisely because of the political distortions, falsifications, and censorship of the Stalin years, historians must double their efforts to assess the source base critically, expand their research perspective by using different types of sources, and share bibliographic information with colleagues. Developing a proficiency in *istochnikovedenie* is a prerequisite to understanding and interpreting the nature of the data provided by the sources. An understanding of content requires an understanding of form. In fact, once a basic understanding of the nature and form of a source is acquired, researchers may find that their approach to content analysis of Soviet documents from the Stalin period is not all that different from that of other fields and other time periods. The study of sources is an integral element in the advancement of our knowledge and understanding of Soviet history as well as a requisite component in the maturation of the field.

The essays in this collection are intended partially to redress the traditional neglect of *istochnikovedenie* in Western studies of Russian and Soviet history. Some of the essays originated as papers presented at the Fourteenth Annual Convention of the American Association for the Advancement of Slavic Studies in Washington,

D.C., on 15 October 1982 in a panel entitled, "Sources for the Social History of the Pre-War Stalin Period," and later published in a special issue of *Russian History/ Histoire Russe* 12, nos. 2–4 (1985). Since that time the original papers have undergone many revisions, and new contributions have been added with the goal of providing wider coverage of source types. In addition, the editors decided to focus exclusively on sources on Soviet Russia; source coverage of the non-Russian republics is an entirely separate matter, deserving a specialized anthology. The contributions contained in this book are not intended as reference works, but, instead, as discussions of sources and presentations of bibliographic surveys. These introductory notes provide some basic information for researchers, but for general reference purposes, the reader is referred to Wojciech Zalewski's extremely helpful *Fundamentals of Russian Reference Work in the Humanities and Social Sciences* (New York: Russica, 1985). Also of use are Karol Maichel's *Guide to Russian Reference Books*, vol. 1: *General Bibliographies and Reference Works* (Stanford: Hoover, 1962) and vol. 2: *History, Historical Sciences, Ethnography, Geography* (Stanford: Hoover, 1964), which, although dated, are still useful as introductory guides to research. The Oxford bibliographer J. S. G. Simmons is perhaps more idiosyncratic in his principles of selection, but his *Russian Bibliography, Libraries and Archives: A Selective List of Bibliographical References for Students of Russian History, Literature, Political, Social and Philosophical Thought, Theology and Linguistics* (Oxford: Anthony C. Hall, 1973) contains some arcane information and a number of items that are not to be found elsewhere. Mention should also be made of the 300-page section on the Soviet Union (by Jenny Brine, the librarian of the Centre for Russian and East European Studies of the University of Birmingham, England) in Gregory Walker, ed., *Official Publications of the Soviet Union and Eastern Europe, 1945–1980. A Select Annotated Bibliography* (London: Mansell Publications, 1982). Although this bibliography formally covers only the postwar period, it is in fact also helpful for the prewar period because of its thoroughness and exceptional clarity of organization. These works may be supplemented with the annual survey articles on reference materials published in *Russian Review* and *Slavic Review*.

For detailed descriptions of specific source types and topics on the Soviet period, the reader should consult the Soviet literature on *istochnikovedenie*. Particularly useful works are *Istochnikovedenie istorii SSSR*, 2nd ed. (Moscow, 1981) and *Istochnikovedenie istorii sovetskogo obshchestva. Ukazatel' literatury* (Moscow, 1987), introductory textbooks on sources for historical research; *Istochnikovedenie istorii sovetskogo obshchestva*, 4 vols. (Moscow, 1964–1982), collections of articles on specific topics and source types with extensive bibliographic sections in each volume; *Massovye istochniki po sotsial'no-ekonomicheskoi istorii sovetskogo obshchestva* (Moscow, 1979), a discussion and survey of statistical sources by a collective of leading Soviet historians; and *Problemy istochnikovedeniia* (Moscow, 1933–1963), a serial issued annually (but now discontinued) with articles on Russian and Soviet historical sources.

Researchers should also be aware of the many guides to current publications of books and serials in the Soviet Union. These reference works form the necessary framework for research in the discipline and allow researchers to stay up to date with recent Soviet publications. The following is a listing of the basic guides:

Bibliografiia izdanii Akademii Nauk SSSR (Moscow-Leningrad, 1957–). Annual.

Ezhegodnik gosudarstvennoi tsentral'noi knizhnoi palaty RSFSR, 5 vols. (Moscow-Leningrad, 1927–1931), covering books published in 1925–1929.

Ezhegodnik knigi SSSR (Moscow, 1936, 1946–). This series continues the above publication with several time lapses. Biannual.

Knizhnaia letopis' (Moscow, 1907–). Weekly listings of new publications.

Letopis' periodicheskikh izdanii SSSR (Moscow, 1933–). From 1954, title varies with separate issues for newspapers, journals, and scholarly serials (e.g., *Uchenye zapiski, Biulleteni, Trudy*). Annual to 1954; from 1956 to 1970, published in 5-year cumulative volumes; annual from 1970–.

Novaia sovetskaia literatura po obshchestvennym naukam. Istoriia, arkheologiia i etnografiia (Moscow, 1947–). Announces Soviet Academy of Sciences publications. Monthly.

Novye knigi SSSR (Moscow, 1923–). Announces forthcoming publications. Weekly.

Obshchestvennye nauki v SSSR. Referativnyi zhurnal. Seriia: istoriia (Moscow, 1973–). Abstracts of new books. Published six times per year. (Readers should also consult the other series of this publication—in particular, the series on law and on economics.)

These works should be used in conjunction with Soviet bibliographies of bibliographies, such as the following:

Bibliografiia sovetskoi bibliografii (Moscow, 1955–). Annual.

B. L. Kandel, *Otechestvennye ukazateli bibliograficheskikh posobii* (Leningrad, 1983).

L. P. Liapunova and L. G. Khomenko, *Katalog bibliograficheskikh ukazatelei spiskov literatury, vypolnenykh za 1971–1980 gg.* (Novosibirsk, 1982).

Western bibliographies of Slavic studies include *American Bibliography of Slavic and East European Studies*, an annual published by the American Association for the Advancement of Slavic Studies and *European Bibliography of Soviet, East European and Slavonic Studies* (Birmingham, 1978–), also issued annually.

In addition to works on *istochnikovedenie* and guides to current publications, there is a large and essential body of reference literature on the periodical press. The most important general reference works for serials are:

Periodicheskaia pechat' SSSR 1917–1949: Bibliograficheskii ukazatel', 9 vols. and index (*svodnyi ukazatel'*) (Moscow, 1955–1963), which enables scholars to identify the journals that were published in their fields of interest (e.g., labor, culture, and so on). Location of these journals is facilitated by *Half a Century of Soviet Serials, 1917–1968. A Bibliography and Union List of Serials Published in the USSR*, compiled by Rudolf Smits, 2 vols. (Washington, D.C.: Library of Congress, 1968), although unfortunately this book is far from a complete list of holdings in U.S. libraries.

Gazety SSSR, 1917–1960. Bibliograficheskii spravochnik, 5 vols. (Moscow, 1970–1984), which lists central and republican newspapers (see newspaper appendices for further information on this valuable source).

Iu. I. Masanov, *Ukazateli soderzhaniia russkoi zhurnalov i prodolzhaiushchikhsia izdanii, 1755–1970 gg.* (Moscow, 1975).

The following indices (along with the aforementioned *Letopis' periodicheskikh izdanii SSSR* are also invaluable reference tools:

Letopis' gazetnykh statei (Moscow, 1936–). Weekly.
Letopis' retsenzii (Moscow, 1935–). Monthly.
Letopis' zhurnal'nykh statei (Moscow, 1926–). Weekly.

Information on periodicals published outside of the Soviet Union may be found in the following:

Abstracts of Soviet and East European Emigré Periodical Literature (ASEEPL). A quarterly from 1982.

Half a Century of Russian Serials, 1917–1968; Cumulative Index of Serials Published Outside the USSR, compiled by Michael Schatoff, ed. by N. A. Hale, 4 vols. (New York: Russian Book Chamber Abroad, 1971–1972).

Ukazatel' periodicheskikh izdanii emigratsii iz Rossii i SSSR za 1919–1952 gg. (Munich: Institut po izucheniiu istorii i kul'tury SSSR, 1953).

Soviet scholars have also published a large body of reference works devoted to bibliography of specific historical topics. These works are indispensable tools of reference. They are often published in very small editions (*malotirazhnye*) and difficult to locate. Some major collections in the U.S., notably the Slavonic Division of the New York Public Library, make special efforts to acquire these materials. In Moscow, the open-access collection (*podsobnyi fond*) of the reading room 3 in the Lenin Library carries many of these works. The following works are among the many available specialized historical bibliographies relevant to the study of the social history of the Stalin prewar years:

G. A. Glavatskikh et al., *Istoriia SSSR. Annotirovannyi ukazatel' bibliograficheskikh posobii, opublikovannykh na russkom iazyke s nachale XIX v. po 1982 g.*, 2 vols. (Moscow, 1983–84).

Istoriia istoricheskoi nauki v SSSR. Sovetskii period. Oktiabr' 1917–1967 gg. Bibliografiia (Moscow, 1980).

Istoriia predpriiatii SSSR. Ukazatel' sovetskoi literatury izdannoi v 1917–1978 gg., 3 vols. (Moscow, 1978).

Istoriia sovetskoi derevni (1917–1967). Ukazatel' literatury (1945–1967 gg.), 4 vols. (Moscow, 1975).

Istoriia sovetskoi derevni (1917–1977). Ukazatel' literatury (1945–1977 gg.), 2 vols. (Moscow, 1984–85).

A. L. Shapiro, *Bibliografiia istorii SSSR* (Moscow, 1968).

Sotsialisticheskaia industrializatsiia SSSR. Ukazatel' sovetskoi literatury, izdannoi v 1926–1970 gg. (Moscow, 1972).

Rabochii klass Rossiiskoi Federatsii, 1917–1980 gg. Ukazatel' sovetskoi litera-

tury, izdannoi v 1917-1980 gg., 5 vols. (Moscow, 1982–85).

Rabochii klass SSSR, 1917-1977 gg. Ukazatel' sovetskoi literatury, izdannoi v 1917-1977 gg., 4 vols. (Moscow, 1978).

In the Soviet Union, Western scholars carry out their research mainly in Moscow and Leningrad. The most important libraries for Western scholars in Moscow are the Lenin Library *(Gosudarstvennaia ordena Lenina biblioteka SSSR imeni V. I. Lenina)*, the State Historical Library *(Gosudarstvennaia publichnaia istoricheskaia biblioteka RSFSR)*, INION *(Institut nauchnogo issledovaniia obshchestvennykh nauk Akademii nauk SSSR)*, and the Gorky Library *(Nauchnaia biblioteka imeni A. M. Gor'kogo Moskovskogo universiteta imeni M. V. Lomonosova)*. (The library at the Institute of Marxism-Leninism appears to be off-limits to Western scholars.) In Leningrad, Western researchers work mainly at the Saltykov-Shchedrin Public Library *(Gosudarstvennaia ordena trudovogo krasnogo znameni publichnaia biblioteka imeni M. E. Saltykova-Shchedrina)* and at BAN *(Biblioteka Akademii nauk SSSR)*. The libraries of the Academy of Sciences (INION and BAN) have the best working conditions for Westerners, although the 1988 fire at BAN has led to the temporary closing of much of the library. Useful guides to Soviet libraries include the following:

Biblioteki Akademii nauk SSSR. Spravochnik (Moscow, 1959).

Biblioteki SSSR obshchestvenno-politicheskogo, filologicheskogo i iskustvovedcheskogo profilia. Spravochnik (Moscow, 1969).

Biblioteki Leningrada. Spravochnik (Moscow, 1965).

Biblioteki Moskvy. Spravochnik (Moscow, 1979).

Biblioteki RSFSR (Moscow, 1974).

Biblioteki soiuznykh respublik (bez RSFSR) (Moscow, 1974).

Biblioteki vysshikh uchebnykh zavedenii SSSR. Spravochnik (Moscow, 1964).

Putevoditel' po Gosudarstvennoi biblioteke SSSR imeni V. I. Lenina (Moscow, 1959).

Putevoditel' po Gosudarstvennoi publichnoi biblioteke imeni M. E. Saltykova-Shchedrina (Leningrad, 1962).

The strongest collections of Soviet materials in the United States are in the Library of Congress, the New York Public Library, the libraries of Columbia and Harvard universities, the Hoover Institution, and the University of Illinois at Urbana-Champaign. One of the finest Slavic reference departments in the United States is at the University of Illinois at Urbana-Champaign where the Slavic bibliographers and librarians have proved particularly helpful to historians trying to locate or order Soviet books and serial publications. The most useful finding aids for Soviet publications in U.S. libraries include *The National Union Catalog*; and *The Slavic Cyrillic Union Catalog for Pre-1956 Imprints* (Totowa, N.J., 1980), which supersedes the *Cyrillic Union Catalog* (New York, 1952). Researchers should also be aware of the catalogs of Slavic research collections issued by Harvard University, the Hoover Institution, and the University of California at Berkeley. Finally, the New York Public Library Reference Department has published a *Dictionary Catalog of the Slavonic Collection*, rev. ed., 44 vols. (Boston: G. K. Hall & Co., 1974), an essential resource for historians of the 1920s and 1930s that can be found in any research library.

These introductory notes are intended to provide an elementary base for research in the social history of the prewar Stalin years. Researchers should consult the general reference works mentioned above and the essays in this collection for more detailed information on specific sources and specialized reference works and finding aids.

A Researcher's
Guide to
SOURCES on SOVIET
SOCIAL HISTORY
in the 1930s

Introduction

Sources on the Social History of the 1930s
Overview and Critique

SHEILA FITZPATRICK

Social history has only recently come to the fore in Western Soviet studies. The bulk of the work so far is on 1917, the civil war, and the NEP period of the 1920s, for which social history sources are abundant and comparatively accessible. The Stalin period presents greater difficulties (especially after the First Five-Year Plan years, 1929–1932), since the sources are fewer than for the earlier period and their contents more heavily censored. Until recently, Western scholars usually avoided this field, partly because of data problems and partly because their attention was focused on political and economic questions rather than social ones. In the past few years, however, serious research has begun on many aspects of the social history of the Stalin period. There are a number of recent dissertations and monographs on the First Five-Year Plan period, and historians are also pushing forward into the 1930s.[1] In the process, they are acquiring expertise on different types of sources, confronting the specific problems of research in this area, and developing techniques and strategies for coping with them. It seems an appropriate time to pool our knowledge and research experience for the benefit of scholars already working in the field as well as students and scholars contemplating social history research on the 1930s.

In this volume, we have set out to cover the basic types of existing source material on the social history of the 1930s: archives, statistics, newspapers and journals, laws and regulations, directories, memoirs and biographical data. Each type of source is dealt with separately in articles by scholars with special expertise or experience in using the source. The task of my introductory article is to provide an overview of sources and resources on the social history of the 1930s, adding information on some types of sources not covered by individual contributors, and discussing the special problems and possibilities of research in this field.

Bibliography

Lynne Viola's Introductory Notes for Researchers provide the basic bibliographical information relevant to Russian historians of the Soviet period. Scholars with previous research experience in earlier periods will find that for the 1930s they need to sift larger amounts of material for relatively smaller yield. In addition to the bibliographies, it is important to master the conventions and problems of library cataloging in this field. Many Soviet books do not have individual authors and have to be cataloged in some other way—either by title or by "corporate author" (that is, under the name of the institution or organization responsible for publication). Many Soviet periodicals appear in library catalogs only under their corporate author and not under title.

The main corporate authors have hundreds of entries in the catalogs of major research libraries, and often the best way of locating works on a particular topic is to pick the most promising of the corporate authors and scan the entries. For Soviet historians, a corporate author of great importance is "Russia (1923-)"[2] (or "U.S.S.R.," "Soviet Union" or, in Soviet libraries, "Soiuz Sovetskikh Sotsialisticheskikh Respublik"). Many entries are to be found under the name of a Soviet government institution: e.g., "Russia, 1923-. Narodnyi komissariat rabochekrest'ianskoi inspektsii," "Russia, 1923-. Tsentral'noe upravlenie narodnokhoziaistvennogo ucheta," and so on.[3]

Another important corporate author—for social as well as political historians—is "Kommunisticheskaia partiia Sovetskogo Soiuza" (the same in both U.S. and Soviet library catalogs). This general heading covers regional and local party organizations as well as central party organs. Reports and materials from party congresses and conferences are entered together under the subheadings "Kommunisticheskaia partiia Sovetskogo Soiuza. S"ezdy (Konferentsii)."

Other corporate authors with many valuable entries on a wide range of topics are "Kommunisticheskaia akademiia" (for the late 1920s and early 1930s) and "Akademiia nauk SSSR." Elusive collectively authored historical works can sometimes be tracked down under "Akademiia nauk SSSR. Institut istorii (Institut istorii SSSR)."

The On-Line Catalog of the Library of Congress (OCLC) and other U.S. national on-line catalogs have so far proved disappointing resources for historians of the 1930s. None of them has done very much retrospective conversion (that is, putting its old cards on line), so they are little use for pre-1970s acquisitions. Moreover, there are intrinsic problems for Soviet historians with the search principles OCLC has built into its system. OCLC cannot handle complex corporate author headings (e.g. "Kommunisticheskaia partiia Sovetskogo Soiuza. Tsentral'nyi komitet"); and its response to a search request for a large corporate author like "Kommunisticheskaia partiia Sovetskogo Soiuza" is to inform the searcher that there are too many titles under this heading to display. The print *Dictionary Catalog of the Slavonic Collection of the New York Public Library* is still the single most useful and usable reference work for historians of the Soviet period, especially those without direct access to a major research collection.

Archives

There are three articles on archives in this volume. Patricia Grimsted (Archival Resources from the 1920s and 1930s) describes the organization of Soviet archives from the perspective of an archival expert who is able to view the system in international comparative perspective. Lynne Viola (Archival Research in the USSR: A Practical Guide for Historians) provides a users' guide to Soviet archives, drawing on her own practical experience of research on the early Stalin period as well as extensive reading of relevant Soviet archival literature. J. Arch Getty (Guide to the Smolensk Archive) discusses the most significant Soviet-period archive available in the West. This is the only archive to which Western scholars have direct, unmediated access, and it is also the only Communist party archive available to Western scholars.

Access to Soviet archives of the Stalin period (in the USSR) has been a major problem for Western scholars. There are a number of reasons for this. First, Soviet authorities have traditionally been suspicious of foreigners and tended to equate scholarly research with intelligence gathering. Second, archival access for *all* scholars, including Soviet, was severely restricted under Stalin, and has continued to be somewhat restricted in the post-Stalin period. Third, much of the political and governmental material that in most countries would be stored in the National Archives is located in the Soviet Union in Communist party rather than Soviet state archives. The rule on access to party archives (for Soviet as well as Western scholars) has been that only Communist researchers are eligible. This poses a peculiar obstacle to any liberalization of archival access for foreign scholars. Fourth, a relatively high proportion of all bureaucratic documents were classified as containing state secrets (marked *"sekretno," "sovershenno sekretno," "strogo sekretno,"* and so on) in the Stalin period. This was partly a function of the prevailing political paranoia of the time, but it also reflected a situation in which there was more bureaucratic paper in circulation than officials were willing and able to read. In practice, the classification of instructions and reports as "secret" was often just a way of flagging the documents as high-priority information. Clearly, however, it creates problems for Soviet archivists in handling foreigners' requests for archival files of the Stalin period.

In the 1960s, Soviet historians started to publish documents from the archives in special series. Publication of archival documents slowed down and virtually halted in the Brezhnev period, but Soviet scholars are now, in the late 1980s, calling for a revival of this type of publication.[4] The two major extant collections for the Soviet period are discussed in this volume by Lynne Viola (Guide to Document Series on Collectivization) and Lewis Siegelbaum (Guide to Document Series on Industrialization). This discussion is supplemented by an analysis, written for this volume by a Soviet historian, of a particular type of industrial archival document, the annual enterprise report (A. B. Bezborodov, Annual Reports of Industrial Enterprises in Soviet Archives as a Historical Source for the 1930s).

In the past, when Western scholars had little direct access to Soviet archives of the Stalin period, there was considerable speculation about the degree to which the archives might have been corrupted by purging and destruction of documents. The more exaggerated fears that the Stalinist regime undertook systematic and wholesale destruction of archival documents to conceal evidence of its crimes were always somewhat implausible, especially after the Smolensk party archive became available to Western scholars (see J. Arch Getty, Guide to the Smolensk Archive). Now, fortunately, we seem to be approaching a time when speculation about the state of Soviet archives may give way to concrete investigations by scholars who are able and willing to bring their conclusions into the public domain. In an article written for this volume, the Soviet historians V. Z. Drobizhev, E. I. Pivovar, and A. K. Sokolov (*Perestroika* and the Study of Sources on Soviet Social History) open up the subject with a frank and illuminating discussion of documents missing from the Soviet archives (for example, the 1937 population census) and types of documents such as personal letters and diaries that were never adequately preserved because of Soviet archival policies in the past. In a similar spirit of *glasnost'*, Bezborodov (Annual Reports of Industrial Enterprises) offers valuable insights into the deficiencies and distortions characteristic of this type of archival document, as well as its utility as a primary source.

In addition to the problems explored by Drobizhev and his colleagues, several other peculiarities of Soviet recordkeeping and bureaucratic practice in the Stalin period should be noted. In Stalin's Russia, as in many other countries at various times, procedures existed to keep certain instructions and even some categories of informational documents out of the bureaucratic record as far as possible. We know from the Smolensk Archive, for example, that from the early 1930s regional party organizations received stenographic reports of the plenary meetings of the party's Central Committee, but were not allowed to retain them for their files. Such material, marked "*Strogo sekretno. Podlezhit vozvratu,*" had to be returned within a few weeks to the Osobyi Sektor of the Central Committee. Thus, the Smolensk Archive does not as a rule contain reports of Central Committee plenums, although it does include records of their receipt and subsequent return.[5] They are reportedly preserved, however, in the secret section of the Soviet Central Party Archives (TsPA IML), where a few Soviet historians have recently been able to study them; and there is even talk of declassifying and publishing them in the next few years.

There are other reasons besides formal restrictions and prohibitions to expect gaps in Soviet archives of the 1930s. Official record-keeping tends to deteriorate in such circumstances as severe internal political crisis and foreign invasion. Judging by the Smolensk Archive, such deterioration occurred toward the end of 1937 and in 1938, presumably because of the impact of arrests, nonreplacement of personnel, and demoralization on the bureaucracy's ability or desire to keep records. The same is apparently true of the early wartime period. According to a Soviet historian who has looked in the Ministry of Defense archives for casualty figures for the first months after the German attack in June 1941, the true figures were not suppressed (as had been suspected), but rather were never collected adequately.[6]

Laws, regulations, and decisions
of central party organs

For years, American Sovietologists tended to focus primarily on *party* decisions and ignore the laws issued by Soviet and republican governments. This was presumably done on the assumption that the party's leadership, not the government, was the real maker of policy, though it may also have been partly a matter of convenience, the party resolutions being fewer and shorter. What might be called the classic Sovietological sources (which, of course, remain essential for Soviet historians) were Stalin's collected works,[7] the party newspaper *Pravda*, the basic collections of party resolutions,[8] and the two party journals *Bol'shevik* (now *Kommunist*) and *Izvestiia TsK* (from 1929, published under the title *Partiinoe stroitel'stvo*).

It was only in comparatively recent years that Western scholars began to make systematic use of the Soviet laws and the administrative regulations of particular government bureaucracies that are the subject of Peter Solomon's article, Laws and Administrative Acts: Sources and Finding Aids.[9] Yet, so rapidly do times change, it is already quite unnecessary to underscore the importance of state laws as a primary source, since nobody who consults this volume is likely ever to have doubted it.

In addition to the basic loci of publication listed in Solomon's article, it is worth noting that many laws and regulations were also published in newspapers. *Izvestiia*, the government newspaper, is the most reliable place to look for laws and other documents issuing from Sovnarkom, just as *Pravda* is the first place to look for resolutions and decisions of the party Central Committee and Politburo. The same principle applies to decisions and regulations of the major government agencies. Those of Vesenkha (the Supreme Council of the National Economy), the Commissariat of Heavy Industry, and other industrial ministries were most likely to be published in the industrial newspaper, *Za industrializatsiiu*. Those of the Commissariat of Agriculture and institutions like Kolkhoztsentr should be sought in the agricultural newspaper *Sotsialisticheskoe zemledelie*. Regulations of the Commissariat of Labor (until its demise in 1933) and decisions of the Central Council of Trade Unions would be carried by the labor newspaper *Trud*.

There are a number of useful contemporary and retrospective collections of laws and party resolutions on specific subjects: the economy,[10] labor,[11] collective farms,[12] trade unions,[13] the soviets,[14] youth,[15] education and culture,[16] and so on.

Government and party institutions were not the only ones to make decisions and issue regulations that are of importance to social historians. The collected resolutions of the Komsomol[17] and the trade unions[18] are of particular importance, not just because of the material they include (which has major omissions) but also because of the additional material they enable one to locate. Both the Komsomol and the trade unions were in a state of crisis and uncertainty throughout most of the 1930s. One of the consequences, in each case, was that they almost ceased to hold national conferences, and generally kept such a low profile that it is difficult to keep track of their activities and policies. But both the Komsomol Central Committee and the Central Council of Trade Unions (VTsSPS) held plenary meetings fairly regularly. The dates of these plenums can be ascertained from the document collections (respectively, *Tovarishch Komsomol* and *Profsoiuzy SSSR*). It is then possible to consult the relevant newspaper (*Komsomol'skaia pravda* in the first case, *Trud* in the second) for detailed and often verbatim reports, not only of the papers and resolutions of the plenum but also of the discussions (*preniia*).

Some general comments on the historian's use of laws are appropriate. Western Sovietologists have often assumed that all orders given in the Stalin period were carried out, since this was an authoritarian government which did not tolerate disobedience from its own officials or the population. Soviet historians of the traditional type were likely to make the same assumption, albeit for different reasons. The assumption is clearly not viable, and historians of the Soviet period should cultivate the same skepticism about implementation of laws and orders as is common in other branches of the historical profession. They should note, moreover, the frequently low standard of drafting of laws—and particularly of party resolutions—which often prevented effective communication of the Center's intentions and the practical responses required from local officials. The drafting was significantly worse in the 1930s than it had been in the 1920s.

Soviet laws and party resolutions were frequently honored in the breach rather than the observance. For example, a law limiting the size of peasants' private plots to *x* hectares cannot be taken as reliable evidence that *x* hectares was the actual real-life maximum after promulgation of the law. However, such a law does enable us to draw the inference that the actual maximum *before* the law was probably often greater than *x* hectares. Similarly, an instruction strictly forbidding new college graduates to take jobs other than those officially assigned to them does not constitute evidence that all or even most graduates took their assigned jobs. On the contrary, the stricter the prohibition, the more strongly it may be inferred that state employers were breaking the rules by offering jobs to graduates not assigned to them, and graduates were breaking the rules by taking them. The careful reader of laws and instructions should always note the penalty, if any, imposed on delinquent institutions and individuals (a low or token penalty implies that authorities may be willing to turn a blind eye on infractions). The reader should also be alert to repetition of the same instructions and admonitions over a period of years, for this implies that official policy has been implemented only partially, if at all, and that the actual situation continues to diverge from that desired by the policymakers.

Statistics

This subject is discussed in this volume by Stephen Wheatcroft. His article, Statistical Sources, provides a survey of the available statistical publications and indicates some of the problems of using them.

It is generally recognized that Soviet statistics of the 1930s are problematic. Their quantity and quality dropped off sharply at the beginning of the 1930s and remained very low until at least the mid-1950s. Comparatively few data were collected and fewer published, and what was published tended to be unreliable, presented in such a way as to exaggerate Soviet achievements and conceal shortcomings. In the postwar period, some economists in the West made valiant efforts to elucidate and clarify the often highly misleading figures issued by the Central Statistical Administration of the Soviet Union.[19] The interest of Soviet historians in demographic history increased noticeably in the 1980s, not just as a by-product of *glasnost'* but as a professional phenomenon related to growing respect for quantitative methodologies (see discussion in Drobizhev, Pivovar, and Sokolov, *Perestroika* and the Study of Sources). Our contributor V. Z. Drobizhev and his colleagues at the Laboratory of the Sector of Soviet History, State Historical-Archival Institute, Moscow, were among the leaders of this trend. Historians working in the Soviet History section of the Institute of History, Philology and Philosophy of the Siberian Division of the Academy of Sciences, Novosibirsk, also made a notable contribution to the study of Soviet demographic history, using statistical data drawn from Siberian archives.[20]

We will presumably never have statistical data on the 1930s and 1940s comparable with that available for the 1920s or the post-Stalin era. One of the reasons is that certain types of social data were simply not collected systematically in the Stalin period. With regard to collective farms, for example, the regime's single-minded preoccupation with output and procurements meant that the farms were required to provide very little information in their annual reports that was not directly related to kolkhoz production.[21] Beyond the most basic data on, for example, the number of kolkhoz households and their breakdown into male and female working-age (*trudosposobnye*) and dependent members, the reports are a meager source on the kolkhozniki themselves. For historians wishing to find out what kinds of data were actually collected on various topics in the 1930s, the TsUNKhU journal *Plan*, which sometimes provided practical instructions for statistical agents in the field, is an excellent source.

Even with regard to the better-quality statistical data of the 1920s and early 1930s, the statisticians' preoccupation with class origins and class position creates problems for the historian. For example, as discussed below, the surveys of Communists, administrative personnel, and specialists created data bases in which class origin is one of the crucial indices. But all the data collected on class must be regarded with a certain skepticism, both because of the elusiveness of the categories themselves and the material advantages to individuals associated with claiming "proletarian" or "poor peasant" origins.

Almost any social historian working with the social statistics of the 1920s and 1930s is likely to encounter problems of interpretation with the ubiquitous class analysis (*sotsial'nyi sostav*) applied in this period. At a minimum, it is necessary to spend considerable effort establishing just what was meant in a given data set by the various class and social categories.[22] But there are also inherent problems, even with the "good" statistical data of the 1920s. The 1926 population census, for example, generated a variety of problems by its rigorous Marxist framework of social analysis, which treated the urban and rural populations as two discrete social bodies, whose members in each case were classified in terms of their relationship to ownership of the means of production. It thus imposed a rigid and unrealistic dividing line between artisan and industrial workers in its analysis of the urban population. At the same time, with regard to the peasantry, it pursued the will-o'-the-wisp of class differentiation to no helpful purpose, and by comparison with other contemporary studies produced a severe undercounting of peasant *otkhodniki* to the towns.

Newspapers and journals

In this volume, a general survey of Newspapers and Journals is provided in an article by Sheila Fitzpatrick, which is supplemented by Appendix I: National, Republican and Regional Newspapers. There are separate treatments of some important types of journals by Peter H. Solomon, Jr. (Legal Journals and Soviet Social History), S. G. Wheatcroft (on economic-statistical journals in his article Statistical Sources) and Mark von Hagen (A Note on Military Sources).

The strict censorship imposed on the press and publishing in general in the Stalin period is obviously one of the historian's major problems. In the newspapers, especially national newspapers, a new rhetoric emerged in the 1930s, high-flown, boosterish, and bland. This was the period of extravagant boasting about real and imaginary achievements (Maxim Gorky even established a new "thick" journal called *Nashi dostizheniia*) and silence about disasters and failures. From the mid–1930s, large sections of the newspapers were devoted to material that many social historians (though not all) may regard as useless filler, for example photographs and formulaic biographies of Stakhanovite workers and peasants.

Two examples can serve to illustrate the problems of the Stalinist press as a source, as well as its utility. The first concerns contemporary press coverage of the 1932–33 famine. It has often been pointed out that the press was silent about the existence of a famine. This is true, though it should be noted that attentive readers of the central press may well have given their own interpretation to the sudden rash of news reports with headings like "Dying villages," "Catastrophe of agriculture," and "Hunger despite a good harvest," whose subject turned out to be Czechoslovakia, China, Poland or one of the numerous other parts of the world allegedly struck by famine in the winter of 1932–33.[23] Nevertheless, some of the regional newspapers, and to a lesser degree the central press, gave extensive and detailed coverage to famine-related problems like confrontation between peasants and officials, "disturbances," peasants refusing to go out into the fields, loss of livestock, and state punitive action against rebellious villages. These were formally attributed to the malicious actions of kulaks. But the North Caucasus newspaper *Molot*, which provided particularly good coverage of the subject, made it clear that this was not the whole story. While commenting darkly that class enemies were "trying to stage (*intsenivorat'*) a famine," the newspaper nevertheless managed to report on the same page a peasant's protest that he should not be asked to deliver seed when "you see [my] family swelling up from hunger,"[24] thus undermining the notion that the famine was "staged." A few weeks later, a correspondent admitted that "some groups of kolkhozniki had come to stare in the eyes of need"—and, moreover, underlined it in an eloquent parenthesis: "Need in the Kuban!" which was left without further commentary.[25]

The second example relates to the Great Purges. Unlike the famine, this was not the subject of a simple press cover-up, since the papers were full of detailed accounts of the process of denunciation, "self-criticism," and ultimate unmasking of "enemies of the people" in the party, government, and other elites, especially in the first half of 1937. True, these reports usually (though not invariably) stopped at the point where the "enemy" was removed from his official position, without spelling out the subsequent process of arrest, imprisonment, dispatch to labor camps, and so on. But both the national and the regional press provided a wealth of information—so far virtually unused by historians—on the Purge process, its victims, and the crimes they had allegedly committed.

When a number of prominent industrial leaders in Dnepropetrovsk were identified as probable "enemies of the people" in the raion party conferences of spring 1937, for example, the local newspaper *Zvezda* gave these discussions extensive coverage, and later followed up with a series of articles on the management of Dnepropetrovsk's major enterprises based on in-depth investigative reporting.[26] The Khabarovsk paper, *Tikhookeanskaia zvezda*, provided a fascinating story of the purges of the party leadership in the region in the spring and summer of 1937. This began with reports of criticism of the Birobidzhan party secretary, Khavkin, for mismanagement of the program of Jewish agricultural settlement in the Birobidzhan autonomous oblast; continued with Khavkin's "non-party" reaction to criticism (he stopped coming to work), and the pressure on the regional party organization to expel him applied by the central Party Control Commission's Far Eastern representative; moved on to Marshal Bliukher's compromise proposal that Khavkin be dismissed from his position as obkom secretary; and concluded with an account of the reckless behavior of the First Secretary of the Far Eastern kraikom, Vareikis (himself soon to be a Purge victim), who not only allowed Khavkin to leave the Far East with party card intact, but even lent him 5,500 rubles from kraikom funds and provided him with a reserved seat on the train so that he could go to Moscow and argue his case in person.[27]

In 1938–39, after a change of policy called a halt to mass purging, the press covered the Great Purges story again, this time detailing rehabilitations of innocent victims and describing the excesses and abuses of the drive against "enemies of the people." This kind of two-shot coverage—the "before" and "after" perspective on notable events—is characteristic of the press and other Soviet sources of the Stalin period; and scholars need to take account of it in organizing their research. A new party or government policy will obviously be decribed in basically positive and optimistic terms at the time it is introduced, although there may be some open or Aesopian argument on the issue in the press prior to the promulgation of the new policy. Almost inevitably, however, the time will come when the policy is abandoned or substantially modified; and this is when the newspapers return to the story, covering it from a quite different angle and often providing much more specific data on the subject than the first time around. (In the case of the 1937 demotions and arrests, there were actually two replays, the first early in 1938 and the second a year later, after the XVIII Party Congress.) The retrospective coverage will feature discussion of the deplorable excesses associated with past "mistakes," giving long-standing critics of the old policy the chance to air their old arguments and present the supporting evidence. For a complete picture, both "before" and "after" coverage should be compulsory reading for the historian.

Stenographic reports

Of the various kinds of publications emanating from official conferences and meetings ("*Rezoliutsii*," "*Doklady*," "*Materialy*," and so on), stenographic reports of proceedings are by far the richest sources for social historians. Their peculiar value as a source lies in the fact that they present data in relatively unmediated and unsifted form. There may be editorial intervention, but the intervention is likely to involve simple cuts rather than rewriting or recasting. Where a controversial remark is cut, its absence can often be detected because other speakers' rebuttals remain in the text. At many conferences and meetings, discussion ranges over a wide area, including the "trivial" and "local" issues that are often of particular interest to social historians. Regional party conferences, in particular, often contained frank and detailed discussion of problems. Only a few types of conference (e.g., those of Stakhanovites) were so highly formalized as to exclude this; and even at the Stakhanovite conferences, speakers were encouraged to report on their own individual experience. Appendix II (Stenographic Reports of Party, Soviet, and Other Meetings) provides lists of these publications, some complete and others comprising all relevant publications that the author has been able to identify in the catalogs of Soviet and U.S. libraries.

The stenographic reports on party congresses and conferences are particularly useful, especially those of regional party conferences (Appendix II, A.3). At the oblast and krai conferences, which were normally held in the month before a national congress or conference, rapporteurs from the Central Committee and Central Control Commission dealt unusually frankly with political and social issues, since they were speaking to a select party audience. The proceedings were often published in numbered copies and for restricted distribution (marked "*tol'ko dlia chlenov VKP(b)*" or "*tol'ko dlia delegatov*"), which means that censorship was minimal. The INION Library in Moscow, which lists a number of restricted items in its regular catalog, has the best accessible collection of republican and regional party conferences. In the West, such material is rare, though there are some items in the Library of Congress.

The range of subject matter may be gathered from the following examples. A 1929 party conference in the Far East dealt extensively with ethnic problems with Chinese and Korean workers, and the danger that the krai might fall into a "colonial" position vis-à-vis European Russia as a consequence of the First Five-Year Plan's emphasis on export of raw materials.[28] A 1933 party meeting in Kazan discussed corruption in the bureaucracy, black-marketeering, and problems associated with the introduction of a new Latin alphabet for the Tatar language.[29] Party meetings in Kazakhstan in 1933 and 1934 shed a dramatic light on the disasters of collectivization in the krai, with the actions of former party secretary Goloshchekin subjected to merciless criticism and mockery, especially by Kazakh Communists who felt that the Russian Jewish Goloshchekin had treated them as inferiors. In addition, the 1934 stenogram contains the text of a long, otherwise unpublished, telegram from Stalin to the kraikom stating that in Kazakhstan, unlike the Ukraine, Russian chauvinism remained a greater danger than local nationalism, because "it would be harder for Kazakh nationalism to link up with foreign interventionists than for Ukrainian."[30]

National, republican, and occasionally regional congresses of soviets also published their stenographic reports (Appendix II, B) which are valuable sources of social documentation. In the 1960s, the Institute of State and Law issued a seven-volume collection of resolutions, speeches, and other materials from congresses of soviets at all levels (national, republican, krai, and oblast, including autonomous republics and oblasts) for the whole of the prewar period.[31] Though it does not include stenographic reports of the proceedings, this is a very useful guide to the congresses. The extraordinarily detailed index to vol. 3, covering national (All-Union) congresses of soviets, provides a convenient overview of the range of social issues discussed at the congresses.[32] It should also be noted that personal data on the deputies to Soviet and Russian congresses of soviets from 1918 to 1936, as well as deputies elected to the Supreme Soviet in 1937, have recently been entered in computerized data bases by Soviet scholars (see Drobizhev, Pivovar and Sokolov, Appendix: Soviet Computerized Data Bases, A: 1–17).

For discussion of policy issues and impending legislation, researchers should also consult the stenographic reports of sessions of the Central Executive Committee of the All-Union Congress of Soviets (TsIK), which became the Supreme Soviet of the USSR in 1937, and its Russian counterpart (VTsIK), which became the Supreme Soviet of the RSFSR. These were published regularly in the prewar period, and are available on microfilm in some major U.S. libraries, including that of the University of Illinois at Urbana-Champaign. The stenographic reports of TsIK include proceedings of the Council of Nationalities (*Sovet natsional'nostei*).

Ad hoc conferences and meetings of various groups including trade unionists, industrial leaders, wives of industrial leaders, and women activists from collective farms also published stenographic reports, a selective list of which is given in Appendix II, C. These vary in quality as sources. The Stakhanovite conferences were the most highly ritualized, featuring reports from workers and peasants on their productivity and how it had been rewarded, jovial banter from the Politburo leaders in attendance, and many photo opportunities. The meetings of industrial leaders, in contrast, were businesslike, relatively informal, and frank.

The various women's conferences provide particularly useful data for social historians. Their stenographic reports are among the few sources of the 1930s that can be relied on to give ample and relatively realistic data on everyday life. Everyday-life (*bytovye*) problems were often considered trivial or otherwise unsuitable for public discussion in the Stalin period, but this conventional prohibition was partially lifted where women were concerned. In the case of the remarkable conferences of wives of industrial and military commanders in 1936–37,[33] improvement of living and working conditions in factories and regiments constituted the central preoccupation of the women's voluntary movement "Obshchestvennitsa" with which the conferences were associated. The delegates also gave valuable testimony on their own lives as volunteers, wives, and mothers which should not be ignored by scholars interested in the mores of the new Soviet elite and its relations with other social groups, as well as those working on problems of women and the family.

Directories and gazeteers

While many types of source material of the 1930s are noticeably inferior in quality and quantity to both the 1920s and the post-Stalin period, directories and gazeteers are at least a partial exception to the rule. There was not a marked falling-off in quality or frequency of issue, compared to the 1920s, until the middle or end of the 1930s. Moreover—somewhat surprisingly—the Soviet public was better served by this type of publication in the 1930s than it was to be at any time in the next half century. To take one of the most striking examples, it was not until after the Second World War that telephone directories came to be regarded as high-security items, and directories listing the names of individual subscribers were published only in very small editions and put on restricted access. In the 1930s, Russians living in Moscow and Leningrad had telephone directories listing the names of individual subscribers, just as they had done (if they were lucky enough to have telephones) in the last years of Imperial Russia and the 1920s. In addition, they had city directories (whose publication was also to be discontinued after the Second World War) and gazeteers.

The city directories of Moscow and Leningrad, published regularly before the First World War and during the 1920s and less regularly in the first half of the 1930s, are described by J. Arch Getty (City Directories). An appendix to his article sets out the table of contents of a representative volume. Social historians working on the two cities should note that both *Vsia Moskva* and *Ves' Leningrad* periodically included lists of street names, matching new ones to old. This renaming process, characteristic of revolutionary societies, is likely to attract more attention from historians in the future, especially in the light of current public-opinion pressure in Leningrad and elsewhere to return to prerevolutionary names of major streets and squares. For Moscow, an authoritative source on the subject is P. V. Sytin, *Iz istorii Moskovskikh ulits (Ocherki)* (3rd ed., Moscow, 1958), which not only traces the history of streets and street names but also gives a virtual house-by-house description of the physical transformation of the central city area in the Stalin period.

Telephone directories were published regularly in the 1930s, at least in the capitals,[34] under the title *Spisok abonentov Moskovskoi (Leningradskoi) gorodskoi telefonnoi seti za . . . g.* As the title implies, these were Western-style telephone directories listing individual subscribers alphabetically. (Since the war, the only telephone directories easily available to the public have listed institutions but not individual subscribers.) The directories are generally listed in library catalogs under city (e.g., "Moskva. Moskovskaia gorodskaia telefonnaia set'."). There appears to be no satisfactory run of Moscow or Leningrad telephone directories in any Western library, but the Lenin Library in Moscow has a complete collection.[35]

Gazeteers (geographical dictionaries) are another important resource for historians. They were published more or less annually for the Soviet Union throughout the 1920s and 1930s under the title *Administrativno-territorial'noe delenie Soiuza SSR na . . . g.*[36] They give information on territorial boundaries of oblasts and raions, which changed frequently as a result of repeated administrative restructuring in the 1920s and 1930s,[37] and also give the most recent figures for regional and city population, and list changes in place names. The Leningrad oblast town of Trotsk, for example, can be identified as the former Gatchina in the 1929 edition of *ATD*, while the 1930 edition discloses that, with Trotsky's fall from grace, Trotsk (formerly Gatchina) became Krasnogvardeisk. The 1930 and 1935 editions show that Zinovevsk, formerly Elizavetgrad, kept Zinoviev's name a few years longer before being renamed Kirovo, while Rykovo (formerly and subsequently Enakievo in the Donbass) was still bearing this name in 1935.[38] Historians interested in pursuing name changes of industrial enterprises should consult another source, *Alfavitno-predmetnyi ukazatel' k prikazam i rasporiazheniim Narodnogo K[omissariata] T[iazheloi] P[romyshlennosti] za 1934 (1936) g.* (Moscow, 1935 and 1937). These data throw a somewhat unexpected light on the cult (or cults) of personality in the 1930s. According to the 1937 volume, ten plants were named or renamed for Ordzhonikidze, the Commissar of Heavy Industry, in 1936, but only one for Stalin.

Memoirs and biographical data

One of the great lacunae for historians of the Stalin period has been the paucity of memoirs and the lack of reliable and systematic biographical data. Hiroaki Kuromiya analyzes the two major types of memoirs in his articles Soviet Memoirs as a Historical Source and Guide to Émigré and Dissident Memoir Literature, in this volume. Until recently, the memoir genre was not well regarded in the Soviet Union. Relatively few memoirs were published, and those that were published are difficult to locate because Soviet bibliographies do not treat memoirs and biography as a distinct category. In addition to providing extensive lists of memoirs by subject area, Kuromiya's Soviet Memoirs directs scholars to the rare bibliographical guides to memoirs in particular areas that have been published.

Under *glasnost'*, memoirs of the 1930s have started to be published in large quantities by the "thick" journals and weeklies like *Moscow News* and *Ogonek*. This is a very welcome development, since the newly published memoirs often deal with previously taboo subjects like the Great Purges and the famine. Their content was to some degree prefigured in the "samizdat" and "tamizdat" publications of the 1960s and 1970s (see Kuromiya, Émigré Memoirs), and they generally follow the conventions of that genre. As with most memoirs, the authors are for the most part intellectuals and political figures, and this situation is likely to continue, since the idea that unremarkable people's lives are worth reporting is tarnished by association with the ghostwritten memoirs of Stakhanovites from the Stalin period. One notable exception, however, is the chilling memoir of a dekulakized peasant-worker—who happened to be a brother of the poet Aleksandr Tvardovskii—published in *Iunost'*.[39]

Biographical dictionaries have been a rarity in the Soviet Union since the 1920s, when the encyclopedia "Granat" included a short *Who's Who* of party and government leaders under its entry on the USSR,[40] and the Society of Former Political Prisoners began to publish a dictionary of revolutionary biographies.[41] Nothing of the kind was published in the 1930s and 1940s. In the post-Stalin period, the Academy of Sciences published a two-volume *Who's Who* in the field of natural science and technology,[42] and a similar one-volume dictionary of Orientalists appeared in the mid–1970s.[43] With the rehabilitation of some Great Purge victims, more biographies of past political figures began to appear in the *Bol'shaia sovetskaia entsiklopediia* (3rd edition) and its supplements, as well as in journals like *Voprosy istorii KPSS*; and the Leningrad branch of the Institute of Party History published a useful two volumes of biographies of participants in the October Revolution in Petrograd.[44] Short biographies of a number of military Purge victims appeared in the journal *Voenno-istoricheskii zhurnal* in the first half of the 1960s, but efforts to publish a more systematic dictionary of military biography were thwarted. It was only at the end of the late 1980s, with the full rehabilitation of former Oppositionists and Purge victims, that large numbers of biographical articles on such persons began to appear once again in scholarly and popular journals. This presumably means that the publication of biographical dictionaries is likely to resume in the 1990s.[45]

In the West, biographical data on Soviet political leaders was systematically collected by monitoring organizations like the U.S. Central Intelligence Agency, Munich Institute for the Study of the USSR, and Radio Liberty/Radio Free Europe.[46] In the 1980s, J. Arch Getty and William Chase used *Vsia Moskva* and other sources to create a computerized biographical data bank on the 1920s and 1930s (see Getty, City Directories, in this volume). About the same time, Soviet scholars led by V. Z. Drobizhev began work on computerized data bases. Their achievement so far can be judged from the annotated listing of 34 data bases which is included in this volume as an Appendix (Soviet Computerized Data Bases) to the article by Drobizhev, Sokolov, and Pivovar on *Perestroika* and the Study of Sources. This constitutes the first detailed description of the data bases to be published either in the Soviet Union or the West.

While individual political biographical data were not published in the Stalin period, there were several surveys of "leading cadres and specialists" (i.e., political-administrative and professional elites) in the late 1920s and early 1930s whose results were published in summary form.[47] The variables in these surveys were those that Communists of the period regarded as politically crucial: social origin, social position, bureaucratic rank and service under the old regime, education, party membership. (The emphases in Soviet personnel data collection changed over time. For a useful overview of the process, see Drobizhev, Sokolov, and Pivovar, Appendix: Soviet Computerized Biographical Data Bases, A: 1–19, where the variables entered for the Congresses of Soviets of the 1920s and early 1930s [Appendix, A: 1–16] may be compared with those for the Supreme Soviet session from 1937 to the 1980s [Appendix, A: 17–19].) In the latter part of the 1930s, Soviet statistical agencies evidently continued to collect data on "leading cadres," but ceased to publish them.[48] The only major survey published in the mid- to late 1930s dealt with personnel in state and cooperative trade.[49]

Communist party membership was intensively surveyed in the 1920s,[50] most notably in the 1927 party census.[51] But such investigations were closely related to the party's preoccupation in the 1920s with the class origins of its members and the promotion (*vydvizhenie*) of working-class Communists into managerial and administrative positions. When class was dropped as a criterion for party admissions and promotions in the 1930s, systematic analysis of party membership data was also abandoned.

**Research possibilities on the 1930s:
past and future perspectives**

The Stalin era is less accessible to researchers than either the preceding period of Soviet history (1917–1929) or the post-Stalin era beginning in 1953. The basic problem is that political circumstances affected the quantity and quality of published data, as well as restricting data collection and inhibiting the dissemination of information within the bureaucracy (thus affecting the quality of archival sources). Censorship severely limited publication of data on social questions, as on economic and, most notably, political ones; and it also introduced distortion and bias in published data in order to give a more favorable picture of the society and gloss over social problems. Foreigners had very restricted contact with Soviet society during the Stalin period, so Western correspondents' reports are less useful as a source than in other periods. Contemporary émigré journals picked up some information, but its reliability is often difficult to judge. Moreover, the journals' contacts inside the Soviet Union were precarious and tended to diminish in the course of the 1930s.

The post-Stalin thaw opened up new sources of information on the Stalin period, especially in the early 1960s. Memoirs were published, both officially by Soviet journals and publishing houses and in unofficial *samizdat* and *tamizdat* form. Soviet historians gained greater access to archives of the Stalin period, and the range and scholarly quality of their publications improved. Regular and detailed publication of statistics resumed in the mid-1950s, and this change brought some retrospective publication of statistical data, including information from the 1939 population census which appeared for the first time when the 1959 census results were published. As Soviet openness to the outside world increased, it became first possible and later routine for historians from the West to make serious research trips to the Soviet Union, and, in many cases, to establish more or less normal relations with their Soviet counterparts. Nevertheless, Western scholarly publications were generally either ignored in Soviet professional journals or criticized as "bourgeois falsification."

Many problems remained for Western researchers, even in the 1970s and the first half of the 1980s. Archival access was still restricted, especially for the Stalin period. Research in Soviet libraries became easier in some ways, but Western scholars still found needed materials missing from the public catalogs or unavailable on request, particularly at the Lenin Library in Moscow. Some types of material like regional and enterprise newspapers were very difficult to obtain.[52] Soviet scholars might share data with Western scholars on an informal basis, but they were uneasy about doing so publicly; and collaborative Soviet/Western scholarly projects were inhibited by a variety of institutional and attitudinal obstacles. Systematic oral history projects could not be undertaken by Western scholars in the Soviet Union, and indeed were rarely conducted even by Soviet scholars. For access to Soviet dissertations, which can be important guides to primary sources that are not available for foreign scholars' use, Western historians were required to obtain special permission from their official Soviet advisors.

In the mid-1980s, *glasnost'* brought further changes. Historical revisionism came in the first instance from novelists and journalists, not from professional historians. Important works in the peculiarly Soviet genre of the politically daring historical novel began to appear in the "thick" journals. Those on the 1930s included B. Mozhaev's *Muzhiki i baby* (*Don*, 1987, nos. 1–3), on the collectivization drive of 1929–30; N. Skromnyi's *Perelom* (*Sever*, 1986, nos. 10–12), on the deportation of kulaks and their resettlement in Kazakhstan; Mikhail Alekseev's *Drachuny* (Moscow, 1982), on collectivization and the famine; A. Rybakov's *Deti Arbata*, a panorama of political and social life in the early to mid-1930s seen from the standpoint of a young Komsomol; and Iurii Trifonov's *Ischeznovenie* (*Druzhba narodov*, 1987, no. 1), on the Great Purges. These novels cannot be read primarily as works of fiction. They are intended as testimonies about Soviet history. Some (for example, the works by Alekseev and Trifonov) are based on personal childhood experience. Others are at least partly based on historical research using published, archival, and oral history sources.[53]

Soviet historians have been harshly criticized for lagging behind the novelists and journalists in the rewriting of Soviet history. At a conference of historians and writers held in Moscow in April 1988, the writer V. P. Astafev said that "the majority of historians . . . do not have the right to use such a sacred word as truth. They have lost the right to that by their deeds, their duplicity. They need to repent and cleanse themselves (*ochistitsia*)."[54] The historians at the meeting admitted that their profession had had a dismal record since the 1920s, that it had been "deformed" in the Stalin and Brezhnev periods, and that it now found itself in a situation of crisis.[55] So strong was the consensus of approval at the meeting for the novelists' portrayal of "the truth (*pravda*)" about Soviet history, in contrast to the "non-truth (*nepravda*)" written by Soviet historians in the past, that only one historian felt able even to hint that there might be potential problems in confusing the genres of history and belles-lettres.[56]

For the time being, the thrust of historical revisionism in the Soviet Union is toward discrediting and overthrowing the old *nepravda* about the Stalin period. Formerly taboo topics like the famine of 1932–33 and the Great Purges have come to the fore, largely through the efforts of the press and the publication of exposé articles, memoirs, and historical novels. A number of well-regarded historians have contributed to this process, notably in such forums as the *"Pravda* Fridays,"[57] where they answer interviewers' questions on major topics of historical controversy like collectivization, and try to separate myth from reality.

The myths of Soviet history, it should be said, are not necessarily Stalinist or of official provenance. There were always unofficial myths—the antitheses, so to speak, of the official ones—that circulated within the intelligentsia and among broader strata of the population. While these may be closer to the truth than the old official myths, historians still need to treat them with caution unless there is solid documentary evidence to support them. One of the problems that Soviet scholars have to confront, as Professor Drobizhev and his colleagues remind us in this volume, is that the Soviet public is currently more interested in seeing old official myths turned on their heads than reading critical analyses of evidence and documentation. The internal monologues Rybakov wrote for Stalin in his *Deti Arbata* are widely perceived as historical "truth" because they are the antithesis of the old "non-truth." Winston Churchill's figure of ten million peasant victims of collectivization is cited in the Soviet press as if it were an established and documentable fact,[58] rather than Churchill's report of an enigmatic remark Stalin made to him more than a decade after the event.

Still, it is cheering (up to a point) to find Western writers cited as authorities on controversial issues of Soviet history, after so many decades of different treatment. From the standpoint of Western historians, the recent Soviet change of attitude toward Western scholarship[59] is one of the most notable products of *glasnost'*. The old pejorative label of "bourgeois falsifier" has been dropped; and works like Stephen Cohen's biography of Bukharin, which only a few years ago might have been confiscated at customs as "anti-Soviet propaganda," are currently in process of translation for Soviet publication.[60] There is great eagerness among Soviet scholars for interchange, discussion, and comparative projects with their Western counterparts. In a striking departure from previous Soviet conventions, the Soviet historian Danilov concluded his discussion on the 1932–33 famine in one of the *"Pravda* Fridays" with a tribute to the work of British and American scholars S. G. Wheatcroft, R. W. Davies, Barbara Anderson, and Brian Silver.[61] Articles by Western scholars, and even Western critiques of Soviet scholarship, are being solicited by Soviet historical journals. Indeed, this volume on sources is itself an example of the new possibilities for U.S.–Soviet collaboration. Our Soviet contributors have given us additional information and insights based on their own formidable expertise, and, moreover, refrained from the kind of self-censorship about "difficult questions" of Soviet scholarly life that has sometimes been characteristic of such collaborations. We are grateful to them for treating their Western scholarly readers as equals and trying to find a common language of discourse.

At the time of writing (February 1989), it is widely assumed that *glasnost'* will mean substantially greater access to materials for both Western and Soviet historians in the future. In Soviet libraries, the old concept of *spetskhran* (restricted access to published materials deemed politically sensitive or otherwise unsuitable) has fallen into disrepute; and in September 1988, the Lenin Library announced that it was opening to the public all but 500 of the 10,000 volumes previously on restricted access.[62] In the archives, Soviet scholars found their access much improved, though this did not apply to all scholars in all archives. Western scholars were being told at the beginning of 1989 that they would have much greater access to state archives like TsGAOR and TsGANKh in the future, and that they would even be able to use *opisi*. With regard to the 1930s, however, this has as yet been only partially confirmed by the actual experience of American scholars and graduate students. Some IREX participants working in Moscow in 1987–88 were still encountering archival problems of the familiar type. Others, particularly graduate students on the junior exchange, report striking successes in their research in archives and elsewhere, and seem to feel that the new era has finally dawned.

To sum up: this is an extremely propitious moment in Western and Soviet scholarship on Soviet social history. The opportunity exists for a significant breakthrough in many areas, including access to sources. The more we know about the sources and their peculiarities and problems, the easier it will be for us—Western *and* Soviet scholars—to take advantage of the new research opportunities and continue the development and improvement of scholarship on the social history of the 1930s.

Notes

1. For practical reasons, we have limited our systematic coverage to Russia, the RSFSR, and Russian-language sources. The vast subject of sources on the non-Russian republics and nationalities, especially in languages other than Russian, must await the attention of other scholars. For two articles on non-Russian sources, see Ronald Grigor Suny, "History from the Outside In: Local and Non-Russian Perspectives—The Case of Georgia," *Russian History/Histoire russe* 12:2–4 (1985), 349–54, and George Liber, "Social History of the Ukraine in the Prewar Period: A Select Bibliography," *ibid.*, 355–65.

2. This was the way the Library of Congress identified the USSR until the early 1980s, when it switched to the classification of "Soviet Union," not only for the USSR but also for prerevolutionary Russia. The change was controversial, and the library is currently considering the possibility of changing back again to "Russia."

3. In Soviet libraries, the equivalent category is "Soiuz Sovetskikh Sotsialisticheskikh Respublik. Narodnyi komissariat . . ." or, in the case of government institutions of the Russian Republic, "Rossiiskaia Sovetskaia Federativnaia Sotsialisticheskaia Respublika. Narodnyi komissariat prosveshcheniia."

4. See, for example, comments by V. I. Startsev, *Voprosy istorii*, 1988, no. 3, 38; Iu. S. Kukushkin, *Voprosy istorii*, 1988, no. 6, 68; Academician S. L. Tikhvinskii, *Istoriia SSSR*, 1988, no. 1, 121.

5. See Smolensk Archive, WKP 191, 2, for the letter from Poskrebyshev, head of the Special Sector of the Central Committee, accompanying the numbered copy of the stenographic report of the December 1935 plenum of the Central Committee sent to the Elnia raikom of the party in January 1936. See also *ibid.*, p. 4, for the Elnia raikom's covering letter

when it returned the report to Moscow on 14 March 1936.

6. Statement by A. G. Khorkov, *Istoriia SSSR*, 1988, no. 4, 16.

7. I. V. Stalin, *Sochineniia*, 13 vols. (Moscow, 1949–51). These volumes cover the period up to January 1934. Publication was suspended and never resumed in the Soviet Union after Stalin's death. In the 1960s, the Hoover Institution sponsored the publication of three additional volumes, covering the period 1934–53: I. V. Stalin, *Sochineniia*, ed. Robert H. McNeal, vols. 1 (XIV) to 3 (XVI) (Stanford, 1967).

8. These were originally published under the title of *VKP(b) v rezoliutsiiakh i reshen- iiakh s"ezdov, konferentsii i plenumov TsK*, later as *KPSS v rezoliutsiiakh i resheniiakh s"ezdov, konferentsii i plenumov TsK*, 8th ed. (Moscow, 1970–); 9th ed. (Moscow, 1983–). For an English-language guide and translations of party resolutions, see Robert H. McNeal, *Guide to the Decisions of the Communist Party of the Soviet Union, 1917–1967* (Toronto: University of Toronto Press, 1972) and *idem.*, *Resolutions and Decisions of the Communist Party of the Soviet Union, 1898–1967*, 4 vols. (Toronto: University of Toronto Press, 1980– 83).

9. The great exception is, of course, the English historian E. H. Carr, who always worked with the collected laws of the Soviet Union (*Sobranie zakonov i rasporiazhenii raboche-krest'ianskogo pravitel'stva SSSR*) close to hand. But, as scholars of the older generation may remember, Carr was often criticized for his choice of sources. In the 1950s, many Sovietologists felt that his extensive use of government in addition to party sources (and his neglect of émigré publications) were signs of a credulous and fellow-traveling attitude to the Soviet Union.

10. *Resheniia partii i pravitel'stva po khoziaistvennym voprosam* (Moscow, 1967–). An earlier publication, M. Savelev and A. Poskrebyshev's *Direktivy VKP(b) po khoziaistvennym voprosam* (Moscow-Leningrad, 1931), is particularly useful because it contains a number of resolutions not included in later collections, as well as giving information that is not available from other sources such as the name of the Central Committee or Politburo rapporteur(s), on the basis of whose report a particular resolution was passed.

11. *Sbornik vazhneishikh zakonov i postanovlenii o trude* (Moscow, 1958).

12. *Istoriia kolkhoznogo prava. Sbornik zakonodatel'nykh materialov SSSR i RSFSR 1917–1958 gg.*, 2 vols. (Moscow, 1958–59); *Kollektivizatsiia sel'skogo khoziaistva. Vazhnei- shie postanovleniia Kommunisticheskoi partii i sovetskogo pravitel'stva, 1917–1935* (Mos- cow, 1957).

13. *KPSS o profsoiuzakh: sbornik* (Moscow, 1974).

14. *KPSS o rabote sovetov: sbornik dokumentov* (Moscow, 1959).

15. *KPSS o Komsomole i molodezhi: sbornik rezoliutsii i reshenii s"ezdov, konferentsii i postanovlenii TsK 1917–1961* (Moscow, 1962).

16. *KPSS o kul'ture, prosveshshenii i nauke: sbornik dokumentov* (Moscow, 1963).

17. *Tovarishch Komsomol. Dokumenty s"ezdov, konferentsii i plenumov TsK VLKSM 1918–1968*, vol. 1 (1918–41), (Moscow, 1969); *Slavnyi put' Leninskogo Komsomola (v dvukh tomakh)*, vol. 1 (1903–37), vol. 2 (1938–), (Moscow, 1974).

18. *Profsoiuzy SSSR. Dokumenty i materialy*, 5 vols. (Moscow, 1963–73), of which vol. 2 (1963) covers the 1930s.

19. See, for example, Naum Jasny's useful analysis of the first statistical handbook issued in the 1950s, *The Soviet 1956 Statistical Handbook: A Commentary* (East Lansing, Mich.: Michigan State University Press, 1957), relevant to historians because this handbook included a good deal of data on the 1930s. For other critiques of Soviet statistics by Jasny, see the bibliography in *To Live Long Enough. The Memoir of Naum Jasny, Scientific Analyst*, ed. and with biographical commentaries by Betty A. Laird and Roy D. Laird (Lawrence, Kans.: University of Kansas Press, 1976).

20. See, for example, *Urbanizatsiia sovetskoi Sibiri*, chief editor V. V. Alekseev (Novosi- birsk, 1987), N. Ia. Gushchin, *Sibirskaia derevnia na puti k sotsializmu (Sotsial'no- ekonomicheskoe razvitie sibirskoi derevni v gody sotsialisticheskoi rekonstruktsii narodnogo*

khoziaistva, 1926–1937 gg.) (Novosibirsk, 1973), A. S. Moskovskii and V. A. Isupov, *Formirovanie gorodskogo naseleniia Sibiri (1926–1939 gg.)* (Novosibirsk, 1984), and V. V. Alekseev and V. A. Isupov, *Naselenie Sibiri v gody Velikoi Otechestvennoi voiny* (Novosibirsk, 1986). The last two works have respectively 32 and 83 statistical tables, largely based on archival and census material, on topics that include territorial sources of urban in-migration, age and sex breakdown of migrants, mortality and birth rates of urban and rural population, marriage and divorce, and ethnic composition of the population.

It should be noted that Alekseev's team is referred to as "the Sverdlovsk group" in Drobizhev, Pivovar, and Sokolov's article in this volume. This is because part of the old Novosibirsk group has recently moved to the Academy of Science's new Institute of History and Archeology of the Urals in Sverdlovsk, of which Professor V. V. Alekseev is director.

21. The meager published data on these questions will be found mainly in *Kolkhozy vo vtoroi stalinskoi piatiletke. Statisticheskii sbornik* (Moscow-Leningrad, 1939) and *Proizvoditel'nost' i ispol'zovanie truda v kolkhozakh vo vtoroi piatiletke* (Moscow-Leningrad, 1939), both published by Gosplanizdat. Note that the title of the first volume is incorrectly listed (without the word *"stalinskoi"*) in E. A. Mashikhin and V. M. Simchera, *Statisticheskie publikatsii v SSSR. Bibliograficheskii ukazatel'* (Moscow, 1975), 107. On kolkhoz annual reports as a data source, see M. A. Vyltsan, "Svodnye godovye otchety kolkhozov za 1935–1939 gg. kak istoricheskii istochnik," and Iu. V. Arutiunian, V. P. Danilov, B. I. Zhuchkov, "Svod otchetov kolkhozov strany za period otechestvennoi voiny," both in *Istoricheskii arkhiv*, 1962, no. 6, and V. I. Zvavich, "Godovye otchety kolkhozov za 1932–1940 gg. i ikh razrabotki kak istoricheskii istochnik," in *Problemy istorii SSSR* (Moscow, 1973).

22. The clearest and most systematic exposition, giving the class status denoted by dozens of specific occupations in analysis of Communist party statistics, was given in a publication of the Central Committee's Statistical Department, *Slovar' zaniatii lits naemnogo truda. Posobie dlia rabotnikov iacheek i komitetov VKP(b) pri opredelenii roda zaniatii kommunistov i prinimaevykh v partiiu* (Moscow, 1928). The occupational and class categories used in the 1926 population census are discussed briefly in *Vsesoiuznaia perepis' naseleniia 17 dek. 1926 g. Kratkie svodki*, vol. 8 (Moscow, 1928), v–xi, and in more detail in *Programmy i posobiia k razrabotke Vsesoiuznoi perepisi naseleniia 1926 g.*, vyp. III: "Klassifikatsiia zaniatii." A guide to the occupational classifications used in the 1939 census is provided in *Sistematicheskii slovar' zaniatii. Posobie dlia razrabotki materialov Vsesoiuznoi perepisi naseleniia 1939 g.* (Moscow, 1957).

23. See, for example, *Sotsialisticheskoe zemledelie*, 12 November 1932, 4; 16 November 1932, 4; 28 November 1932, 1; 17 December 1932, 4. *Izvestiia*, 17 February 1933, 3, also developed this theme, publishing reports on Ireland, India, the African colonies, Japan, Germany, and the Balkans under the general heading "In capitalist countries, the agricultural crisis is destroying the peasant farm and setting adrift millions of ruined peasants and farmers throughout the world."

24. *Molot* (Rostov), 10 March 1933, 1.

25. *Molot*, 28 March 1933, 2.

26. There are almost daily reports in *Zvezda* (Dnepropetrovsk) through April and May 1937. See also articles in *ibid.*, 5 July 1937, 2; 27 July 1937, 2; 3 August 1937, 2.

27. *Tikhookeanskaia zvezda*, 9 May 1937, 3; 16 October 1937, 3; 17 October 1937, 3.

28. *IX Dal'ne-vostochnaia kraevaia partiinaia konferentsiia. Stenograficheskii otchet. 22 fevralia–1 marta* (Khabarovsk, 1929).

29. *Ob"edinennyi plenum [Tatarskogo] O[blastnogo] K[omiteta] i O[blastnoi] K[ontrol'-noi] K[omissii] VKP(b) (19–23 fevralia 1933 g.). Stenograficheskii otchet* (Kazan, 1933).

30. *Shestoi plenum Kazakskogo kraevogo komiteta VKP(b), 10–16 iiulia 1933 goda. Stenograficheskii otchet* (Alma-Ata, 1936) and *VIII Kazakhstanskaia kraevaia konferentsiia VKP(b), 8–16 ianvaria 1934 g. Stenograficheskii otchet* (Alma-Ata, 1935). Stalin's telegram,

which was read out by lst Secretary Mirzoian, is in *VIII Kazakhstanskaia kraevaia konferentsiia*, 222.

31. *S"ezdy Sovetov Soiuza SSR, soiuznykh i avtonomnykh sovetskikh sotsialisticheskikh respublik*. Sbornik dokumentov, 7 vols. (Moscow, 1959–65). Editors: F. I. Kalinychev, V. M. Kuritsyn, S. S. Orlov, S. L. Ronin, and K. U. Chernenko.

32. (Moscow, 1960). The index is 116 pages long.

33. *Vsesoiuznoe soveshchanie zhen khoziaistvennikov i inzhenerno-tekhnicheskikh rabotnikov tiazheloi promyshlennosti. Stenograficheskii otchet* (Moscow, 1936) and *Vsesoiuznoe soveshchanie zhen komandnogo i nachal'stvuiushchego sostava RKKA. 20–23 dekabria 1936 g. Stenograficheskii otchet* (Moscow, 1937).

34. Moscow telephone directories were issued in 1926, 1928, 1930, 1932, 1934, 1935, 1937, and 1939. Leningrad telephone directories appeared in 1932, 1934, and 1937 (incomplete list).

35. Unfortunately, this collection has not always been accessible to Western scholars. For an account of one scholar's problems of access, see Sheila Fitzpatrick, "The Impact of the Great Purges on Different Elite Strata: A Case Study from Moscow Telephone Directories for 1937 and 1939," paper delivered at 20th National Convention of the American Association for the Advancement of Slavic Studies, Honolulu, November 1988, footnote 3.

36. New editions of *Administrativno-territorial'noe delenie Soiuza SSR* appeared in 1929, 1930, 1931, 1932, 1934, 1935, 1938, 1939, 1940, and 1941. (The last four volumes were entitled *Administrativno-territorial'noe delenie soiuznykh respublik na . . . g.*) If volumes were published for 1933, 1936, and 1937, the author has been unable to trace them. A similar series for the Russian Republic, *Administrativno-territorial'noe delenie RSFSR*, began publication in 1940.

37. A useful introduction and handbook on this subject is V. Z. Drobizhev, I. D. Kovalchenko, and A. V. Muravev, *Istoricheskaia geografiia SSSR* (Moscow, 1973).

38. *Administrativno-territorial'noe delenie* (1929), 63–65; *ibid.* (1930), 65–66; *ibid.* (1935), 463.

39. Ivan Tvardovskii, "Stranitsy perezhitogo," *Iunost'*, 1988, no. 3, 10–30.

40. *Entsiklopedicheskii slovar' Russkogo bibliograficheskogo instituta Granat*, 7th ed., vol. 41 (parts 1–3, Moscow, 1925–29): supplement to "SSSR" entry: "Deiateli Soiuza Sovetskikh Respublik." Some of these biographies have been translated in Georges Haupt and Jean-Jacques Marie, compilers, *Makers of the Russian Revolution* (Ithaca: Cornell University Press, 1974).

41. *Deiateli revoliutsionnogo dvizheniia v Rossii: bio-bibliograficheskii slovar'. Ot predshestvennikov dekabristov do padeniia tsarizma*, ed. V. Vilenskii-Sibiriakov, 5 vols. (Moscow, 1927–34). Publication was interrupted when the society fell into disrepute and was dissolved in 1935. Vol. 5 (2 parts), which deals with Social-Democrats, got no further in the alphabet than "Gm."

42. *Biograficheskii slovar' deiatelei estestvoznaniia i tekhniki*, 2 vols. (Moscow, 1958–59).

43. S. D. Miliband, *Biobibliograficheskii slovar' sovetskikh vostokovedov* (Moscow, 1975).

44. *Geroi Oktiabria. Biografii aktivnykh uchastnikov podgotovki i provedeniia Oktiabr'skogo vooruzhennogo vosstaniia v Petrograde* (Leningrad, 1967). A smaller and inferior volume on participants in the revolution in the Moscow armed uprising of October appeared under the same title: *Geroi Oktiabria* (Moscow, 1967).

45. The recent appearance of a two-volume dictionary of military biography, *Geroi Sovetskogo Soiuza* (Moscow, 1987–8?), containing 12,632 entries, was discussed in an article in *Pravda*, 11 January 1989, p. 6.

46. For historians working on the 1930s, the most useful collections include B. Lewytskyj, *The Soviet Political Elite: Brief Biographies* (Stanford: Hoover Institution, 1970) and

Who was Who in the USSR: A Biographic Directory containing 5,015 Biographies of Prominent Soviet Historical Personalities (Munich: Institut zur Erforschung der UdSSR, 1972).

47. Notably Ia. M. Bineman, *Kadry gosudarstvennogo i kooperativnogo apparata SSSR* (Moscow, 1930) and *Sostav rukovodiashchikh rabotnikov i spetsialistov Soiuza SSR* (Moscow, 1935), a publication of TsUNKhU, based on a survey of over 850,000 senior officials and specialists conducted in November 1933.

48. A survey of "leading cadres and specialists" made by the Central Statistical Administration in 1940 was reportedly published as *Sostav spetsialistov s zakonchennym vysshim obrazovaniem na 1 ianvaria 1940 g.*, vyp 1 and 2 (Moscow, 1940) (see citation in *Massovye istochniki po sotsial'no-ekonomicheskoi istorii sovetskogo obshchestva* [Moscow, 1979], 126), but I have been unable to locate this volume in any Western or Soviet library. An extract from TsSU's report on the survey was published in *Industrializatsiia SSSR 1938–1941 gg. Dokumenty i materialy* (Moscow, 1973), 269–76.

49. *Itogi torgovoi perepisi 1935 g.*, vyp. 2: *Kadry sovetskoi torgovli* (Moscow, 1936).

50. For a survey of this body of source material, see Peter Gooderham, "Party Publications and Other Sources on Cadres in the 1930s," *Russian History/Historie russe* 12:2–4 (1985), 283–92. Gooderham is particularly informative on data on the Leningrad party organization.

51. The results of the census were published in *Vsesoiuznaia partiinaia perepis' 1927 goda. Osnovnye itogi perepisi* (Moscow, 1927) and *Sotsial'nyi i natsional'nyi sostav VKP(b). Itogi Vsesoiuznoi partiinoi perepisi 1927 g.* (Moscow, 1928). *Kommunisty v sostave apparata gosuchrezhdenii i obshchestvennykh organizatsii* (Moscow, 1929) elaborated the results with reference to Communists holding official and managerial positions. For other quantitative analyses of party membership, see the series of publications issued by the Central Committee's Statistical Department under the title *R.K.P.(b)* [Later, *V.K.P.(b)*] *v tsifrakh* (9 vols., 1924–29), which investigated such topics as Communists in the armed forces, women Communists, and party saturation of the industrial working class.

52. The Lenin Library created extraordinary problems for Western scholars in the 1970s, perhaps unintentionally, by sending its newspaper collection to Khimki, a northern suburb of Moscow which is off-limits to foreigners.

53. On internal evidence, Mozhaev's *Muzhiki i baby* makes extensive use of contemporary newspapers, and he cites an archival source as well as various published sources in his afterword to the novel (*Don*, 1987, no. 3, 99–106). Skromnyi does not identify his sources, but parts of his novel read very much as if they were based on archival material (see, for example, the okrug party meeting described in the first section [*Sever*, 1986, no. 10, 52–64]).

54. *Voprosy istorii*, 1988, no. 6, 33.

55. See comments of Kasianenko, Chubarian, and Iskenderov in *ibid.*, 15, 48–49, 50.

56. This was V. A. Shishkin, who suggested that the history/fiction genre might be liable to sensationalism and distortion. But the instance he cited was trivial, and from a minor literary work. *Voprosy istorii*, 1988, no. 6, 103.

57. The *"Pravdinskie piatnitsy"* started appearing in 1988 under the editorship of G. L. Smirnov, Director of the Institute of Marxism-Leninism under the Central Committee of the CPSU. Topics have included collectivization and the famine (with V. P. Danilov and N. V. Teptsov), *Pravda*, 16 September 1988, 3; Stalin and the struggles with Left and Right Oppositions, and the nature of Stalinism (with G. Bordiugov and V. Kozlov), *Pravda*, 30 September 1988, 3, and 3 October 1988, 3; Stalinist industrialization and the alternatives (with V. S. Lelchuk and L. P. Kosheleva), *Pravda*, 21 October 1988, 3.

58. See, for example, Roy Medvedev, "The Suit against Stalin," *Moscow News*, 1988, no. 48 (Dec. 4–11), 8. Churchill's figure, to be sure, is by no means the least reliable of the data cited in this woolly attempt by Medvedev to quantify Stalin's victims.

59. See the roundtable discussion "Contemporary non-Marxist historiography and Soviet historical science" in *Istoriia SSSR*, 1988, no. 1. The change is even more marked in face-to-

face contacts between Soviet and Western historians.

60. An excerpt from Stephen F. Cohen's *Bukharin and the Bolshevik Revolution. A Political Biography, 1888-1938* (New York, 1973) has already appeared under the title of "Duumvirat: Bukharin i Stalin," with a full-page introduction by Cohen, in *Ogonek*, 1988, no. 45, 29-30.

61. *Pravda*, 16 September 1988, 3.

62. Reported in *The New York Times*, 3 September 1988, 4. It was stated that only works of "anti-Semitic and Zionist content, those promoting ethnic conflict, and pornography" would remain in *spetskhran*.

Archival Resources from the 1920s and 1930s

Soviet Archival Developments and Reference Aids for the Social Historian

PATRICIA KENNEDY GRIMSTED

Recent calls for more *glasnost'* about the history of Soviet society suggest new possibilities for serious scholarship and more honest publications in the USSR about events and developments during the tumultuous decades of the 1920s and 1930s. But if there is to be real *perestroika* in historical scholarship, there will necessarily have to be fresh archival research and a more careful examination of the remaining archival documentation from those years. Several published Western commentaries on the recent Soviet discussion of history are likewise forced to conclude that until historians start turning seriously to the archives, many of the pending historical controversies will remain unresolved.[1]

Public discussion in the spirit of *glasnost'* has extended to archival problems, and archival leaders have been involved in the controversy about the study of history, as well as about pending plans for archival reform.[2] Considerable alarm has been raised "about the state of archival affairs in the country," as, for example, in an open letter to the newspaper *Sovetskaia kul'tura*. In the letter, the Scholarly Council of the Moscow State Historico-Archival Institute (MGIAI) complains that although archives are "[s]upposed to be recognized as a center of culture and science, during

This article results from research experience in the Soviet Union over the last twenty-five years, most of which was undertaken under the auspices of academic exchange programs between the American Council of Learned Societies and the Academy of Sciences of the USSR, administered by the International Research and Exchanges Board (IREX). I am grateful for the extensive support and facilitating arrangements provided by IREX and by exchange partners in the USSR. I further appreciate assistance over the years from many Soviet archivists, librarians, and other colleagues. The article was originally prepared in 1984 and has been revised and updated several times since for use in IREX orientation programs. During this entire period, my work has been supported by a series of research grants from the National Endowment for the Humanities, a federal agency, to which I am deeply indebted. Some portions of this article have been drawn from my more general reference work, *A Handbook for Archival Research in the USSR* (Washington, D.C.: Kennan Institute for Advanced Russian Studies and International Research and Exchanges Board, 1989). Researchers should refer to that handbook for further information and bibliographic data.

the years of stagnation they turned into a bureaucratic organization with the main aim of 'preserving' agency secrets.'' The MGIAI council calls for ''decisive *perestroika*'' for ''the service of social memory—the archives of the USSR.''[3]

As of October 1988, a new high-level council on archives was being established, as recommended by MGIAI. Questions remain, however, about the extent to which reform will be realized and about the extent to which the Soviet state and Party archives from the 1920s and 1930s are really ready for the historians. Complicated questions still require answers:

First, to what extent have archival records been retained from the 1920s and 30s, and what records have been destroyed beyond recall?

Second, has an adequate reference system been developed for historians to explore and select appropriate sources?

And third, to what extent will historians be allowed access to Party archives as well as records in state archives and, once admitted, to what extent will they be encouraged to explore freely for sources they might deem relevant and to publish the results of their research or the documents they find?

The recent open discussion of archival problems in the press may be the harbinger of reform in the archival service. But changes in present policies and practices cannot resurrect documentation that went to the paper factories in earlier decades, and user-oriented reference systems cannot be produced overnight. Recordkeeping practices and archival policies of earlier decades have left indelible stamps on the nature, content, and arrangement of that documentation, as well as on its present archival configuration. Since changes necessarily come slowly in the archival realm, researchers need to understand the organizational pattern and archival procedures as they have developed since 1917.[4]

1. The organization and administration of Soviet archives

The revolution that brought Lenin and his Bolshevik Party to power in October 1917 was soon followed by revolutionary developments in the archival realm, including nationalization and government control not only of all archives and manuscripts, but also of records management in all ongoing agencies of state and society as well as temporary or abolished ones. The archival decree issued under Lenin's signature on 1 June 1918 provided a theoretical and practical basis with legal and administrative authority for total archival control.[5]

The State Archival Fond

Nationalization and legal control over all archival materials has been extended through the institutionalization of the so-called State Archival Fond—GAF (*Gosudarstvennyi arkhivnyi fond*, initially the *Edinyi gosudarstvennyi arkhivnyi fond*), a legal concept that embraces all archival materials under state control, including manuscript collections, throughout the Soviet Union. Following the organization of the union structure in the early 1920s, correlated ''State Archival Fonds'' were established for each separate union republic—although with control from Moscow. Similar legal entities were extended to the Baltic republics and to the Moldavian SSR, following their annexation during World War II.

Initially the concept would have extended to records created by the Communist Party, but then a separate system of Party archives was created in the late 1920s. Later the Archival Fond of the Communist Party (AF KPSS) was legally defined as a separate entity, and it is administered entirely independently from the State Archival Fond.[6] The exclusion of Communist Party records from the State Archival Fond obviously grossly limits its comprehensiveness and places many of the most crucial and historically revealing post-1917 archival materials outside of state control.

The most recent Soviet archival regulations issued in 1980 update earlier provisions for the GAF, and also list eight separate agencies that have authorization for the long-term retention of their own archives.[7] Most notably, the ministries of Foreign Affairs and Defense, the Academy of Sciences, and libraries and museums under the Ministry of Culture all have permanent jurisdiction over their own archival records and related manuscript collections. Other independent archives are maintained by the All-Union Geological Fond, the Cartographic and Geodesic Fond, the All-Union State Fond of Feature Films (*Gosfil'mofond*), the All-Union Registry of Standards, and the Fond of Hydro-Meterology and Environmental Data. Thus, while the inception of the State Archival Fond has brought nationalization to much of the Soviet archival wealth, a significant level of administrative decentralization remains. There is no mention of the KGB archives.

The State Agency for Archival Administration— Glavarkhiv

The centralization and planning that has undergirded Soviet archival achievements and the total state control of the historically valuable and politically sensitive records of state and society have been coordinated, and largely made possible, by the existence of an independent agency charged with the overall administration of the State Archival Fond.

Known since 1938 as the Main Archival Administration (*Glavnoe arkhivnoe upravlenie*), the formal name has changed a number of times, reflecting the agency's place within the Soviet bureaucratic hierarchy, but its general function has been relatively constant. Initially from 1918 to 1922 under the jurisdiction of the People's Commissariat of Education, it was subsequently directly subordinate to the Central Executive Committee, but in 1938 the Archival Administration came under the jurisdiction of the People's Commissariat (and later Ministry) of Internal Affairs. In 1960 it was shifted to a quasi-ministerial status attached to the Council of Ministers of the USSR, with the official name of *Glavnoe arkhivnoe upravlenie pri Sovete ministrov SSSR*.[8] The earlier official acronym "GAU" has since the early 1980s been replaced by "Glavarkhiv." While the Moscow-based Glavarkhiv of the USSR is charged with the administration of archival affairs on the all-union level and the coordination of archival administration throughout the USSR, parallel agencies are organized under the Councils of Ministers of each union republic and on the oblast or other local level under the appropriate Executive Committees.

A new archival law under discussion in 1988 projected the transfer of the state archival service to the Ministry of Justice as a means of streamlining and reducing its present top-heavy, centralized administrative structure. Early in 1988, plans were announced in the Baltic republics and Armenia to shift their archival services to the republic-level Ministries of Justice, but these reforms were implemented only sporadically. Opposition to the proposed change was extensive, and by the fall of 1988, these plans were forestalled or reversed. Further archival reform is still planned, and comprehensive archival laws are being drafted on republic and all-union levels.[9]

The functions of Glavarkhiv are extremely broad and comprehensive, and much more centralized than is the case in the non-Communist world. Of particular importance to researchers, a division known as the Scientific Reference Service (*Nauchno-spravochnyi apparat*), handles archival reference systems, including centralized files for registration of all fonds in the republic-level or all-union State Archival Fond (GAF). All such activities are—at least in theory—standardized throughout the USSR by published rules and regulations.[10] Glavarkhiv has a research and development function, which includes the operation of the All-Union Scientific-Research Institute, VNIIDAD (*Vsesoiuznyi nauchno-issledovatel'skii institut dokumentovedeniia i arkhivnogo dela*), the only high-level research institute devoted to archival affairs in the world.[11] Glavarkhiv has a special foreign relations division which controls exchange programs with foreign archives and the admission of foreign researchers to state archives throughout the USSR.[12]

Records management (deloproizvodstvo/dokumentovedenie)

As part of its total control over the national documentary legacy, Glavarkhiv directly supervises records management (*deloproizvodstvo*) in all government agencies, economic enterprises, and other organs of state and society. The Russian term might better be translated "recordkeeping practices," as it was traditionally used in the Russian Empire before the Revolution with reference to chancery functions in government offices and other agencies. In the contemporary Soviet context, however, and in line with contemporary Western usage, the English-language term "records management" would be the closest equivalent in terms of the selection, care, and management of records produced by a given office or agency.

Since the 1970s, Soviet specialists use the newly coined Russian term *dokumentovedenie*, which would be literally translated as "the science of documentation," to denote their study and planning efforts in standardizing document forms, systematizing documentary functions, and recording optimal documentation of official activities with an eye to future information retrieval. This term is now more frequently encountered for the general field of records management, although the term *deloproizvodstvo* will be found in earlier literature on the subject. It should be understood, however, that records management as practiced in Soviet agencies under the direction of Glavarkhiv is a much more comprehensive, regulated process than corresponding practices in the United States and many Western countries. Glavarkhiv control starts with the prescription of standardized forms for documents for most official uses, the supervision of document management, and paper flow within government offices, including standard office registers to be kept for various transactions.

In fact, usually the documentary registers, indexes, and other parts of the reference apparatus produced by government agencies later become the basic finding aids once the records involved are transferred to permanent state archives. Published regulations ensure that the registers prepared will eventually serve as inventories (*opisi*) when the records reach their archival destination. Such control over agency recordkeeping practices ensures a level of continuity between agency records and archival deposits—including continuity in their registration—that is not found in many countries.

Regulations published in 1974 establish the so-called General State System of Records Management, which applies to offices in all state agencies, with sample forms and/or format guidelines for many of the processes involved.[13] A new edition in preparation reportedly would make adherence to the prescribed practices mandatory in all offices.

The importance assigned to the field of records management is further evidenced by the special division devoted to research and planning on the subject in the high-level Soviet archival research institute—VNIIDAD, the research and development arm of Glavarkhiv. In 1973, Glavarkhiv published a fundamental monograph, prepared under the auspices of VNIIDAD, setting forth a "contemporary documentary arrangement system" for document management within government offices, including the arrangement of records in permanent file units, with an eye to stricter control and coordination between the records being produced in government offices and their eventual archival storage and retrieval.[14] Since the early 1970s, even more attention has been devoted to the forms of documents being used in government offices. For example, a 1981 publication provides guidelines for standardized forms and practices to be used in many state agencies.[15] Under the auspices of VNIIDAD, Glavarkhiv specialists are developing theoretical plans for what they now term a Unified State System for Improved Records Management (*Edinaia gosudarstvennaia sistema dokumentatsionnogo obespecheniia upravleniia*) that will provide a model for coding, filing, and retrieving both traditional standard forms and computerized documentary records.[16]

Although such systems will dramatically affect the records being preserved from contemporary years, they have little bearing on the nature of records from the 1920s and 1930s. In earlier decades of Soviet rule, recordkeeping practices were regulated, but conformity with regulations was often highly erratic. Prescribed standards—and in the republics, prescribed linguistic usage—were changed several times. Frequently, the lack of forms and rapid turnover or poorly qualified staff, among other factors, meant that records kept fell well below the norm. A collection of selected earlier Soviet laws and decrees regarding records management was issued in 1973.[17] An in-depth impression of some of the recent work being done in the area of automated records systems and related problems of records management from an archival perspective is apparent in a 1976 collection of reports published by MGIAI, a few of which relate to records from the earlier Soviet period.[18]

The close coordination between records management within ongoing agencies and the transfer of records to permanent archival repositories means that the historian must be intricately acquainted with the internal structure and function of Soviet institutions, their documentary forms, recordkeeping practices, and guidelines for records management and eventual archival transfer. Some reference literature and introductory textbooks are available on the subject.[19] Yet from the standpoint of the researcher interested in the 1920s and 1930s, a detailed, carefully documented analytic study still needs to be made regarding recordkeeping practices in early decades of Soviet rule, together with more precise information about the appraisal and disposal policies that were followed in various agencies.

Appraisal

In the Soviet context, appraisal—as Western archivists would term the selection of documentary records for permanent storage—is intricately tied into the process of records management. Glavarkhiv formulates retention schedules and file disposal lists, based on the type of document and level of the agency, i.e., raion, or oblast, with priority going to agencies on the union-republic and all-union level.

At the heart of the system is the Glavarkhiv Central Expert Appraisal Commission (*Tsentral'naia ekspertno-proverochnaia komissiia Glavarkhiv*), sometimes translated simply as the Central Appraisal Commission, which controls appraisal on the all-union level and supervises subsidiary commissions on union republic and lower administrative levels, down to the representatives responsible for each and every agency. Through the auspices of these commissions, Glavarkhiv establishes guidelines for which documents will be preserved and for how long, thus determining what documents will be available for future researchers and others who might need to use them for official purposes.[20] This formalized appraisal system is a relatively new development from the post-Stalin period, but it draws on basic practices already being followed in earlier decades of Soviet rule.

Initially, all records were to remain in their producing agency for five years, but after several fluctuations in time-span, the normal period of initial office retention came to be five, ten, or fifteen years, depending on the level of the agency and the nature of the documentation involved. A seventy-five year retention period in the local agency is required for all records of vital statistics.[21] Records designated for permanent storage are usually consigned to their appropriate archive on the oblast, krai, union republic, and all-union levels after fifteen years, although in many cases the creating agency retains control over them for an additional designated period.

Although the figure of four to five percent is usually quoted as the portion of records designated for permanent preservation in the USSR, naturally, in many cases, various records may be needed by their creating agencies for different periods before disposal. Hence an extensive system of local or intermediate temporary archives has been developed on the raion level. Some agencies not under Glavarkhiv, such as the Communist Party, the Ministry of Foreign Affairs, the KGB, and the

Ministry of Defense, retain a larger percentage of the documentation they create, and they maintain their own agency archives to house it.[22]

Soviet records management functions naturally have a vital impact not only on the organization and function of contemporary archives and their access in the USSR, but also on the nature and type of documents to be preserved for future generations. In connection with the more open approach to various social and political problems in the last two years, more probing questions are being raised about the nature and scope of retention and disposal programs, and the strictness of adherence to established guidelines.

For example, an article published in the "unofficial" Moscow journal *Glasnost'* in July 1987 decries the continuing destruction of court records relating to victims of the Stalin purges. According to the author, "archives of the USSR Procurator's Office and the Ministry of Justice were 'cleaned' of such cases (i.e., all of them were burned) in the 1960s and 1970s." The Joint Special Archives of the Military Council and the USSR Supreme Court, however, still preserved "cases of Soviet citizens who had been falsely charged, sentenced, and [who] for the most part, died in the 1930s–1950s" and these regulations called for the files "to be transferred . . . , primarily to the Central State Archive of the October Revolution [TsGAOR SSSR], where all documents are to be preserved in perpetuity." Following recent personnel changes, however, the author contends, "the Special Archives underwent an emergency 'cleaning,'" to the extent that "all the cases of people sentenced in the 1930s–40s . . . have intentionally been destroyed." According to the author, even today files are being burned—"up to 1,500 files on one 'volunteer Saturday' . . . under the pretext of 'insufficient space' for the current documentation that is needed."[23] The report is accompanied by a moving appeal by the journal editor, Sergei Grigoriants, to General Secretary Mikhail Gorbachev "to stop the barbaric destruction of those documents and to allow historians to study what little has remained in the archives. Otherwise there is no hope that we will avoid another age of Stalinism."[24]

Related questions along somewhat less specific lines were raised by MGIAI rector Afanas'ev during his visit to the United States in October 1988. In a press interview on the eve of his departure, he was questioned about the fate of documentation regarding the period of collectivization, mass famine, and the Great Terror. Afanas'ev replied:

> There is absolutely no basis to think that archives remained inviolable. Needless to say, a regime that destroyed millions of people would not have stopped before the destruction of a few hundred sheets of paper. . . .[25]

The issues raised are fundamental ones. If major court records and, presumably, many others of a long-term significance, have been destroyed—and even in a period of *perestroika* are continuing to be destroyed—more liberal policies of access to archives are not going to help the more open writing of the history of the Stalin years. If the appropriate retention schedules have not been followed, then obviously Glavarkhiv is not carrying out its responsibilities or is unable to enforce compliance.

Alternatively, if such court records were designated for disposal after a given number of years, then it is the appraisal policies and practices of Glavarkhiv and its predecessors, rather than any more liberal access policies, that will have dictated the limited historical documentation that will be available for future generations.

Documentary publications

Glavarkhiv has extensive publication functions, including supervision of publication programs for all archives under its direct administration. These include documentary publications, reference materials, and methodological literature. Professional archival journals are issued on the all-union level and by several union republics.

Particular emphasis is placed on the publication of selective collections of documents from state archives, some of which are prepared with the collaboration of research institutes under the Academies of Sciences on both all-union and republic level. Following successive Party imperatives, Soviet archival authorities emphasize documentary publication programs as one of their most important functions, with the aim of making highly selected documents available to the public, and usually with recognizable political restraints and ideological objectives. Scholars frequently complain that such politically inspired publication functions are given a much higher priority than the publication of detailed finding aids and reference compendia that might permit researchers to know the complete contents of the archive and to find those documents that might interest them.

As a spinoff of the recent discussion of *glasnost'* in history, there have been many calls for more open, scholarly, and historically revealing publication of documents. For example, the Learned Council of MGIAI complained in May 1988, "For the three years of *perestroika*, . . . not a single document has been published, nor a single documentary collection, on Glavarkhiv's initiative, enlightening themes of the blemishes of our history."[26] Comments by Glavarkhiv director F. M. Vaganov, however, give little hope of improvement.[27]

2. Archival reference systems and archival access

Archival arrangement

Centralization in Soviet archival administration has brought significant standardization in internal organization, arrangement, and descriptive schemes in all Soviet repositories. Standardized rules drawn up by Glavarkhiv to be used in all repositories throughout the Soviet Union define the different components of archival arrangement and the different types of finding aids that should be prepared.[28] But the extent to which the guidelines have been applied still varies considerably from one repository to another.

The cardinal principle of Soviet archival arrangement, not unlike usage in many national archives, is that records should be kept together and grouped as closely as possible in the order in which they were kept in their originating agency or office of provenance. The close coordination between records management and archives administration since the revolution further ensures that this principle is followed once materials are transferred to their permanent archival depository.

Fonds (fondy). The most important organizational unit within all Soviet repositories is the *fond* (Russian plural, *fondy*). All records, groups of manuscripts, and other documentary complexes in archives and other manuscript repositories are now divided into fonds and assigned fond numbers.[29] Individual fonds comprise the records, or complex of documentary materials, from a single institution or organization, produced in the exercise of its institutional functions, or in the course of its normal business activities, i.e., those records that have been designated for permanent preservation. Fonds may range in size and complexity from a tiny group of records from a small agency that lasted only a few years, to a gigantic body of materials from a large administrative agency, with over a million files extending over several centuries.

Once assigned, fond numbers are supposed to be permanent. In many instances, however, archival reorganization and the transfer of records among different institutions have necessitated changes in fond numbers, much to the confusion of researchers. Researchers should also be alert to possible variants in the assignment of fond divisions. Changes in arrangement guidelines in different periods since the 1920s have been the cause for major restructuring in some cases. Accordingly, researchers should always cite the official institutional name for the fond in addition to its number, because if numbers have been reassigned or delineations between fonds changed, archivists can still usually locate materials by reference to the official institutional name of the records.

In contrast to Western usage, the term "fond" is also used in the Soviet Union for personal and family papers, and also for papers from private institutional sources. All personal papers from a particular family or individual are normally classified as a single numbered fond.

Collections (sobraniia, *or* kollektsii). Like institutional records and personal papers, collections are also assigned fond numbers in all Soviet repositories. Researchers should nonetheless be aware of the traditional, basic distinction between "records," or "archives," and "manuscript collections." Manuscript collections differ from archives in that their common feature is usually their collector or the broad subject matter that they represent. Collections are not systematic records of any organization but are rather miscellaneous manuscripts or documents that have been artificially assembled apart from their creating agencies or designated receiving agencies, and they usually possess some historical, artistic, or literary value.

For example, in the 1920s artificially structured archival collections (Russian singular *kollektsiia*) were assembled of the highly prized documentation relating to the revolutionary movement. Relevant materials were extracted from their natural order and related records, such as key groups of police files, and were moved *in toto* from their original agency archival environment to form special "historico-revolutionary'' archives or separate divisions within regional repositories. Such practices help to explain some lingering organizational anomalies in some Soviet archives, including Communist Party archives.[30]

File unit (delo) *subdivisions*. All fonds are divided into basic filing units, and each file unit (*delo*)—the smallest grouping within the fond—bears a separate item number. The Russian term *delo* (plural, *dela*) has been used by Glavarkhiv in state archives officially since the 1970s, and is actually the traditional Russian term for files in government offices. Before the 1970s, however, the term *edinitsa khraneniia* (literally, storage unit) was standard, and hence that designation (abbreviated *ed. khr.*) will be found in published guides and citations predating the 1970s, and even later in other forms of citations. The file unit may be an individual manuscript volume or discrete folder of documents, since the term is now used for both manuscript collections and agency records.

In the case of official records, file units are usually formed in the office of origin, where they are arranged to comprise logical and easily identifiable categories. It may be a large dossier with several folders on a related subject, or a single folder containing a group of letters, memoranda, or reports, which may be related by date, author, addressee (institutional or individual), or type of document.

In English usage, the term ''folio'' rather than ''page'' is used for individual sheets—or leaves—within a file folder or bound manuscript volume. The Russian-language equivalent would be *list* (plural, *listy*, abbreviated *l.*, or *ll.*). In traditional archival usage, within each file unit that consists of more than one folio or leaf, folios are numbered consecutively, normally only on the recto; the verso is usually cited in Russian as the *oborotnaia storona* (*ob.*). In some institutions or collections, volumes may be numbered, or foliated, on both sides of a single sheet, to produce foliation as page numbers of a book.

Inventory (opis') *divisions*. In the course of arrangement, even within the originating office, individual file units are numbered and listed in an office register, or master inventory, known in Russian as an *opis'* (plural, *opisi*, abbreviated *op.*). Depending on the office and its volume of records designated for preservation, registers might list all the files for a particular chronological period, or they might reflect specific functional, structural, or geographic divisions within the agency. Fonds from large agencies will accordingly have many *opisi*. When the records are transferred to the archive, the files themselves are usually not rearranged, but the original *opisi* are numbered and serve as structural divisions within the fond. For most large institutional fonds from the 1920s and 1930s, the registers now used as the basic *opisi* were actually prepared in the originating chancery or office as the office transaction or correspondence register.

In addition to providing the permanent registration of all file units, the *opis'* also serves as the archival shelf list, providing official administrative registration and security control of file units in the fond. Even more importantly for researchers and archivists, the *opis'* also serves as a descriptive inventory and hence as the basic finding aid for the fond.

In Soviet agencies, and later in archives, the *opisi* themselves are not assigned formal names as structural series within the fond as would be the practice in most Western archives. In some cases *opisi* do in fact represent such normal divisions within office records, and a given *opis'* does contain all the files from a specific office, or may be delimited by function, types of documents, dates, or geographic area that might be covered by the file units listed. Divisions by different inventories may reflect the bureaucratic structure of the agency, with separate *opisi* containing records of the secretariat (*sekretariat*), planning office (*planovyi otdel*), financial office (*finansovyi otdel'*), and so forth. In other cases, file units for office records are ordered in registers by reference to the type of document involved—orders (*prikazy*), plans (*plany*), reports (*otchety*), correspondence (*perepiska*), and so forth.[31]

Regrettably for the researcher, reference systems in Soviet archives seldom note this crucial information. Rarely are there systematic, user-oriented descriptive lists of *opisi* available for individual fonds, and even if such information can be determined from archival card files or accession registers, it is not often available to researchers. Researchers can only discover such schema by perusing the *opisi* themselves, by sampling specific files, by consultation with knowledgeable archivists or colleagues.

Since the fall of 1988, foreign researchers have been given access to inventories for postrevolutionary records in many state archives, which means that they can now choose for themselves the files they want to consult. In some cases, however, the *opisi* available, particularly from the 1920s and 1930s, are grossly inadequate for efficient information retrieval. But for the vast majority of fonds in state archives, *opisi* are still the only internal finding aids available. It is to be hoped that the new Glavarkhiv policy of communicating these vital finding aids to researchers will be continued, since the withholding of *opisi* heretofore was one of the severely criticized problems of research in Soviet archives, particularly for foreigners.

3. General reference aids for archival researchers

The lack of adequate internal finding aids in Soviet archives is paralleled by the lack of adequate published directories and bibliographies. Most of the reference resources available for those dealing with social history in the 1920s and 1930s have been described in earlier publications.[32] Nevertheless, it might be well to comment on a few basic Soviet reference works here, particularly those of most relevance for the prewar Stalin period.

Archival directories

In the hierarchy of Soviet archival reference publications, a directory or handbook (*spravochnik*) usually describes holdings in a variety of different institutions on an institutional level.

All-union directory. The most important single Soviet publication for the archival researcher is the second (1983) edition of a handbook compiled by I. M. Grossman and V. N. Kutik published by Lviv University.[33] Published far away from the resources of Glavarkhiv and its Moscow research institute, this volume nonetheless provides the most extensive directory and bibliography of finding aids available for repositories throughout the USSR, including those under the Academy of Sciences, the Ministry of Culture, and universities, as well as those of Glavarkhiv itself. Its coverage is highly uneven, and by no means comprehensive. Its rich bibliography is exceedingly awkwardly arranged and difficult to use (especially by the foreign scholar), and tends to emphasize the most recent publications. Despite such drawbacks, it deserves the serious attention of researchers. It should be noted that the second edition, although much more extensive in terms of institutional coverage and bibliography, does not repeat all of the bibliography in the earlier edition, and omits the helpful chapters with historical and procedural information.[34]

Glavarkhiv directories. The new, long-awaited, two-volume Glavarkhiv directory of state archives throughout the USSR down to the oblast level appeared in 1989.[35] A second volume promised for 1990 will cover repositories under the Academy of Science and libraries and museums under the Ministry of Culture. Although this directory now provides an up-to-date starting point for identifying archival institutions throughout the country, its repository-level coverage is a big disappointment, with no lists of individuals fonds or even all major groups of fonds, and inadequate bibliography of published finding aids.

The previous general Glavarkhiv directory was issued in 1956, but it covered only state archives throughout the USSR under Glavarkhiv administration. It is now seriously outdated and its minimal bibliography of published guides is also obsolete.[36] In 1982, Glavarkhiv issued an extremely popularized short directory (*kratkii spravochnik*) of the eleven central state archives of the USSR.[37] Virtually useless for the serious researcher, it provides no bibliography whatsoever, and does not even mention the published guides that, however now out-of-date, still constitute the basic means for specific identification of individual fonds.

Much more helpful historical and descriptive data about the central state archives of the USSR will be found in the 1977 textbook prepared for the Moscow State Historico-Archival Institute by G. A. Dremina.[38] Dremina accesses new developments in the reference facilities of each institution, outlines major changes in profile and acquisition policies, and explains major changes in the structure and delineation of holdings among the central state archives since 1960. A subsequent small textbook by Dremina covers activities and developments in each archive during the period 1971 through 1975, and more limited coverage of the period 1978–1980 appears in a pamphlet issued in 1986.[39]

The permanent state archives of the Russian Soviet Federated Socialist Republic (RSFSR), are covered briefly in a comprehensive directory published by Glavarkhiv in 1980.[40] Brief, but disappointingly superficial, descriptions are provided for each of the central state republic-level repositories, as well as those for autonomous republics, krais, and all oblasts. Its bibliography is minimal—and grossly incomplete—in terms of available guides and documentary publications.[41]

A new, popularized Russian-language directory of Ukrainian state archives appeared in mid–1988 with minimal bibliography of finding aids but with no definition of major fonds.[42] More detailed coverage and bibliography of finding aids is provided in my own English-language directory which appeared at the end of 1988.[43] Short directories have been published separately for other Soviet republics.[44]

Academy of Sciences directory. Much more satisfactory coverage has been published for archival holdings under the Academy of Sciences than for those under Glavarkhiv, at least on an all-union level. A basic and most helpful directory issued in 1979 lists major archival fonds in all of the Academy institutes in Moscow and Leningrad.[45] It cites fond numbers, dates, and the number of storage units in all cases, and its coverage of personal papers is much more extensive than the general all-union directory of personal papers mentioned below.

Personal papers. In terms of directories covering archival materials in more than one institution, the three-volume directory—or literally index (*ukazatel'*)—of personal papers in repositories throughout the USSR is a significant achievement that should be known to researchers in all periods.[46] Anyone who has tried to locate and use family papers in many Western countries can appreciate the value to scholars of this centralized descriptive effort. Yet the published version has disappointingly excluded many important individuals. Gaps are particularly distressing in listings for papers of politically sensitive individuals from the 1920s and 1930s, particularly those who perished during the purges of the 1930s. There are also major lacunae among non-Russians, especially those active in pre-Soviet periods. Communist Party archives did not participate in the survey; hence most papers among their holdings are also excluded. It is to be hoped that in the spirit of *glasnost'* another supplemental volume will be issued listing the many individuals omitted from the 1980 volume as well as other groups of personal papers that have come to light subsequently.

Archival guides. In the hierarchy of Soviet archival reference publications, in contrast to a directory, which provides generalized repository-level coverage of many different archival institutions, a guide (*putevoditel'*) provides a comprehensive annotated list of the major fonds within a given repository. The *putevoditel'* systematically gives the number and designation of each fond, and basic data about the agency from which it came. It records the total number of file units in the fond, their inclusive dates, and a brief description of their contents. However, the description rarely reflects the actual structure or arrangement of the fond, since lists of *opisi* or designation of *opis'* divisions are not provided. And, since there is no indication of *dela* numbers either, the guide cannot be the basis for specific researcher requests for documentation within the fond.

Regrettably, many of the guides prepared by state archives under Glavarkhiv in the 1970s or 1980s are significantly less detailed, with much less annotation than those published in the 1950s and 1960s. Accordingly, Glavarkhiv has started using the title *kratkii spravochnik*, or "short directory," rather than *putevoditel'*, although these should be considered in the category of guides. The amount of detail furnished in archival guides (or short directories) varies considerably from one archive to another, and researchers cannot assume that all important holdings are mentioned, especially those from the 1920s and 1930s. Furthermore, researchers should not assume that the mention of a fond, or specific files within a fond, in an earlier guide, but not in a later edition, means that the materials are no longer there. It should be assumed that the most recent fond numbers and archival designations are the most current, and more likely to be correct than citations in a previously published monograph, but references should always be checked in earlier guides and descriptions, particularly when the latter contain more detail or if the referenced materials are not cited in the most recent finding aids.

According to the projected plans for Glavarkhiv, guides are to be prepared for all state archives, but, particularly for central state archives, there is a long way to go to fulfill such a plan. Nonrestricted, or openly available, and relatively up-to-date guides are available for only two of the eleven central state archives on the all-union level, and for only four of the eleven state archives under the RSFSR in Moscow and Leningrad. Glavarkhiv RSFSR has a better track record outside of Moscow, since guides or short directories have been published for fourteen out of the sixteen central state archives of autonomous republics, five out of six krai-level state archives, and for forty-three out of the forty-eight oblast-level state archives of the RSFSR. Yet many of these are not widely available. Statistics vary for the non-Russian union republics.[47]

The appalling lack of distribution of, and hence the basic lack of access to, published finding aids for state archives is one of the most serious problems facing researchers. The problems have multiplied in the late 1970s and 1980s, at least partly as a result of changes in Glavarkhiv reference priorities and publication economies. Apparently, in an effort starting about a decade ago to lower production costs and save paper, most of the Glavarkhiv guides are being issued as small press-run (*tirazh*), in-house editions, and they are not distributed through normal book distribution channels. Although all but a few bear a censorship number as legitimate publications, many are not registered with the All-Union Book Chamber. Some are issued as unpriced (*bezplatno*) official publications, which apparently further limits their distribution requirements and technically prohibits export. Such lack of registration and distribution requirements may also explain why obligatory deposit copies have not been received by the Lenin Library and other major libraries in Moscow and Leningrad.[48]

Bibliographies of archival literature

The lack of adequate bibliography of finding aids and other descriptive literature, along with the generally superficial quality of recent Glavarkhiv directories, makes it an imperative for researchers to consult a wide range of other literature in attempting to track down the reference information they need and to identify the holdings they might wish to consult in various archival institutions. Unfortunately, there is as yet no single cumulative compendium that can adequately serve them in this task, but there are a number of bibliographic aids worth consulting.

Several basic Soviet historical bibliographies have some cumulative coverage of archival finding aids and documentary publications, as do some of the more specialized bibliographies on specific subjects, but there is no satisfactory single compendium to be recommended covering sources for the 1920s and 1930s. Most helpful as a guide to historical bibliographies is the latest edition of the annotated bibliography of historical bibliographies prepared by the State Public Historical Library (GPIB RSFSR) and the Lenin Library (GBL) in Moscow.[49] The careful annotations and precise bibliographic details can assist researchers in locating appropriate bibliographies that might lead them to additional historical sources or secondary literature.

The most helpful general compendium of archival literature specifically oriented for study of the 1920s and 1930s is the recent two-volume cumulative bibliography specifically devoted to historical source study issued in 1987–1989 by the Institute of History of the USSR in Moscow.[50] The first volume includes two parts, one with imprints from the period 1917–1937 and the second from the years 1938–1967. The second volume covers literature that appeared from 1968 to 1984. Most relevant for those using archives is the rubric within each part for surveys of archival holdings, which includes archival guides as well as more general survey descriptions of specific fonds or groups of materials. The coverage, although it remains incomplete, is more oriented to the researcher than the Glavarkhiv archives mentioned below. Emphasis is on holdings on the all-union level, with only scattered coverage of Ukraine in terms of non-Russian areas. Also of note are the rubrics for literature on records management, archival affairs, and the appraisal and the collecting function of archives. Other separate rubrics of archival relevance in each part are devoted to CPSU sources, legal acts, statistical sources, memoirs and diaries, audiovisual sources, and the historiography of source study. Despite lacunae, this is the most important bibliography available for archival research on the 1920s and 1930s.

Glavarkhiv cumulative bibliographies. The cumulative bibliographies of archival publications issued by Glavarkhiv usually list only official, Glavarkhiv-sponsored publications, and they are much less up to date than the Lviv handbook. They attest to the range of publications available, but are in themselves poorly organized as reference aids.

In 1961 two separate bibliographies were issued by Glavarkhiv, one listing archival literature published officially by state archives, including finding aids and other methodological and technical publications regarding archival affairs,[51] and a second for published editions of documents, again primarily from state archives.[52] Three supplemental volumes were issued, combining the coverage of archival literature and documentary publications, but with a dramatically increasing time lag in imprints covered. Indeed, the last volume issued in 1977 extends the coverage so far only through 1970 imprints. The latest supplement, extending the coverage through 1975 imprints, was prepared, but the hefty manuscripts have been deposited in typescript in the VNIIDAD manuscript depository.[53] Coverage of literature in the field of records management and documentation studies for the period 1971–1975 was completed as a separate work, but also remains unpublished in VNIIDAD.[54] Unfortunately, according to specialists in VNIIDAD, the series is not scheduled to continue, and there is no adequate replacement.

The bibliographic coverage of Glavarkhiv documentary publications has now been assumed by a separate series, which is continuing in published form. The series started with a more purely methodological orientation, covering literature on problems and methodology of documentary publishing, for which Soviet archivists use the term "archeography" (*arkheografiia*). A retrospective bibliography covering Glavarkhiv imprints during the period 1917–1970 appeared in 1974.[55] Starting with the supplements covering literature from the years 1971–1973 and 1974–1975, which appeared in 1976 and 1980 respectively, major documentary publications are also listed, as well as methodological literature.[56] The latest volume (1989), extending the coverage through 1980 imprints, is much more extensive in terms of the institutional coverage, but there is an eight-year time lag.[57] As far as documentary publications are concerned, this continuing series (*Sovetskaia arkheografiia*) actually replaces the discontinued Glavarkhiv series described above. Bibliographic entries in all volumes of this series are listed alphabetically under the year of publication. Again the indexes are inadequate, with listings of neither subject nor repository, but, given the extent of their coverage, the volumes merit attention. Since these bibliographies are prepared by VNIIDAD, the Glavarkhiv research institute, they usually exclude documentary publications that were not officially undertaken by or with the cosponsorship of Glavarkhiv or by the state archives under its jurisdiction.[58]

Glavarkhiv bibliographic bulletins. More recent and up-to-date Glavarkhiv bibliographic coverage is now being produced only in monthly bibliographic bulletins with no provisions for cumulative indexing. As a result, ongoing bibliography in the field of archival literature and documentary publications is almost impossible to follow abroad, because the most extensive in-house monthly bibliographic serial publication prepared by VNIIDAD (under Glavarkhiv auspices) is not available through international library exchange or normal export channels. Issued with a complicated publication history of changing titles and separate subseries, it can be consulted in bibliographic reference collections only in a few selected Soviet libraries. The series covering archival literature and archeography is most relevant to the archival researcher, although the series covering records management (*dokumentovedenie*) may also have some important leads.[59] Like other Glavarkhiv bibliographies, the series invariably contains references only to Glavarkhiv/VNIIDAD publications and to those produced jointly with the Academy of Sciences or other institutions.

Starting in the 1980s, an increasing amount of serious archival literature produced under Glavarkhiv was not being openly published at all, but rather deposited in the VNIIDAD depository for approved, but unpublished, manuscripts. Since 1978 VNIIDAD has issued an abstract series, *Ekspres-Informatsiia*, that provides lengthy summaries of many of these important works,[60] and some of them are listed sporadically with annotations in *Sovetskie arkhivy.*[61]

Archival and archeographic serials

Glavarkhiv journals. The professional bimonthly archival journal published by Glavarkhiv, *Sovetskie arkhivy*, tends to be increasingly political and generally less scholarly in content compared to Academy publications. It has been published with title variations since 1956.[62] Although its masthead claims it is prepared with the participation of the Institute of History of the Academy of Sciences of the USSR, there is scant evidence of scholarly contribution from that institute. The journal is nonetheless important for the researcher because it continues to include frequent survey descriptions of selected fonds and of archival documentation on specific subjects, as well as reviews of arbitrarily selected new publications, texts of selected documents, and news of developments in the archival realm. Before 1986 this journal did not attempt to provide bibliographic coverage even of Glavarkhiv publications and basic reference aids for archival researchers. As an important new step in this direction, *Sovetskie arkhivy* printed an initial list of fifty-five finding aids issued during the years 1981–1985 for state archives under Glavarkhiv. Curiously, however, the list was not introduced as a formal bibliography, but was rather printed on the inside back covers of several issues.[63] Several other issues have included similar lists of documentary publications.[64]

A separate journal was also issued by the Archival Administration of the RSFSR during the years 1956 through 1962. However, it was never registered as a regular periodical and is not generally available.[65] Researchers interested in Ukrainian lands should also follow the bimonthly journal of the Ukrainian archival administration, which was started under an earlier title in 1947.[66] A new index appeared in mid–1988, but it covers articles published only since 1971.[67] Some of the other non-Russian republics also have their own national archival journals, but few are available abroad.[68]

Archeographic Commission serials. Much more scholarly in tone and comprehensive in scope are the publications of the Archeographic Commission of the Academy of Sciences. Traditionally, the Archeographic Commission was concentrated principally on research regarding the prerevolutionary period, with most of its attention to pre-nineteenth century sources. In more recent decades, however, the Archeographic Commission has been concerned more widely with unpublished archival and manuscript sources of all periods, and some important efforts have been devoted to postrevolutionary developments. Reflecting its honored position under the Academy of Sciences, its orientation has continued to be much more scholarly than that of Glavarkhiv, and its varied archeographic efforts have been much more oriented to the serious researcher than those of its Glavarkhiv counterparts. Its distinguished yearbook, *Arkheograficheskii ezhegodnik*, should draw the careful attention of archival researchers in many fields.[69]

During the first decade of its publication, *Arkheograficheskii ezhegodnik* assumed a major bibliographic role with annual compendia of recent literature in the archival field. Since 1967, however, such functions were regrettably dropped. A separate cumulative bibliography of archival and archeographic literature issued in 1984 covers imprints during the years 1968 to 1972, including documentary publications, archival finding aids, and related reference works.[70] Organized for easier reference use than the Glavarkhiv bibliographies mentioned above, and with a separate rubric for publications pertaining to the Soviet period, there were high hopes for its continuation. Most regrettably, this essential bibliographic function is not being continued by the Archeographic Commission.[71]

Several series have appeared under the sponsorships of regional branches of the Archeographic Commission, but these rarely have coverage pertaining to sources from the Soviet period.[72] The Leningrad Branch of the Archeographic Commission publishes the annual series *Vspomogatel'nye istoricheskie distsipliny*, which is the most important publication vehicle for articles relating to the ancillary historical disciplines. Its principal focus tends to be prerevolutionary, but many volumes include a few articles discussing important sources from the Soviet period.[73]

4. Major individual archives

The archival directories mentioned in the general bibliographic section above will orient the researcher to most of the important archives with holdings of relevance to social history for the interwar Stalin period. It might be helpful, nonetheless, to list a few of the most important repositories, particularly on the all-union level, along with others in the Moscow-Leningrad region, since these will undoubtedly be most often utilized by foreign researchers, and updated information on finding aids is sparse.[74]

TsGAOR SSSR

The Central State Archive of the October Revolution of the USSR, or TsGAOR SSSR (*Tsentral'nyi gosudarstvennyi arkhiv Oktiabr'skoi revoliutsii, vysshikh organov gosudarstvennoi vlasti organov gosudarstvennogo upravleniia SSSR* (address: 119817 Moscow, Bol'shaia Pirogovskaia ul., 17), houses the majority of records of the Soviet all-union central government and various organs of state administration since 1917. Since 1961, when TsGAOR took over most of the former Central State Historical Archive in Moscow (TsGIAM), it has had a prerevolutionary division, but these holdings will not be of present concern. In that same year, its own holdings from the Soviet period were subdivided, and those groups of fonds relating to the economic sphere, such as central economic planning agencies, as well as ministries responsible for various phases of the economy, were transferred out to form a new Central State Archive of the National Economy (TsGANKh) (see below).

An earlier major reorganization involved shifting out all records from the 1920s specifically relating to the RSFSR. These were all transferred to the relatively new Central State Archive of the RSFSR, after its establishement in Moscow in 1957 (see below). These changes are explained in earlier published descriptions of TsGAOR, along with references to relevant literature and finding aids.[75] The most complete historical account of the archive with explanations of these major changes in profile is to be found in Dremina's 1977 volume and in her later pamphlets which chronicle developments through 1980.[76] The most recent openly published Glavarkhiv description is the nine-page survey in the 1982 short directory of cental state archives, but it does not identify specific fonds, gives no fond numbers, and is otherwise completely useless for research purposes.[77]

A short guide listing major fonds in TsGAOR was issued in 1979, but until late 1988 it was restricted for internal staff use and few copies will be found outside the archive.[78] Hence most researchers have been in the extremely disadvantaged situation of having to plan their work blind. A new, up-to-date guide with minimal annotations of each fond is in preparation. The first volume, covering prerevolutionary fonds, is due to be published in mid–1989, and the second, covering postrevolutionary holdings, is scheduled for issue by the end of 1989. A supplement is in process, listing the many fonds recently declassified. Brochures listing recent TsGAOR accessions were issued in 1986, 1987, and 1988, but few fonds from the 1920s and 1930s are involved.[79]

A guide to TsGAOR holdings as they were organized at the end of World War II was issued in 1946, and is openly available in Soviet libraries.[80] It lists major fonds from the period of the 1917 revolutions through the early 1930s, with brief annotations of their contents. Many of the holdings covered, however, are now divided among TsGA RSFSR, TsGANKh SSSR, and TsGAOR SSSR itself. Although the guide is thus of little value for identifying the present archival location or fond numbers of the fonds it describes, it has yet to be superseded in the details it provides for the contents of individual fonds and thus it retains prime research value. A second volume issued in 1952 potentially extends the coverage, but it still remains under restricted access.[81]

Although until the fall of 1988 not even a basic list of fonds in TsGAOR was made publicly available, there are a number of more specialized surveys, and analyses or citations of more limited groups of holdings, that will assist the foreign scholar in research planning before actually reaching the archive. Many of these are identified (but without fond numbers) in the Grimsted bibliographies and the Grossman and Kutik directory.

It should be noted that TsGAOR, in addition to the records in its custody, serves as a center for collecting mirofilms from archives abroad relating to the history of areas now constituting part of the USSR. Mention should accordingly be made of the 1978 published list of foreign microfilms acquired by TsGAOR, of importance to scholars working with Soviet-related materials held in foreign archives.[82]

Helpful for the identification of appropriate fonds in TsGAOR relating to labor history in the Soviet period (although unfortunately with no fond numbers) is the survey article by A. F. Butenko in the 1962 collected volume on labor history mentioned above.[83]

Of more particular interest and special note is the detailed 1958 guide to trade-union records, prepared by the Central Archive of the All-Union Central Council of Trade Unions (VTsSPS).[84] All of the trade-union records from the 1920s and 1930s described in this guide have now been transferred to TsGAOR custody, but it should be noted that there have been some changes in fond numbers in the process of transfer. The guide also lists trade-union fonds transferred earlier to TsGAOR and other fonds in TsGAOR relating to trade unions. A 1961 article by I. I. Belonosov surveys VTsSPS archival holdings for the 1940–1960 period and also explains the transfer process.[85] For a short report on the general organization of trade-union records in the Soviet Union, see the official Soviet contribution in the 1980 international guide to records for labor history.[86] As of early 1989, all trade-union records scheduled for permanent retention (approximately 5–6 percent of those records produced) through 1974 have been transferred to TsGAOR, while the VTsSPS archive retains only more recent files. In the past, VTsSPS authorities retained jurisdiction over access to their records even after transfer to TsGAOR. This problem has eased since the fall of 1988, and relatively few trade-union materials now require VTsSPS approval prior to consultation.

Access to materials from the 1920s and 1930s in TsGAOR SSSR has significantly improved since the fall of 1988. In a 1988 report in *Sovetskie arkhivy* on *perestroika* in state archives, TsGAOR SSSR was singled out for its progress in declassifying archival holdings. It is reported that during 1987–88 TsGAOR had removed restrictions from 318,000 file units and had declassified over 156,000 files. Special mention was made of declassification of major fonds from the 1920s and 1930s, with specifications on records of the Council of People's Commissars of the RSFSR, the Central Executive Committee of the USSR, a card file on individuals in the White Army and in emigration during the interwar period, the Council on Relations with the Orthodox Church, and the Committee for Cultural Ties with Foreign Countries.[87] This progress in declassification was also confirmed in a newspaper report published in September in *Sovetskaia kul'tura*.[88] According to the TsGAOR director, by the spring of 1989 the number of file units declassified had doubled again, and researchers abroad are to be assured that such declassification applies to foreign as well as Soviet scholars.[89]

Access to reference facilities in TsGAOR has also improved significantly within the past year. Not only are foreign scholars now permitted access to the 1979 guide, but, even more important, since late 1988 foreigners are at last being given access to internal *opisi*, which can be seen as one of the most encouraging developments in recent years.

TsGANKh

As its name indicates, the Central State Archive of the National Economy, or TsGANKh SSSR (*Tsentral'nyi gosudarstvennyi arkhiv narodnogo khoziaistva*

SSSR) (address: 119817 Moscow, Bol'shaia Pirogovskaia ul., 17), serves as the all-union central repository for records relating to the national economy. Most of the initial fonds were transferred to TsGANKh from TsGAOR SSSR after the archive was founded in 1961. Those fonds transferred include the records of central planning agencies such as GOSPLAN SSSR, the Central Statistical Administration, the State Bank of the USSR, and all those of ministries (and earlier, commissariats) involved with heavy industry, food and light industry, construction and metallurgy, finance, agriculture, and transportation and communication. Despite the transfer to the separate Central State Archive of the RSFSR of many fonds previously held in TsGAOR, fonds of all-union significance relating to the economy from institutions of the RSFSR, particularly from the 1920s, are now housed in TsGANKh. Some fond numbers have been changed in the process, but many remain unchanged. Some additional groups of fonds, principally from the 1940s and 1950s, came directly from the institutional records of their creating agencies, especially those from various agencies liquidated in the course of the Khrushchev economic reforms.

A guide, or short directory, listing the major fonds in TsGANKh was published in 1973, but was initially restricted for internal use only.[90] The restriction has now been lifted, but, since the guide was prepared for internal use, it was not distributed to libraries. The guide lists with brief annotations the major fonds held by the archive under various rubrics representing the major categories of records held in the archive: records of institutions involved with planning, statistics, and population censuses; financial institutions including credit, savings, and insurance agencies; institutions of science and technology (excluding the Academy of Sciences); manufacturing; agriculture; forestry; transportation and communication; construction and architecture (although technical plans and drawings are held in TsGANTD); trade; storage and supply; geological, geodesic, cartographic, and hydrometric services (although some such records are held in more specialized independent archives); records of cooperatives; and personal fonds. A new, more detailed guide to the archive is now in the final stages of preparation and is scheduled for publication at the end of 1989. Some of the earlier records from the 1920s transferred from TsGAOR are described briefly in the 1946 guide to TsGAOR, but there is no published key to indicate which fonds were transferred.[91]

A detailed guide covering personal fonds in TsGANKh was issued in 1987, but has not been widely distributed.[92] An earlier article by one of the compilers describes many of the personal fonds that have been brought together in the archive; more important, a sizable volume by the same author describing work with personal papers in TsGANKh was deposited in typescript in the VNIIDAD depository, and is also available to researchers in the archive.[93]

In terms of other general descriptions of TsGANKh, the initial brief treatment of the archive in the Grimsted 1972 directory has now been largely superseded by the short coverage in the Grossman and Kutik directory (again without fond numbers), which also lists a few more articles published about its holdings.[94] The 1982 directory of central state archives provides a superficial six-page survey of the holdings with no fond numbers or dates for specific archival groups.[95] The Dremina studies mentioned above provide more detailed historical background on the structure and profile of the archive, which is a helpful orientation for researchers trying to figure out the transfers. Dremina also mentions the recent activities in the archive including the preparation of much-needed finding aids.[96]

Access to holdings in TsGANKh has eased for foreigners in the past decade, and particularly since the fall of 1988. Some fonds deposited in TsGANKh still have restrictions by their creating agencies, and there have been a number of complaints in the Soviet press about the difficult process of securing permission to use such records. Soviet scholars further complain that even if they are finally shown the materials they need after the long bureaucratic process of securing permission, they are not permitted to cite the documents.[97] According to a 1988 comment by the director, two-thirds of the fonds in TsGANKh had been subject to such restrictions by their depositing agencies, but that number has now been reduced to one third.[98] According to current policy, the lifting of such restrictions and the declassification process extends to foreign as well as Soviet researchers. This is a most welcome change in policy, since in recent years TsGANKh SSSR has shown considerable reluctance to communicate many otherwise open records to foreign researchers, particularly if they have not been studied in detail by Soviet scholars.

As an additional important development in the past year, reference facilities have become more available to foreign scholars. Not only are foreign scholars now permitted access to the 1973 guide, but, even more important, since late 1988 foreigners are at last being given access to internal *opisi*, thus permitting better understanding of the contents and organization of individual fonds and the possibility of ordering appropriate materials directly.

Other central state archives of the USSR

Among all-union archives, the two central state archives mentioned above will undoubtedly be the most important for social historians of the prewar Stalin years. Several other all-union central state archives also maintain records from the period and may deserve attention.

TsGAKFD SSSR. Documentary films and photographs from the Soviet period are maintained in the special Central State Archive of Film and Photo Documents—TsGAKFD SSSR (*Tsentral'nyi gosudarstvennyi arkhiv kinofotodokumentov SSSR*), in Krasnogorsk, outside of Moscow (address: 143400 g. Krasnogorsk, Rechnaia ul., 1). Feature films are kept in the special feature film archive, the so-called Gosfil'm-ofond in Belye Stolby, not far from Moscow, which is administered apart from the state archival system.[99]

TsGAZ SSSR. Sound recordings are apt to be less relevant, but these are now housed separately in the Central State Archive of Sound Recordings—TsGAZ SSSR (*Tsentral'nyi gosudarstvennyi arkhiv zvukozapisi SSSR* Moscow (address: 107005 Moscow, 2-ia Baumanskaia ul., 3).[100]

TsGALI SSSR. Records of institutions in cultural fields, including literature and the arts, along with many personal fonds of individuals are housed in the Central State Archive of Literature and Art of the USSR—TsGALI SSSR (*Tsentral'nyi gosudarst-vennyi arkhiv literatury i iskusstva SSSR*) (address: 125512 Moscow, Vyborgskaia ul., 3/k.2). This archive is the best described of all of the eleven central state archives in terms of up-to-date guides and published inventories of many individual fonds. Indeed, there are now six volumes in the series of guides to TsGALI, the latest of which appeared in 1988 and covers accessions during the years 1978 to 1983.[101] Of tremendous relevance for the social historian, TsGALI SSSR traditionally has been more accessible to foreigners in terms of holdings from the Soviet period than other central state archives. Unlike the situation for foreigners in other central state archives in Moscow, readers are allowed access to the main TsGALI reading room, and since the spring of 1988, they are being permitted access to *opisi* and many of the rich card catalogs covering various parts of the holdings.

TsGASA. The Central State Archive of the Soviet Army—TsGASA (*Tsentral'nyi gosudarstvennyi arkhiv Sovetskoi Armii*) contains military records extending through the 1930s. The 1982 Glavarkhiv directory provides a brief, superficial survey of TsGASA holdings. The only published guide, as well as published inventories, covers only materials from the period of World War I and the Civil War up to the early 1920s.[102]

Military archives with records from the Soviet period still remain the least accessible to foreigners, yet their holdings may well be of considerable interest in terms of the potential for topics of social history.

TsGAVMF SSSR. Holdings for the Soviet period in the Central State Archive of the Navy of the USSR—TsGAVMF SSSR (*Tsentral'nyi gosudarstvennyi arkhiv Voenno-Morskogo Flota SSSR*) are not listed in any guide.[103]

State archives of the RSFSR

The existence of a 1980 directory of state archives of the RSFSR[104] makes it less important to enumerate the various state archives on the level of the RSFSR now located in Moscow and Leningrad. Nevertheless, it might be well to mention several of the most important institutions along with available guides, particularly since their official designations have been changed since most of the earlier directories and guides were published.

TsGA RSFSR. The separate Central State Archive of the RSFSR—TsGA RSFSR (*Tsentral'nyi gosudarstvennyi arkhiv RSFSR*) (address: 121059 Moscow, Berezhkovskaia naberezhnaia, 26), established in 1957, is of high importance for social historians of the 1920s and 1930s. As mentioned earlier, it received many groups of records earlier held by TsGAOR SSSR and listed in the 1946 published TsGAOR guide.[105] These are principally the holdings of high-level agencies of the

RSFSR, after its establishment in 1923, which during the 1920s also served many all-union functions. There are records of a few of these agencies that have scattered holdings going back earlier than 1923 in TsGA RSFSR. It should be noted that there is a separate Central State Archive for the RSFSR (*TsGA RSFSR Dal'nego Vostoka*) in Tomsk that holds records of provenance in Far Eastern regions, with holdings dating back to the eighteenth century. No guide is available for this archive, although there is a brief survey of holdings in the general 1980 directory of RSFSR state archives.

A new short guide for TsGA RSFSR in Moscow was issued in 1973, initially for public circulation, but, unfortunately, as an example of restrictive Glavarkhiv policies regarding more recent guides, it was withdrawn and classified "for internal use only." As of fall 1988, that restriction has still not been lifted.[106] Before that, a very preliminary list of fonds in TsGA RSFSR was issued in 1959, two years after its establishment, but before it received the transfers from TsGAOR SSSR.[107] That guide describes an extensive group of institutional records from ministries and related agencies in the RSFSR, particularly in areas of manufacturing and trade that were liquidated in 1957, as part of the major regional economic administrative reforms under Nikita Khrushchev. These massive records, predominantly dating from the 1940s and early 1950s, were transferred for permanent preservation to the newly established archive. Few of these fonds date from earlier than the end of the 1930s, so this early guide will have relatively little to offer the researcher for the social history of earlier decades. In addition to brief coverage in the 1980 RSFSR directory, there are several other descriptions of TsGA RSFSR that merit attention.[108]

Moscow oblast archive—TsGAMO. The Central State Archive of Moscow Oblast—TsGAMO (*Tsentral'nyi gosudarstvennyi arkhiv Moskovskoi oblasti*) (address: 113149 Moscow, Azovskskaia ul., 17) as currently organized, houses only postrevolutionary records from oblast-level institutions. Although oblast-level archives in the past were always known simply as the "State," rather than the "Central State" archive of a particular oblast, the Moscow oblast archive was given the higher status in 1980. Now administered by the Archival Administration of the Moscow Oblast Executive Committee (AU Mosobispolkom), it has been subjected to a series of complicated reorganizations in recent decades along with other local Moscow state archives.[109] Its current organization and holdings are reflected in the comprehensive new guide issued in 1983.[110] This recent guide is essential for researchers, although for the description of some fonds, it is well to compare the earlier 1963 guide issued under the earlier name of the archive (GAORSS MO).[111] Those interested in labor history will also want to consult the lists of early factory and labor records held by the archive included in a publication from the early 1930s.[112] A later 1959 listing of factory records in the archive has less detail, although some additional fonds are included, and all have the then current fond numbers.[113] Labor-related sources from the Moscow region for the period of the First Five-Year Plan, including trade-union records, are surveyed in a 1961 article by Ia. Z. Livshits.[114] Researchers should be aware, however, that some of these holdings of more purely municipal provenance or pertinence earlier held by the former GAMO (earlier GAORSS MO) have been transferred to the newly established Moscow city archive for postrevolutionary holdings (TsGAORSS g. Moskvy) (see below). This would include records from some factories physically located in the city of Moscow itself and trade-union fonds from city union organizations and councils.

Moscow city archives. As a result of the reorganization of Moscow city archives in 1976, there are now three separate municipal-level central state archives in the capital. From 1976 to 1988 they were all responsible directly to the Archival Administration of the Moscow City Executive Committee (AU Mosgorispolkoma), but starting in 1988 they were administratively linked more closely under the Moscow City Associated Archives (*Moskovskoe gorodskoe ob"edinenie arkhivov*). Two of these are relevant here for postrevolutionary holdings, since the third—the Central State Historical Archive of the City of Moscow (TsGIA g. Moskvy)—holds purely prerevolutionary records.[115] All three are located in a new building adjacent to the Kaluzhskaia metro station (Address: 117393 Moscow, Profsoiuznaia ul., 80), and are serviced by modern research facilities including a large reading room. As of spring 1989, foreign scholars are permitted direct access to this facility.

TsGAORSS g. Moskvy. Most important for the Soviet period, the Central State Archive of the October Revolution and Socialist Construction of the city of Moscow—TsGAORSS g. Moskvy (*Tsentral'nyi gosudarstvennyi arkhiv Oktiabr'skoi revolutsii i sotsialisticheskogo stroitel'stva g. Moskvy*)—now holds postrevolutionary records designated for permanent preservation from all state institutions centered within the capital city itself. Theoretically, there is now a strict, distinct territorial division between city and oblast archives in terms of the postrevolutionary institution from which they receive records, but although the allocation of records is supposed to follow a logical pattern, lines of demarcation are occasionally blurred. Following the reorganization in 1976, TsGAORSS g. Moskvy accordingly took over some city-based records from the former GAMO (now TsGAMO). A guide with brief annotations of major fonds in TsGAORSS g. Moskvy has been prepared and is scheduled for issue at the end of 1989. Details of fonds listed earlier as being held in the oblast archive and subsequently transferred to the city archive should be clarified by this new guide.[116]

TsGAKFFD g. Moskvy. Audiovisual materials of a documentary nature originating in the city of Moscow are now held in the separate Central State Archive of Film, Photo-, and Phonographic Documentation of the city of Moscow—TsGAKFFD g. Moskvy (*Tsentral'nyi gosudarstvennyi arkhiv kinofotofonodokumentov g. Moskvy*). A short guide to the holdings of this local Moscow audiovisual archive was issued in 1987.[117]

Leningrad city and oblast archives. Local state archives in Leningrad have also been reorganized in recent decades. There are now five state archives for the city of Leningrad and one additional one for Leningrad oblast, all of which are administered by the Leningrad Oblast and City Executive Committee (AU Lenoblgorispolkom). Five of these have pertinent holdings for the postrevolutionary period. The sixth is the Central State Historical Archive of Leningrad (TsGIAL), before 1969 officially known as the Leningrad State Historical Archive (LGIA), which holds all prerevolutionary records from the city and guberniia of St. Petersburg.[118]

Given this complete reorganization, researchers should be wary of the listings in the 1960 short directory of holdings in Leningrad state archives.[119]

TsGAORSSL. Most basic for the social historian of the 1920s and 1930s is the Central State Archive of the October Revolution and Socialist Development of Leningrad—TsGAORSSL (*Tsentral'nyi gosudarstvennyi arkhiv Oktiabr'skoi revoliutsii i sotsialisticheskogo stroitel'stva Leningrada*), which is the new name of the principal postrevolutionary repository. Before 1974, it was known as the Leningrad State Archive of the October Revolution and Socialist Development (LGAORSS), and earlier, the State Archive of the October Revolution and Socialist Construction of Leningrad Oblast (GAORSS LO). The present archive still retains many of the holdings described in the 1962 guide.[120] But, along lines similar to the case in Moscow, some of those holdings—most specifically those from oblast-level institutions located outside the city itself—are held by the newly reorganized Leningrad Oblast State Archive in Vyborg (LOGAV). In addition to those changes, some holdings from cultural organizations in Leningrad are held by the newly constituted central State Archive of Literature and Art of Leningrad (TsGALIL).

An article describing sources for labor history in the former LGAORSS was published in a 1961 miscellany volume and two more articles appeared in a 1962 volume. Most of them remain in TsGAORSSL, as do the extensive factory records that were listed in a 1959 volume.[121]

LOGAV. The former LGAORSS branch archive in Vyborg has now become the separate Leningrad Oblast State Archive in Vyborg—LOGAV (*Leningradskii oblasnyi gosudarstvennyi arkhiv v g. Vyborge*). The Vyborg repository holds predominantly postrevolutionary records from Leningrad Oblast institutions based outside the city of Leningrad, but it also holds some scattered local records from Vyborg guberniia dating to the eighteenth century.

TsGALIL. Unlike the situation in Moscow, there is a separate Central State Archive of Literature and Art of Leningrad—TsGALIL (*Tsentral'nyi gosudarstvennyi arkhiv literatury i isskustva Leningrada*), until 1969 known officially as the Leningrad State Archive of Literature and Art—LGALI (*Leningradskii gosudarstvennyi arkhiv literatury i isskustva*), to which has been transferred all of the fonds of postrevolutionary cultural institutions earlier held by LGAORSS. Its holdings date only from the postrevolutionary period, and are accordingly of great importance to the social historian of the early decades of Soviet rule.

TsGAKFFDL. Like the situation in Moscow, there is also a separate Central State Archive of Film-, Photo-, and Phonographic Documents of Leningrad—TsGAKFFDL (*Tsentral'nyi gosudarstvennyi arkhiv kinofotofonodokumentov Leningrada*). As of 1988, however, it is functioning only on a limited scale for photographs, pending construction of a new facility. In the meantime documentary films and sound-recordings remain in their creating agencies.

TsGANTDL. There is also a separate Central State Archive for Scientific-Technical Documentation of Leningrad (*Tsentral'nyi gosudarstvennyi arkhiv nauchno-tekhnicheskii dokumentatsii Leningrada* (TsGANTDL), which houses engineering and construction drawings and similar technical documentation. Before 1969 its was known simply as the Leningrad State Archive for Scientific-Technical Documentation (LGANTD).

*   *   *

Postrevolutionary state archives with local records outside of Moscow and Leningrad are surveyed briefly in the RSFSR archive directory mentioned above.[122]

Communist Party archives

Obviously one of the most important archives for the social historian of the prewar 1920s and 1930s is the Central Party Archive of the Institute of Marxism-Leninism under the Central Committee of the Communist Party of the Soviet Union—TsPA (*Tsentral'nyi partiinyi arkhiv IML pri TsK KPSS*).

There has been much bitter recent criticism in the Soviet press of access prohibition to Party archives. For example, MGIAI rector Afanas'ev has called for "wider access to Party documents for all researchers."[123] And Professor Ilizarov, also from MGIAI, has put the current restrictive access policy to Party archives in appropriate perspective: "When one considers the fundamental political and organizational power that the Party has wielded over society during the past seventy years," he complains, one would have to project that "today, up to fifty percent of all retrospective information on the history of Soviet society is locked away from wide scholarly societal consciousness. . . ."[124] Despite the publication of his and similar complaints, there has been little indication of improved access to Party archives in recent years, even for trusted Soviet scholars. Researchers should continue to try and to hope that sources in Party archives will become more accessible. One American exchange scholar was admitted to the library of the Institute of Marxism-Leninism during the academic year 1987–1988. From limited reports, the institute is more prepared than in the past to communicate with foreign researchers, but as of the academic year 1988–1989 there has been no progress in terms of access for foreign scholars.[125]

The most research-oriented survey of holdings in TsPA appears in the Grossman and Kutik directory, which also has a rich bibliography of descriptive literature.

That directory also includes a separate description of the separate Central Archive of the *Komsomol* (*Tsentral'nyi arkhiv VLKSM*), and an additional survey of local Party archives, which, as mentioned above, parallels the system of state archives down to the oblast level.[126] Otherwise, the most informative description remains the 1956 article by A. A. Struchkov.[127] Grossman and Kutik fail to mention the whole series of survey reports on new acquisitions to the Central Party Archive that were published from 1958 through 1974.[128] Two rather superficial textbooks on the early history of Party archives were prepared by V. E. Korneev for MGIAI,[129] and the 1979 survey by D. I. Antoniuk contains considerable bibliography on Party archival history.[130] Also helpful is the 1984 survey by V. V. Anikeev.[131] Other studies of relevance to the Party archive include the general 1968 textbook by Maksakov (see n. 30) and the Varshavchik surveys of sources for Party history.[132]

Other major repositories in Moscow and Leningrad

Foreign researchers should not overlook the often abundant archival materials for social history located in the wide range of libraries and museums in Moscow and Leningrad, as well as those in other institutes under the Academy of Sciences. Published information about these holdings is still inadequate, but in many cases the repositories themselves as well as their internal finding aids are more open to foreign researchers than is the case in state archives.[133]

* * *

The recent calls for *perestroika* in historical scholarship and the more open discussion of historical problems of those decades in the press give cause for hope that Soviet historians will soon turn to a more honest, serious, and archival-based examination of existing sources. The extent to which archival resources and the requisite archival finding aids will be more open to foreign researchers remains to be seen, but researchers from abroad need to keep trying. Fundamental changes in policies and practices within the archival establishment, and in the extent to which foreigners are accepted without discrimination, are not going to come overnight. Yet historians will continue to find the wealth of documentary materials that have been preserved from the 1920s and 1930s well worth the many frustrations of gaining access to them. If there is to be true *perestroika* in historical interpretation, leading to a more honest interpretation and understanding of the formative decades of the Soviet Union, Soviet and foreign historians alike will need to start with more open archival investigation.

Notes

1. For a perceptive English-language account of some of the recent developments relating to the study of history, see R. W. Davies, "Soviet History in the Gorbachev Revolution: The First Phase," *Socialist Register,* 1988, pp. 37–78. See also the more journalistic two-part article by Dev Murarka, likewise covering developments through the first half of 1987:

"Soviet History I: Recovering the Buried Stalin Years," *The Nation*, 24 October 1987, pp. 447–51; and "Soviet History II: A New Revolution in Consciousness," *The Nation*, 31 October 1987, pp. 486–90. A much longer, two-part chronicle by Stephen Wheatcroft covers many of these developments in more detail to the end of 1987: "Unleashing the Energy of History, Mentioning the Unmentionable, and Restructuring Soviet Historical Awareness: Moscow, 1987," *Australian Slavonic and East European Studies* 1, no. 1 (1987): 85–132; and "Steadying the Energy of History and Probing the Limits of *Glasnost'*: Moscow July to December 1987," *Australian Slavonic and East European Studies* 1, no. 2 (1987): 57–114. See also the somewhat more politically oriented account by Thomas Sherlock, "Politics and History under Gorbachev," *Problems of Communism* 37, nos. 3–4 (May–August 1988): 16–42; and the insightful paper by Mark von Hagen, "History and Politics under Gorbachev: Professional Autonomy and Democratization," *Harriman Institute Forum* 1, no. 11 (November 1988).

2. See my article, "*Glasnost'* in the Archives? Recent Developments on the Soviet Archival Scene," *American Archivist* 52, no. 2 (Spring 1989): 214–36.

3. "Spasti sluzhbu sotsial'noi pamiati, Pis'mo v gazetu," (Signed) Uchenyi sovet Moskovskogo gosudarstvennogo istoriko-arkhivnogo instituta, *Sovetskaia kul'tura,* 31 May 1988, p. 6. See also the supporting comments in answer to this article by A. Prokopenko, "Dela arkhivnye . . . ," *Sovetskaia kul'tura,* 13 August 1988, p. 7.

4. My survey of archival history since 1917, presented as an historical introduction in *Archives and Manuscript Repositories in the USSR: Moscow and Leningrad* (Princeton: Princeton University Press, 1972), pp. 23–60, needs considerable amplification and updating. More bibliography on the history of Soviet archives is included in my *Archives . . . : Moscow and Leningrad*, Supplement 1: *Bibliographical Addenda* (Zug, Switzerland: Inter-Documentation, 1976). Additional selected literature through 1985–1986 is included in my study *Recent Soviet Archival Literature: A Review and Preliminary Bibliography of Selected Reference Aids* (Washington, D.C.: Kennan Institute for Advanced Russian Studies, 1987; *Occasional Paper,* No. 204). See my more recent but briefer survey in *A Handbook for Archival Research in the USSR* (Washington, D.C.: Kennan Institute for Advanced Russian Studies and International Research and Exchanges Board, 1989), chapter 1. Bibliographic references cited in my directory series that are also cited in the present article are accompanied by the corresponding "PKG" code number. Included with the publication data for citations in this article is the corresponding microfiche order number for those items now available in microfiche editions from Inter Documentation Company (IDC), Leiden, The Netherlands.

Several surveys of archival development in the USSR have been published, especially as textbooks for the Moscow State Historico-Archival Institute (MGIAI), but for the most part they provide only the bare administrative details. Soviet archival developments up to the end of World War II are narrated in some detail by V. V. Maksakov in a volume based on the author's lectures at the Moscow State Historico-Archival Institute: *Istoriia i organizatsiia arkhivnogo dela v SSSR, 1917–1945* (Moscow: "Nauka," 1969; [IDC—R–10,772]); see PKG—A–98. See also the more recent superficial text by V. I. Vialikov, *Arkhivnoe stroitel'-stvo v SSSR (1917–1945 gg.) Uchebnoe posobie* (Moscow: MGIAI, 1976). Also covering the early decades of Soviet rule and somewhat more readable are the brief texts by V. N. Samoshenko, *Arkhivnoe delo v period postroeniia sotsializma v SSSR, 1917–1937 gg. Uchebnoe posobie* (Moscow: MGIAI, 1982), and V. V. Sorokin, *Arkhivy uchrezhdenii SSSR (1917–1937 gg.). Uchebnoe posobie* (Moscow: MGIAI, 1982).

Published collections of basic Soviet archival decrees and legislation provide the legal framework. Many of the successive regulations for archival affairs are included in the official collection *Sbornik rukovodiashchikh materialov po arkhivnomu dely 1918–1982 gg.* (Moscow: GAU, 1985), and the even briefer 1968, *K 50-letiiu sovetskogo arkhivnogo dela* (Moscow: GAU, 1968).

5. See more details and citations to the relevant Soviet literature in my article "Lenin's

Archival Decree of 1918: The Bolshevik Legacy for Soviet Archival Theory and Practice,''
American Archivist 45, no. 4 (Fall 1982): 429–43.

6. See "Polozhenie ob Arkhivnom fonde KPSS" (28 December 1966), as described in
"Ob Arkhivnom fonde KPSS," *Partiinaia zhizn'*, 1967, no. 2, pp. 52–55.

7. "Polozhenie o Gosudarstvennom arkhivnom fonde Soiuza SSR," 13 August 1958,
was reprinted in *Sovetskie arkhivy,* 1980, no. 4, pp. 3–11. The entire text is reprinted in
Osnovye dekrety, pp. 49–66. See also the previous regulations, "Polozhenie o Gosudarstvennom arkhivnom fonde Soiuza SSR," 13 August 1958, reprinted in *K 50-letiiu sovetskogo arkhivnogo dela,* pp. 26–41.

8. The regulation defining the functions of GAU dated 28 July 1961 is printed in *K 50-
letiiu sovetskogo arkhivnogo dela,* pp. 42–48, and in *Osnovye dekrety,* pp. 27–32. It was
earlier published in *Voprosy arkhivovedeniia,* 1961, no. 3, pp. 3–8, followed by a commentary (pp. 9–20). The most recent updated regulation dated 4 April 1980 is published in
Sovetskie arkhivy, 1980, no. 4, pp. 12–16, and reprinted in *Osnovye dekrety,* pp. 49–66.

9. Among the most extensive critical comments on the proposed change were the interview with VNIIDAD director A. I. Chugunov: R. Armeev, "Bez arkhivov net istorii,"
Izvestiia, 2 June 1988, p. 4; the open letter against the draft law by the Scholarly Council of
the archival training institute (MGIAI), "Spasti sluzhbu sotsial'noi pamiati, Pis'mo v gaze-
tu," (Signed) Uchenyi sovet Moskovskogo gosudarstvennogo istoriko-arkhivnogo instituta,
Sovetskaia kul'tura, 13 August 1988, p. 7; the open letter by MGIAI professor Boris Ilizarov,
"Komu vygodny tainy. Trevozhnye voprosy po povodu proekta Zakona o gosarkhive,"
Literaturnaia gazeta, 1988, no. 22 (1 June), pp. 7, 12; and the more recent article by Boris
Ilizarov, "Ob arkhivakh—i tainyi bor'be za sokhranenie ikh 'tain,'" *Ogonek,* 1989, no. 2 (7–
14 January), pp. 10–11.

10. See the latest compendia, *Osnovnye pravila raboty gosudarstvennykh arkhivov,* ed.
F. M. Vaganov, A. V. Elpat'evskii et al. (Moscow: Glavarkhiv, 1984; [IDC—R–17,256]),
with the authority of the official edict of Glavarkhiv, no. 352, dated 7 December 1983. English
edition: *Basic Rules for the Work of the USSR State Archives* (Moscow: Glavarkhiv, 1984).
The awkward translation into unprofessional English makes it very difficult to understand, so
readers are urged to compare the Russian version. Compare the earlier edition under the same
title, edited by L. L. Smoktunovich (Moscow: GAU, 1962; [IDC—R–11,076]); see PKG—
A-99.5.

11. VNIIDAD was the focus of a visit by two American archivists participating in the first
exchange of archival specialists under the new Soviet-American Commission on Archival
Cooperation. See the report by Edwin C. Bridges, "The Soviet Union's Archival Research
Center: Observations of an American Visitor," *American Archivist* 51 (Fall 1988): 486–500.
Bridges emphasizes its research and development in the field of records management and
appraisal.

12. See more details about the functions of Glavarkhiv in Grimsted, *Archives: Moscow
and Leningrad,* pp. 27–34, and the more recent *Handbook for Research,* pp. 8–18.

13. *Edinaia gosudarstvennaia sistema deloproizvodstva (Osnovnye polozheniia),* ed.
V. N. Avtokratov, A. P. Kurantov, M. T. Likhachev, et al., under the direction of F. I.
Dolgikh (Moscow: GAU, 1973). The publication carries the Council of Ministers registration
number as an official regulation (Postanovlenie no. 435, dated 4.IX.73). See also the relevant
sections in the latest edition of the basic Soviet textbook for archival affairs, *Teoriia i praktika
arkhivnogo dela v SSSR,* 2d ed., ed. F. I. Dolgikh and K. I. Rudel'son (Moscow: "Vysshaia
shkola," 1980; [IDC—R–14,837]); a German translation of this textbook was prepared by the
East German Archival Administration: *Theorie und Praxis des Archivwesens in der UdSSR.
Lehrbuch für Studenten im Fach Geschichte/Archivwissenschaft,* 2d ed., ed. E. Schetelich
(Berlin: Staatliche Archivverwaltung der DDR, 1983). Earlier records management regulations were issued in 1963: *Osnovnye pravila postanovki dokumental'noi chasti deloproizvodstva i raboty arkhivov uchrezhdenii, organizatsii i predpriiatii SSSR* (Moscow: GAU,
1963).

14. K. I. Rudel'son, *Sovremennye dokumentnye klassifikatsii* (Moscow: "Nauka," 1973).

15. *Unifitsirovannaia sistema organizatsionno-rasporiaditel'noi dokumentatsii. Unifitsirovannye formy, instruktivnye i metodicheskie materialy po ikh primeneniiu,* 2d ed. (Moscow: VNIIDAD, 1981).

16. R. Armeev, "Bez arkhivov net istorii," p. 4.

17. *Sbornik zakonodatel'nykh aktov po deloproizvodstvu (1917–1970 gg.). Uchebnoe posobie,* ed. Ia. Z. Livshits (Moscow: MGIAI, 1973). This volume was not widely distributed publicly in the USSR and is still not available abroad.

18. *Aktual'nye voprosy metodiki dokumentovedeniia i arkhivovedeniia,* ed. M. S. Seleznev (Moscow: MGIAI, 1976).

19. See the literature cited on records management in the bibliographic section below.

20. Soviet procedures for appraisal (in Russian, *ekspertiza tsennosti dokumentov*) and the function of the Appraisal Commissions are described in *Teoriia i praktika,* pp. 60–107.

21. The latest regulations are summarized in the decree of 4 April 1980, outlining the State Archival Fond: "Polozhenie o GAF SSSR," *Sovetskie arkhivy,* 1980, no. 4, p. 8, especially paragraph 16.

22. For regulations in the 1920s and early 1930s, see also the article by O. E. Bogdanova, "Iz istorii vedomstvennykh arkhivov (1918–1936 gg.)," in *Aktual'nye problemy sovetskogo arkhivovedeniia,* ed. S. P. Liushin et al. (Moscow: MGIAI, 1976), pp. 88–107.

23. Dmitri G. Iurasov, "Unichtozhenie poslednego sudebnogo arkhiva 30-x—50-x godov," *Glasnost'. Informatsionnyi biulleten'* (Moscow), July 1987, nos. 2–4, p. 2; I quote the text republished in English translation, *Glasnost* (New York), July 1987, nos. 2–4, p. 3.

24. *Ibid.* (Moscow edition), p. 3; English edition (New York), pp. 3–4.

25. "Iurii Afanas'ev ob unichtozhenii dokumentov . . . ," *Novoe russkoe slovo* (New York), 4 November 1988, p. 1.

26. Uchenyi sovet Moskovskogo gosudarstvennogo istoriko-arkhivnogo instituta, "Spasti sluzhbu sotsial'noi pamiati, Pis'mo v gazetu," *Sovetskaia kul'tura,* 31 May 1988, p. 6.

27. See Vaganov's comments quoted by V. Molchanov, "Dostup ogranichen. Netraditsionnye razmyshleniia v sviazi s iubileem," *Pravda,* 1 June 1988, p. 4. A short summary of the article, under the title "Access Restricted," appears in the *Current Digest of the Soviet Press* 40, no. 22 (1988): 22–23.

28. The latest (1984) rules for archival work in the USSR include several sections devoted to arrangement and description practices for Soviet state archives: *Osnovnye pravila raboty gosudarstvennykh arkhivov,* especially pp. 17–34, and 61–106. Many of the specifications are presented in more general terms in *Teoriia i praktika arkhivnogo dela v SSSR* (1980), especially pp. 20–60, 117–32, and 147–65.

29. I prefer to anglicize the term "fond" with reference to Soviet archives, because there is no precise English equivalent, and because Soviet usage differs in a number of ways from the American "record group" or the British "archive group." See the helpful compendium of Soviet archival terminology, *Kratkii slovar' arkhivnoi terminologii,* ed. I. S. Nazin et al. (Moscow: GAU, 1968; [IDC—R–9886]) (PKG—H–63). See the detailed explanation of Soviet practices in the formation of archival fonds in *Teoriia i praktika arkhivnogo dela,* 2d ed., especially pp. 28–60.

30. The early development of the Communist Party archival system is discussed in the posthumous booklet by V. V. Maksakov, *Organizatsiia arkhivov KPSS (Uchebnoe posobie),* ed. Iu. F. Kononov (Moscow: MGIAI, 1968; [IDC—R–10,831]) (PKG—D–1). See also the more recent textbooks by Valentin Efimovich Korneev, *Arkhivy VKP(b) v 1917–1925 gg. Uchebnoe posobie* (Moscow: MGIAI, 1979) and *Arkhivy VKP(b) (1926–1941 gg.). Uchebnoe posobie* (Moscow: MGIAI, 1981).

31. See more details about these arrangement processes with examples in *Teoriia i praktika arkhivnogo dela,* 2d ed., especially pp. 43–54.

32. See the most recent Grimsted coverage in *Handbook for Research,* especially chapter 5. For more detailed coverage of institutions in Moscow and Leningrad and some general bibliography, see my initial 1972 directory, *Archives . . . : Moscow and Leningrad,* and 1976 Supplement 1, as well as the 1986 Kennan Institute pamphlet, "Recent Soviet Archival Literature." The first book of my coverage of Ukrainian archives provides considerable general bibliography and a directory of archival repositories, *Archives and Manuscript Repositories in the USSR: Ukraine and Moldavia,* book 1: *General Bibliography and Institutional Directory* (Princeton: Princeton University Press, 1988).

33. Iurii Mironovich Grossman and Vitalii Naumovich Kutik, *Spravochnik nauchnogo rabotnika: Arkhivy, dokumenty, issledovatel',* 2d ed. (Lviv: "Vyshcha shkola," 1983; [IDC—R-14,560]); see PKG—NG-1. See the Grimsted detailed review and bibliography relating to this volume, *Recent Soviet Archival Literature,* and the shorter review essay, "A New Soviet Directory of Archives and Manuscript Repositories: A Major Contribution in Light of Recent Reference Aids," *Slavic Review* (Fall 1986): 534–44.

34. Iurii Mironovich Grossman and Vitalii Naumovich Kutik, *Spravochnik nauchnogo rabotnika: Arkhivy, dokumenty, issledovatel',* (Lviv: "Vyshcha shkola," 1979; [IDC—R-14,870]). See the detailed Grimsted review article, "Recent Publications on Archives and Manuscript Collections in the Soviet Union: A Selective Survey," *Slavic Review* (Fall 1982): 511–33.

35. *Gosudarstvennye arkhivy SSSR. Kratkii spravochnik,* 2 vols. (Moscow: "Mysl'," 1989). With a pressrun of 35,000, in *Novye knigi,* the directory should be widely available. Compare the comprehensive list of state archives throughout the USSR together with their available published guides in the Grimsted *Handbook for Research,* Appendices 1–3.

36. *Gosudarstvennye arkhivy Soiuza SSR. Kratkii spravochnik,* ed. G. A. Belov, A. I. Loginova, S. V. Nefedova, and I. N. Firsov (Moscow: GAU, 1956; [IDC—R-3533]); (reprint ed.: Cambridge: Oriental Research Partners, 1973); see PKG—A-7/NG-82.

37. *Tsentral'nye gosudarstvennye arkhivy SSR. Kratkii spravochnik,* comp. T. N. Dolgorukova, O. Iu. Nezhdanova, and S. I. Iudkin; ed. F. I. Dolgikh et al. (Moscow: Glavarkhiv, 1982).

38. G. A. Dremina, *Tsentral'nye gosudarstvennye arkhivy SSSR 1945–1970 gg. (Uchebnoe posobie)* (Moscow: MGIAI, 1977). Again, unfortunately, this text was issued in a small pressrun and is not widely available in foreign libraries. See the Grimsted directory, *Archives . . . : Moscow and Leningrad,* pp. 121–95, and Supplement 1, pp. 29–65, for additional bibliography.

39. G. A. Dremina, *Tsentral'nye gosudarstvennye arkhivy SSSR v deviatoi piatiletke. Uchebnoe posobie* (Moscow: MGIAI, 1984); G. A. Dremina, *Tsentral'nye gosudarstvennye arkhivy v period razvitogo sotsializma. Tekst lektsii* (Moscow: MGIAI, 1986). The 1986 pamphlet covers only TsGAOR SSSR, TsGANKh, and TsGALI SSSR.

40. *Gosudarstvennye arkhivy RSFSR. Spravochnik-putevoditel',* comp. E. M. Korneva et al.; ed. V. A. Tiuneev et al. (Moscow: "Sovetskaia Rossiia," 1980).

41. See also the brief survey and bibliography for archives of the RSFSR in the Grossman and Kutik directory, pp. 62–71 (bibliography pp. 368–72).

42. *Gosudarstvennye arkhivy Ukrainskoi SSR,* comp. K. M. Arkhipenko, V. N. Volkovinskii, S. N. Kirzhaev et al.; ed. A. G. Mitiukov (Kiev: "Naukova Dumka," 1988). This volume updates the highly popularized Ukrainian-language directory that was issued in 1972: *Derzhavni arkhivy Ukrains'koi RSR. Korotkyi dovidnyk* (Kiev: "Naukova dumka," 1972; [IDC—R-14,303]).

43. Grimsted, *Archives . . . : Ukraine and Moldavia,* book 1.

44. These are all listed in my *Handbook for Research,* chapter 5 and Appendix 3.

45. *Kratkii spravochnik po nauchno-ostraslevym i memorial'nym arkhivam AN SSSR,* ed. B. V. Levshin (Moscow: "Nauka," 1979).

46. *Lichnye arkhivnye fondy v gosudarstvennykh khranilishchakh SSSR. Ukazatel',* vols. 1–2 (Moscow: GAU/GBL/Arkhiv AN SSSR, 1962–1963; [IDC—R-10,655]) and vol. 3

(Moscow: "Kniga," 1980; [IDC—R-10,655]), see PKG—A-9 and NG-407.

47. Lists of published guides for all state archives throughout the USSR as of 1988, appear in the Grimsted *Handbook for Research*. There is no comparable up-to-date Soviet bibliographic coverage of these basic guides, which are the essential starting point for planning research in a specific institution.

48. In the spring of 1988, over fifty of the guides listed in the appendices to this volume were not available in the Lenin Library, which boasts of receiving a copy of every Soviet publication. Neither were copies to be found in other major research libraries. See further explanation of this problem in the Grimsted *Handbook for Research*, pp. 80-85.

49. *Istoriia SSSR. Annotirovannyi ukazatel' bibliograficheskikh posobii opublikovannykh na russkom iazyke s nachala XIX v. po 1982 g.*, 3d ed., 2 vols. + supplement (Moscow: GBL/GPIB RSFSR, 1983-1985; [IDC—R-14,932]); see PKG—NG-153; pt. 1, comp. and ed. G. A. Glavatskikh et al. (1983); pt. 2, comp. I. A. Guzeeva et al.; ed. G. A. Glavatskikh et al. (1984). The supplement with indexes and additional reference materials was issued in 1985. Since some entries are not repeated from the previous edition, researchers should also consult that second edition, *Istoriia SSSR. Annotirovannyi perechen' russkikh bibliografii izdannykh do 1965 g.*, comp. M. L. Borukhina et al.; ed. Z. L. Fradkina et al., 2d ed. (Moscow: "Kniga," 1966; GPIB RSFSR; [IDC—R-14,765]); see PKG—NG-153.

50. *Istochnikovedenie istorii sovetskogo obshchestva. Ukazatel' literatury*, comp. V. Kh. Bodisko, Iu. P. Bokarev, A. V. Grebeniuk, et al., ed. G. A. Trukhan, 2 vols. (Moscow: Institut istorii SSSR, 1987-1989). It was issued in a rotaprint in-house edition and hence is not widely available.

51. *Katalog arkhivovedcheskoi literatury, 1917-1959 gg.*, comp. A. A. Silaeva, I. F. Kovalev, and S. V. Nefedova; ed. A. I. Loginova and I. N. Firsov (Moscow: GAU, 1961; [IDC—R-10,649]); see PKG—A-1/H-1/NG-48. The organization of the volume according to major types of publications by subject or archival repository makes retrieval very difficult. For example all the guides are listed in one section organized by date of issue, and there is no indexing by subject or repository.

52. *Katalog sbornikov dokumentov, izdannykh arkhivnymi uchrezhdeniiami SSSR 1917-1960 gg.*, comp. E. V. Markina, L. I. Shekhanova, et al.; ed. A. I. Loginova and L. I. Iakovlev (Moscow: GAU, 1961; [IDC—R-10,750]); see PKG—A-65.

53. *Katalog arkhivovedcheskoi literatury i sbornik dokumentov (1960-1963 gg.)* (Moscow: GAU, 1964; [IDC—R-10,650]); see PKG—A-2/H-1/NG-48; *Katalog . . . (1964-1967 gg.)* (Moscow: GAU/VNIIDAD, 1970; [IDC—R-10,651]); see PKG—A-3/ H-1/ NG-48; and *Katalog . . . (1968-1970 gg.)* (Moscow GAU/VNIIDAD, 1977; [IDC—R-14,697]); see PKG—NG-48. "Katalog arkhivovedcheskoi literatury za 1971-1975 gg.," comp. M. G. Artsruni et al.; ed. V. N. Avtokratov et al.; 2 parts, typescript (Moscow: VNIIDAD, 1985; deposited in CTsNTI po dokumentovedeniiu i arkhivnomu delu [14.XI.85], no. 35).

54. "Katalog dokumentovedcheskoi literatury za 1971-1975 gg.," comp. M. G. Artsruni et al.; ed. V. D. Banasiukevich; 2 parts, typescript; (Moscow: VNIIDAD, 1985; deposited in OTsNTI po DAD, no. 8160).

55. *Sovetskaia arkheografiia. Annotirovannyi katalog nauchno-metodicheskoi literatury (1917-1970 gg.)*, vol. 1, comp. I. F. Astrakhantseva et al. (Moscow: GAU/VNIIDAD, 1974; [IDC—R-14,629]); see PKG—NG-62. Traditionally the term *arkheografiia* had been used with particular reference to the location, description, and publication of early historical sources, especially medieval charters and early manuscript books, but Soviet archivists—as indicated by this series—use the term increasingly with reference to official, politically oriented documentary publication activities for any period, including postrevolutionary archival documents.

56. *Sovetskaia arkheografiia . . . (1971-1973 gg.)*, vol. 2, comp. V. R. Kopylev et al. (Moscow: GAU/VNIIDAD, 1976); and *Sovetskaia arkheografiia . . . (1974-1975 gg.)*, vol. 3, comp. A. L. Panina et al. (Moscow: GAU/VNIIDAD, 1980; [IDC—R-14,629]); see PKG—NG-62.

57. *Sovetskaia arkheografiia . . . (1976–1980 gg.)*, vol. 4, comp. A. L. Panina et al. (Moscow: VNIIDAD, 1987).

58. Many of the major publication projects undertaken by other organizations such as the Ministry of Foreign Affairs, the Communist Party, and the Academy of Sciences, especially those involving documentation from the Soviet period, are cosponsored by Glavarkhiv, but this is not always the case. Hence, the diligent researcher must turn to other bibliographic compendia.

59. Starting in 1986, there are two series, one with the title *Arkhivovedenie, arkheografiia. Bibliograficheskii ukazatel'*, and the other *Dokumentovedenie, dokumentatsionnoe obespechenie upravleniia. Bibliograficheskii ukazatel'*. From 1978 through 1985 there were three subseries with the overall series title *Ukazatel' neopublikovannykh i vedomstvennykh materialov*, Series 1: *Dokumentovedenie;* Series 2: *Arkhivovedenie, arkheografiia;* and Series 3: *Normativye i tekhnicheskie usloviia khraneniia dokumentov* (1978–1982) and *Obespechenie sokhrannosti dokumentov* (1983–1985). See PKG—NG–49. In 1976–1977, the same three subseries were issued with the overall series title of *Novosti nauchnoi literatury.* From 1971 to 1975 a combined bulletin covering Soviet publications appeared under the title *Novaia literatura po voprosam dokumentovedeniia i arkhivnogo dela,* which replaced the earlier serial, *Bibliograficheskii ukazatel' po otechestvennym materialam. Dokumentovedenie i arkhivnoe delo* (Moscow: VNIIDAD, 1968–1971).

60. *Ekspres-Informatsiia* (Moscow: VNIIDAD, 1978–), provides relatively long summaries of selected foreign literature and some internal state archival technical and methodological publications, as well as unpublished deposit manuscripts.

61. See, for example, *Sovetskie arkhivy*, 1984, no. 1, p. 94, and no. 5, p. 94; 1986, no. 4, p. 95, and no. 6, p. 84; 1987, no. 1, p. 96, and no. 4, p. 111; and 1988, no. 2, pp. 110–11.

62. Before 1966 it was titled *Voprosy arkhivovedeniia* (Moscow, 1959–1965), and earlier *Informatsionnyi biulleten' GAU pri MVD SSSR* (Moscow, 1956–1959); see PKG—A–76/H–32a/NG–478. All issues are available in microfiche edition: from 1956 to 1965 [IDC—R–10,786], and from 1966 to 1984 [IDC—R–10,756]. An index has been announced as forthcoming.

63. "Spravochno-informatsionnye izdaniia o dokumentakh gosudarstvennykh arkhivov, vyshedshie v svet v 1981–1985 gg.," *Sovetskie arkhivy*, 1986, nos. 5 and 6, and 1987, no. 1. Because these important lists are printed on the inside back covers, they are not picked up in the tables of contents, nor in other bibliographic compendia.

64. Most recently a list of documentary publications issued in 1985 appears in *Sovetskie arkhivy*, 1987, no. 2, inside back cover; lists for 1986 and 1987 appear in ibid., 1988, nos. 1 and 3, inside back covers.

65. *Informatsionnyi biulletin' [AU MVD RSFSR]* (Moscow, 1956–1962). It is listed in the bibliography *Sovetskaia arkheografiia. Annotirovannyi katalog nauchno-metodicheskoi literatury (1917–1970 gg.)*, but it does not appear in *Letopis' periodicheskikh izdanii SSSR* for those years.

66. *Arkhivy Ukrainy*, 1965, no. 4+. Earlier issues were entitled simply *Naukovo-informatsiinnyi biuleten'* (Kiev, 1947–1965, no. 3); titles varied slightly, and in some years it was published only in the Russian language (see PKG—NG–456). The entire series since 1952 is available in a microfiche edition [IDC—R–14,324].

67. *Arkhivy Ukrainy. Naukovo-informatsiinyi biuleten'. Systematychnyi pokashchyk, 1971–1987 rr.*, comp. L. M. Vas'ko et al.; ed. V. M. Volkovyns'kyi (Kiev: Holovne arkhivne upravlinnia pry Radi Ministriv URSR, 1988). This index is available as part of the microfiche edition.

68. Insofar as data is available, see full listings in the Grimsted *Handbook for Research*, chapter 5 and Appendix 3.

69. For fuller bibliographic details see PKG—A–69/H–27/NG–470. The series, from its inception with the issue *za 1957* (Moscow, 1958) through the volume *za 1981* (Moscow, 1982), is available on microfiche [IDC—R–10,754].

70. S. S. Barantseva, *Publikatsii i opisaniia dokumental'nykh pamiatnikov istorii i kul'-tury. Trudy po arkheografii i smezhnym nauchnym distsiplinam. Bibliograficheskii ukazatel'*, pt. 1: (1968–1972) (Moscow: Arkheograficheskaia komissiia AN SSSR, 1984). It was issued in a rotaprint edition of only 500 copies. Full references to the previous bibliographic coverage in the first ten volumes of *Arkheograficheskii ezhegodnik* are cited in the initial note in Barantseva's preface.

71. Barantseva no longer works with the Archeographic Commission, and in March 1988 I was told that there are no plans for continuing the bibliography.

72. A complete bibliography of those available through 1986 is included in the Grimsted 1987 bibliography, *Recent Soviet Archival Literature*, pp. 8–12.

73. Nineteen volumes have appeared through 1988. The serial started publication in Leningrad in 1968. See PKG—A–77/NG–479.

74. Grimsted's *Handbook for Research*, Appendix 1, gives current phone numbers and names of many directors for institutions in Moscow and Leningrad. In all cases, more bibliography of finding aids is listed in the earlier Grimsted directory and bibliographies.

75. See Grimsted, *Archives: Moscow and Leningrad*, pp. 123–32; and Grossman and Kutik, *Spravochnik*, pp. 17–23.

76. Dremina, *Tsentral'nye gosudarstvennye arkhivy SSSR 1945–1970*, pp. 79–109. See Dremina's supplemental accounts of archival activities in the period 1971–1975 in *Tsentral'-nye . . . v deviatoi piatiletke* (1984); and in the period 1976–1980 in *Tsentral'nye . . . v period razvitogo sotsializma* (1986), pp. 8–17.

77. *Tsentral'nye gosudarstvennye arkhivy SSSR* (1982), pp. 8–16.

78. *Kratkii spravochnik o fondakh Tsentral'nogo gosudarstvennogo arkhiva Oktiabr'skoi revoliutsii, vysshikh organov gosudarstvennoi vlasti i organov gosudarstvennogo upravleniia SSSR*, comp. L. I. Burkutskaia and A. V. Dobrovskaia (Moscow: GAU/TsGAOR, 1979; 278 p. rotaprint).

79. *Tsentral'nyi gosudarstvennyi arkhiv Oktiabr'skoi revoliutsii, vysshikh organov gosu-darstvennoi vlasti i organov gosudarstvennogo upravleniia SSSR. Novye postupleniia*, vol. 1: comp. O. Iu. Nezhdanova and L. G. Aronov (Moscow: Glavarkhiv, 1986; 34 p. rotaprint); vol. 2: *1987* (Moscow: Glavarkhiv, 1988). See also *Novye postupleniia v Gosudarstvennykh arkhivakh SSSR*, vol. 1: *TsGAOR SSSR*, comp. I. S. Sokolova and L. G. Aronov (Moscow: Glavarkhiv, 1987; 18 p.; rotaprint). These brochures are hard to find because of the small pressrun and limited distribution, but copies of all three are available at Harvard University.

80. *Tsentral'nyi gosudarsvtennyi arkhiv Oktiabr'skoi revoliutsii i sotsialisticheskogo stroitel'stva. Putevoditel'*, ed. I. I. Nikitinskii et al. (Moscow: GAU, 1946; [IDC—R–10,676]); see PKG—B–1.

81. Vol. 2 (Moscow: GAU, 1952). I was not permitted to examine a copy in 1989, when the TsGAOR director claimed there was no copy in the archive. According to Soviet scholars, the guide, now available in the regular TsGAOR reading room, provides detailed coverage of the formerly secret Prague collection.

82. *Tematicheskaia ukazatel' k kollektsiiam mikrofotokopii dokumentov zarubezhnykh ar-khivov, khraniashchikhsia v TsGAOR SSSR*, comp. R. Ia. Buss-Breiger, N. A. Karpunova, V. A. Robova, and A. I. Tsvetkova (Moscow: GAU/TsGAOR, 1978; 92 p. rotaprint). Since this list was initially issued with the restriction "*dlia sluzhebnogo pol'zovaniia*," few copies are likely to be found outside the archive.

83. A. F. Butenko, "Materialy po istorii rabochego klassa SSSR v fondakh Tsentral'nogo gosudarstvennogo arkhiva Oktiabr'skoi revoliutsii i sotsialisticheskogo stroitel'stva SSSR," in *Voprosy istoriografii i istochnikovedeniia istoriia rabochego klassa SSSR*, pp. 75–88; see PKG—B–5.

84. *[Vsesoiuznyi tsentral'nyi sovet professional'nykh soiuzov. Tsentral'nyi arkhiv.] Pute-voditel'*, ed. P. I. Kabanov et al., vol. 1 (Moscow: Profizdat, 1958; [IDC—R–10,677]); see PKG—B–3.

85. I. I. Belonosov, "Obzor dokumental'nykh materialov Tsentral'nogo arkhiva

VTsSPS,'' *Voprosy istoriografii i istochnikovedeniia istorii rabochego klassa SSSR* (Leningrad, 1962), pp. 234–316.

86. "Les archives des syndicats et l'histoire du mouvement ouvrier en U.R.S.S.,'' *Labour Trade Union Archives/Les archives des syndicats et mouvements ouvriers*, published as *Archivum. International Review on Archives/ Revue internationale des archives* 27 (1980): 130–35.

87. "Arkhivnye uchrezhdeniia strany na puti uskoreniia i perestroiki,'' *Sovetskie arkhivy*, 1988, no. 4, pp. 5–6.

88. A. Mosesov, "Arkhivy raskryvaiut tainy,'' *Sovetskaia kul'tura*, 29 September 1988, p. 2.

89. As explained to the present author by TsGAOR director B. I. Kaptelov in April 1989.

90. *Kratkii spravochnik fondov Tsentral'nogo gosudarstvennogo arkhiva narodnogo khoziaistva SSSR*, comp. E. P. Butskaia, N. M. Kleman, M. E. Kucherenko, et al.; ed. V. V. Tsaplin (Moscow: TsGANKh SSSR, 1973; 413 p. rotaprint). Since this guide was initially issued with the restriction *"dlia sluzhebnogo pol'zovaniia,''* few copies are found outside the archive.

91. See the TsGAOR guide listed in note 80 above; for the second volume, published in 1952, see note 81.

92. *Tsentral'nyi gosudarstvennyi arkhiv narodnogo khoziaistva SSSR. Fondy lichnogo proiskhozhdeniia. Putevoditel'*, comp. M. I. Kul'kova, A. A. Novikova, and L. E. Tatievshaia; ed. V. V. Tsaplin et al. (Moscow: Glavarkhiv, 1987; 263 p. rotaprint). A copy is available for open consultation in the Lenin Library.

93. A. A. Novikova, "Sobiranie lichnykh arkhivov deiatelei narodnogo khoziaistva v TsGANKh SSSR,'' in *Voprosy sobiraniia, ucheta, khraneniia i ispol'zovaniia dokumental'-nykh pamiatnikov istorii i kul'tury*, vol. 1: *Pamiatniki novogo vremeni i sovetskoi epokhi*, ed. S. O. Shmidt et al., pp. 139–43 (Moscow, 1982). The deposited manuscript is listed and described in *Sovetskie arkhivy*, 1987, no. 4, p. 111: A. A. Novikova, "Komplektovanie Gosudarstvennogo arkhivnogo fonda SSSR dokumentami deiatelei narodnogo khoziaistva na primere TsGANKh SSSR'' (Moscow, 1986; 356 p.; VNIIDAD OTsNTI depository MS no. 043).

94. Grossman and Kutik, *Spravochnik*, pp. 23–24. See the earlier coverage in Grimsted, *Archives . . . : Moscow and Leningrad*, pp. 133–34. See also a few additional bibliographical listings in Supplement 1, p. 33; however, none of these are of prime interest for the period in question.

95. *Tsentral'nye gosudarstvennye arkhivy SSSR* (1982), pp. 17–23.

96. Dremina, *Tsentral'nye gosudarstvennye arkhivy SSSR 1945–1970*, pp. 110–26. See also Dremina's supplemental coverage in *Tsentral'nye . . . v deviatoi piatiletke* (1984) and in *Tsentral'nye . . . v period razvitogo sotsializma* (1986), pp. 18–32.

97. See for example the specific complaints about these problems in TsGANKh cited by V. Molchanov, "Dostup ogranichen,'' *Pravda*, 1 June 1988, p. 4. The report is summarized in *Current Digest of the Soviet Press* 40, no. 22 (1988): 22.

98. A. Mosesov, "Arkhivy raskryvaiut tainy,'' *Sovetskaia kul'tura*, 29 September 1988, p. 2.

99. See the coverage of TsGAKFD and Gosfil'mofond with bibliography of descriptive literature and finding aids in Grimsted, *Archives . . . : Moscow and Leningrad*, pp. 190–94, and 257–58; and with more recent bibliography in Grossman and Kutik, *Spravochnik*, pp. 25–27 (the latter directory does not mention Gosfil'mofond). See also the more recent data in Grimsted, *Handbook for Research*.

100. See descriptive literature cited in the directories cited in *ibid*.

101. *Tsentral'nyi gosudarstvennyi arkhiv literatury i iskusstva SSSR. Putevoditel'*, 6 vols. (Moscow: GAU/TsGALI SSSR, 1959–1988). See Grimsted, *Archives . . . : Moscow and Leningrad*, pp. 143–52, Supplement 1, pp. 36–37, and "Recent Publications,'' p. 521 (esp.

notes 53 and 54), and the additional coverage in Grossman and Kutik, *Spravochnik*, pp. 35–38. A short general brochure describing the history, holdings, and activities of TsGALI was issued in 1988, with an extensive bibliography of published descriptions and documentary publications issued by the archive: *Tsentral'nyi gosudarstvennyi arkhiv literatury i iskusstva SSSR. Kratkii spravochnik*, ed. N. B. Volkova (Moscow: GAU/TsGALI SSSR, 1988).

102. See Grimsted, *Archives . . . : Moscow and Leningrad*, pp. 135–37; *Tsentral'nye gosudarstvennye arkhivy SSSR* (1982), pp. 27–31; and Grossman and Kutik, *Spravochnik*, pp. 30–32. All military records of World War II are kept in the separate permanent Central Archive of the Ministry of Defense (*Tsentral'nyi arkhiv Ministerstva oborony SSSR*—TsAMO SSSR) in Podol'sk near Moscow, but this facility is not under Glavarkhiv administration.

103. See the brief descriptions in Grossman and Kutik, *Spravochnik*, pp. 32–33, and in Grimsted, *Archives . . . : Moscow and Leningrad*, pp. 138–42, as well as the briefer, superficial sketch of holdings in *Tsentral'nye gosudarstvennye arkhivy SSSR* (1982), pp. 32–35.

104. See note 40 above.

105. See note 80 above.

106. *Arkhivnye fondy Tsentral'nogo gosudarsvennogo arkhiva RSFSR. Kratkii spravochnik*, ed. N. P. Eroshkin (Moscow: GAU, 1973). In line with its initial public issue the guide has been mentioned in several Soviet publications.

107. *Spravochnik o sostave i soderzhanii dokumental'nykh materialov Tsentral'nogo gosudarstvennogo arkhiva RSFSR*, comp. T. P. Korzhikhina (Moscow: TsGA RSFSR, 1959). A xerox printout from microfilm is available at Harvard College Library.

108. See the short article celebrating the twentieth anniversary of the archive by V. A. Sidorova and F. I. Sharonov, "Tsentral'nyi gosudarstvennyi arkhiv RSFSR (1957–1977 gg.)," *Sovetskie arkhivy*, 1977, no. 6, pp. 40–48. See also the short coverage in Grossman and Kutik, *Spravochnik*, pp. 62–73 (both editions of their directory cite the 1973 guide). A few additional publications regarding the archive are cited in Grimsted, *Archives . . . : Moscow and Leningrad*, p. 361.

109. From 1965 to 1980 this archive was named the State Archive of Moscow Oblast (GAMO); from 1941 to 1965 it was known as the State Archive of the October Revolution and Socialist Construction of Moscow Oblast (GAORSS MO), and, from its foundation in 1930 to 1941, it was called the State Archive of the October Revolution of Moscow Oblast (GAORMO).

110. *Spravochnik po fondam Tsentral'nogo gosudarstvennogo arkhiva Moskovskoi oblasti i ego filial v g. Bronnitsy*, comp. V. O. Sedel'nikov, S. S. Buzinova, T. A. Vargina et al.; ed. M. V. Krivenko (Moscow: Glavarkhiv, 1983; 276 p. rotaprint). The guide was issued in a pressrun of 1,000, but as an unpriced (*bezplatno*) in-house publication, which explains its limited distribution, even in Soviet libraries.

111. *Gosudarstvennyi arkhiv Oktiabr'skoi revoliutsii i sotsialisticheskogo stroitel'stva Moskovskoi oblasti. Kratkii spravochnik*, comp. Iu. Ia. Vlasov et al.; ed. A. E. Grishanov (Moscow: GAU, 1962; [IDC—R–10,938]); see PKG—G-4. See also the earlier listings in Grimsted, *Archives . . . : Moscow and Leningrad*, pp. 363–64, and in Grossman and Kutik, *Spravochnik*, pp. 66–67.

112. *Arkhivnoe delo v Moskovskoi oblasti. Sbornik materialov* (Moscow, 1931–1932; [IDC—R-10–937]), vol. 1, pp. 5–21; see PKG—G-2/Sup. 1, p. 145.

113. See the appendix in *A. M. Gor'kii i sozdanie istorii fabrik i zavodov* (Moscow, 1959), pp. 255–344.

114. Ia. Z. Livshits, "Kratkii obzor dokumental'nykh materialov po istorii bor'by rabochikh tiazheloi promyshlennosti Moskvy za vypolnenie pervogo piatiletnego plana (po fondam Gosudarstvennogo arkhiva Oktiabr'skoi revoliutsii i sotsialisticheskogo stroitel'stva Moskovskoi oblasti)," in *Izmeneniia v chislennosti i sostave sovetskogo rabochego klassa* (Moscow, 1961), pp. 335–52.

115. See the brief survey of all of these local Moscow archives in the 1980 directory of RSFSR archives, and in Grossman and Kutik, *Spravochnik*, pp. 64–67. See also the explana-

tion of local changes in Moscow archives in Grimsted, "Recent Publications," pp. 524–25.

116. In the meantime, with the publication of the 1983 guide to TsGAMO (see note 110), one can verify holdings that remain there.

117. *Tematicheskii perechen' kinofotofonodokumentov, khraniashchikhsia v Tsentral'-nom gosudarstvennom arkhive kinofotofonodokumentov g. Moskvy,* comp. L. V. Mokrousova (Moscow: Glavarkhiv, 1987; 94 p. rotaprint).

118. See the explanation of local changes in Leningrad archives in Grimsted, "Recent Publications," pp. 524–25, and in Grossman and Kutik, *Spravochnik,* pp. 67–71.

119. *Leningradskie gosudarstvennye oblastnye arkhivy. Kratkii spravochnik,* comp. V. A. Zubkov et al.; ed. P. V. Vinogradov (Leningrad, GAU, 1960; [IDC—R–10,937]); see PKG—G–1.

120. *Gosudarstvennyi arkhiv Oktiabr'skoi revoliutsii i sotsialisticheskogo stroitel'stva Leningradskoi oblasti. Kratkii putevoditel',* comp. M. V. Kiselev et al.; ed. P. V. Vinogradov (Leningrad, 1962; [IDC—R–10,943]); see PKG—G–13.

121. V. I. Startsev and O. I. Shkaratan, "Fondy Gosudarstvennogo arkhiva Oktiabr'skoi revoliutsii i sotsialisticheskogo stroitel'stva Leningradskoi oblasti kak istochnik po istorii sovetskogo rabochego klassa," in *Izmeneniia v chislennosti i sostave sovetskogo rabochego klassa,* pp. 317–34; Iu. S. Tokar, "Obzor fondov leningradskikh gosudarstvennykh arkhivov po istorii sovetskogo rabochego klassa," in *Voprosy istoriografii i istochnikovedeniia rabochego klassa SSSR,* pp. 89–98 (PKG—G–14.5); and V. I. Startsev, "Statisticheskie istochniki Gosudarstvennogo arkhiva Oktiabr'skoi revoliutsii i sotsialisticheskogo stroitel'stva Leningradskoi oblasti po istorii rabochego klassa SSSR," in *ibid.,* pp. 99–109 (PKG—G–14.6). For lists of factory records with fond numbers, see *A. M. Gor'kii ki sozdanie istorii fabrik i zavodov* (Moscow, 1959), pp. 255–344.

122. See a full list of available published guides to RSFSR state archives in Grimsted, *Handbook for Research,* Appendix 2.

123. Iurii Afanas'ev, "Perestroika i istoricheskoe znanie," *Literaturnaia Rossiia,* no. 24 (17 June 1958), p. 9.

124. B. Ilizarov, *Literaturnaia gazeta,* 1988, no. 22 (1 June), p. 12.

125. In March 1988, however, neither the Central Party Archive, nor the foreign office of its controlling Institute of Marxism-Leninism, were willing to receive me in connection with the preparation of my research handbook. I had hoped to clarify policies and procedures for prospective foreign applications and to expand my coverage of literature regarding the Party archival network.

126. Grossman and Kutik, *Spravochnik,* pp. 38–46 (bibliography, pp. 360–65).

127. A. A. Struchkov, "Tsentral'nyi partiinyi arkhiv Instituta Marksizma-Leninizma pri TsK KPSS," 1956, no. 4, pp. 188–200; see PKG—D–2. See also the additional bibliographic data on Party archives in Grimsted, *Archives . . . : Moscow and Leningrad,* pp. 243–47, Supplement 1, p. 81, and "Recent Publications," p. 521 (esp. note 55).

128. "Popolnenie fondov Tsentral'nogo partiinogo arkhiva IML pri TsK KPSS," *Voprosy istorii KPSS,* 1958, no. 2, pp. 217–21; 1959, no. 2, pp. 191–95; 1960, no. 2, pp. 202–207; 1961, no. 2, pp. 164–70; 1962, no. 3, pp. 217–21; 1963, no. 2, pp. 117–21; 1964, no. 3, pp. 114–18; 1965, no. 2, pp. 150–55; 1966, no. 4, pp. 138–41; 1968, no. 3, pp. 150–56; 1972, no. 7, 114–22 (for 1968–1971); and 1974, no. 6, pp. 113–18 (for 1972–1973). This entire series was issued in a separate microfiche edition (IDC—R–9890); see PKG—D–8. Grossman and Kutik refer only to the last report in the series.

129. V. E. Korneev, *Arkhivy RKP(b) v 1917–1925 gg. Uchebnoe posobie* (Moscow: MGIAI, 1979), and V. E. Korneev, *Arkhivy VKP(b) v 1926–1941 gg. Uchebnoe posobie* (Moscow: MGIAI, 1981).

130. D. I. Antoniuk, "Istoricheskii opyt KPSS v osushchestvlenii leninskikh idei partiinogo arkhivnogo stroitel'stva," in *Voprosy partiinogo arkhivnogo stroitel'stva sotsialisticheskoi sistemy* (Moscow: IML, 1979).

131. V. V. Anikeev, *Iz istorii obrazovaniia arkhivnogo fonda KPSS* (Moscow: 1984);

published as *Novoe v zhizni, nauke, tekhnike. Seriia istoriia i politika KPSS*, 1984, no. 4.

132. M. A. Varshavchik, *Istoriko-partiinoe istochnikovedenie. Teoriia, metodologiia, metodika* (Kiev: "Vyshcha shkola," 1984; [IDC—R-17,253]); see PKG—NG-245. This volume updates, but does not repeat, all of the coverage in Varshavchik's earlier text on source study for Party history: *Istochnikovedenie istorii KPSS* (Moscow: "Vysshaia shkola," 1973; [IDC—R-11,181]); see PKG—NG-246. A new edition with the same title and publisher appeared in 1988, but a copy has not been available for review.

133. An outline survey and bibliography of many of these institutions is provided in Grimsted, *Archives . . . : Moscow and Leningrad* directory and the 1976 Supplement, with some additional bibliographical comments in the 1982 and 1986 *Slavic Review* articles and the 1987 Kennan Institute bibliography *Recent Soviet Archival Literature*. There is also extensive coverage of some of them provided in the 1983 edition of the Grossman and Kutik *Spravochnik*. Current institutional names, addresses, and published guides are referenced in Grimsted, *Handbook for Research*, especially Appendix 1.

Archival Research in the USSR
A Practical Guide for Historians

LYNNE VIOLA

In a brilliant series of lectures later published under the title *What is History?* E. H. Carr ascribed to the historian enormous power and control over the selection, classification, and use of "facts" to, in a manner of speaking, "make history." He stated: "The facts speak only when the historian calls on them: it is he who decides to which facts to give the floor, and in what order or context."[1] When Carr made this statement at Cambridge University in 1961, however, he clearly did not and could not have had in mind those "facts" which nowadays Western historians can occasionally cull from Soviet archives, for in the case of data derived from Soviet archives, the contemporary Western historian quickly loses his nineteenth-century unbound Promethean powers of historical creation and finds himself subject to the forces of the less rational twentieth century and other more mundane considerations of state and politics.

Soviet archives present something of an obstacle course to Western historians. Preparation for research in Soviet archives, as well as access to and actual work in the archives, is, in general, a difficult undertaking for any Western historian, but it is perhaps most difficult of all for the Western historian whose research topic falls into the Soviet period and, in particular, the Stalin years. These were years wrought by intense struggle, and they remain an object of sensitivity and often high secrecy in the Soviet Union. Soviet authorities are reluctant to grant "bourgeois" historians access to archival material from those years given the sensitivity of the historical issues, the unfortunately enduring legacy of cold war historiography, and the vagaries of East-West political relations. As a consequence, archival access is highly restricted and working conditions in Soviet archives are often of a tenuous nature.[2]

Yet despite a plethora of persisting problems, there has been a marked, although

The author worked in Soviet archives in 1981–82 while a participant on the IREX graduate student/young faculty exchange and wishes to thank the following people for their aid in preparing for archival work or preparing this article subsequently: Eugene Beshenkovskii, Sheila Fitzpatrick, Patricia Kennedy Grimsted, and Richard Wortman. The author would also like to express her gratitude to the Main Archival Administration and its fine staff, especially L. E. Selivanova. Although the author worked in Soviet archives again for a very brief period in 1988, the practical aspects of this article are based largely on the earlier experience.

relative, improvement in the last decade. An increasing number of Western scholars have received archival access for work on postrevolutionary topics, and a handful among them have had access to materials on the 1930s, or, more precisely, the First Five-Year Plan period.[3] Western historians of Soviet Russia can no longer simply dismiss the prospect of archival research in the USSR. Archives, as a major primary source of social history, must be given due consideration as Western scholars consider research strategies and project plans for work in the Soviet Union.

Given that necessity, the object of this article is to offer some practical guidelines on the use of Soviet archives with an emphasis on pre-archival preparation, as well as to present a survey of document terminology and several types of archival documents which are of particular importance to social historians. My own experience in Soviet archives, like that of most Westerners working on topics in the postrevolutionary period, was limited in terms of both time and access. Therefore, the article is not intended to be in any way all-inclusive or the reflection of a solidly acquired expertise. Instead, it is intended to serve as a practical introduction for Western social historians working on the prewar Stalin period and preparing to request permission to work in Soviet archives.

Preparing to work in Soviet archives

Serious and thorough pre-archival preparation is one of the most crucial elements in the grand strategy of approaching archival research in the USSR. If initially denied access to archives, good preparation and a demonstration of basic familiarity with the material at issue may very well enhance the likelihood of eventual access, increasing the legitimacy and/or credibility of a second or third application to the Main Archive Administration (GAU). Once in the archives, good preparation is essential to the exercise of optimal control in the selection and ordering of documents and to the attempt to derive the maximum value from materials, given limited time resources and other constraints. This is especially so in light of the customary inability of Western scholars to obtain permission to use the *opis'* (unpublished archival inventory), card catalogs, and other internal archival finding aids in the Soviet archives. Preparation for work in the archives, however, is difficult because the information available in the West on archival holdings from the Stalin years is limited, scattered, and highly incomplete and because so few Western social historians of the postrevolutionary period have had experience in Soviet archives which could be shared with other scholars. Consequently, the essential work of preparing for archival research in the Soviet Union involves a large measure of innovation, tracking down sometimes obscure sources, and recognizing the limits of what is possible.

The two cardinal rules of archival preparation are "know your archival sources" and "know your topic from an archivist's perspective." Observance of these rules of preparation will aid in the ordering of materials in the archives, where Western scholars, in lieu of the *opis'*, must, to a great extent, work blind. A researcher should attempt to enter the archives with knowledge of exact archival code numbers, exact dates of documents, and the correct terminology with respect to desired types of documents or files.[4]

The best introduction to Soviet archives for Western scholars is the work of Patricia Kennedy Grimsted.[5] Dr. Grimsted describes the historical evolution and the organization of archives in the USSR, as well as providing valuable practical information and useful bibliographies of Soviet scholarly works on or related to the subject of archives. After gaining a familiarity with the information presented by Grimsted, it is best to determine whether or not the specific archival repository of concern has issued a guide (*putevoditel'*) or directory (*spravochnik*) describing its holdings.[6] These publications vary according to thoroughness and usefulness, but they are helpful in providing some indication of the scope and nature of the holdings, main archival divisions according to *fondy* (sometimes providing *fond* numbers and titles, as well), types of documents available on various topics, and document terminology.

The published archival guides do not always provide certain, very important types of information, such as the location of a specific document or holding, *opis'* and *delo* numbers within a *fond*, and more thorough descriptions of individual holdings. In order to obtain more detailed information of this nature, it is essential to use the bibliographical surveys (usually in prefaces or first chapters) and complete archival references in Soviet monographs and articles on the topic of research interest, published surveys (*obzory*) of specific archival materials (in relevant scholarly journals, journals published by the archives, collections of articles on the relevant research topic, etc.),[7] and collections of published documents related to the research topic.[8] The materials provided in these sources are useful aids in preparing a list of archival references according to specific categories of records, titles, and code numbers, as well as allowing for a preliminary formulation of a clear description of archival materials which is necessary both for the initial application to work in Soviet archives and, in lieu of the *opis'* and, in most cases, complete archival references, for ordering purposes once in the archives.[9] The more complete and the more exact the information available on a particular holding, the easier it will be for the Soviet archival attendant to locate the material in question. In addition, this approach to solid preparation may grant the researcher more control in ordering and access. It should be noted, however, that no matter how thorough the preparation, the Western scholar is bound to fall short of the goal in terms of thoroughness and accuracy, especially in reference to precise archival citations, because much needed information is lacking and the available information on Soviet archival holdings does not always answer specific needs and interests.

There are, therefore, definite limits to the returns that can be expected from following the rule of "know your archival sources." For this reason, it is essential to pay serious attention to the second rule: "know your topic from an archivist's perspective." The second rule is a necessary supplement to the first and, like the first rule, serves only to maximize the degree of preparedness possible for archival research in the USSR rather than to guarantee any expertise or foolproof readiness for entry into Soviet archives.

It is important to examine the research topic from the perspective of the archivist and future archive needs in order to attempt to formulate some idea of the types of documents and information available and the probable location of documents, as well as to be prepared to make maximum use of often minimal time resources without needless waste. A detailed knowledge of the chronology of an event or events within the research topic may be helpful for ordering purposes since many records are arranged according to month or year. It is also useful to draw up a list of all relevant *published* laws, statistical collections, and collections of documents on the research topic. Quite often, published materials can surface among the documents in a portfolio, along with clippings from Soviet newspapers available in the West. A knowledge of what has been published and what is available in the West in terms of these categories of sources will help in order to avoid either duplication of earlier work or wasting valuable time in the archives.

The most important step in getting to know the research topic from the archivist's perspective, however, is to obtain a general understanding of *deloproizvodstvo*. *Deloproizvodstvo*, a difficult term to translate and one lacking a clear English equivalent, can best be understood as the way in which documents are organized in the process of administering an institution; in short, *deloproizvodstvo,* within this context, pertains to the recordkeeping practices (or even filing system) of an institution or organization.[10] In order to understand the *deloproizvodstvo* of an institution or organization, it is necessary to understand the internal organization and administrative divisions of a particular institution. This knowledge will provide an important key to an understanding of the types of documents which an institution produced, their subsequent archival location, arrangement, and classification, for the original administrative divisions of an institution are generally maintained in the archives. For example, depending on the time period, internal organization of Soviet institutions was often fairly standard with many of the same departments, such as departments of cadres, planning, statistics, organization and instruction, etc. These institutional subdivisions normally are retained as the basic organizational framework for the records of the given institution and may appear as individual *dela* or *opisi* within the *fond* representing the institution. If it can be determined that a document was produced within a certain department within an institution, this information may prove very useful in narrowing down the possible location of the document. Therefore, a knowledge of *deloproizvodstvo* is necessary in order to obtain an idea of what materials are available in instances where other sources have proved insufficient and in order to provide the archival attendant with the information necessary for locating materials.[11]

A knowledge of administration and recordkeeping practices can provide virtually unlimited and highly innovative clues to obtaining familiarity with an archival holding from afar. Information on the procedural functioning of an institution can be quite valuable. If it can be ascertained in what sector or unit and at what time intervals various types of standard accounts, records, reports, and plans were issued (and for how long they were preserved), then the researcher will be provided with a clue for a potentially valuable source of information available in most institutional holdings. Another type of information that may prove useful is knowledge of the position of an institution or organization in the administrative (and regional) hierarchy. If, for example, the researcher can identify an organization's subordinates and superiors, this information will enable him to request such materials as official correspondence and different types of interdepartmental directives and orders.

There are many sources to which the researcher can turn in order to obtain an understanding of Soviet institutions. The first and most obvious are histories of Soviet governmental organization and individual institutions and organizations.[12] There are also Soviet textbooks on *deloproizvodstvo*, as well as information on *deloproizvodstvo* within handbooks on sources and archival guides and directories.[13] Individual archival guides will often provide information on the internal organization of institutions according to departments, sectors, or administrative units (e.g., presidium, secretariat, etc.).[14] Finally, an examination of published documents can be helpful, for the published collections generally provide full archival citations, the institution and department of issue of a document, and the institution and department of the recipient of the document for each individual document.[15] These sources will also provide an introduction to document terminology, a good working knowledge of which is perhaps the most useful tool the Western researcher can have as he enters the archives. This subject will be discussed in detail in the second part of the article.

The central goal of preparation for work in Soviet archives is to obtain an understanding of how the archives are organized, and the location and general content of various sets of documents. As is clear from the above, achievement of this goal requires a good deal of detective work which, even according to the standards of the social historian of the Stalin years, can often lead down rather elaborate and irregular paths. However, there is one excellent source which is both obvious and easily accessible and which provides a good introduction to Soviet archival research. This is the Smolensk Communist Party Archive.[16] Although incomplete in certain respects and, as a Communist Party archive, organized somewhat differently from Soviet government archives, the Smolensk Party Archive can be used as a guide to document terminology, an introduction to the value of certain types of documents, and a practice tool for gaining familiarity with handwritten documents.[17] In addition, it will provide the researcher with an opportunity to make use of one of the more valuable and comparatively underutilized sources of Soviet history on the prewar Stalin years available in the West.

This brief sketch of practical hints and suggestions on preparation for archival research should not be considered anything but a rough introduction and, moreover, one which happened to suit the research aims and strategy of the author. Different research needs and goals may dictate a different course of preparation. Furthermore, it should be emphasized that not all topics lend themselves to archival research in the first place. A topic that is too broad, too vague, or somehow politically objectionable is probably not suited to archival research in the Soviet Union or anywhere else for that matter. In addition, it is necessary to consider whether a Western formulation of a research topic will be understandable to Soviet archivists and historians both in political and professional terms. Once these factors have been taken into account, the researcher may plan a course of preparation for archival research according to specific needs and goals. It should be noted, however, that although careful preparation is prerequisite to, it is not necessarily a guarantee of, entry and work in the archives.[18]

Document typology and terminology

Archives hold many different types of documents. An important part of preparation for work in Soviet archives is gaining an understanding of the typology of Soviet documents produced in the period under study. The typology of documents is closely related to the *deloproizvodstvo* and administration of an institution or organization and, therefore, these aspects of archival preparation are, to a large extent, interrelated. A knowledge of the typology of documents will allow the researcher several advantages when attempting to determine the location of a certain type of information and the nature of the holdings of a particular record group. It is also of immense value in describing archival documents when filling out orders in the archives. It should also be noted that in cases when an archival *fond* is very large and is therefore subdivided into *opisi* according to institutional sectors or departments, *dela*, at least in part, may be titled according to the types of documents contained within (in addition to more descriptive wording pertaining specifically to the contents of the documents).[19] Finally, a knowledge of the correct terminology of specific types of documents is prerequisite to meaningful work in the archives.

A government and its institutions produce many different categories of documents. Not all of them are of use to social historians, but before indicating those that are of greatest value to the social historian, it is necessary to outline a typology of documents. In order to do this, the classification system used in a recent Soviet textbook on sources for historians will serve as a basic guide.[20] The typology is outlined below, along with brief descriptions of each category of document and examples of document types to help clarify categorization and to acquaint the reader with the basic terminology:

1. *Organizational documentation* (organizatsionnaia dokumentatsiia)

These documents define the order of a function or administrative activity of some kind within an institution or organization or the relation between several institutions or organizations. They relate especially to administration and serve to define the order of a structural form, the implementation of a task, the rights and responsibilities of employees, etc. Documents in this category include the following:

polozheniia (regulations, statutes)
ustavy (regulations, statutes, rules of an organization)
pravila (rules)
statuty (statutes)
normativy (norms)
obiazatel'stva (obligations)

dogovory (agreements, contracts, treaties)
kontrakty (contracts)
trudovye soglasheniia (labor agreements, contracts)

2. Administrative or directional documentation (rasporiaditel'naia dokumentatsiia)

These documents serve to realize or implement an administrative function whose basis is laid down in the documents of the organizational category. In this sense, they are a continuation of category one as they follow up on the implementation of guidelines set out in those documents. (These sets of documents are closely interrelated and therefore categorization is often merged into the category of *"organizatsionno-rasporiaditel'naia dokumentatsiia."*) Examples of this type of documentation are:

resheniia (decisions)
rezoliutsiia (resolutions)
prikazy (orders, commands)
instruktsii (instructions)
tsirkuliary (circulars)
rasporiazheniia (orders, instructions)
porucheniia (commissions)
predpisaniia (directions, instructions)
nakazy (mandates, instructions)

Also included in this category are *afishi* (posters or placards), *ob"iavleniia* (advertisements or notices), *plakaty* (posters), and *biulleteni* (bulletins) of an informative or directive nature. Within the broader, merged category of *organizatsionno-rasporiaditel'naia dokumentatsiia* are included *protokoly* (protocols) and *stenogrammy* (stenographic records) of official proceedings.

3. Routine correspondence (tekushchie perepiski)

This category speaks for itself and includes the following types of correspondence: *telegrammy* (telegrams), *telegrafnye i teletaipnye soobshcheniia* (telegraph and teletype messages), *radiogrammy* (radiograms), *telefonogrammy* (telephonograms), and *pis'ma* (letters). This category of documentation is further subcategorized by correspondence within institutions (*vnutrennye perepiski*) and between institutions (*vneshnye perepiski*). Also included in this category are letters from citizens to institutions, such as *predlozheniia* (suggestions), *zaiavleniia* (requests), *raporty* (reports), and *zaprosy* (inquiries).

4. Diplomatic correspondence (diplomaticheskaia perepiska)

This category is self-evident and, because it is, in general, outside the sphere of social history, will not be discussed further.

5. *Planning documents* (planovaia dokumentatsiia)

These documents relate to various aspects of planning and include the following:
  plany raboty (plans of work)
  proekty (drafts)
  proektnye zadaniia (planned targets)
  programmy (programs)
  smety (budgetary estimates)
  grafiki (graphs, charts)
  setevye grafiki (graphs)

6. *Accounting records* (uchetnye dokumenty)

These documents constitute an amorphous and large group and relate to various types of records and accounts. The records may relate to simple bookkeeping and accounting, financial information, or personnel information of an institution. The following types of documents are included in this category:
  ankety (questionnaires)
  listki (forms)
  zhurnaly i knigi ucheta (account ledgers and books)
  reestry (rolls, registers)
  kadastry (land cadastral surveys)
  perechni (lists)
  tabeli (tables)
  tarify (tariffs, rates)
  scheta (accounts)
  balansy (balances)

7. *Control or verification documents*
(kontrol'naia dokumentatsiia)

This type of document is closely related to the accounting group and therefore is sometimes classified as *"uchetno-kontrol'naia dokumentatsiia."* The following types of documents are included in this category:
  materialy revizii (audit materials)
  proverki (audits)
  zakliucheniia o rabote (conclusions from a specific piece of work)
  spravki o deiatel'nosti (information on activities)
  registratsii (registrations)
  edinovremennye obsledovaniia (special inspections or investigations)

8. *Reporting/accounting material*
(otchetnaia dokumentatsiia)

These documents represent summations, conclusions, and generalizations of information derived from the other types of documents. They are both summaries and analyses, and generally are required of organizations and institutions on some regular time basis. The following are examples of these documents:

otchety (accounts, reports)
obzory (surveys, summaries)
trudovye raporty (work reports)
svodki (reports, progress reports)
doneseniia (reports, dispatches)
doklady, dokladnye zapiski (reports, memoranda)

9. Statistical documents
(statisticheskie dokumenty)

This category is self-evident and includes as "types" many of the documents listed above rather than constituting a specific form of document itself.

This listing of document typology should not be considered all-inclusive either as to general types or individual document examples described within each category. Moreover, the categories presented above, as indicated in several places, are not necessarily mutually exclusive categories; nor are the individual document types limited to representation only in the given category. Before concluding this general survey of document typology, it is necessary to note that there are several, broader approaches to classification of documents which should be mentioned briefly as well.

The typology presented above is based, to a large extent, on the function of a document; there are several approaches to typology which are based on the form or general nature of a document. The first general classification of documents is related to whether documents are drawn up according to standardized forms. Standardized forms of documents (*razrabotannye* or *typovye*) include, for example, *ankety, tipovye blanki* (standardized forms), *obraztsy* (sample forms), *trafarety* (model forms), *formuliary* (record cards), *vedomosty* (registers), and *listki*. Another further general distinction among documents is according to whether they are primary (*pervichnye*) materials or of a derivative nature (*proizvodnye*) based upon primary materials (e.g., *otchetnye* documents). The final general classification of documents is a division of archival materials into official (*sluzhebnye, ofitsial'nye*) and unofficial (*neofitsial'nye*) materials. The former consist of government papers of the various types described above. The latter are of diverse nature but are, in general, distinguished as emanating or relating to an individual and include *pis'ma, kharakteristiki* (personal references or evaluations), and other materials of a less official nature.[21] In general, these categories of document typology are less important to the researcher in terms of determining location and content of archival records. However, some of the terminology and document type examples given are useful for ordering and interpretive purposes. In addition, this broader typology is useful to an understanding of the general nature of Soviet documentation and the types of documents that an institution preserves within its files and which are eventually transferred to the archives as a part of its records.

This rudimentary introduction to Soviet document typology, classification, and terminology is intended to serve as a base for understanding the general content and nature of archival holdings. Such a general understanding is useful in narrowing down the range of documents and document categories in order to determine more precisely what is most useful and necessary from the perspective of the individual researcher and his topic. There are several categories or types of documents that are especially pertinent to the study of social history. The following pages will survey selected document types deemed to be of particular interest to social historians.

Archival documents from the First Five-Year Plan period

The social historian of the First Five-Year Plan period is necessarily interested in access to any and all of the categories of documents presented in the typology above. At the same time, however, he is subject to a number of processes of selection. The first—a process of more or less natural selection—is shaped by the proportion of documents that belong to any given category. For example, documents of the accounting (*uchetnyi*) category account for almost half of all archival materials, while planning documents make up a little over one quarter of all documents for the Soviet period.[22] It is, therefore, more likely that a researcher will chance upon document types that are more widely represented in the archives than those of a rarer variety. The second process of selection—a process determined by the individual archival staff member working with the scholar and the Main Archive Administration—is largely beyond the control of the researcher and will not be examined here. The final process of selection is that which is related to a historian's own classification of sources or, in this case, documents, according to value and usefulness.

Two of the most important categories of sources for the social historian are the accounting (*uchetnyi*) and reporting (*otchetnyi*) categories of documents. These two categories can provide much of the raw material that the social historian seeks: statistical data, records and registers, personnel reports, questionnaires, etc. Within each of these categories, there are many different types of documents, but several can be singled out as of particular value to the social historian. Discussion here will accordingly be devoted to documents from these two categories, in addition to letters, another type of document, which are not so easily categorized according to typology but which are of immense value to social historians.

Documents of the reporting category are of major importance to the study of social history and are, perhaps, the easiest of the document types to work with. These types of documents appear rather frequently in the archives. The *doklad*, *dokladnaia zapiska*, and *otchet*—each a form of report on an event, activity, the implementation of a policy, etc.—are the most common. These documents can contain a variety of different types of information depending upon the author of the report, what he considered important, and what his intended audience was interested to learn. Reports can include statistical data, excerpts of letters or statements of individuals, tables and charts, and lists of various types. They are mainly of a descriptive nature, and the larger part of the report is narrative.

These were the most widespread types of documents among the archival materials to which the author had access within the *fondy* of individual trade union central committees for the period 1929–31.[23] These documents were among the records of the trade unions' rural departments and derived from sources on all levels, ranging from city-level, raion, okrug, and oblast/krai/republic trade union organizations to factory committees and individual trade union representatives, workers, and workers' brigades pursuing rural work. The reports generally provided surveys on work done by the trade unions in the countryside and work with new factory workers (recent arrivals from the countryside) and included statistical materials, excerpts of workers' letters and statements, and comments on the political mood in the village or factory. These reports provide an insight into the major issues of the times as articulated by the trade union officials and factory workers who compiled these documents. For example, the most frequent issues raised in these reports as they pertained to the factories were the food problem of 1929 and the problem of so-called "petit-bourgeois" contamination of the working class due to the influx of peasants into the labor force.[24] Perhaps the main significance of the report type of document, apart from facts and figures in the narrative, is the way in which the documents' authors perceive particular subjects or events, define and interpret major issues, and present solutions to those issues.

The *svodka*, usually a report issued on a sequential basis similar to a progress report, is another very useful type of document of the reporting category. The information provided in the *svodka* is similar to that of other forms of reports only differing in its sequential nature. The sequential nature of the *svodka* makes this type of source more current and allows the researcher a day-to-day glimpse of the process and progress of a particular activity, subject, or event. For example, the author had access to a set of *svodki* compiled by the Moscow oblast committee of the metal workers' trade union on the subject of the implementation of the recruitment campaign of the 25,000ers (factory workers recruited for work in the collective farms in late 1929–early 1930) and covering the period from 10 December to 31 December 1929.[25] Each report contained general information and statistics on recruitment among Moscow metal workers, followed by individual factory breakdowns on the course of the campaign. The factory breakdowns on the campaign included information on the number of volunteers for recruitment, the personal profile of the volunteers according to age, sex, skill, etc., recruitment quotas per factory, campaign problems, methods of campaign implementation, and the reaction of workers to the campaign. This information presented the opportunity to follow the development of the campaign as it progressed. This type of presentation of information is, moreover, somewhat more direct, more routine, and closer to events than the more reflective *doklad* or *otchet*, thereby allowing somewhat less room for the author of the report to impose his own opinions and impressions.

The *anketa*, or questionnaire or data sheet, is an example of a document type from the accounting category as well as an example of a standardized (*typovyi*) form of document. This type of document represents raw material for the social historian and, in most cases, is required in fairly large quantity to be of real use. The *anketa* contains personal and professional information on employees, workers, or partici-pants in some specific activity, including information on birth date, social origin, party membership, skill level, family data, and so on. In theory, there are *ankety* for all Soviet workers and employees in the archival records of factories (which are generally stored in local or regional archives). The author had access to two sets of a limited number of *ankety* on the 25,000ers from the Moscow Tormoznoi and Kolomenskii factories.[26] The following information was provided in these *ankety:* birth dates, party membership and year of entry into the party, professional special-ity, length of service (*stazh*) in production and in the trade union, public service record (*stazh obshchestvennoi raboty*), Red Army service, educational level, num-ber of family dependents, rural assignment, and method of recruitment. The value of this source for prosopography, labor history, and other aspects of social history is both self-evident and unlimited. Moreover, a document type like the *anketa*, and for that matter the majority of the accounting types, are less vulnerable to conscious or unconscious subjective shaping by their authors as can often be the case in reports and, to a lesser degree, in the *svodki*.

One source or document type which is almost entirely given to such subjective shaping and whose main value, to a great extent, resides precisely in this shaping is the letter. There are many different types of letters, ranging from official or semi-official reports in letter form to personal letters. There are also many types of letter writers including individuals representing an official interest or institution as well as average civil servants, workers, and peasants. Letters are dispersed throughout the institutional records, usually mixed in with other types of documents, and their location will depend upon such factors as author, addressee, subject of concern, and purpose of the letter. This type of document is often handwritten and generally the most difficult of documents to read for the non-native Russian speaker especially if the author of a given letter was a representative of the laboring classes. In the case of letters written by workers and peasants, this source often represents one of the very few types of documents that these social groups have left to posterity. Moreover, given the traditional propensity of Soviet citizens to petition higher authorities and to write letters of complaint as a normal matter of recourse, one can surmise that the quantity of letters among institutional records (provided they were preserved) must indeed be massive.

The author had access to almost one hundred letters written by 25,000ers work-ing in the collective farms in 1930–31.[27] These letters provided very interesting details on rural conditions, the collective farms, rural officials, and peasants, treat-ing a multitude of issues. The letters reveal a great deal about how the worker viewed his surroundings and, in this case, collectivization and life in the countryside. This group of letters, in particular, and probably other similar sets of letters as well, is important for several other auxiliary purposes. First, the letters of 25,000ers pro-vided a source of information on rural issues for the central committees of the trade unions, who, in turn, relayed the information to the party central committee. The workers were often requested to report on various issues and to answer specific sets of questions. Second, the letters provided an outlet for grievances and a way to seek aid in conflicts with, for example, former factories, local officials, and various institutions. The trade unions frequently intervened for workers in cases of conflict with local rural organs, party expulsions, housing problems, financial problems, etc. In this instance, letters are significant not only due to content and the authors' points of view, but due to the light they shed on the other purposes of the letters as sources of information and an outlet for workers' grievances, as well as the light they shed on the trade unions' role as ombudsmen. Letters, therefore—and not only those written by workers—are a valuable source for social historians and may be used in a number of ways in historical investigations. Letters from this time period and especially those of workers have been published in a variety of sources but nowhere except in the archives can the historian read the original letters in addition to responses and continuing correspondence.

Conclusion

The value of archival research to social historians and especially to social historians of the Stalin period is clear. There is much in the Soviet past and in the Stalin prewar years, in particular, that remains a cipher. Increasing access to archival data on this period will contribute much to our attempts to decode the cipher. Apart from the "facts" of history which are buried in the archives, the value of archival research can be defined more concretely in terms of practical usefulness. The first evident strength of archival materials is that they are easier to work with than most published sources. The data is better organized and thematically concentrated. The researcher need not pore over twenty to thirty newspapers in search of bits and pieces of scattered evidence. The second strength of archival materials is that they can provide an understanding of events and policies (through, for example, the *svodki*) on a day-to-day basis. The researcher can see precisely *how* the history of the times was made. Finally, and perhaps most important, archival materials provide detailed information that cannot be matched in any other source.

The value of the archives and, particularly, archival research within the constraints of a concentration on the Stalin period should not be overstated. Archival records are not the repository of truth. They can contain as much bias as any other source. The authors of many of the types of documents listed in the preceding pages were no less politically biased than, for example, journalists who wrote for the contemporary press. Moreover, they often worked under similar political constraints. It is necessary to keep this in mind when working with archival materials and to remember, to quote once again from Carr, that, "No document can tell us more than what the author of the document thought—what he thought had happened, what he thought ought to happen or would happen, or perhaps only what he wanted others to think he thought, or even only what he himself thought he thought."[28] Further on in the text, Carr goes on to say: ". . . the facts of history never come to us 'pure,' since they do not and cannot exist in a pure form: they are always refracted through the mind of the recorder.''[29] This is true of the "facts," or data, contained in Soviet archival repositories as well. It is the historian's task to recognize such bias, to weed it out when necessary and if possible, or simply to harness it and to put it to use. The bias of a document's author tells the historian much about not only the author, but also his social group or class and his times. As Carr concludes in his discussion of the recorder of history: "The language he speaks is not an individual inheritance, but a social acquisition from the group in which he grows up."[30] The language of archival documents is as important as the individual letters of the alphabet in a document, which, when combined together, put forth the "facts" and evidence of the times.

The bias of a source can, to some extent at least, be controlled provided the historian can rein in his own biases and those of the times in which he is writing. To return to the initial problem stated in the introduction, it is necessary to point out another problem of archival research which, unlike the problem of bias, is largely beyond the control of the researcher. Problems of control in the selection of sources, and therefore of evidence, in Soviet archives is the most serious problem that the Western historian must confront in his research. For unlike Carr's imaginary and, in some ways, omnipotent historian, the historian working in the archives cannot simply "call upon" the "facts," or data, lay them out according to size and shape, and then proceed to select, categorize, and classify. Even in the era of *glasnost'* and *perestroika*, Western historians continue to face major problems in archival access. These problems are, to some extent, survivals from the period of stagnation when all Western historians were treated as ideological "enemies." Such problems, however, serve to make Soviet archives something of an anomaly (with the exception of certain third-world nations) within the context of international norms and standards of archival access. Therefore, given the problems of source and evidence selection, the Western historian will necessary fall short of the unbound Prometheus in many respects, but nonetheless can struggle against his chains by making use of certain skills derived in preparatory work. A basic knowledge of administration, record-keeping practices, and document typology and terminology will provide the researcher with more control in the selection and ordering process and a better understanding of how to classify specific types of evidence culled from Soviet archives when set against a background of such factors as the administrative purpose of a particular document, its institutional or individual author and addressee, and so on. In addition to this, the researcher can compare evidence derived from archival data with evidence derived from other (published) sources in order to determine bias, accuracy, and usefulness. These and a variety of other measures can be applied to archival evidence in order to classify its use and value and to offset the problems of diminished control over the selection process.

Despite the problems and numerous difficulties confronted in working in Soviet archives, the assets of archival research in the USSR far outweigh the debits. Archival research is an important part of professional training for young historians and, in terms of Western historians of the Stalin period, not simply the younger generation. Furthermore, continued and expanded access to Soviet archives is a necessity if the legacy of Cold War historiography—which has led to a neglect of Soviet society and a view of Soviet history often solely from the standpoint of the vista offered from the Kremlin walls—is to be overcome. Social history is changing the face of Western historiography on the 1930s; expanded access to Soviet archives will contribute immeasurably to the further development of the study of the social history of the Stalin years in the West.[31]

Notes

1. Edward Hallett Carr, *What is History?* (New York: Vintage, 1961), 9.

2. It should be noted that scholars working on the prerevolutionary period often face problems similar to those of scholars working on the postrevolutionary period. This is most notably the case in regard to the problem of viewing the *opis'* and the selection of documents within the archives.

3. Western scholars working on postrevolutionary topics and particularly topics on the First Five-Year Plan period have had the most success in obtaining access to the central government archives, TsGAOR SSSR (Central State Archive of the October Revolution, Higher Organs of State Government and Organs of State Administration of the USSR) and TsGANKh SSSR (Central State Archive of the Economy of the USSR). To date, the archives of the Communist Party remain closed to Western scholars.

4. Archival code numbers are the basic citation form of archival reference and take the following form: a) *fond* number (the equivalent of a record group; the first major subdivision of an archive usually based on the records of an individual institution or organization); b) *opis'* number (basically, the inventory listing the contents of a *fond* or part of it; the *opis'* serves as the next subdivision of an archive in cases when there is more than one *opis'*, and may represent individual sectors or departments within an institution); c) *delo* number (sometimes entitled *edinitsa khraneniia*; this is the smallest unit in the archive divisions and is a portfolio containing documents); d) list number (the folio numbers of a *delo* consisting of more than one item are called *listy* [plural] but need not be given when ordering documents). See note 24 below for examples of archival citation models.

5. Patricia Kennedy Grimsted, *Archives and Manuscript Repositories in the USSR: Moscow and Leningrad* (Princeton, N.J.: Princeton University Press, 1972); *idem.*, "Regional State Archives in the USSR: Some Notes and a Bibliography of Published Guides," *Slavic Review* 28:1 (1969); and *idem.*, "Recent Publications on Archives and Manuscript Collections in the Soviet Union: A Selective Survey," *Slavic Review* 41:3 (1982). See citations in *idem.*, "Archival Resources for Social History of the 1920s and 1930s: Soviet Archival Developments and Reference Aids for the Social Historian," *Russian History/Historie russe* 12:2–4 (1985) for other references to Dr. Grimsted's many articles and books on Soviet archives.

6. There is a *putevoditel'* for TsGAOR SSSR which also must be used as a guide to TsGANKh SSSR. The latter was organized in 1961 and many of its holdings were transferred from TsGAOR and retain their original citation numbers. Because other holdings besides those from TsGAOR are contained in TsGANKh, it is difficult to determine its holdings exactly. In general, however, according to Grimsted's 1972 directory (p. 133), TsGANKh's main divisions are on the following lines: (a) heavy industry, (b) food and light industries, (c) construction and metallurgy, (d) plans of financial organs, (e) agriculture, (f) transportation and communications. For further information and sources on these two archives see Grimsted (1972, 123–134); and *Tsentral'nyi gosudarstvennyi arkhiv Oktiabr'skoi revoliutsii i sotsialisticheskogo stroitel'stva. Putevoditel'* (Moscow, 1946). For information on TsGA

RSFSR (Central State Archive of the RSFSR), see Grimsted's 1972 directory (pp. 361–362) and her "Archival Resources," 181, note 94, discussing the publication of a guide for TsGA RSFSR. The regional archives in Moscow and Leningrad have undergone a number of reorganizations in recent years which Grimsted has largely clarified in the 1982 *Slavic Review* article (pp. 524–525). For further information on these archives, see Grimsted's 1972 directory (pp. 363–364, 368–369), along with the 1982 *Slavic Review* article and the two general directories pertaining to archival holdings from the Soviet period held under Moscow and Leningrad regional auspices: *Gosudarstvennyi arkhiv Oktiabr'skoi revoliutsii i sotsialisticheskogo stroitel'stva Leningradskoi oblasti. Kratkii putevoditel'* (Leningrad, 1962) and *Gosudarstvennyi arkhiv Oktiabr'skoi revoliutsii i sotsialisticheskogo stroitel'stva Moskovskoi oblasti. Kratkii spravochnik* (Moscow, 1962). For a bibliography of published guides to other regional archives in the USSR, see Grimsted's 1969 *Slavic Review* article. For information pertaining to Communist party archives, see V. V. Maksakov, *Organizatsiia arkhivov KPSS* (Moscow, 1968); V. E. Korneev, *Arkhivy VKP (b) v 1917–1925 gg. Uchebnoe posobie* (Moscow, 1979); and *idem., Arkhivy VKP (b) (1926–41 gg.). Uchebnoe posobie* (Moscow, 1981). It is also useful for the researcher to consult at this point the more general guides and directories to Soviet archives, such as *Gosudarstvennye arkhivy RSFSR. Spravochnik-putevoditel'* (Moscow, 1980) and *Gosudarstvennye arkhivy Soiuza SSR. Kratkii spravochnik* (Moscow, 1956). Finally, for general introductions to the archives, summaries of archival holdings, and further sources on the archives, see G. A. Dremina, *Tsentral'nye gosudarstvennye arkhivy SSSR, 1945–1970 gg. Uchebnoe posobie* (Moscow, 1977) and I. M. Grossman and V. N. Kutik, *Spravochnik nauchnogo rabotnika. Arkhivy, dokumenty, issledovatel'* (Lvov, 1979).

7. For further information on these types of sources, the reader should consult *Katalog arkhivovedcheskoi literatury, 1917–1959 gg.* (Moscow, 1961); *Katalog arkhivovedcheskoi literatury i sbornikov dokumentov (1960–1963 gg.)* (Moscow, 1964); *Katalog arkhivovedcheskoi literatury i sbornikov dokumentov (1964–1967 gg.)* (Moscow, 1970); *Katalog arkhivovedcheskoi literatury i sbornikov dokumentov (1968–1970 gg.)* (Moscow, 1977), as well as Grimsted (1972, 1982), Dremina (1977), and Grossman and Kutik, *Spravochnik nauchnogo rabotnika*. Useful bibliographies on this type of source are contained in *Istochnikovedenie istorii sovetskogo obshchestva*, 4 vols. (Moscow, 1964–1982) and *Istoriia istoricheskoi nauki v SSSR. Sovetskii period. Oktiabr' 1917–1967 gg. Bibliografiia* (Moscow, 1980), 477–489. For surveys of specific holdings, the researcher should consult *Istoricheskii arkhiv* (Moscow, 1955–1962); *Problemy istochnikovedeniia* (Moscow, 1933–1963); and *Sovetskie arkhivy* (a publication of GAU which superseded *Voprosy arkhivovedeniia* in 1966). For further information on archival periodicals, the reader may consult T. B. Bataeva and A. D. Stepanskii, "Arkhivnaia periodika i razvitie sovetskogo arkhivovedeniia," *Voprosy istorii*, no. 9 (Sept. 1983).

Finally, mention should be made of the following works which are of exceptional value to a study of the First Five-Year Plan period. *A. M. Gor'kii i sozdanie istorii fabrik i zavodov* (Moscow, 1959) contains an invaluable series of appendices on the archival holdings of individual factories and plants. Each factory or plant archival holding is presented individually with a description of the nature of the documents contained in the holding, an indication of the archival repository in which the holding is located, and archival code numbers. For descriptions of specific archival holdings and topics, the reader should consult A. Butenko, "Materialy po istorii rabochego klassa SSSR v fondakh TsGAOR SS SSSR," *Voprosy istoriografii i istochnikovedeniia istorii rabochego klassa SSSR* (Leningrad, 1962); N. A. Ivnitskii, "Fond Kolkhoztsentra SSSR i RSFSR kak istochnik dlia izucheniia kollektivizatsii sel'skogo khoziaistva v SSSR," *Problemy istochnikovedeniia*, vyp. IV (Moscow, 1955), which covers the years of Kolkhoztsentr's existence (1927–1932); Ia. Z. Livshits, "Kratkii obzor dokumental'nykh materialov po istorii bor'by rabochikh tiazheloi promyshlennosti Moskvy za vypolnenie pervogo piatiletnego plana. (Po fondam Gosudarstvennogo arkhiva Oktiabr'skoi revoliutsii i sotsialisticheskogo stroitel'stva Moskovskoi oblasti)," *Izmeneniia v chislennosti i sostave sovetskogo rabochego klassa* (Moscow, 1961); V. I. Startsev, "Statisticheskie istochniki Gosudarstvennogo arkhiva Oktiabr'skoi revoliutsii i sotsialisticheskogo stroitel'stva Leningradskoi oblasti po istorii sovetskogo rabochego klassa,'' *Voprosy istoriografii i istochnikovedeniia istorii rabochego klassa SSSR*; and V. I. Startsev and O. I. Shkaratan, "Fondy Gosudarstvennogo arkhiva Oktiabr'skoi revoliutsii i sotsialisticheskogo stroitel'stva Leningradskoi oblasti kak istochnik po istorii sovetskogo rabochego klassa,'' *Izmeneniia v chislennosti i sostave sovetskogo rabochego klassa.*

8. For general finding aids to published archival documents, *Sovetskie arkhivy* and *Katalog sbornikov dokumentov, izdannykh arkhivnymi uchrezhdeniiami SSSR* (Moscow, 1961) are helpful. *Sovetskie arkhivy* and *Istoricheskii arkhiv* have published valuable archival materials in their issues. The seven volume series, *Materialy po istorii SSSR (dokumenty po istorii sovetskogo obshchestva)* (Moscow, 1955–1959), contains excellent collections of documents. Among other publications of archival materials (sometimes mixed with other types of sources), particularly noteworthy are: *Industrializatsiia SSSR, 1926–1941. Dokumenty i materialy*, 4 vols. (Moscow, 1969–1973); *Partiino-politicheskaia rabota v Krasnoi Armii. Dokumenty, 1921–1929 gg.* (Moscow, 1981) which goes up to July 1929; *Politicheskoi i trudovoi pod"em rabochego klassa SSSR (1928–1929 gg.). Sbornik dokumentov* (Moscow, 1956); *Profsoiuzy SSSR. Dokumenty i materialy, 1905–1963*, 5 vols. (Moscow, 1963–1974); *Sotsialisticheskoe sorevnovanie na predpriiatiiakh Leningrada v gody pervoi piatiletki, 1928–1932 gg. Sbornik dokumentov i materialov* (Leningrad, 1961); *Sotsialisticheskoe sorevnovanie v SSSR, 1918–1964. Dokumenty i materialy profsoiuzov* (Moscow, 1965); *Vnutrennie voiska v gody mirnogo sotsialisticheskogo stroitel'stva. 1922–1941 gg. Dokumenty i materialy* (Moscow, 1977); and *Zheleznodorozhnyi transport v gody industrializatsii SSSR (1926–1941 gg.)* (Moscow, 1970). Perhaps the most valuable published collections of archival and other materials are those produced by the various regional archive administrations on collectivization and industrialization. For bibliographies on these series, see my article and the article by Lewis H. Siegelbaum in this collection.

9. It should be noted that it is useful to bring a complete and accurate listing of sources of citation to the archives in order to aid the archival attendant in locating materials if some problem arises.

10. This is a difficult term to translate and define. The authors of *Spravochnik nauchnogo rabotnika* (p. 293) define it as, "that activity encompassing questions of documentation and the organization of work with documents in the process of fulfilling administrative actions." For another definition, see Walter McKenzie Pintner and Don Karl Rowney, eds., *Russian Officialdom. The Bureaucratization of Russian Society from the Seventeenth to the Twentieth Century* (Chapel Hill: University of North Carolina Press, 1980), 9–10. For more detailed treatments of *deloproizvodstvo*, the reader should consult a general work on archival theory and practice or on the study of sources, such as *Istochnikovedenie istorii SSSR* (Moscow, 1981), chap. 25; K. G. Mitiaev, *Teoriia i praktika arkhivnogo dela. Uchebnoe posobie* (Moscow, 1946); *idem.*, *Istoriia i organizatsiia deloproizvodstva v SSSR. Uchebnoe posobie* (Moscow, 1959); *Teoriia i praktika arkhivnogo dela v SSSR* (Moscow, 1966); and V. V. Sorokin, *Arkhivy uchrezhdenii SSSR (1917–1937 gg.). Uchebnoe posobie* (Moscow, 1982).

11. Grossman and Kutik, *Spravochnik nauchnogo rabotnika*, 47–49.

12. For general histories of Soviet state institutions and organizations, see A. A. Nelidov, *Istoriia gosudarstvennykh uchrezhdenii SSSR, 1917–1936 gg.* (Moscow, 1962); and V. A. Tsikulin, *Istoriia gosudarstvennykh uchrezhdenii SSSR, 1936–1965 gg.* (Moscow, 1966). Also see T. P. Korzhikhina, *Istoriia gosudarstvennykh uchrezhdenii SSSR* (Moscow, 1986), for a guide that is less complete but more concise and still in print.

13. See notes 6 and 10 above.

14. For examples of institutional structural divisions, see Grossman and Kutik, *Spravochnik nauchnogo rabotnika*, 48–49 and sources listed in note 6 above. In order to illustrate this point further, here is an example of the internal structure of VTsSPS (All-Union Central Council of Professional Trade Unions) as depicted in the *putevoditel'* for TsGAOR SSSR (pp. 229–34):

prezidium (1917–1931)
organizatsionno-instruktorskii sektor (1917–1931)
informatsionnyi sektor (1917–1932)
tarifno-ekonomicheskii otdel (1917–1929)
sektor proizvodstva i zarabotnoi platy (1930–1931)
sotsial'no-bytovoi sektor (1930–1931)
sektor profkadrov (1930–1931)
massovyi sektor (1930–1931)
iuridicheskoe biuro (1925–1929)
kul'totdel (1917–1931)
finansovyi sektor (1920–1931)
statisticheskii sektor (1917–1935)
upravlenie delami (1920–1931)

Soviet city directories are also a useful source of information on administrative subdivisions within an institution or organization. See J. Arch Getty's article in this collection for further information.

15. See note 8 above.

16. For information pertaining to the Smolensk Communist Party Archive, see *Guide to the Records of the Smolensk Oblast of the All-Union Communist Party of the Soviet Union, 1917–1941* (Washington, D.C.: National Archives and Records Service. General Services Administration, 1980). This guide is discussed in J. Arch Getty's article on the Smolensk archives.

17. Most official documents (e.g., reports) from the period under consideration were typed and not handwritten. However, the researcher is very likely to come across handwritten materials in the case of letters or, if my experience in working with raion and local-level materials in GAMO in 1988 is any indication, certain types of documents from the raion or local levels of government.

18. For an interesting account of one Western scholar's approach to and experience in Soviet archives, see Sheila Fitzpatrick, "A Student in Moscow, 1966," *Wilson Quarterly* 6:3 (1983). See also the interesting letter by Donald J. Raleigh printed in *Moscow News* 33 (August 21–28, 1988), discussing the problems that Western scholars face in Soviet archives. (My thanks to William Husband for bringing this article to my attention.)

19. Grossman and Kutik, *Spravochnik nauchnogo rabotnika*, 52. See also Mitiaev (1946), 171–175, for further details on designing titles for *dela*.

20. A. K. Sokolov, "Deloproizvodstvennaia dokumentatsiia gosudarstvennykh uchrezhdenii, predpriiatii i obshchestvennykh organizatsii," *Istochnikovedenie istorii SSSR* (1981), 399–405.

21. *Ibid.*, 403, 405. For slightly different, more complex typologies, see Mitiaev (1946), 61–82.

22. Sokolov in *Istochnikovedenie istorii SSSR* (1981), 406.

23. My selection of document types is necessarily influenced by the types of materials to which I had access. Among the trade union *fondy* treated here (all from TsGAOR SSSR) are the following:

fond 5466: TsK soiuza sel'skokhoziaistvennykh i lesnykh rabochikh.
fond 5469: TsK soiuza rabochikh metallistov.
fond 5453: TsK soiuza kozhevnikov.
fond 7676: TsK soiuza rabochikh obshchego mashinostroeniia.
fond 5475: TsK soiuza stroitelei.
fond 5525: TsK soiuza pechatnikov.
fond 5452: TsK soiuza gornorabochikh.
fond 5470: TsK soiuza rabochikh khimikov.
fond 5457: TsK soiuza sherstianoi, shelkovoi i trikotazhnoi promyshlennosti.

24. TsGAOR SSSR, *f.* 5469, *op.* 13, *d.* 122, *ll.* 2–7, 162–169; *f.* 5469, *op.* 13, *d.* 123,

ll. 72–76, 78–91; *f.* 5469, *op.* 13, *d.* 124, *ll.* 90, 93–94, 99–100; *f.* 5469, *op.* 13, *d.* 126, *ll.* 12, 56, 63.

25. TsGAOR SSSR, *f.* 5469, *op.* 13, *d.* 124, *ll.* 37–56.

26. TsGAOR SSSR, *f.* 5469, *op.* 13, *d.* 125; *f.* 7676, *op.* 6, *d.* 180.

27. TsGAOR SSSR, *f.* 5453, *op.* 14, *d.* 57 (all letters); *f.* 5453, *op.* 14, *d.* 150 (part letters); *f.* 5470, *op.* 14, *d.* 204 (part letters); *f.* 5475, *op.* 13, *d.* 66 (letter excerpts in reports); *f.* 7676, *op.* 1, *d.* 160 (part letters).

28. Carr, *What is History?*, 16.

29. *Ibid.*, 24.

30. *Ibid.*, 36–37.

31. As a postscript to the article, it is useful to note, in addition to the above bibliography on Soviet archives, several useful guides to archives on Russia and the Soviet Union located in the West. See Steven A. Grant, *Scholars' Guide to Washington, D.C. for Russian/Soviet Studies* (Washington, D.C.: Smithsonian Institution Press, 1977); Steven A. Grant and John H. Brown, *The Russian Empire and Soviet Union. A Guide to Manuscripts and Archival Materials in the United States* (Boston: G. K. Hall and Co., 1981); *Russia in the Twentieth Century: The Catalog of the Bakhmeteff Archive of Russian and East European History and Culture, The Rare Book and Manuscript Library, Columbia University* (Boston: G. K. Hall, 1987); Richard C. Lewanski, *Eastern Europe and Russia/Soviet Union. A Handbook of West European Archival and Library Resources* (New York: K. G. Saur, 1980); and Gregory Walker, ed., *Resources for Soviet, East European and Slavonic Studies in British Libraries* (Birmingham: University of Birmingham, Centre for Russian and East European Studies, 1981).

Guide to the Smolensk Archive

J. ARCH GETTY

To date, the documents of the Smolensk Archive comprise the only archival material from the Soviet Communist party available to Western researchers. The general story of the archives is well known: invading German army units found the files as they passed through Smolensk in July 1941. The files were taken back to Germany, where in 1945 they were found again, this time by the advancing American army. They then came into the custody of the National Archives and Records Service which, in cooperation with the U.S. Department of the Army and the American Historical Association, microfilmed the collection.[1]

It has been thirty years since Merle Fainsod first tapped the Archive for his tour de force, *Smolensk Under Soviet Rule*.[2] Touching on party affairs, religion, agriculture, youth, and women—among other topics—this important book was the first to show how the system worked on the inside. It provided vivid color and breathed life into the structural and model-oriented analyses of its day. Fainsod discovered documents unknown in the West and introduced us to real people of the 1930s. It is a measure of his achievement that no one bothered to study the Archive for twenty years. When scholars cited the Smolensk documents, they cited Fainsod.

Only in the last ten years or so have students of the Stalin period rediscovered the Smolensk Archive. Partly because they questioned the totalitarian model[3] and partly because they suspected that Fainsod had not been able to mine the whole vein, scholars have begun to incorporate systematic use of the Smolensk Archive into their research on various topics.[4]

Archival coverage, strengths and weaknesses

The records of the Smolensk regional Communist party committee encompass the years from before 1917 to about 1941. The territory was known variously as Smolensk guberniia (1917–1929), the Western oblast (1929–1937), and Smolensk oblast (from 1937). The Smolensk Archives are therefore the records of a rather large entity: a regional/provincial party organization (gubkom, later obkom).

The Archive does not contain the primary files of any district (raion) party committee (raikom); the Archive's files pertaining to specific raions are the obkom's files on correspondence and contact with the raikoms. Similarly, the Archive does

Table 1

Chronological Coverage of the Smolensk Archive

Period	Number of files
1917–1920	24
1921–1924	49
1925–1928	124
1929–1932	122
1933–1936	156
1937–1941	50
misc. dates	16
Total	541

not contain files that were the property of soviet, police, or other non-party organizations, but rather includes files reflecting the obkom's relations with those institutions.

Files on non-party organizations found their way into the obkom files through one of two channels: either they pertained to the party cell of the organization or else they recorded communication between the obkom and the non-party organization. These files thus reflect only the "party" side of the activities of these organizations. Thus file WKP 106 promises to tell the reader about the Tumanovo Raion NKVD, but only contains reports on its party cell and its activities: preparations for Youth Day, indoctrination of Komsomol NKVD members, party propaganda, etc.

As we know it today, the Smolensk Archive consists of 541 numbered files containing over 200,000 pages on the activities of the Smolensk regional party organization before 1941. The files are now consecutively numbered WKP 1 through WKP 541.[5] The distribution of chronological coverage is reflected in Table 1.

Parts of a few of the files in the first period relate to events before the October Revolution of 1917, but most pertain to the Civil War. Similarly, most of the files in the 1937–1938 category end in 1938; only a few extend beyond that year.

The period covered by the Smolensk Archive is a function of document storage dispositions in Smolensk in 1941. When the Germans entered Smolensk, the local Bolshevik leadership was able to destroy or evacuate party records for the current period, which were kept at party headquarters. Stored, or archived, files on previous years were apparently kept in a different building across town, and it was this collection which the Germans found.

Like all document collections, the Smolensk Archive has strengths and weaknesses. In terms of topical coverage, the Archive is relatively strong on political affairs (especially the relationship among various levels of the apparatus), purges, agriculture, education and propaganda, youth, women, and Jewish affairs. It is relatively weak on industry and industrial planning, urban affairs, and the activities of police and other non-party organizations.

Another weakness or difficulty relates to the organization and presentation of the documents. Even a first look at the Archive reveals the disorganized nature of most of the files, which suffer from what Fainsod called a "random character." Documents on agriculture can be found among protocols of meetings; a swine-breeding report might be next to a Central Committee circular. This chaotic and unpredictable quality sharply reduces the value of various finding aids (discussed below). Moreover, some of the documents are difficult to read. Illegible handwriting, primitive typewriters, smudged papers, and blurred microfilm have turned many of the papers into optical puzzles which strain the eyes and often defy decoding.

Provenance of the documents

A perusal of the Smolensk Archive will quickly show that these could not be all the files of an oblast party organization.[6] There are files on some raions and not on others; chronological gaps exist within the files on a given subject; and we do not find files on subjects we should expect.[7] Within a given file, it is difficult to know what may have been removed by Russians, Germans, or Americans.

We do not know the criteria used by Smolensk officials in deciding what to save in a given file. We do not know whether the Smolensk party officials kept all back files in the area the Germans found. We do not know whether or not the Germans took all the files they found or only a selection.[8] And we do not know if all the files the Germans took ended up in American hands.

However, we do know with a fair degree of certainty that the integrity, order, and provenance of the individual files have remained intact. Many of the microfilmed files begin with a "*delo*" page (often a copy of the cover of the file itself) listing in Russian the number of "*listy*" in the folder. The pages are hand numbered, probably by the Soviet party archivist, and the page numbers match the *delo* cover.[9] Although individual files are intact, the Archive is incomplete in ways we cannot explain. (Of course, the same can be said of virtually every archival collection used by historians.) More to the point, researchers who have used the Archive seem to agree that the collection is complete enough to provide what archivists call "evidential value": the obkom's files "provide an authentic and adequate documentation of its organization and functioning."[10]

How typical was Smolensk?

This perennial question is difficult to answer. What was a "typical" oblast? The Western Region was largely a rural area specializing in industrial crops: flax was its claim to fame.[11] In its level of urbanization, ratio of party members to population, density of communications, and industrial base it was far behind Moscow and Leningrad. Yet so were most regions in the USSR, as the following data show.

Tables 2 and 3 give seven standard demographic variables for the fourteen administrative regions used in the 1926 census. Particularly interesting is a comparison of the figures for the Western Region with the median scores. For six of the seven variables, the Western Region is at or very near the median.

In terms of these demographic measures, then, there is no reason to believe that the Western Region was demographically atypical; indeed it seems almost the "typical" region.

Figure 1 shows the estimated party membership in the 25 Russian-speaking oblasts and krais represented at the 17th Party Congress in 1934.[12] Although the Western Region did not boast one of the largest memberships, it ranks 12th of 25: almost exactly in the center of the spread. So, in terms of level of urbanization, distribution of labor force, literacy, per capita income, infant mortality, and size of party organization, the Western Region was in fact a typical region.

And while it is true that the Smolensk party organization was smaller and more rural than many others across the country, indices of party saturation were not markedly different from the norm. Nationally in the 1930s, only about 0.3 percent of the rural population belonged to the Communist Party. In Belyi raion (the best documented rural raion in Smolensk), the figure was 0.33 percent. Nationally in 1932–33, one in five kolkhozy had a party cell and about half of all kolkhozy had at least one communist. The figures for Smolensk were almost exactly the same.[13] Indeed, in some ways, the rural party in Smolensk was better organized than elsewhere. In 1935, 14 percent of all rural communists in the Western region were classified as "isolated"; that is, they belonged formally to no organized cell. For Ivanovo, the figure was 28 percent, for Sverdlovsk, 47 percent, and for Leningrad, 53 percent.[14]

Of course, historians are rightly concerned about the generalizability of local or regional studies, and it always pays to be careful. But statistics aside, there seem few other reasons to believe that the Western Region was dramatically unusual. The center/periphery relationship and internal problems documented by the Smolensk Archive are echoed in national press reporting on other regions. Smolensk does not seem to have been singled out for criticism or discussion any more than other oblasts or krais. Actually, we have been generalizing from Smolensk for three decades inasmuch as most of our understanding of party structure, chains of command, and institutional actors comes from Fainsod.

In some ways the typicality of Smolensk is a non-question. Even were we to suspect somehow that the Western Region was in some way peculiar—and the above data suggest that it was not—its party archive would be worth studying in its own right. It is all we have, and research from it is vital for that reason alone.

What types of documents are in the files?

Some key documents are available only in the Smolensk Archive. The Stalin/Molotov letter of May 1933 ordering the release of detainees,[15] and the Central Committee secret letter announcing the first show trial in 1936[16] are examples. The vast majority of the documents are perhaps not so dramatic as the CHEKA's 1918 order

Table 2

Population Density, Urbanization, Dependency on Agriculture, Working in Industry by Census Region, 1926

Region	Pop./km	% urban	% working in agric.*	% working in industry
Belorussia	39.3	17.0	81.5	4.8
Central Black Earth	57.5	9.5	88.7	3.4
Central Industrial (incl. Moscow)	45.8	25.6	66.7	15.0
Central Volga	30.3	11.4	86.9	4.0
Leningrad/Karelia	13.1	34.5	60.8	16.3
Lower Volga	17.1	17.7	77.5	7.0
N. E. Region	2.2	9.9	86.3	4.8
N. Caucasus	28.5	19.8	74.1	8.2
Siberia	2.1	13.0	81.3	5.9
Transcaucasus	31.7	24.1	72.0	8.5
Ukraine	64.3	18.5	84.5	8.4
Ural	3.9	20.7	74.9	11.5
Viatka	21.5	6.8	90.6	3.3
Western	**43.6**	**11.9**	**85.5**	**5.5**
median	29.2	12.4	81.4	6.5

Source: Soviet census of 1926 presented in Frank Lorimer, *The Population of the Soviet Union: History and Prospects* (Geneva, 1946), 67–71.
*Percentage of the population dependent on agriculture.

Table 3

Literacy, Income, and Infant Mortality by Census Region, 1926

Region	% literate	Per capita income (rubles)	Infant mortality*
Belorussia	53.3	85	102
Central Black Earth	49.6	84	200
Central Industrial	68.7	140	175
Central Volga	47.5	82	195
Leningrad/Karelia	72.2	135	165
Lower Volga	54.3	125	168
N. E. Region	59.8	106	203
N. Caucasus	55.0	135	155
Siberia	41.5	?	235
Transcaucasus	37.0	?	?
Ukraine	57.6	104	141
Urals	50.3	107	247
Viatka	51.5	100	232
Western	**52.9**	**96**	**175**
median	52.2	102	175

Source: Soviet census of 1926 in Lorimer, *Population*, 76, 81–82.
*Deaths per 1,000 live births.

Figure 1. **Regional Party Membership in 1934.**

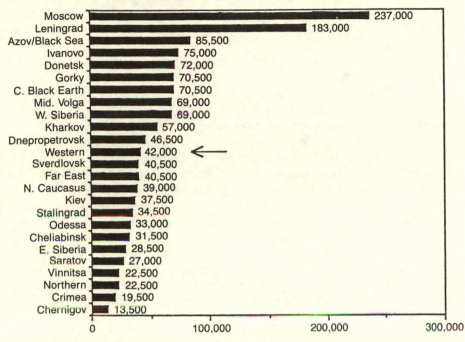

to turn in weapons[17] or the 1937 writers' meeting resolution against "Trotskyist-Averbakhist, Right-Trotskyist, and Trotskyist-Bukharinist wrecking in literature."[18] But because this is the only available party archive collection, virtually all its documents are unique.

In general, the files can be grouped into several categories. The majority are files comprising runs of obkom records on particular organizations in roughly chronological sequence. Thus, WKP 166 includes correspondence between the Krasnyi raion party committee and the Smolensk obkom in 1932 and 1933. Another category includes non-sequential files on particular subjects: WKP 315 is a file of reports to the obkom from the chief of the Machine Tractor Station political sections in the region, describing conditions on collective farms. Still another group of files concerns specific campaigns, operations, or events: WKP 384 is about the 1935 party membership screening in the city of Smolensk; WKP 510 concerns preparations for the celebration of the tenth anniversary of the October Revolution in 1927.

Among the files and across the years, we find several standard types of documents.

1. Protocols of party meetings

The party protocol is almost surely the most common document in the Smolensk Archive. Summary records of the proceedings of a specific meeting, these protocols are found throughout the chronological period of the Archive from the spring of

1917 into 1938. They cover meetings of organizations at every level from small party cells in various enterprises to raion committees to meetings of the Western obkom itself.[19] They are usually (and mercifully) typed, often in several copies, and follow a specific format.[20]

The top of the protocol lists the name of the organization, date of the meeting, and the number of members present and absent (and why). It also contains the agenda for the meeting: a list of specific reports and "theses" to be presented by reporters to the membership.[21] In all cases, unfortunately, the texts of the reports or theses themselves were not recorded in the protocol.

The next section of the protocol consists of paraphrases or summaries and frequently quotations of the remarks of the speakers made in the course of discussing the reports. These discussions are often quoted in full. The final section of the protocol is a record of the decisions taken *po dokladu* (on the basis of the report) or otherwise, and is signed by the secretary of the party organization. Sometimes, reports were given *k svedeniiu* (for information) and did not produce corresponding resolutions.

The Western obkom kept protocols not only of its own meetings, but of those in various raions in the region. Raikom protocols were circulated to the obkom and vice-versa. Additionally, an extract (*vypiska*) of a protocol might be sent to a particular non-party institution or enterprise if the decision affected its affairs. Frequently, such institutions requested extracts.[22]

2. Party correspondence

These are memoranda, telegrams, and letters between the Western obkom and various other obkoms and raikoms. They are usually on blank paper with the stamp of the originating party committee in the upper left corner.[23] Such correspondence consisted of requests for information on specific party members, checks of references, or less often, requests for a *vypiska* of one of the meetings of the addressee's committee.[24] They are in the forms of either letters or telegrams. There is, however, little in the way of interactive written communication between the Western obkom and the Moscow Central Committee. One does find printed circular letters or Central Committee advisories pertaining to certain operations or campaigns which evidently went out to all obkoms. But aside from routine requests for information on local conditions, there are few "personal" or two-way communications on this level.

There might be two explanations. Perhaps such sensitive material was not kept in the remote archive in Smolensk and was therefore not available to the Germans. It is also possible, though, that much of the communication between Moscow and the leaders of the Western obkom was oral. The Archive contains reference to a number of reports First Secretary I. P. Rumiantsev delivered to his followers after his trips to Moscow. Like many obkom secretaries, Rumiantsev was a member of the Central Committee and seems to have traveled to the capital frequently to report on various activities and to lobby for his region, perhaps obviating the need for extensive written correspondence.[25]

3. Central requests for information

Obkoms and raikoms were bombarded with requests for information from Moscow. Specific departments of the Central Committee (Cadres, Accounting, Agitprop) sent printed forms to the localities on such topics as the number and composition of cells and committees, the participation of members in agitprop activities, or (especially in the 1930s) reports on those admitted and expelled from the party. These forms often had lengthy instructions printed on the reverse telling local party officials exactly how to fill out the lines of the form. Adjacent to these forms, one often finds in the Archive the rough drafts and working notes of the official who completed the form.[26]

4. Central circulars

In order to provide information to local and regional party committees, Moscow circulated a variety of memos and bulletins on various topics. Variously labeled *pis'-mo, tsirkuliar, svodka,* or *biulleten'*, these missives did not have the character of a party decision or order.[27] Often marked "secret," they rather contained current events information, local examples of good or bad conduct, or advisories about changes in the political winds. The material in these circulars was meant to provide regional party officials with guides to correct conduct and propaganda material on the general line.

Such communications, especially the *pis'mo* and *svodka*, became common in the 1930s. The most famous example is the July 1936 "Top Secret" letter "On the Terrorist Activity of the Trotskyist-Zinovievist Counterrevolutionary Bloc," which announced the upcoming trial of Zinoviev, Kamenev, et al. and set the stage for the Ezhovshchina. The letter contains alleged examples of treason from around the country, extracts from the pre-trial depositions of the accused, and concludes with exhortations to unmask the enemy. No official operation was ordered; this was not a formal party decision or resolution of the Central Committee. Unofficially, though, the message was clear: "vigilance" was to increase and local party officials were to use the information and examples provided to prepare the party for a new direction.[28] Later on, various *svodki* were produced to provide more examples of enemy activity for local consumption.[29]

5. Other central material

In addition to requests for information and circular letters, the Central Committee occasionally sent specific instructions on the conduct of a party campaign or operation. Usually an *instruktsiia* or, less commonly, a *pis'mo*, this type of document gave detailed instructions and timetables for the prosecution of the operation. Like the circular, it was not in itself a party decision or formal resolution. Rather it made reference to the official decision and provided details on implementation. In some cases, the instructions were conveyed in the form of an extract from the protocol of an Orgburo meeting in Moscow.[30]

6. Lists

The Smolensk Archive contains a wide variety of lists of people. They include lists of those mobilized for military or other special tasks, lists of those selected to attend propaganda or educational courses, lists of party members (often with their social origins, party *stazh*, etc.), and lists of those purged or promoted.

7. Miscellaneous

Because of the random nature of the files, this is a large category. Some documents are simply brief notes or handwritten summaries on certain topics. There are numerous reports, plans of work, pamphlets, and newspaper clippings from local or national papers.[31]

Some files contain letters or complaints from average citizens. These letters are often accompanied by notes giving the disposition of the complaint: reference to a party committee or official for investigation. Some of these letters were referred to the Western obkom by newspaper editors or higher party bodies. It seems that nearly all of them were investigated.[32]

Some files contain a single item or collections of non-records. WKP 461 contains only blank membership cards for the League of Militant Atheists. WKP 472 is full of propaganda material suitable for radio broadcast, and WKP 478 and 480 contain specifically anti-fascist propaganda material. WKP 479 is a writing book with notes on a series of Marxism-Leninism lectures in a political course, and WKP 493 is a cash ledger.

Finding aids

Because of the disorganized nature of the Smolensk Archive, the existing finding aids are of quite limited value. Scholars accustomed to working in well-organized and cataloged archives will be disappointed with the tools available here.

Historically, the first finding aid was the annotated list of files compiled by Merle Fainsod in the process of writing *Smolensk Under Soviet Rule*.[33] Grouped by subject, this list of files reflects the topics used by Fainsod in the chapters of the book. Most entries contain only the date and a one-line annotation of the file's contents. Its main weakness is that it is not complete; some files covering material related to Fainsod's topics are not listed. It is a useful tool primarily for those needing an introduction to some of the topics that interested Fainsod.

The official guide is the National Archives and Records Service's *Guide to the Records of the Smolensk Oblast of the All-Union Communist Party of the Soviet*

Union, 1917–1941. It consists of three parts: a subject index, a register of the files, and computer-generated index to the register.

The subject index, compiled by Daniel Ipson, is more complete than Fainsod's but is not annotated. Under each subject ("Agriculture," "Komsomol," etc.), a list of files that contain something on the topic is given. Because of the dubious pagination in the Archive, page numbers are not provided. The Ipson index is useful for narrowing down the number of files related to a given topic and as a check on the completeness of one's research, but the lack of page references means that, in most cases, the researcher still has to page through sometimes hundreds of files to locate relevant material.

The register of files is based on a transcription of the descriptive note cards compiled by Fainsod and Michael Halyshyn. (In the microfilm, most files are preceded by such a card.) Each provides a paragraph or so of Fainsod's and/or Halyshyn's views of the most important contents of the file. Their views, and thus their annotations, tended to reflect their own interests and the spirit of the 1950s. Some files mainly concerning agriculture or youth activities are reduced to annotations solely concentrating on the "structure of control," "Communist infiltration," or the purges of those organizations. Important documents are often not mentioned at all on the cards.

Some of the cards in the register contain value judgments which seem strained and anachronistic. To researchers following the conflicts and struggles within a primitive and confused apparatus, it comes as a surprise to read the flat annotation that "According to documents, full cooperation existed within the party administrative structure."[34]

Other cards contain misinformation and misinterpretation. Thus the annotation for WKP 84 says of Stalin's "Cadres Decide Everything" speech that "Stalin said that communist achievements up to 1935 were largely due to the efforts made by the leaders of the nation."[35] Actually, he said the opposite and denigrated the contributions of leaders. The card for WKP 178 claims that a famous 1933 letter from Stalin and Molotov "instructed all agencies on procedures for arresting and deporting small property owners."[36] The document, correctly cited by Fainsod, actually gave instructions on releasing those falsely arrested. Because of these flaws, the register and computer list derived from it are of little use except as very rough and untrustworthy hints of some subjects that may be in the file.

Because of the limited help available from existing finding aids, researchers necessarily find themselves laboriously paging their way through many files looking for random pages relating to their topics. A good procedure is to use the Ipson index to generate a list of the possibly relevant files and the Fainsod/Halyshyn cards to augment the list with files which, despite the purported annotation, merely touch on the dates of the research topic. Then, there is unfortunately no substitute for going through the files page by page.

The Smolensk Archive is a unique collection. We have no other records of the inner functioning of local party institutions, no other source on local personnel issues, and no equally detailed local account of agricultural collectivization and administration. Despite the tedium and difficulties involved in using the collection, the Smolensk Archive is an indispensable source on local history before World War II, and it can pay rich dividends to the persevering researcher.

Notes

1. Known formerly as the "Records of the All-Union (Russian) Communist Party, Smolensk District, Record Group 1056," the official title of the collection is now the "Records of the Smolensk Oblast of the All-Union Communist Party of the Soviet Union, 1917-1941." Fainsod's shorthand "Smolensk Archive" has become the accepted name. Nearly all of the originals are in the custody of the National Archives and Records Service (NARS). (Seven of the more than 500 original files were inadvertently returned to Germany.) See Robert Wolfe and Daniel R. Brower, "Introduction," in *Guide to the Records of the Smolensk Oblast of the All-Union Communist Party of the Soviet Union, 1917-1941* (Washington, D.C.: National Archives and Records Service, 1980). The Smolensk Archive microfilm is available for purchase from NARS as Microfilm Publications T87 (rolls 1-69), T84 (rolls 27-28), and T88 (rolls 1-4). See the *Guide to the Records* for the contents of each roll. Researchers are cautioned to use only the microfilm copies of the Smolensk Archive. Some photocopied versions are incomplete. The paper version of the Archive at Harvard's Widener Library is missing several files, and many of the key documents Fainsod cited have been pilfered.

2. Merle Fainsod, *Smolensk Under Soviet Rule* (New York, 1958).

3. Because of the time in which he wrote, Fainsod used the language of the monolithic totalitarian model. But his findings frequently contradicted the usual understanding of the paradigm. "But the totalitarian machine, at least in the Smolensk area, was far from perfect. . . . Drunkenness, bribery, and self-serving behavior were endemic, and they persisted despite repeated efforts to stamp them out. Paradoxically, it was the very inefficiency of the state machine which helped make it tolerable." Fainsod, *Smolensk*, 449-450. For an interpretation of Fainsod's ambivalent attitude toward the reigning model, see Jerry Hough and Merle Fainsod, *How the Soviet Union is Governed* (Cambridge, Mass., 1979), preface.

4. Works that have made systematic use of the Smolensk Archive include: Daniel Brower, "Collectivized Agriculture in Smolensk: The Party, the Peasantry, and the Crisis of 1932," *Russian Review* 36:2 (1977), 151-166, and "The Smolensk Scandal and the End of NEP," *Slavic Review* 45:4 (1986), 689-706; J. Arch Getty, "Party and Purge in Smolensk, 1933-1937," *Slavic Review* 42:1 (1983), 60-96, and *Origins of the Great Purges: The Soviet Communist Party Reconsidered, 1933-1938* (Cambridge, 1985); Daniel A. Ipson, "The Struggle to Control Agriculture in the Smolensk Region," Ph.D. dissertation, (University of California, Davis, 1979); Roberta T. Manning, "Government in the Soviet Countryside in the Stalinist Thirties: The Case of Belyi Raion in 1937," *Carl Beck Papers in Russian and East European Studies*, no. 301, n.d.; Gabor T. Rittersporn, "The State Against Itself: Social Tensions and Political Conflicts in the USSR, 1936-1938," *Telos* 41 (1979); *idem.*, "Stalin in 1938: Political Defeat Behind the Rhetorical Apotheosis," *Telos* 46 (1980-81), 6-42; *idem.*, "Soviet Officialdom and Political Evolution: Judiciary Apparatus and Penal Policy in the 1930s," *Theory and Society* 13 (1984), and *idem.*, "Rethinking Stalinism," *Russian History* 11:4; William Rosenberg, "Smolensk in the 1920s: Party-Worker Relations and the 'Vanguard' Problem," *Russian Review* 36:2 (1977), 125-150; Constantine S. Shelly, "Scenes from the Smolensk Scandal: Power and Corruption in the Communist Party," M. A. thesis, (University of California, Davis, 1984); Peter H. Solomon, Jr., "Soviet Criminal Justice and the Great Terror," *Slavic Review* 46:3-4 (1987), 391-413. Selected documents have been published in Nicholas Werth, *Etre Communiste en URSS sous Staline* (Paris, 1981); Mikhail Voslenskii, *Nomenklatura* (London, 1985); and Sergei Maksudov, *Neuslyshannye golosa: dokumenty Smolenskogo arkhiva* (Ann Arbor, 1987).

5. WKP is a German acronym for "Vsesoiuznaia Kommunisticheskaia Partiia" (All-

Union Communist Party). Formerly, files WKP 528 through WKP 534 were known as 116/154 e, f, g, h and 116/155, 116/156, and 116/171, respectively. Files WKP 535 through WKP 538 were formerly labeled RS 921 through RS 924. Some older copies of the Archive, including the paper photostats at Harvard's Widener Library, retain the old numbering system. In addition to this renumbering of all files into the WKP system, some of the files seem to have been renumbered for other reasons. The *"delo"* pages show, for example, that WKP 9 was formerly labeled WKP 190. WKP 10 was formerly known as WKP 16, and before that, "Arkhiv 210."

6. Indeed, Soviet works have referred to two other archival collections in the USSR relating to Smolensk in the prewar period: Gosudarstvennyi arkhiv Smolenskogo oblasti (GASO), and Partiinyi arkhiv Smolenskoi oblasti (PASO). Western scholars have had access to neither. Citations of these two archives in Soviet works suggest that their *fondy* cover the same years and some of the same organizations as the Smolensk Archive but do not contain the same documents.

7. For example, there are no comprehensive party membership files or personnel dossiers, and not nearly enough on transportation, land tenure, and other vital topics.

8. There are many files on Jewish affairs, agriculture, and the party. These might have been the files the Germans found most interesting and worth taking.

9. Based on a spot check of the files with a *delo* page and pagination. Many files have neither.

10. T. R. Schellenberg, *Modern Archives: Principles and Techniques* (Chicago, 1956), 140.

11. For information on the region in this period see Fainsod, *Smolensk; Vsia Zapadnaia oblast' RSFSR: spravochnik* (Moscow, 1932); T. G. Timokhina et al., *Smolenskaia oblast': Kraeved. slovar'* (Moscow 1978); M. E. Klimenko, *Ocherki istorii Smolenskoi organizatsii KPSS*, kn. 1 (Moscow, 1985) and *Na zemle Smolenskoi* (Moscow 1985). Scholarly and documentary collections include *Materialy po izucheniiu Smolenskoi oblasti* (Moscow 1952–1976); *Kollektivizatsiia sel'skogo khoziaistva v Zapadnom raione RSFSR (1927–1937 gg.)* (Moscow, 1968).

12. Membership estimated by multiplying the number of delegates with voting rights by the stated representation figure (1:1500); candidate members are excluded. Figures include all delegations except: Kara-Kalpak ASSR, Karelia, Kazakhstan, Turkmenia, Kirgizia, Tajikistan, Uzbekistan, Azerbaijan, Armenia, Tatar ASSR, Moldavia, Bashkiria, Georgia, S. Caucasus, Iakutsk.

13. *Istoriia KPSS*, vol. 5, part 1 (Moscow, 1970), 49; V. M. Selunskaia, *Izmeneniia v strukture sovetskogo obshchestva, 1921–seredina 30-kh godov* (Moscow, 1979), 230; I. Glazyrin, *Regulirovannie sostava KPSS v period stroitel'stva sotsializma* (Moscow, 1957), 89–90; *Partiinoe stroitel'stvo*, no. 17–18, September 1932, 26 (hereafter, PS); WKP 313, pp. 130–131; WKP 85, pp. 352–368.

14. F. Iosifov, "Partiinaia rabota s kommunistami-odinochkami," PS, nos. 1–2, January 1935, 44; F. Chivirev, "K voprosu o rabote s kommunistami-odinochkami," PS, no. 14, July 1935, 30–34.

15. WKP 178, pp. 134–135.

16. WKP 499, pp. 322–328.

17. WKP 2, item 8.

18. WKP 532, pp. 130–134.

19. File WKP 538 (RS 924) is a complete collection of the Western obkom's meeting protocols for 1936.

20. Rarely, one finds preprinted forms for protocols. See WKP 6, p. 57 for an example.

21. The agenda nearly always included a *"raznoe,"* *"tekushchie dela,"* or miscellaneous category.

22. See WKP 6, pp. 75 and 81 for examples.

23. Obkom committees had their own printed stationery, but few raikoms did.

24. WKP 361 contains many of these.

25. WKP 238, pp. 14–15 is a report on one of Rumiantsev's trips to Moscow. WKP 538 contains obkom protocols which suggest that Rumiantsev was absent frequently.

26. WKP 572, p. 178; WKP 532, *passim.*; WKP 11, *passim.*

27. An exception is the "Closed Letter" of the Central Committee ordering the Verification of Party Documents in 1935, WKP 499, pp. 308–309. The Smolensk City Committee used the "Closed Letter" to prepare its own "Information Summary" for the local membership: WKP 384, pp. 66–67.

28. WKP 499, pp. 322–328.

29. WKP 538 (116/154e), pp. 44, 85–88.

30. *Ibid.*, p. 38. The first *Instruktsiia* in the Archive is dated November 27, 1918. (WKP 2, item 3).

31. WKP 9, p. 35 is an "*Otchet*" on the Guberniia Land Administration; WKP 532, p. 31 is a raikom plan of work; WKP 238, pp. 87–88 is a plan of work for the obkom.

32. See WKP 190, 195, and 355 for examples. See also Roberta T. Manning "The Collective Farm Peasantry and the Local Administration: Peasant Letters of Complaint in Belyi Raion in 1937" (unpublished paper).

33. Fainsod's index can be found at the beginning of Roll #1 of T87.

34. Annotation to WKP 215, *Guide to the Records*, 121.

35. *Guide to the Records*, 93.

36. *Guide to the Records*, 111.

Annual Reports of Industrial Enterprises in Soviet Archives as a Historical Source for the 1930s

A. B. BEZBORODOV

In the years of *perestroika* there has been an inevitable increase of interest in the period of Soviet history that laid the foundations of the socialist structure—that is, of that system which now requires renewal. The present phase of the scientific-technical revolution presents social scientists with the challenge of providing a more detailed interpretation, based on documentary evidence, of the social processes related to the different stages of Soviet industrial development. For this project to be carried out successfully, a full analysis is needed of the structural changes in the labor force of workers, engineering-technical personnel, white-collar employees, and other categories employed in industrial enterprises during the 1930s, the period of the industrialization of the Soviet Union.

It is natural in this context that Soviet and American historians should pay special attention to broadening the source base of their respective researches. In this essay, the author presents some conclusions from his study of the annual reports (*otchety*) of industrial enterprises in the 1930s as historical sources.

The reports in question were drawn from two archives, the Central State Archive of the National Economy of the USSR (TsGANKh) and the Central State Archive of the October Revolution and Socialist Construction of the City of Moscow (TsGAORSS g. Moskvy). The relevant documents were found in seventeen separate archival *fondy*, some of which were intensively studied by the author, others reviewed more superficially. The reports studied in depth came from the archives of the Commissariat of Heavy Industry of the USSR (TsGANKh, *fond* 7297) and the Commissariat of Light Industry of the USSR (TsGANKh, *f.* 7604), as well as those of very large industrial plants and groups of enterprises in Moscow—"Dinamo" (TsGAORSS g. Moskvy, *f.* R–100), "Serp i molot" (TsGAORSS g. Moskvy, *f.* R–176), "Kalibr" (TsGAORSS g. Moskvy, *f.* R–487), "Krasnaia Roza" (TsGAORSS g. Moskvy, *f.* R–370), and others.

A few words are in order about the completeness of the runs of documents preserved in these archives. The TsGANKh *fondy* contain annual reports only for the year 1936. The Moscow city archive (TsGAORSS g. Moskvy) contains annual reports for the whole decade of the 1930s.

The type of document discussed here is a complex source. It incorporates basic indices on the enterprises' fulfillment of the industrial-financial plan: gross and commodity output, and production of finished goods, including consumer goods (*shirpotreb*). There are data on the factory and commercial cost price of production, productivity of labor, sales, the chief technical and production indices, indices of wastage, losses classified by type of goods, as well as violations of safety regulations and accounting and financial-payroll discipline.

Of particular note in the annual reports are the special sections devoted to the enterprises' activity in developing the social sphere. These include the system of training and retraining of cadres; the level of wages and salaries of workers, engineering-technical personnel, white-collar employees, and junior service personnel (*mladshii obsluzhivaiushchii personal*); provision of housing and communal services for these categories of employees (and also apprentices), with indication of the type of accommodation provided. The reports also show the expenses of the enterprises for the maintenance of hospitals, pharmacies, schools, nurseries, kindergartens, public baths and laundries, cultural facilities, and so on.

The information given in the reports on labor turnover in the plants and enterprise groups, together with analyses of the sources of labor recruitment, are of special interest. The reports also provide data on the dynamics of the Stakhanovite and shock-work movements.

Statistical data which form the basis of the reports are presented both in tables and in narrative form. As a rule, the narrative consists of explanatory notes on the basic activities covered by the annual reports. The most informative form of reporting is the one mandated by the Commissariat of Finance of the USSR and the Central Administration of National-Economic Accounting (TsUNKhU) of Gosplan USSR in 1936.

It is not easy to determine the reliability of the documents analyzed in this essay. These documents are, of course, products of a very contradictory epoch. As the Soviet scholar O. R. Latsis justly remarks, ". . . it was a heedless disregard for the material aspect of things that explains the collapse of the second half of the Five-Year Plan. With everything so tightly stretched and no reserves to fall back on, a failure in one place started a chain reaction, and one disproportion produced another."[1]

The annual reports reflect a quite variegated picture of the labor collectives' success in reaching their production targets. As far as the chief types of production were concerned, the plan was likely to be fulfilled and over-fulfilled. On the remaining indices, however, there were often severe shortfalls.

With regard to expenditures in the social sphere, we find clear evidence in the reports that a "left-over principle" (*ostatochnyi printsip*) of financing was emerging in this area. Thus, for example, the reports show that planned expenditures at the Kharkov Tractor plant, the First State Ball-Bearings factory, the Auto-tractor Instruments plant (Pavlov-on-the-Oka, Gorky region), and the Kirzhach plant "Red October" were actually reduced in 1936 from what they had been in 1935.[2] Despite the cuts in these figures dictated from above, the plants nevertheless managed to increase expenditures (albeit not to the level of the previous year), but how they did this remains undisclosed.

The reports sometimes offer the explanation that the enterprises' economic failures were the result of intentional sabotage. For example, the compilers of the annual report of the "Dinamo" factory in 1937 included a special section on "Struggle with the consequences of wrecking in 1937."[3] In our opinion, such explanations are unfounded.

Confidence in the reliability of the statistics in the annual reports is undermined by the fact that pencilled additions and corrections to the figures are often encountered in the texts.[4] Thus, in our judgment there is no firm basis for assuming that the sources at our dispoasl are fully reliable. In a more general context, it is impossible to disagree with the conclusion of a Soviet scholar, G. I. Khanin, who writes that in the period from the 1930s to the 1950s, "a vicious circle was created—unreal drafting of plans, distorted statistical information, unreal plans—which we have not been able to break out of to this day."[5]

Nevertheless, it is worth trying to characterize the workforce of the enterprises of the 1930s, its living and working conditions, labor turnover, and the sources of labor recruitment on the basis of the reports.

The working class was naturally the basic element at the plants and factories. As is well known, the cadre stratum of workers grew in the 1920s. Then the proportion of workers with less experience started to increase rapidly. In the second half of the 1930s, the cadre stratum began to grow again. The new part of the labor force came in part from the collective farms in the countryside and in part from urban working-class youth and women from working-class families who had not previously worked in industry.

In the course of the industrial transformation of the country that occurred during the first two Five-Year Plans, there was a dramatic increase in the number of persons with industrial skills. The working class now constituted one third of the population. In 1937, the ranks of industrial workers (not counting apprentices and junior service personnel) grew to 9.1 million persons.[6] The workers that emerged in that difficult epoch became the social support of the industrialization of the country.

Individual documents from those years enable us to form an idea of the breakdown of the workforce in terms of length of work experience at a particular enterprise. At the Moscow silk-dyeing and -finishing enterprise group "Krasnaia Roza" at the beginning of 1937, for example, 896 persons had worked for less than a year, 1,586 for 1–3 years, 813 for 3–5 years, and 1,563 for more than 5 years.[7]

It is important to note the trend toward qualitative improvement in the ranks of the working class. That trend was closely associated with the introduction and mastery of new technology, and was manifest in the Stakhanovite movement. By the beginning of 1936, changes were starting to occur in the Stakhanovite movement, with a shift in emphasis from individual record-breaking to collective Stakhanovite work and increases in the production output of the enterprise as a whole. Various mass forms of the movement became widespread in 1936 and 1937. In 1939–40, whole Stakhanovite shifts, brigades, sections, and shops appeared at the machine-building plants. As a result, the productivity of labor increased at the enterprises.

The annual reports of industrial enterprises allow us to see a direct connection between the development of Stakhanovism as a mass movement and the growth of labor productivity,[8] and also to study the dynamics of the mass movement. On 1 January 1941, 48.7 percent of all cadre workers (2,082 persons) at the "Krasnaia Roza" group of enterprises were Stakhanovites, which represented a 3.8 percent increase from the level of 1 January 1940.[9]

The technical experience acquired by workers opened new possibilities for the mechanization of work and the emergence of new labor professions—coal-combine operators, electric welders, crane operators, and so on. However, as the reports show, efforts to overcome the country's technical and economic backwardness were not universally successful in industry. For example, at the "Dinamo" plant, despite the existence of an integrated network for the training and retraining of worker cadres by the end of the Second Five-Year Plan, the proportion of auxiliary workers stayed at the same level—51 percent—in 1936 and 1937.[10] In 1940 the plant's warehouses still lacked almost any kind of mechanization of labor-intensive processes.[11]

The factory reports contain information not only about workers but also about other categories of employed persons: engineering-technical workers, employees, junior service personnel, apprentices. But it is limited in quantity. The data include numbers in each category, broken down by shop,[12] the percentage of administrative and managerial personnel within the ITR (engineering-technical) group,[13] and the planned and actual number of engineering-technical personnel at each enterprise.[14]

These documents do not provide information on the relations between workers and the technical intelligentsia, nor do they fully illuminate the role of engineering-technical personnel in norm-setting (NOT).

It is obvious from the documents that the potential for growth of labor productivity on the basis of new technology was not completely realized. In economic terms, men were valued less highly than machines, which constituted the basic capital investment. It was generally acknowledged that the factories had a surplus of labor at their disposal, but machines were in short supply. This gave rise to a labor culture oriented toward quantity rather than quality (*ekstensivnyi tip kul'tury truda*), especially during the First Five-Year Plan. In later years, the time came when the machines too were not fully utilized.

This attitude to labor use inevitably produced a technocratic type of thinking on the part of managers, which in its turn led to acceptance of a relatively low standard of living for blue- and white-collar workers. In consequence of the ambitious tempos required by the development strategy favored by I. V. Stalin and his associates, capital investment in industry had to be increased in every possible way, even if that meant cutting back on consumption and the most stringent economies with regard to expenditures that determined the people's standard of living. For the same reasons, it was considered necessary and possible to redistribute resources from the consumption sphere to the production sphere, regardless of the fact that this kind of redistribution produces acute shortages of consumer goods—a "goods famine," in the terminology of the time.

Although labor productivity in industry increased by 41 percent during the First Five-Year Plan, the average wage doubled over the same period. Since the number of workers and employees also doubled, that means that the general fund of wages grew by a factor of four, which the plan had not anticipated.

Drawing on archival sources, let us investigate the situation in enterprises of the leather and shoe industry in 1933. Here average wages exceeded the plan by 4.7 percent for engineering-technical workers, 6.5 percent for employees, 12.4 percent for junior service personnel, 14.8 percent for apprentices, and 15.5 percent for workers in training (*obuchaiushchikhsia rabochikh*).[15] Offering an explanation for the situation that had developed, the authors of the reports write that local authorities allowed them to raise wages if they reduced the number of persons employed.[16]

In contrast, the production of consumer goods increased more slowly than it was supposed to according to the plan. In the same year, 1933, factories and groups of enterprises in the leather and shoe industry failed to meet their delivery quotas by about 6.7 million pairs of shoes.[17] A natural consequence of these unplanned changes in the relationship of the supply of money to the supply of goods was a rapid rise in retail prices.

Let us investigate the enterprises' expenditures from the Director's Funds on social and cultural amenities, taking the Auto-tractor Instruments plant as an example. In 1935–36, funds were allocated for the upkeep of nurseries, kindergartens, Pioneer camps, hospitals, pharmacies, schools, and cultural facilities; for sanatoria and rest homes (beds and *putevki* for employees using them); for various medical expenses including salaries of medical personnel; for long-service bonuses; for grants to families of deceased employees; for public dining rooms and a subsidy to improve nutrition; for losses in the market gardens supplying the public dining rooms; for public baths and laundries serving employees and their families; and for miscellaneous purposes.[18] Total expenditures for 1935 amounted to 410,000 rubles, and for 1936 to 368,000 rubles.[19]

A study of the reports of factories like Kharkov Tractor, "*Krasnyi Oktiabr'*" (Kirzhach), First State Ball-Bearings, and Auto-tractor Instruments helps us to see a definite pattern: when expenditures on the collective's social and cultural needs were reduced, the enterprises failed to meet their plan targets.[20]

The housing problem became particularly acute for industrial enterprises in the 1930s. During the first two Five-Year Plans, the state spent 17,215 million rubles on housing construction.[21] In the towns, apartment blocks with a total floor space of 124.2 million square meters were added to the housing supply.[22] By the end of 1933, houses built since the Revolution constituted more than a third of all housing space. Construction of individual workers' housing increased.

All the same, given the exigencies of large-scale industrial construction, shortages of equipment and construction materials, and rapid increase in the size of the urban population, housing construction still lagged behind demand. A substantial portion of the urban population, especially new arrivals from the countryside, had to live for years in barracks, basements, and other unsuitable premises. In fact, barracks were as common a type of accommodation as communal apartments.

Judging by the documents, virtually all labor collectives suffered from housing shortages. The housing problem was worst in the neighborhood of new construction sites (*novostroiki*) and recently built enterprises. The Auto-tractor Instruments plant, for example, came on line in 1932. After three years, 220 of its workers were living in houses and 234 in barracks. After four years, the number in houses had fallen to 132, while the number in barracks had risen to 375.[23] As for the construction workers, all of them (79 persons in 1935 and 164 persons in 1936) lived in barracks.[24] At this plant, the average living space for one member of a working-class family living in regular housing (*v zhilykh domakh*) in 1935 was 4.2 square meters,[25] compared to the national average of 4.3 square meters in 1932.[26]

Often the living conditions of blue- and white-collar workers were adversely affected by the mushrooming of the local bureaucracy. This was what happened in 1936 at the Iaroslavl State Auto plant. When the city of Iaroslavl became an oblast center, the enterprise's ability to lease residential accommodation was significantly reduced.[27]

In virtually all the reports at our disposal, the information on housing includes data on the provision of basic communal services in apartment blocks and barracks. At the Moscow Brakes factory in 1936, for example, 100 percent of apartment blocks had running water, sanitation, and electricity, but in the barracks only electricity was universally provided. Not much more than a third of the apartment blocks, and none of the barracks, had central heating.[28]

Safety precautions and observance of industrial safety laws should have been a prime concern of factory managements and trade unions, given the constant intake of raw and half-trained workers. The archival documents include statistics on this subject, most of them showing a reduction in the incidence of trauma and the number of accidents.[29] But it is difficult at this distance to be sure whether these statistics are accurate. In the report of the "Dinamo" plant for 1937, the serious shortcomings in regard to safety measures were attributed to sabotage[30]—and that was the end of the discussion. In our opinion, the simplistic character of this judgment casts some doubt on the reliability of the authors' claims that the number of industrial accidents and illnesses had been reduced.

The archival documents we are using allow us to study the turnover of cadres at the enterprises and the sources of labor recruitment. Fluctuation in the labor force was a real scourge of industrial managers right up to the very end of the 1930s. The main causes of labor turnover were the acute housing shortages[31] and difficulty in adapting to the conditions of factory work. Of the workers who left the Iaroslavl Auto plant or were fired in 1936, 63 percent had been 6 months or less on the job, and only 1 percent had worked for more than 7 years.[32] At the "Dinamo" plant in the third quarter of 1937, 76 percent of those fired were workers with factory experience of not more than a year. The loss of cadre workers, in contrast, occurred mainly through death.[33] The situation was similar everywhere.

On 26 June 1940, the Supreme Soviet of the USSR passed a law "On the transfer to the 8-hour working day and the 7-day working week, and on prohibition of departure without permission for workers and employees of enterprises and institutions."[34] Corresponding orders were issued in all commissariats on 27–28 June, and new work schedules taking account of the peculiarities of each branch of industry were established for the enterprises.[35] As the sources demonstrate, these measures for strengthening industrial discipline made it possible to reduce labor turnover.[36]

In the 1930s, workers who had recently come from the countryside, including those recruited through contracts with the collective farms, made up a substantial part of the young working class.[37] Organized recruitment (that is, recruitment via enterprise contracts with collective farms) provided industry with its main source of unskilled labor. Skilled cadres, according to the reports, were trained in the FZU (factory apprenticeship) schools.[38]

In 1938 and 1939, the party and government took measures to improve the process of state organized recruitment (*organizovannyi nabor*) of labor. A resolution of Sovnarkom USSR "On the proper regulation of recruitment of the work force from the collective farms" dated 21 July 1938 gave exact instructions indicating in which oblasts, krais, and republics various commissariats should recruit labor. Particular attention was paid to the training of new workers and their material circumstances and living conditions.[39]

As we have seen, the annual reports of industrial enterprises of the 1930s possess definite value as a historical source. Future work on these sources should involve further checking of their reliability, so that they can be used, in particular, in the writing of the history of plants and factories. The large volume of formalized statistical information contained in the reports makes them an appropriate object of computer analysis. The use of computer technology makes it possible to obtain summary data (on labor turnover, work time lost, and similar topics), calculate average statistical indices (wages of blue- and white-collar workers, provision of different kinds of housing, and so on), and make comparative analyses of data.

Notes

1. O. Latsis, "Perelom," in *Stranitsy istorii KPSS. Fakty, problemy, uroki* (Moscow, 1988), p. 360.
2. See TsGANKh, *f.* 7297, *op.* 23, *d.* 4, *l.* 7 (obverse side); *d.* 8, *l.* 14 (ob.); *d.* 13, *l.* 19 (ob.); *d.* 15, *l.* 7 (ob.).
3. TsGAORSS g. Moskvy, *f.* R–100, *op.* 1, *d.* 24, *ll.* 43–50.
4. See, for example, TsGANKH, *f.* 7297, *op.* 23, *d.* 4, *l.* 7 (ob.)
5. G. Khanin, "Ekonomicheskii rost: al'ternativnaia otsenka," *Kommunist*, 1988 no. 17, p. 8.
6. See *Trud v SSSR. Statisticheskii sbornik* (Moscow, 1968), p. 81.
7. TsGAORSS g. Moskvy, *f.* R–370, *op.* 1, *d.* 43, *l.* 127.
8. See TsGANKh, *f.* 7297, *op.* 23, *d.* 16, *l.* 5; TSGAORSS g. Moskvy, *f.* R–370, *op.* 1, *d.* 43, *l.* 132; *op.* 2, *d.* 85, *l.* 72.
9. TsGAORSS g. Moskvy, *f.* R–370, *op.* 2, *d.* 85, *l.* 72.
10. TsGAORSS g. Moskvy, *f.* R–100, *op.* 1, *d.* 24, *ll.* 66–70, 86.
11. TsGAORSS g. Moskvy, *f.* R–100, *op.* 1, *d.* 54, *l.* 115.
12. TsGAORSS g. Moskvy, *f.* R–176, *op.* 4, *d.* 6, *ll.* 218–23.
13. TsGAORSS g. Moskvy, *f.* R–100, *op.* 1, *d.* 24, *l.* 88.
14. *Ibid.*, *l.* 87.

15. TsGANKh, *f.* 7604, *op.* 2, *d.* 84, *l.* 122.
16. *Ibid.*
17. *Ibid.*, *l.* 81.
18. TsGANKh, *f.* 7297, *op.* 23, *d.* 4, *l.* 7 (ob.).
19. *Ibid.*
20. See TsGANKh, *f.* 7297, *op.* 23, *d.* 13, *ll.* 14 and 19 (ob.); *d.* 8, *l.* 14 (ob.); *d.* 15, *ll.* 2 and 7 (ob.); *d.* 4, *ll.* 2 and 7 (ob.).
21. See *Sotsialisticheskoe stroitel'stvo Soiuza SSR, 1933–1938 gg. Statisticheskii sbornik* (Moscow-Leningrad, 1939), p. 115.
22. See *Rabochii klass—vedushchaia sila v stroitel'stve sotsialisticheskogo obshchestva, 1921–1937 gg.* (Moscow, 1984), vol. 2, p. 248.
23. *Ibid.*
24. *Ibid.*
25. TsGANKh, *f.* 7297, *op.* 23, *d.* 4, *l.* 6 (ob.).
26. See D. Buzin, "Zhilishchno-kommunal'noe khoziaistvo za 20 let," *Problemy ekonomiki*, 1937, no. 5–6, p. 188.
27. TsGANKh, *f.* 7297, *op.* 23, *d.* 4, *l.* 6 (ob.).
28. TsGANKh, *f.* 7297, *op.* 23, *d.* 11, *l.* 8 (ob.).
29. See, for example, TsGAORSS g. Moskvy, *f.* R–100, *op.* 1, *d.* 24, *l.* 45; *f.* R–176, *op.* 4, *d.* 17, *l.* 521; TsGANKh, *f.* 7297, *op.* 23, *d.* 16, *ll.* 60, 65–67.
30. TsGAORSS g. Moskvy, *f.* R–100, *op.* 1, *d.* 24, *l.* 45.
31. See, for example,. TsGANKh, *f.* 7297, *op.* 23, *d.* 7, *l.* 15; *d.* 16, *l.* 47; TsGAORSS g. Moskvy, *f.* R–176, *op.* 4. *d.* 6, *ll.* 217–218; *f.* R–370, *op.* 1, *d.* 43, *ll.* 129–30.
32. TsGANKh, *f.* 7297, *op.* 23, *d.* 16, *ll.* 46–47.
33. TsGAORSS g. Moskvy, *f.* R–100, *op.* 1, *d.* 24, *l.* 75.
34. *Resheniia partii i pravitel'stva po khoziaistvennym voprosam* (Moscow, 1967), pp. 757–58.
35. See *Rabochii klass SSSR nakanune i v gody Velikoi Otechestvennoi voiny. 1938–1945 gg.* (Moscow, 1984), vol. 3, p. 125.
36. See TsGAORSS g. Moskvy, *f.* R–176, *op.* 4, *d.* 17, *l.* 42; *f.* R–370, *op.* 2, *d.* 85, *ll.* 75–76.
37. See TsGANKh, *f.* 7297, *op.* 23, *d.* 7, *l.* 13; *d.* 12, *l.* 7; TsGAORSS g. Moskvy, *f.* R–176, *op.* 4, *d.* 6, *ll.* 217–18.
38. TsGAORSS g. Moskvy, *f.* R–100, *op.* 1, *d.* 24, *l.* 66; *f.* R–176, *op.* 4, *d.* 6, *ll.* 217–18.
39. See *Sobranie postanovlenii pravitel'stva SSSR*, 1938, no. 34, art. 208.

Guide to Document Series on Collectivization

LYNNE VIOLA

In 1961, the Main Archival Administration of the Soviet Union resolved to publish several large series of document collections devoted to major topics in the history of the nation. Among those topics was the history of the collectivization of Soviet agriculture. The series on collectivization was launched under the title *Istoriia kollektivizatsii sel'skogo khoziaistva SSSR*. The Main Archival Administration initially intended to publish thirty volumes, but the series eventually grew into some forty volumes of documents based on twenty-nine regions of the nation.[1]

The decision to publish this series represented a major step for Soviet historiography. Before the mid–1950s, almost no primary materials on collectivization had been published, the exceptions being collections of statistical materials devoted to various aspects of agriculture and rural life.[2] Indeed, before the mid–1950s, Soviet scholars' access to archival documents on collectivization was highly restricted. Conditions in the archives vastly improved with the 7 February 1956 publication of a Council of Ministers of the USSR decree which widened archival access for Soviet researchers.[3] The relative liberalization of archival access made possible the publication of a number of important sets of documents in the second half of the 1950s and the early 1960s. Two collections of laws and decrees on collectivization and collective farming were published at this time,[4] along with several individual books[5] and periodical publications of documents.[6]

The series *Istoriia kollektivizatsii sel'skogo khoziaistva SSSR* proved to be the first concerted national attempt to publish archival material on collectivization and collective farming. The Main Archival Administration (under the jurisdiction of the Council of Ministers of the USSR), the Institute of Marxism-Leninism (under the jurisdiction of the Central Committee of the Communist party of the Soviet Union), and the Institutes of History and Economics of the Academy of Sciences of the USSR jointly published the series.[7] The publishers appointed a central editorial board composed of senior scholars in the field of Soviet rural history. In addition, smaller editorial boards, consisting of leading regional specialists, were appointed for each individual collection.[8] The publication of the series began in the early 1960s and continued into the 1980s.

Work on this article was assisted by a grant from the Joint Committee on Soviet Studies of the Social Science Research Council and the American Council of Learned Societies with funds provided by the National Endowment for the Humanities and the Ford Foundation.

The document collections encompass twelve of the fifteen union republics[9] and seventeen regions within the RSFSR.[10] The publishers of the series apparently initially planned to issue three volumes of general documents pertaining to the USSR as a whole, but these volumes have not yet appeared nor is it clear that they will appear in the future.[11] The language of the majority of volumes is Russian, and although the volumes on the union republics contain some native language documents, the larger part of these collections (with the exceptions of Ukraine and Belorussia) is either in Russian or has been translated into Russian. Most volumes in the series contain a preface with a general introduction to the region and its history and a discussion of the sources used in the compilation of the collection. Most volumes also contain lengthy endnotes which serve as annotation to the texts of the documents. The prefaces and endnotes range in quality from volume to volume, but in some cases include very valuable information from the archives, making them (and especially the endnotes) as important as the documents themselves.[12] Each volume contains a table of contents. In some volumes, the table of contents is a simple (and useless) chronological outline based on standard periodization without specific listing of documents; in other volumes, the table of contents is a complete listing of the documents by title and date. In keeping with Soviet tradition, very few volumes contain indices. Finally, the majority of the collections are arranged chronologically according to the following standard Soviet periodization framework:

First phase (1927–29): "Preparation for collectivization"

Second phase (1930–32): "Wholesale collectivization and the elimination of the kulak as a class"

Third phase (1933–37): "The organizational-economic strengthening of the collective farm system."

For the third phase, some collections deviate slightly from this periodization by extending forward in time to 1941.

The majority of the documents in the collections are from Soviet state and Communist party archives. In addition to various central and regional Communist Party archival materials, materials from the *fondy* of the Soviet government (i.e., republic-level *sovnarkomy*; regional, *okrug*, and district *ispolkomy*; and *sel'sovety*); the People's Commissariats of Agriculture, Finance, Justice, and Labor and their regional affiliates; the trade unions; the Workers' and Peasants' Inspection (Rabkrin); and other agencies are represented in the collections. Most of the documents presented in the collections have not been published previously.[13] However, each volume (to a greater or lesser degree) does contain some number of previously published materials from the periodical press, published statistical collections, collections of published laws and decrees, and so on.

A broad range of document types are included in the collections.[14] Soviet reviewers of the series have presented the following document typology as representative of the bulk of the collections' contents:[15]

1. directives (*resheniia partiinykh, sovetskikh i kolkhozno-kooperativnykh organov po voprosam kollektivizatsii sel'skogo khoziaistva; direktivy, tsirkuliary, pis'ma etikh organov nizovym organizatsiiam*)

2. reports (*doklady i otchety na s"ezdakh, konferentsiiakh, soveshchaniiakh par-tiinykh i sovetskikh organizatsii; dokladnye zapiski i informatsionnye svodki; mate-rialy obsledovanii i soobshcheniia s mest; korrespondentsii v periodicheskoi pechati*)

3. institutional materials (*protokoly sobranii, zasedanii pravlenii kolkhozov; ustavy kolkhozov; obrashcheniia kolkhoznikov; dogovory o sotsialisticheskom sorev-novanii*).

Also included among the documents are letters of peasants, workers, and offi-cials; statistical charts and tables; and newspaper reports on various topics.

The quality of the collections is very uneven. In general (but with major excep-tions), the volumes published in the 1960s are of a higher caliber than those pub-lished in later years. In fact, according to one Soviet reviewer, the size of the later volumes was formally limited.[16] The best volumes in the series are those covering the Northern region, Central Volga, Siberia, the Western region, the Northwestern region, the Central Industrial Region, the North Caucasus, the Urals, the Nizhegorodskii-Gor'kovskii (Upper Volga) region, and Ukraine; the remaining volumes are of a somewhat lower (although varied) quality, but are still extremely useful research tools. One Soviet reviewer claims that the editing of documents within the collections is minimal, but nonetheless there are cases where documents either are presented in excerpted form or include elipses indicating a cut has been made.[17]

The document series on collectivization is a rich and useful source for the social history of the Soviet countryside in the period from 1927 to 1937. This article is intended as an introduction to the series, and should be read as a selective survey of the collections rather than an exhaustive description of this large and multi-faceted work. This survey includes an examination of the collections in the collectivization series as well as other collections of documents which are on collectivization but not formally part of the series.[18]

The document series as a source on the first phase of collectivization (1927–1929)

Each collection in the series includes coverage of the countryside during the last years of the New Economic Policy, 1927–29. Information is provided on the region-al development of agriculture, the regional party and soviet organizations, the collective farms, the grain requisitioning campaigns, and the first phase of collec-tivization. The evidence presented in the documents illuminates the life of the Soviet countryside during the transitional years of crisis leading into the Stalin revolution, painting a picture of a collective farm movement at an impasse and a state at war with its peasantry.

Data on collective farms

The documents in the collectivization series provide detailed statistics on collective farming in the late 1920s, including information on the number of collective farms, the type of farms (i.e., TOZ, artel, or commune), the size of the farms, and the social composition of the farms. Data on collective farm membership shows that the social base of the collective farm movement was the *bedniak*, or poor peasant.[19] The collective farms, on the whole, had difficulty attracting other strata of the peasantry in more than minimal numbers. The *seredniak*, or middle peasant, and kulak tended to be more attracted to consumer and (especially) machine cooperatives than to production collectives.[20] Collective farms with the lowest degree of socialization of the means of production (i.e., the TOZ) dominated the movement.[21]

In addition to the poverty of the collective farm movement and its low level of socialization, the collective farms tended to be very small, sometimes little more than associations of relatives.[22] In some cases, only the male heads of households were members (echoing the predominant form of membership in the *skhod* or traditional village assembly).[23] Membership in general was unstable with high rates of turnover throughout the 1920s. High turnover was caused at least in part by the fact that the early collectives tended to be poorly organized with management in total disarray. Remuneration of labor most often came in the traditional form of payment "per eater" or, somewhat less frequently, payment per worker.[24] To some degree, many of the early collective farms depicted in the documents appear as relatively spontaneous peasant associations based on some hybrid of peasant farming and socialist principles.

Regional reports continually complained of the dismal state of affairs within the collective farms. These reports also bemoaned the lack of communist and/or soviet leadership of the movement, often implying that in this respect the collective farms were not all that different from the distrusted village which had warded off party-state intervention relatively successfully throughout the 1920s.[25] Problems of leadership were compounded by the large percentages of collective farms that were unregistered ("*dikie*") and therefore not subject even to the minimalist control of the central collective farming agencies.[26]

The picture emerging from these documents is of a collective farm movement which may very well have reached its limits of growth within the perimeters of Communist acceptability.[27] The problems of the movement frustrated central and regional authorities, leading them to step up attempts to gain control over the collective farms. Periodic purges of cooperative and collective farm leadership and membership were carried out in 1927–28 and again in late 1929.[28] The purges, however, tended less to bolster the confidence of the authorities than to convince them that the farms were full of socially and politically alien elements almost to the point of hopelessness.[29] This sense of hopelessness over the state of the collective farms was reinforced during the grain procurement crisis when some farms behaved in much the same fashion as private peasants—they resisted the state's forcible procurements by hiding their grain or by selling it on the black market.[30]

Violence and terror in the countryside

The document series tells a story of crescendoing chaos and violence in the years leading up to wholesale collectivization. Increasingly desperate to escape the state's repressive policies, peasants responded to force with force. Violence tended to erupt during key campaign periods when the state forcibly intervened into the life of the village—in particular, during soviet elections and grain requisitioning. The documents provide vivid evidence of the tensions stirred up by soviet election campaigns, the accompanying waves of disenfranchisement, and the authorities' response to local attempts to elect undesirable elements to office.[31]

Reports on grain requisitioning tell a similar, if often more violent, story of peasant resistance. For example, in Moscow oblast in October 1929, there were reports about well-to-do peasants (*zazhitochnye*) breaking up village meetings on requisitioning, threatening activists, and committing arson. There were rumors that activists' homes would be burned down, and, possibly as a consequence, poor peasants refused to serve on requisitioning commissions.[32] In the North Caucasus in the summer of 1929, the regional party committee responded to alleged kulak sabotage of requisitioning by ordering village and poor-peasant assemblies to draft decrees exiling and expropriating kulaks who did not fulfill grain requisitioning assignments or who hid their grain. The directive suggested that these measures be applied to one or two farms per stanitsa for "educational purposes," and warned not to allow such measures to be applied on a mass scale, but to apply them only under the supervision of the okrug and district committees of the party.[33]

Repression of all kinds was indeed applied on a rather large scale in this period, feeding into the dialectics of an escalating wave of state and peasant violence.[34] The document series provides a detailed glimpse of this violence by including statistical data on cases of peasant "terrorist acts" and state repressive measures. "Terror," in this context, usually denoted murder, attempted murder, and assault, but could also include arson, riots, and threats. From 1927–29, the documents refer to some 74 murders and 138 beatings or assaults directed against (in the main) lower-level rural officials and activists. Also reported are 138 cases of arson, 51 cases of arson or vandalism of activists' or officials' homes, 93 riots, 4 cases of lynching (*samosud*), and numerous instances of threats, attacks on collective farms, and disrupted meetings. These figures were compiled by a simple counting of cases reported throughout the series. The documents also provide aggregate figures on terrorist acts for a number of regions and districts over specific time periods. For example, in Siberia, 226 terrorist acts were reported in 1927, 702 in 1928, and 1,135 in 1929.[35] In the Urals, 1,027 terrorist acts were reported in 1928.[36] Relatively detailed breakdowns on such cases are given for the Central Black Earth Region in 1928 and 1929. From August to 15 December 1928, for example, out of 122 terrorist acts recorded in this region, 22 were murders, 46 attempted murders, and 18 assaults. The largest number of these acts were directed against lower soviet officials (especially *sel'sovet* chairmen) and rural activists. From March to April 1929, 24 terrorist acts were recorded; from May to June 1929, 111 terrorist acts were recorded (among which were 5 murders, 4 woundings, 28 assaults, 26 attempted murders, and 48 cases of arson).[37]

The document series also provides some statistical data on cases of repression of peasants prior to wholesale collectivization. In the Western region, for example,

1,382 farms had been subject to individual taxation as kulaks by 1 October 1929. In the same period, for failure to fulfill requisitioning obligations or for hiding grain, courts in the Western region prosecuted 207 kulaks and millers, 32 clergy, and 42 traders; of these 146 were sentenced to prison terms, 73 were sentenced to forced labor, 62 were fined (to a total of 44,061 rubles), and 96 were subject to some form of expropriation.[38] In Leningrad oblast, 2,051 people were charged under article 107 of the penal code in the month of July 1928.[39] Data are reported for several other parts of the country but in a much more partial way than for cases of peasant terror.[40]

From the summer of 1929, if not earlier, the documents begin to tell a story of increasing peasant unrest related, in one form or another, to collectivization, collective farming, or collective farmers. In fact, from 1928, some regions began to initiate plans for collectivization by creating special departments of rural affairs within the party organization (at various regional levels) devoted to collectivization or by creating special instructors whose task it was to push for collectivization.[41] Along with increasing organizational attention to collectivization came reports of the use of force in organizing collective farms in some regions from as early as 1928.[42]

The documents also indicate an increasingly intransigent attitude to the kulak on the part of some regional party organizations from 1928. Even before 1928, party officials in Turkmenistan had firmly opposed admission of kulaks to the collective farms.[43] In the Western region in November 1928, following a village disturbance, a representative of a provincial kolkhoz union recommended expropriating kulak lands.[44] Such extremism escalated in 1929 and especially in the fall of 1929 when, for example, an MTS director in the North Caucasus demanded that kulaks be expropriated and exiled to Solovki.[45] In the Central Volga, in December 1929 (i.e., before the central directives on dekulakization), the regional party committee suggested to the Central Committee the possibility of exiling kulaks to the end of the fields, a practice that had been taking place for some time in parts of Central Volga.[46] Similar suggestions were made in October and December 1929 in Tatariia where kulaks were given distant lands during *zemleustroistvo*, despite the regional party committee's warning that the formation of kulak settlements (*poselki*) should be allowed only in exceptional cases.[47] In Astrakhan, on 28 November 1929, the okrug party committee ordered a survey of all farms dividing households into four basic social categories (*batrak, bedniak, seredniak,* and kulak); this survey, which was supposed to be completed by 15 January 1930, was later used as the basis of dekulakization.[48] These examples provide interesting evidence of the degree of radicalism in the rural party-state apparatus at various regional levels, offering some insights into the background of central decisions on collectivization and dekulakization.

Peasant attitudes to the collective farm

Most documents included in the collectivization series contain reference to the peasants' alleged enthusiasm for the collective farms and eagerness to join them. In some instances, this may have been an accurate representation of the reality (or perceived reality) of the moment, though it doubtless also reflects the biases of the series' editors as well as those of the contemporary authors of the documents. Nevertheless, the documents also provide a good deal of evidence of peasant hostility to collective farming, or to the form collectivization was assuming.

One expression of such hostility comes from a letter written by a peasant of the Western region, Ivan Borzenkov, to the editors of the newspaper *Tovarishch'* on 8 April 1928.[49]

I ask the editor to publish my letter in the newspaper. I read "Tovarishch" and I see that Soviet power strongly recommends peasants to join collectives.

But we had collectives and we have not forgotten them. Our Staninskii collective existed for three years and all the property was squandered. Loafers and spongers got together in the collective. Why join a collective, it is better to quit your farm and voluntarily leave for "greener pastures."

The peasants want to live freely (*vol'no*) but [they] force us to join collectives. The bedniaki and seredniaki do not want to live in collectives and will not go into them.

A volley of letters followed Borzenkov's in the newspaper. Two respondents, "*sel'-kor* no. 161" and Ivan Minaev, took issue with the implication that poor peasants were loafers. A third writer argued that Soviet power used only persuasion, not force, and that the peasants would be freer in the collectives than in private farming due to the presence of machines and newspapers.[50]

The collections contain many examples of peasant doubts and suspicions about the collective farms. In one village in the Central Industrial Region in October 1929, peasants asked members of a visiting workers' brigade no less than ten times whether enlisting in a collective farm would be voluntary or forced ("*Zapisyvat' v kolkhoz budet nasil'no ili dobrovol'no?*"). Rumors were spread that only loafers and drunkards would join the collective farms. Women, in particular, were said to be opposed to the farms, although they may just have been more vocal in their opposition than the men.[51] Documents from the Western region, for example, include reports of attacks on collective farmers as they worked in the fields, disrupted meetings on and riots against collectivization, anti-collective farm placards, and women "categorically" refusing to enter the collectives (often after their husbands had already joined).[52]

Hostility to the collective farms sometimes became indistinguishable from hostility to the state. This was the case in a lynching attempt which occurred in August 1929 in the village of Santalovka in the Kaluga region, where a collective farm had been organized the previous March. From the beginning, the collective farm was a source of fierce strife between local collective farmers and villagers (labeled "kulaks" in the sources). In August, the people's court judge Borisov and the school inspector Smirnov attended an apparently innocuous meeting at the collective farm.

On their way back to the district center, they were attacked and beaten by a group of local kulaks. Borisov protested that the two officials had nothing to do with collective farms and attempted to prove this by showing his briefcase. In response, he heard, "you with the briefcase . . . , beat him harder." Eventually Borisov and Smirnov managed to escape back to the village where they sought out the collective farm chairman. After another attempt to convince the kulaks who they were, the orgy of violence began again. Smirnov finally escaped into the woods and Borisov was somehow rescued by some collective farmers. As Smirnov ran off, the kulaks yelled "Shoot down the Moscow reptile."[53] Borisov and Smirnov, as Moscow officials, were representative of the city, the capital, and Soviet power, and, as such, allies of the detested collective farm.

Rumors

The degree of peasant alienation from the state is eloquently attested by the reports from the countryside's dense unofficial news network—purveying both wild rumor and what may be described as enhanced reality—contained in the document collections. The rumor mill generally fed off of three common peasant fears: invasion, apocalypse, and a fear of the destruction of traditional ways of life and work in the village. In the Northwestern region, for example, there were rumors about impending war. Peasants said, "in spring there will be a war and then there will be no bread in the USSR. Poland and England are breaking off relations in view of the coming war. Poland and Rumania do not recognize us. In order to delay war they [the state] export grain and leather. . . ."[54] Such rumors were surely exaggerated and, for some peasants, useful in creating a mood of distrust and anxiety, but they also reflected current international tensions and were not surprising as sources of worry given a recent history of war and civil war. Rumors also spread about the evils of the collective farm and, by implication, the Soviet state. Talk of apocalypse, the second coming, and the reign of anti-Christ (presumably equalling Soviet power plus the collective farm) was common.[55] In the village Nizhnee Olgovo, as was the case elsewhere, rumors were spread that "unclean forces" emanated from the homes of new collective farm members, thereby linking them with anti-Christ.[56] Other rumors were simply variations on themes from real life and told of coming famine, the seizure of all grain and livestock, the socialization of wives and children (based on tales of the collective life), and so on.[57] In an atmosphere of fear and uncertainty, rumors were seized upon and spread (the sources say by peasant women) like wildfire. And they tended to be most pervasive in areas in which collectivization had already made incursions into the village by summer and fall of 1929.

The potency of the underground news network can be judged by an episode that took place in the Kuban in August 1929 and which is typical of war times. Rumors spread in a Kuban stanitsa of an impending "black night." (Elsewhere in the Soviet countryside such episodes are referred to by peasants as "Bartholomew's Nights."[58]) This rumor was supposedly counterposed to the impending "red day of 1 August," a day of protest against the threat of imperialist war. Rumor had it that

Cossack troops would enter the village and massacre the poor and non-Cossack peasants. Reportedly, these rumors scared the women to tears. On the night of 1 August, the non-Cossack peasants (*inogorodtsy*) gathered armed, twenty to a hut, or hid in the steppes.[59] Such rumors, along with cases of "terrorist acts," present vivid evidence of the fragility of state-peasant relations on the eve of wholesale collectivization.

The document series as a source on the
second phase of collectivization (1930–1932)

The collectivization series is strongest in documenting the second phase of collectivization: the period of "wholesale collectivization and the elimination of the kulak as a class." The series has broken much new ground in publishing previously inaccessible documents and in presenting a relatively full picture of collectivization. Perhaps the primary significance of the collections in this respect is the sense of regional developments and diversity that can be gleaned from the documents.

Collectivization

The collectivization campaigns of the First Five-Year Plan period and especially of the winter of 1929–30 are treated at length in the documents. Most of the collections include statistical data on the percentages of collectivized farms per region and sometimes per okrug or district within regions; in many cases monthly breakdowns are given for 1930, 1931, and sometimes beyond.[60] Some information is included on the size of collective farms.[61] Several of the collections also provide information on what size collective farms were *supposed* to be. For example, a December 1929 Donskii okrug commission on collectivization planned for the collective farm to be the size of the communal land society (*zemel'noe obshchestvo*).[62] Later information from the Central Volga in 1932 suggested that the collective farm should be organized according to the size of the village; this instruction came in response to reports of the "recidivism" of gigantomania in collective farm organization.[63] The collections are also excellent sources of information for following the way in which the collectivization campaigns developed in different agriculture regions, showing that while the "big push" came in winter 1929–30 for the grain producing regions, it came only in 1930–31 and sometimes later for the grain deficit regions and more backward areas of the country. Researchers can get an idea of some of the forces propelling upward the rates of collectivization in these documents. The Central Industrial Region collection, for example, includes a number of documents from various regional levels which contain directives to revise upward the plans for collectivization.[64] The Ivanovo oblast party committee, for instance, urged in January 1930 that collectivization be completed in spring, arguing that work on collectivization would be too difficult in the summer.[65]

The collections on the Western region and the North Caucasus provide evidence on the important connection between the destruction of livestock (often based on early collectivization attempts) and the further escalation of the rates of collectiviza-tion and the socialization of livestock.[66] In general, coverage of the fate of socialized and nonsocialized livestock is very strong in the collections. For example, reports from the Don okrug indicate that peasants preferred to starve their horses to death, rather than sell them cheaply on the free market, in order to obtain the insurance premium which remained higher than current market value.[67] Reports from Siberia in early 1930 and from the Central Volga in November 1930 show regional authori-ties issuing decrees forbidding the slaughter of livestock for any reason.[68] Statistical data on the decline of livestock during the massive slaughters and sales are given for many regions for the years of the First Five-Year Plan.[69]

Dekulakization

The series contains important documents on the elimination of the kulak as a class. Although the key central directives on dekulakization from late January and early February 1930 have never been published, many of the corresponding regional directives have been published in the document series. Such decrees are available for the Aleksandrovskii okrug of the Ivanovo region, the Western region, the Central Volga, Siberia, Astrakhan okrug in the Lower Volga, the Far Eastern region, Dage-stan, Tatariia, Turkmenistan, the Northern region, and Kazakhstan.[70] In addition, regional directives on the implementation of dekulakization in 1931 are published from the Western region and Eastern Siberia.[71] These documents demonstrate that regional differences could exist even in such a politically sensitive and centralized operation as dekulakization. The 1930 decrees from the Western region, Central Volga, Tatariia, and the Northern region all spoke of the organization of kulak settlements for the third category of kulaks. In the Central Volga, the settlement's intended size was indicated in the directive and it was suggested that the settlements be organized along the lines of a labor colony. The 1931 Eastern Siberia directive calls for the exile of *all* kulaks (in the presence of at least one able-bodied worker and excluding certain categories of families) thereby eliminating the 1930 divisions of kulak households into three categories. The 1931 Western region directive warns the district party committees that dekulakization must occur throughout the region on the same day to avoid the panic and violence of 1930.

Some of the collections include statistical data on the numbers of households scheduled for or actually subject to dekulakization in 1930. Data on the number of households dekulakized in 1930 are provided for the Urals (30,000), Central Volga (28,000), the Tatar Republic (13,668), Leningrad oblast (10,023, with a breakdown into the three categories of kulak), Astrakhan (5,000 planned) and Siberia (30,000 planned for second category only).[72] Information on the actual or planned numbers of kulak farms exiled from their native region in 1930 is given for the Western region (6,950), Leningrad oblast (6,658), and Central Volga (6,000 planned).[73] Data for the Vladimir district of Ivanovo oblast in 1930 show that 2,271 farms were assigned to the second category of kulaks and 1,097 farms were assigned to the third category, thereby clearly violating central orders that about four-fifths of all kulak farms be allotted to the third category.[74] Data on the Ukraine—presumably for 1930 and 1931, although this is not entirely clear—indicate a figure of 200,000 peasant households dekulakized.[75]

The best coverage of dekulakization is contained in the documents on Astrakhan, a collection that is not formally part of the collectivization series. The most significant feature of this collection consists of fifty-odd pages of protocols from the Astrakhan okrug special commission on the elimination of the kulak as a class dated from 4 February to 18 March 1930.[76] These protocols provide the most detailed information available on the implementation of dekulakization. The Astrakhan collection also contains an information report on dekulakization in the okrug (dated 19–23 March 1930) which discusses peasant riots and other forms of resistance as well as the punishment of *peregibshchiki*.[77] Finally, the Astrakhan collection includes what may be one of the best accounts of a peasant uprising during the period of wholesale collectivization—an account of the uprising in Nachalova on 22 February 1930 in which 700 people participated, 227 were arrested, six were killed, and eight wounded. (Those killed and wounded were mainly Communists and collective farm members.) The documents include a report on the incident by Sheboldaev, secretary of the Lower Volga kraikom, to Stalin. Sheboldaev was clearly very concerned about the Nachalova uprising. He ordered that no information on the uprising be issued to the press and that the dead be buried quickly and quietly in the village.[78]

Episodes like the Nachalova uprising also occurred elsewhere and contributed to the reassessment of policy epitomized in Stalin's article of 2 March 1930, "Dizziness from Success." But the document collections on the North Caucasus and the Northern region indicate that some regions were attempting to restrain lower-level cadres from excesses *before* the publication of Stalin's article.[79] Most of the collections contain reports on excesses and the punishment of *peregibshchiki* after the retreat.[80] Documents from Western Siberia and Bashkiriia provide information on the rehabilitation of incorrectly dekulakized farms as well.[81]

Documents in several collections discuss the chaos in property relations and the hostility that developed between collective farmers and peasants who quit the collective farms after the retreat. In the Lower Volga, such hostility led to an unwillingness to readmit peasants to collective farms in later months.[82] In the Western region, the hostility led to the formation of what the documents called "two camps," and cases are cited where quitters stormed the collective farms to take back their property by force. In many parts of the Western region it was frankly admitted that no one knew how much land belonged to the collective farm and how much to the private farmers, thus further complicating the return of property.[83] A Central Volga regional party committee decree of 21 March 1930 on the exodus from the farms suggested that peasants first be warned that they would pay higher taxes, receive the worst lands, and be deprived of many government privileges if they left the collective farm; if such warnings had no effect, the decree continued, exits were not to be blocked. Departing peasants were to receive their property back, but not their seed or forage and they were to be given land at the end of the fields (similar to what third category kulaks received in the Central Volga).[84]

Violence in the countryside

The excesses, against which Moscow struggled in March 1930, remained an intrinsic feature of policy implementation in the countryside and contributed to a wave of peasant violence in 1930 and 1931. The document series provides ample coverage of "kulak" terrorist acts and resistance in these years. There is less aggregate statistical data on violence in this period than for the preceding period, but the descriptions of violence given are much more vivid, thereby compensating in narrative for what is missing in hard data. The documents tell the story of a countryside in the grip of war.

The document series contains references to a total of 68 murders of officials in connection with collectivization in 1930 and 1931, as well as large numbers of beatings and assaults. In the Western region, for example, 70 terrorist acts were recorded in the period from 15 April to 1 June 1931.[85] In Uzbekistan, 90 terrorist acts were reported for the period from January to April 1931.[86] Most of these acts of violence were reportedly directed against rural activists. The collective farms were also targets of attack. In Western Siberia in 1931, 10.6 percent of all collective farms experienced arson, 3.3 percent experienced illegal slaughter of livestock, 18 percent experienced some sort of attack on the collective farm *aktiv*, and 10.4 percent experienced damage of farm machinery.[87] In Azerbaidzhan, 831 acts of sabotage were reported for the first half of 1931.[88] And in Turkmenistan, reference is made to the *basmachi* uprising of March–August 1931 (put down by the army) which is said to have engulfed the entire republic.[89] These figures by no means tell the whole story of the dimensions of the violence of those times.[90]

In some parts of the countryside, it was dangerous for officials and city people to travel or to visit villages. From the fall of 1929, for example, Siberia was declared unsafe due to banditism.[91] In the mountainous regions of the North Caucasus, traditionally untamed areas, travel during collectivization resembled that of the civil war days. In February 1930, the secretary of the Ingush oblast party committee, a North Caucasus regional party committee instructor, and their driver were ambushed and murdered on their way back from working on collectivization in the villages. In June 1930, a similar fate was shared by a member of the Kabardino-Balkar oblast committee, the secretary of one of the region's okrug party committees, an oblast soviet executive committee member, and their driver.[92] F. A. Makeev, reportedly the chair of the Kuban Association of Proletarian Writers, was murdered in March 1930 while at work as an okrug plenipotentiary on collectivization.[93]

Within the village, a similar vengence was wreaked upon peasant activists who sided with the authorities and took part in collectivization or dekulakization. The most frequent motive in these acts of violence was revenge. For example, in the North Caucasus in late 1929, a young Komsomol woman was brutally murdered for her part in a play that unmasked the local kulaks.[94] In July 1930 in Pokrovskii district in Siberia, a group of eight kulaks shot a village activist to death and then broke into his house, killing his wife and children and later burning down the house.[95]

Less violent forms of peasant resistance were also widespread. "Agitation and propaganda" against the collective farm and state policy are reported throughout the series and include articulated opposition from all strata of the peasantry, non-peasants, and clergy.[96] Peasants frequently collected signatures for petitions and held "secret meetings" in support of dekulakized peasants.[97] The singing of anti-collective farm *chastushki* was reported in the Northwestern territories, and in Ukraine "kurkuls" (that is, kulaks) reportedly destroyed portraits of Lenin and Stalin in one village.[98] The practice of submitting petitions to quit collective farms with peasant signatures arranged in a circle (so no one could guess who was the first to sign) is reported in the documents, and there is at least one case of a collective farm meeting successfully rejecting the accusation that one of its members was a kulak.[99]

Rumors

The rumor mill continued to operate during these years, with an emphasis on themes of apocalypse, war, and the destruction of traditional ways. There were wild rumors that women and children would be socialized and all would sleep under the ten metre blanket on a common bed, and more down-to-earth rumors about the closing of bazaars and churches.[100] Whether verging on the fantastic or closer to reality, these types of rumors generally had some basis in the wild excesses of the times.[101] Peasants also began to circulate rumors—again not entirely fantastic—that the collective farm meant a return to serfdom.[102] Rumors of war were now frequently accompanied by forecasts of impending starvation and famine. Peasants continued to talk of war with Poland (especially in the Western parts of the country), but also of war with China following the hostilities on the Far Eastern railroad.[103]

Many rumors instilled fear in the hearts of peasants and seem to have been a conscious device for turning peasants away from the collective farms. In most cases, this type of rumor drew upon fears of anti-Christ and the end of the world. During a meeting on dekulakization in the village of Dmitrievo in the Vladimir okrug, there was talk of an impending Bartholomew's night. It was said that the night would be dry, and then a humid spell would follow and all would be destroyed "according to God's writ."[104] A report from the Tiumen okrug in the Urals noted that rumors spoke of collective farmers' foreheads being stamped (presumably with the mark of anti-Christ); these rumors often proclaimed that everyone with stamped foreheads would be killed when the anti-Communist uprising began.[105] In Astrakhan, there were rumors that the Virgin Mary had sent down a letter (written in gold letters) warning peasants that sickness and punishment would descend upon those who joined the collective farm.[106] In the Pskov area, local evangelists called workers' brigades anti-Christs who had come to plant a "devil's lair" (i.e., the collective farm) and to leave the mark of the devil.[107] Rumors about war, invasion, and murderous bands of horsemen recalled the civil war era in the minds of many peasants and so were not entirely fantastic. In the context of the momentous upheaval of the First Five-Year Plan period, it may have seemed to many peasants as if the end of the world were at hand; and, in fact, it was for an entire way of life.

The document series as a source on the third phase of collectivization (1932–37)

The strengths of individual collections vary enormously for this final period treated in the document series. In general, the coverage of these years is much weaker than that of the earlier periods. Nevertheless, many of the collections include valuable information on the crisis of collective farming in 1932, the famine, and the problems of collective farming in the mid–1930s.

The collective farms

Weak organization, poor leadership, and, above all, oppressive state requisitioning policies prevented the consolidation of collective farming following the massive wholesale collectivization campaigns of the First Five-Year Plan era. Many of the documents in the collectivization series indicate that the collective farms suffered from high rates of turnover and sometimes even collapsed due to the instability of collective farm membership. Although membership turnover was a problem in 1930 and 1931,[108] it appears to have reached epidemic proportions in many regions in 1932 and, to a perhaps lesser extent, in 1933. In Western Siberia, mass departures of kolkhoz members in early 1932 caused a drop in the proportion of peasant households collectivized from 60.6 percent in December 1931 to 58.7 percent.[109] In Central Volga, similarly, the percentage of collectivized peasant households declined from 82.5 percent to 76.6 percent in early 1932, and then dropped down further to 68–70 percent by May 1933.[110] In the Western region, where the overall proportion of households collectivized dropped from 51.9 percent to 48.4 percent in the first half of 1932, departure rates in some individual districts were as high as 7–8 percent of collective farm members.[111]

A renewed campaign to force the socialization of livestock in the winter of 1931–32 is one of the reasons cited in the documents for increased peasant departure. This problem was reported in the North Caucasus, Western Siberia, and Central Volga, and led to the publication of a special Central Committee decree aimed against the "excesses" of this campaign in March 1932.[112] Renewed attempts to enlarge collective farms ("gigantomania") through mergers was another reported reason for departures in some areas.[113] In the Western region, departures were blamed on kulak agitation: according to an August 1932 report, the kulaks made use of the difficult food situation and "in particular . . . stress the difficult situation of those Ukrainian kolkhozniki coming [to the Western region] for bread," saying, "this is the way it will be for everyone."[114]

Many of the reasons for the departures from the collective farms in 1932 derived from the general lawlessness of the countryside. Lawlessness and its consequences became a major (albeit short-lived) concern of central authorities in the summer of

1932, leading to a spate of information in the press and elsewhere on the consequences of lawlessness.[115] This concern is reflected at the local level in regional decrees warning against the following (apparently common) violations of legality: imposition of unlawful taxes or levies on revenues derived from collective farmers' private plots; reduction in the size of private plots; arbitrary and frequent "reelections" of collective farm officers imposed from the outside; high turnover of collective farm officials through arbitrary dismissals; attempts to force collective farms to purchase unnecessary or defective agricultural inventory; and illegal and excessive demands for the labor or produce of collective farms.[116]

The famine

The famine of the early 1930s is a very delicate issue in Soviet historiography. Before the era of *glasnost'*, the Soviet government routinely denied the existence of famine in the Soviet countryside in the early 1930s.[117] With the exception of a couple of indirect references in Soviet historical works of the Khrushchev era and in literary works,[118] little information on the famine was available. The document series on collectivization is only a partial exception to this rule of silence. Even on this subject, however, the collections do yield data if carefully mined.

Drought is reported in Central Volga (1931 and 1933), Lower Volga (1931) and parts of Kazakhstan (1932).[119] Crop failures are reported in the documents of the Western region (1933, due to heavy rains), parts of Voronezh region in the Central Agricultural Region (1934), parts of Western Siberia (1934), Central Volga (1933, mainly in the southeastern districts of the left bank of the Volga), and the North Caucasus (1932).[120] The documents sometimes also refer directly to food difficulties. This is the case in the Western region in 1932, the Kuban in late 1931, and the North Caucasus generally in 1932 and 1933, Central Volga in spring 1932, Kazakhstan in 1932, and Moldavia in 1932.[121] A report from the Ukraine refers to allegedly "false information" in a report by the deputy head of an MTS *politotdel* (i.e., state security representative) which spoke of cases of people swelling up from starvation. This same report, however, acknowledged that there were cases when collective farmers had no food except that provided by the farm's cafeteria, and recommended food aid for some collective farmers.[122] A document from Kazakhstan refers to the "difficult winter of 1933" and to the "significant successes" in the rehabilitation of the Kazakh aul, after "the famine which took place in 1932 and the beginning of 1933. . . ."[123]

A number of documents note various kinds of peasant insubordination associated with famine. Cases of theft and collective farms not fulfilling their obligations are reported, as are cases of collective farmers not going out to work and thus leaving fields unharvested.[124] A "conspiracy of silence" was reported at collective farm meetings in the North Caucasus where collective farmers refused to respond to reports or questions at the meetings.[125] There are also scattered references to resistance to central policy by lower-level officials. In Kazakhstan, where regional party secretary Goloshchekin reported the existence in one district of an "underground party" against requisitioning, a raikom secretary was quoted as saying, "I will not requisition grain for the government on the bones of the kolkhozniki."[126] A report from the Ukraine on the work of the MTS *politotdels* in 1933–34 suggested that many *politotdel* chiefs opposed giving grain to the government because of the need to shore up collective farm reserves.[127]

In a very different spirit, negative references to mass searches and the encirclement of villages on the part of officials in the "struggle for bread" are made in documents on Moldavia, and editorial notes mention the use of "naked repression" and the exile of entire villages in the Don and Kuban.[128] Finally, several documents note government assistance to famine-stricken areas (without necessarily labeling them thus)—a food and seed loan of five tons of grain to the Western region in 1933 and two seed and food loans to Kazakhstan in February and September 1932.[129] Much of the information on the famine comes from reports submitted by MTS *politotdel* leaders. These reports also sometimes include information on the widespread purges of rural officialdom, specialists, and collective farms.[130]

The post-famine years

The document series' coverage of the post-famine years concentrates on problems of internal collective farm management and organization, the introduction of the 1935 collective farm charter, and violations of that charter in the later 1930s. Reports on internal collective farm organization note the following problems: the tendency of families to split up in order to increase the size of their private plot;[131] the assignment of collective farm draught animals and/or parcels of collective fields to their former (pre-collectivization) owners;[132] and the continued existence up to the 1935 charter of strip farming in the collective farms.[133]

The 1935 collective farm charter, which was intended to remedy many of the problems of the collective farm system, is discussed in many documents in the collectivization series. In the Ivanovo region, for example, there was a good deal of negative agitation about the charter. Peasants on one collective farm revised the charter by crossing out the clause that stated it was necessary to give certain products to the government. On another collective farm, peasants interpreted statements on the acceptance of some kulaks and their children to mean a general rehabilitation of all kulaks; and in yet another case, the peasants interpreted the clause on granting land to collective farms "forever" as meaning a legislated return to serfdom.[134]

The collections that cover the last years of the 1930s focus on the state's crackdown on the collective farms in light of the many violations of the 1935 charter. The documents discuss the tendency of many farmers to increase private plots at the expense of collective lands, the violation of the law on the nationalization of the land (through illegal land sales and rentals), the increase in the number of livestock owned privately by collective farmers, and the continued presence of strip farming in some collective farms.[135] Finally, there are scattered references to the state's attempts in 1936 and after to complete at long last the collectivization and resettlement of *khutor* owners in the Western and Northwestern parts of the country.[136]

As might be expected, the information on peasant rumors contained in the collections for this period is much less rich than for earlier periods, though there are some interesting reports from national minority areas, which underwent wholesale collectivization later than the major grain-producing regions.[137] There are also relatively few reports of violence in comparison with the earlier periods. A total of ten murders and eleven assaults are reported in the collections for the years from 1932 to 1935. Arson continued to be a problem noted in several areas.[138] There are also several reports of attacks on female shock workers and Stakhanovites as well as attacks on farm machinery.[139]

Coverage of the years after wholesale collectivization is much weaker than earlier years. Nonetheless, if carefully mined, the documents provide a small glimpse into an otherwise veiled period of time. Most significantly, the documents paint a picture of a collective farm system in disarray and a rural economy in distress.

Conclusion

The document series on collectivization provides an excellent source of primary materials for the study of the countryside in the late 1920s and 1930s. In addition to the topics discussed above, social historians will find materials on women,[140] demobilized Red army soldiers,[141] Cossacks,[142] private farmers (*edinolichniki*),[143] and the fate of dekulakized peasants in the 1930s.[144] Needless to say, the document series provides neither an exhaustive nor a complete picture of the processes of collectivization and dekulakization. The process of selection of documents clearly was informed by a Soviet political and scholarly bias which left untouched many essential types of information in the archives. Nevertheless, the series remains one of the best published sources available on the countryside in this time period and a source that has yet to be fully mined by Western scholars.

Notes

1. For further information and analysis of the series, see G. A. Belov, "O nekotorykh voprosakh publikatsii dokumental'nykh istochnikov po istorii kollektivizatsii sel'skogo khoziaistva SSSR," *Voprosy istorii*, no. 4 (1962); M. L. Bogdenko, "Pervye toma obshchesoiuznoi serii dokumentov i materialov po istorii kollektivizatsii sel'skogo khoziaistva SSSR," *Voprosy istorii*, no. 8 (1966); N. A. Ivnitskii, "O publikatsii dokumentov po istorii kollektivizatsii sel'skogo khoziaistva," *Arkheograficheskii ezhegodnik za 1967 g.* (Moscow, 1969); V. V. Kabanov, "Dokumenty po istorii kollektivizatsii sel'skogo khoziaistva," *Istoriia SSSR*, no. 5 (1978); M. M. Kudiukina, "Dokumenty po istorii kollektivizatsii sel'skogo khoziaistva RSFSR (1927–1937 gg.)," *Sovetskie arkhivy*, no. 4 (1984); I. M. Volkhov, "Istoriia kooperativno-kolkhoznogo stroitel'stva v SSSR i zadachi podgotovki publikatsii dokumentov," *Sovetskie arkhivy*, no. 3 (1982). Readers are also advised to consult the six-volume bibliography on the history of the Soviet countryside, *Istoriia sovetskoi derevni* (see above, Viola, "Preface," p. xii, for full bibliographic information).

2. See the article by S. G. Wheatcroft in this collection for references to statistical collections on the countryside.

3. Bogdenko, "Pervye toma," 147.

4. *Istoriia kolkhoznogo prava. Sbornik zakonodatel'nykh materialov SSSR i RSFSR, 1917-1958 gg.*, 2 vols. (Moscow, 1958–59); and *Kollektivizatsiia sel'skogo khoziaistva. Vazhneishie postanovleniia Kommunisticheskoi partii i sovetskogo pravitel'stva, 1917–1935* (Moscow, 1957).

5. The following early publications are not formally a part of the series: *Iz istorii kollektivizatsii sel'skogo khoziaistva Riazanskoi oblasti, 1927–1935 gg.* (Riazan, 1962); *Iz istorii sotsialisticheskogo preobrazovaniia sel'skogo khoziaistva na Khersonshchine, 1918–1941 gg.*, 3 vols. (Kherson, 1957–59) (a fourth volume covering the post-1941 period was published in Simferopol' in 1978); *Kollektivizatsiia sel'skogo khoziaistva na Kubani (1918–1927 gg.)* (Krasnodar, 1959); and the multi-volume collection on the Lower Volga region, *Saratovskaia partiinaia organizatsiia v gody sotsialisticheskoi industrializatsii strany i podgotovki sploshnoi kollektivizatsii sel'skogo khoziaistva, 1926–1929 gg.* (Saratov, 1960); *Saratovskaia partiinaia organizatsiia v period nastupleniia sotsializma po vsemu frontu. Sozdanie kolkhoznogo stroia, 1929–1932 gg.* (Saratov, 1961); *Saratovskaia partiinaia organizatsiia v gody bor'by za zavershenie sotsialisticheskoi rekonstruktskii narodnogo khoziaistva, 1933–1937 gg.* (Saratov, 1963).

6. See, in particular, the extremely valuable documents published in *Istoricheskii arkhiv* and *Materialy po istorii SSSR: Dokumenty po istorii sovetskogo obshchestva*, 7 vols. (Moscow, 1955–59).

7. Ivnitskii, "O publikatsii dokumentov," 243; Kabanov, "Dokumenty," 160.

8. The composition of the central editorial board (and of the chief editors) changed slightly over the years. See Bogdenko, "Pervye toma," 148; and Kabanov, "Dokumenty," 160, n. 1, for a list of central editorial board members.

9. The union republics (so far) covered are Ukraine (3 vols.), Belorussia (3 vols.), Uzbekistan (3 vols.), Kazakhstan (2 vols.), Georgia (1 vol.), Azerbaidzhan (3 vols.), Lithuania (1 vol.), Moldavia (2 vols.), Kirgiziia (1 vol.), Tadzhikistan (1 vol.), and Turkmenistan (2 vols.).

10. The RSFSR regions (so far) covered are the Urals, Eastern Siberia, Western Siberia, Far East, Kuban, North Caucasus, Bashkiriia, Dagestan (2 vols.), Iakutiia, Tatariia, Central Industrial Region, Central Black Earth Region, Nizhegorodskii-Gor'kovskii krai, Northern region, Northwestern region, Central Volga, and Western region.

11. See Bogdenko, "Pervye toma," 147; Ivnitskii, "O publikatsii dokumentov," 243; and Kabanov, "Dokumenty," 160, for mention of these volumes and also of a card index for the series.

12. E.g., *Kollektivizatsiia sel'skogo khoziaistva na Severnom Kavkaze* (Krasnodar, 1972), 740, n. 62, for data on the number of farms exiled from thirteen districts of the region on 9 March 1931; *Kollektivizatsiia sel'skogo khoziaistva v Srednem Povolzh'e* (Kuibyshev, 1970), 15, for information on the number of peasants dekulakized by May 1930; *Istoriia kollektivizatsii sel'skogo khoziaistva v Vostochnoi Sibiri* (Irkutsk, 1979), 18, for the number of peasants dekulakized in 1930; and *Kollektivizatsiia sel'skogo khoziaistva v Severnom raione* (Vologda, 1964), 681–82, n. 43, for plans on the numbers of peasants to be exiled to the Northern region in 1930. (All further references to individual collections will be abbreviated in the notes after the first citation by reference to the name of the region.)

13. Kabanov, "Dokumenty," 162, estimates that 75–80 percent of the documents in the RSFSR collections have not been published previously.

14. See the discussion of document typology in my article in this collection, "Archival Research in the USSR."

15. Bogdenko, "Pervye toma," 149. Later reviews use a similar typology. See Ivnitskii, "O publikatsii dokumentov," 244; and Kabanov, "Dokumenty," 161.

16. Kudiukina, "Dokumenty," 74.

17. Kabanov, "Dokumenty," 165.

18. I.e., the works referred to in note 5 above, as well as the later collections on Astrakhan

and Adzhariia: *Put' trudovykh pobed. Sbornik dokumentov i materialov. Iz istorii vozniknoveniia i razvitiia sel'skokhoziaistvennykh i rybolovetskikh kolkhozov v Astrakhanskom krae* (Volgograd, 1967); and *Bor'ba za zavershenie sotsialisticheskoi rekonstruktsii narodnogo khoziaistva v Adzharii. Sbornik dokumentov i materialov, 1933–41 gg.* (Batumi, 1986). Occasional reference will also be made to the very valuable *Vnutrennie voiska v gody mirnogo sotsialisticheskogo stroitel'stva, 1922–1941. Dokumenty i materialy* (Moscow, 1977). This survey will not discuss collections of documents published in the periodical press or the collections of laws. For a complete listing of the collections in the document series, see the bibliography at the end of this article.

19. *Kollektivizatsiia sel'skogo khoziaistva Tsentral'nogo promyshlennogo raiona* (Riazan, 1971), 281; North Caucasus, 96, 180–81; Astrakhan, 140; *Kollektivizatsiia sel'skogo khoziaistva Zapadnoi Sibiri* (Tomsk, 1972), 25.

20. North Caucasus, 180; Astrakhan, 113.

21. Central Industrial Region, 97; North Caucasus, 106; Astrakhan, 106–107.

22. Central Industrial Region, 187, 232; North Caucasus, 154; Astrakhan, 106–107; *Kollektivizatsiia sel'skogo khoziaistva v Zapadnom raione RSFSR* (Smolensk, 1968), 46. In Astrakhan, according to an October 1928 report, 26.6 percent of collective farm and cooperative members were related.

23. In Vladimir province of the Central Industrial Region in 1928, 79 percent of collective farm members were male and only 21 percent female. Central Industrial Region, 281.

24. Astrakhan, 106–107; Central Industrial Region, 117, 285.

25. North Caucasus, 102; Astrakhan, 106–107.

26. In Iaroslavl province in the Central Industrial Region, in June 1927, 262 of 366 collective farms were said to be *"dikie."* Central Industrial Region, 28.

27. In the Kuban, a report predicted the slowdown of the collective farm movement as early as 1927 due to the near exhaustion of excess government lands on which to establish collective farms. Kuban (1918–1927), 190–91. Elsewhere, regional authorities also predicted a crisis for the movement if problems were not overcome. See Central Industrial Region, 117; and *Kollektivizatsiia sel'skogo khoziaistva Belorusskoi SSR*, 3 vols. (Minsk, 1973–85), vol. 1, 177.

28. *Istoriia kollektivizatsii sel'skogo khoziaistva Urala* (Perm, 1983), 96–97; *Kollektivizatsiia sel'skogo khoziaistva v Nizhegorodskom-Gor'kovskom krae* (Kirov, 1985), 140; Northern region, 198–99; Western region, 214; Astrakhan, 140, 152–54; Eastern Siberia, 100–102; Western Siberia, 107–109, 110–11; Central Volga, 45; Belorussia, vol. 1, 140–42; *Kollektivizatsiia sel'skogo khoziaistva v Severo-Zapadnom raione* (Leningrad, 1970), 138–52.

29. Western region, 214; Western Siberia, 107–109, 110–11. Apparently there were fairly universal purges of collective farms ordered in October and November 1929 to be completed by 15 January 1930. This information is from the Western Siberia collection, 107–109, 110–11. Here a Siberian regional decree of 25 November orders the purge to be completed by 15 January; another decree of 5 December again called for a purge, this time to be completed by 15 February. This second decree suggests some degree of indecision or sluggishness in implementation vis-à-vis the kulak question. The 5 December decree, moreover, refers to an earlier 19 March 1929 directive ordering a purge of the collective farms.

30. Central Industrial Region, 240–41.

31. Urals, 73–75; Riazan, 120, 125–26; Western region, 130; Northern region, 123–25; Northwestern region, 76–78; *Kollektivizatsiia sel'skogo khoziaistva Bashkirskoi ASSR* (Ufa, 1980), 51–52; *Iz istorii kollektivizatsii sel'skogo khoziaistva Dal'nego Vostoka* (Khabarovsk, 1979), 74; *Kollektivizatsiia sel'skogo khoziaistva v Azerbaidzhana*, 3 vols. (Baku, 1982–), vol. 1, 152–56, 158–59, 186–97.

32. Central Industrial Region, pp. 240–43.

33. North Caucasus, 150–51.

34. For other discussions of struggle during procurements, see North Caucasus, 63–64, 81, 193–94; Central Volga, 81; Northwestern region, 31–37, 153–54. Violence also tended to break out during tax campaigns (Northern region, 123–25; Bashkiriia, 51–52) and *zemleustroistvo*. The latter process often pitted collective farmers against private farmers within the same village (Western region, 123–24; *Kollektivizatsiia sel'skogo khoziaistva Tatarskoi ASSR* (Kazan, 1968, 105–106, 109, 111–12). The documents on Tatariia include information of October 1929 from the Tatar kolkhoz union indicating the use of force to create collective farms during *zemleustroistvo* and the practice of moving kulaks out to the worse land and threatening other peasants with a similar fate if they did not join the collective farm. The Tatariia obkom responded to these occurrences in October 1929 by forbidding the resettlement of kulaks in *poselki* except in extreme cases.

35. Eastern Siberia, 16; Western Siberia, 8.

36. Urals, 12. In the Western region, 284 terrorist acts were reported in 1929 (Western region, 233), of which 37 percent were directed against activists and 63 percent against lower soviet officials. In the Northern region, 49 terrorist acts were reported in 1928 and 95 in the first half of 1929 (Northern region, 14). Partial data are provided for other regions and for okrugs and districts within regions; e.g., Riazan, 125–26; Central Industrial Region, 331–32; Western region, 130–33; Central Volga, 81, 141–43; Tatariia, 326, n. 32; Azerbaidzhan, vol. 1, 187; Belorussia, vol. 1, 16, 194. In addition, there were reports of 30 *vystupleniia* in the Central Volga (p. 81) in May 1929 and 60 in June 1929 during grain requisitioning. Compare the figures on terrorist acts with the supposedly aggregate figures in *Vnutrennie voiska*, 18, 202, which claim 1,400 terrorist acts in all in 1928 and 1,202 in 1929 for the Leningrad region, Central Volga, and Central Black Earth Region alone.

37. *Kollektivizatsiia sel'skogo khoziaistva v Tsentral'no-Chernozemnoi oblasti* (Voronezh, 1978), 57–58, 74–76. The targets of terror included 55 lower soviet officials, 2 policemen, 12 collective farm/cooperative workers, 1 *sel'kor*, 21 *bedniak* activists, and 8 Communist and Komsomol members. The source claims that the perpetrators of violence included 163 kulaks, 25 *seredniaks*, and 8 *bedniaks*. The majority of acts (50) were committed during requisitioning, one occurred during the tax campaign, 10 were related to zemleustroistvo, and 15 to the "struggle with the kulaks."

38. Western region, 224–25. (Not all of these sentences were mutually exclusive; many were fined and subject to some form of harsher punishment.)

39. Northwestern region, 32.

40. E.g., Urals, 116–18; Nizhegorodskii, 128–29; Central Black Earth Region, 11.

41. Astrakhan, 69; Central Industrial Region, 59–60, 68.

42. Nizhegorodskii, 74–75; Central Industrial Region, 169.

43. *Kollektivizatsiia sel'skogo khoziaistva Turkmenskoi SSR*, 2 vols. (Ashkhabad, 1968, 1972), vol. 1, 119, 165, 177, 324.

44. Western region, 123–24; also see *Kollektivizatsiia sel'skogo khoziaistva Dagestana ASSR*, 2 vols. (Makhachkala, 1976), vol. 1, 113. The decision of the North Caucasus kraikom of 18 July 1929 to purge collective farms of kulaks and not to allow their further entry to the collective farms, which was given the "force of a general party directive" (pp. 13–14), is printed in North Caucasus, 158.

45. North Caucasus, 179.

46. Central Volga, 140, 141–43.

47. Tatariia, 105–109, 111–12.

48. Astrakhan, 17, 154–55.

49. Western region, 83–86.

50. *Ibid*.

51. Central Industrial Region, 257–58.

52. Western region, 141, 161–62, 171–72, 183–84.

53. Central Industrial Region, 244–46.

54. Northwestern region, 75–76.

55. See, for example, N. A. Ivnitskii, ed., "Dokladnaia zapiska Kolkhoztsentra v TsK VKP (b) o kolkhoznom stroitel'stve v 1928-1929 gg.," *Materialy po istorii SSSR: Dokumenty po istorii sovetskogo obshchestva*, 7 vols. (Moscow, 1955-59), vol. 7, 245. In Elansk district in the Urals, where wholesale collectivization had become a reality by fall 1929, rumors of anti-Christ and the end of the world understandably abounded. Here wandering women (seemingly former nuns) met an old man in the woods, gave him a copy of the Gospels, and told him always to carry it with him if he wanted to find the correct path. But he was told that he must quit the collective farm if he wanted the Gospels to work.

56. Northwestern region, 91.

57. See rumors reported in *ibid.*, 153-54; Tatariia, 98; Azerbaidzhan, vol. 1, 153; Bashkiriia, 79.

58. Ivnitskii, "Dokladnaia zapiska," 242.

59. *Kollektivizatsiia i razvitie sel'skogo khoziaistva na Kubani* (Krasnodar, 1981), 52-53. (Hereafter referred to as Kuban, vol. 2.)

60. E.g., Western Siberia, 147, 165-66, 181; Saratov (1930-32), 251; Western region, 352, 366; Central Industrial Region, 363, 432, 446-47, 460, 488, 542, 635, 708-710, 757.

61. Central Industrial Region, 16, 493; Western region, 301.

62. North Caucasus, 16. Another document in this collection (p. 195) indicates that the collective farm should equal the size of the *sel'sovet* (which may or may not be similar in size to the land society).

63. Central Volga, 315-16.

64. Central Industrial Region, 301, 304, 327, 340.

65. *Ibid.*, 327.

66. Western region, 309; North Caucasus, 217-18.

67. North Caucasus, 226.

68. Eastern Siberia, 118-19; Western Siberia, 117-18; Dagestan, vol. 1, 182-83; Central Volga, 215-18. In the Central Volga, authorities used a tenfold fine for slaughter, adjusting the size of the fine to correspond to local procurements prices.

69. E.g., Western region, 309; Central Black Earth Region, 199; Eastern Siberia, 17; Central Volga, 372; Tatariia, 25. Less information is given on problems of *socialized* livestock. Documents from the Central Black Earth Region indicate that an obkom decree of 14 February 1930 ordered socialized livestock to remain in the care of their former owners in lieu of socialized stables and barns.

70. Only the TsIK law on dekulakization was published, not the party decree or TsIK instructions. Regional variants are in Central Industrial Region, 333-36; Western region, 246-50; North Caucasus, 248-52; Central Volga, 156-58; Western Siberia, 135-38; Astrakhan, 209-15; Far East, 105-108; Dagestan, vol. 1, 203-204; Tatariia, 135-38; Turkmenistan, vol. 2, 62-66; Northern region, 272-77; *Kollektivizatsiia sel'skogo khoziaistva Kazakhstana*, 2 vols. (Alma-Ata, 1967), vol. 1, 279-80.

71. Western region, 357-61; Eastern Siberia, 162-65.

72. Urals, 17; Eastern Siberia, 18; Western Siberia, 134-35; Central Volga, 15; Tatariia, 145 (district breakdowns given); Northwestern region, 407, n. 26; Astrakhan, 17, 212. (The plan changed over time here. There were four categories of kulaks—category one: 800; two: 1,210; three: 200; four: 3,450.)

73. Western region, 248; Northwestern region, 407, n. 26; Central Volga, 15. Also see Northern region, 16, 316-19, 681-82, n. 43, 682, n. 45, for plans on resettlement of kulaks in this region.

74. Central Industrial Region, 384-85.

75. *Istoriia kolektivizatsii sil's'kogo gospodarstva Ukrains'koi SSR*, 3 vols. (Kiev, 1962-71), vol. 2, 7.

76. Astrakhan, 215-70. (Includes other types of documents as well.)

77. *Ibid.*, 270-75.

78. *Ibid.*, 236-48. In his original report to Stalin, Sheboldaev indicated that dekulakiza-

tion was proceeding without complications following the Nachalova incident. This statement, however, contradicted a report by a regional party committee plenipotentiary that indicated that other uprisings similar to Nachalova were likely in the northern part of the region.

79. E.g., North Caucasus, 197–99, 236–38, 259–60; Northern region, 679–80, n. 39. Also see documents from the Central Industrial Region, 351; and Central Volga, 147–51.

80. See, for example, Astrakhan, 275 on punishment of *peregibshchiki*; and Western Siberia, 144–45, 150.

81. Western Siberia, 144–45, 150; Bashkiriia, 142–43.

82. Saratov (1930–32), 130–31. Such unwillingness to admit new members was a problem throughout the early 1930s. Many collective farms could not absorb a larger membership and remain economically stable. See North Caucasus, 474, for references to refusals to admit new members in 1931.

83. Western region, 279, 282–83. (It was reported that in Rzhev okrug, 30–50 percent of men left for the city after the retreat.)

84. Central Volga, 174–75.

85. Western region, 387–88.

86. *Sploshnaia kollektivizatsiia sel'skogo khoziaistva Uzbekistana* (Tashkent, 1980), 347, n. 6.

87. Western Siberia, 197. The total number of cases reported in this survey is almost 2,000.

88. Azerbaidzhan, vol. 1, 13.

89. Turkmenistan, vol. 2, 274–75, 635, n. 27.

90. E.g., *Vnutrennie voiska*, 310, notes that fifty OPGU officials were killed during operations against bandits; and at least fifty 25,000ers were murdered in 1930–31. See Lynne Viola, *The Best Sons of the Fatherland: Workers in the Vanguard of Soviet Collectivization* (New York, 1987), 159. *Vnutrennie voiska*, 18, also reports 65 violent incidents (*vystupleniia*) in Siberia between January and March 1930; 718 in Central Volga in 1930; and 190 armed uprisings in Central Asia in January to March 1930.

91. N. Ia. Gushchin, "Likvidatsiia kulachestva kak klassa v Sibirskoi derevne," *Sotsial'naia struktura naseleniia Sibiri* (Novosibirsk, 1970), 122.

92. North Caucasus, 738, n. 59.

93. Kuban, vol. 2, 82.

94. North Caucasus, 218–19.

95. Western Siberia, 163–64.

96. E.g., a nun in the Northwestern region (pp. 162–63) "agitated" against the state by saying: "Why do they not take kulaks into the collective farm? Christ taught us to love one's neighbor."

97. E.g., Central Industrial Region, 443.

98. Northwestern region, 162–63; Ukraine, vol. 2, 547.

99. Nizhegorodskii, 210; Riazan, 158; Kazakhstan, vol. 1, 409–10.

100. Central Industrial Region, 398–99; Western region, 256; Kuban, vol. 2, 73–75.

101. See my article, "Bab'i Bunty and Peasant Women's Protest During Collectivization," *Russian Review* 45:1 (1986), for some ideas about the reality behind the common blanket.

102. Central Industrial Region, 398–99; Western region, 256; Kuban, vol. 2, 73–75.

103. *Ibid.*

104. Central Industrial Region, 336.

105. Urals, 115–16.

106. Astrakhan, 270–75.

107. Northwestern region, 162–63.

108. For turnover in 1931, see Western region, 368.

109. Western Siberia, 14, 208–209.

110. Central Volga, 23; also see 274–75, 642, n. 51.

111. Western region, 368–69, 419–20.

112. E.g., North Caucasus, 517–18; 755, n. 126; Central Volga, 291–94; Western Siberia, 14.

113. Western region, 664, n. 69. (Such expansion led to the collapse of some collective farms; this type of expansion was ordered to be halted in July 1932.)

114. *Ibid.*, 419–20. According to a December 1932 Western region report which called the spring 1932 departures "mass exits," the departures led to the collapse of entire farms. Many farms were left with too few hands to work too much land. Conflict between quitters and those who remained in the farms was also reported as were cases of families splitting up with members leaving the collective farm in order to increase the size of their private plots (Western region, 432).

115. The campaign for revolutionary legality came to an unofficial end with the issue of the infamous decree of 7 August 1932 imposing draconian punishment for offences against state and collective farm property.

116. Western region, 414–16; Central Industrial Region, 550–59.

117. For some recent scholarly references to the famine, see *Istoriia krest'ianstva SSSR*, 5 vols. (Moscow, 1986–), vol. 2, 256, 265; G. I. Shmelov, "Ne smet' komandovat'!" *Oktiabr'*, no. 2 (February 1988), 10; V. Danilov, "U kolkhoznogo nachala," *Sovetskaia Rossiia*, 11 October 1987, 4; and especially *idem.*, "Diskussiia v zapadnoi presse o golode 1932–1933 gg. i 'demograficheskoi katastrofe' 30–40—kh godov v SSSR," *Voprosy istorii*, no. 3 (1988), 116–21.

118. For earlier (mostly literary) references to the famine, see Dana Dalrymple, "The Soviet Famine of 1932–34," *Soviet Studies* 15:3 (1964) and continuation in 16:4 (1965). One of the few scholarly references (pre-*glasnost'*) is in I. E. Zelenin, "Politotdely MTS (1933–1934 gg.)," *Istoricheskie zapiski* 76 (1965), 47.

119. Saratov (1930–32), 285; Central Volga, 22, 24; Kazakhstan, vol. 1, 496–97.

120. Western region, 14, 454, 664, n. 70; Central Black Earth Region, 263; Western Siberia, 268–69; Central Volga, 417, 438; North Caucasus, 31.

121. Western region, 419–20; Kuban, vol. 2, 124–25; Central Volga, 294; Kazakhstan, vol. 1, 21, 480; *Sotsialisticheskoe pereustroistvo sel'skogo khoziaistva Moldavskoi ASSR* (Kishinev, 1964), 310.

122. Ukraine, vol. 3, 376. A document from the Western region refers to the return of private peasants in August 1934 from the Ukraine after finding that conditions in the south were worse. Peasants from the Western region were also reported arriving in Western Siberia in 1933–34 and leaving in 1934 and 1935 when Western Siberia experienced intensified food problems following two years of crop failures (Western region, 522). Also see references to Ukrainian peasants fleeing to the Western region (Western region, 420); and Siberian collective farmers quitting the farms in entire groups in 1935 due to food difficulties (Western Siberia, 268–71).

123. Kazakhstan, vol. 2, 103, 141–42. The source is a letter from the party and government leadership of Kazakhstan to the Central Committee and Soviet government in Moscow, dated November 1934.

124. Central Industrial Region, 497, 547; Western region, 429; Kuban, vol. 2, 132–33; Central Volga, 294, 482; Moldavia, 310; North Caucasus, 32, 522–23. See North Caucasus, 522–23, where the failure to go out to work was punished by expulsion from the collective farm, or, in the case of private farmers, expropriation or deportation. By December 1933, the head of the *politotdel* in the North Caucasus could report that collective farmers' attitudes to labor had changed. He noted that earlier it was necessary to force the farmers to work. Now they worked voluntarily because "for the kolkhoznik expulsion from the kolkhoz is the same as death. If someone is excluded, he cries and pleads not to be excluded" (North Caucasus, 567).

125. North Caucasus, 530–33.

126. Kazakhstan, vol. 1, 547; and vol. 2, 102, 104 notes that eight raikom leaderships

LYNNE VIOLA

were removed and 16.6 percent of all collective farm officials fired according to a report of December 1933.

127. Ukraine, vol. 3, 398–401; also Far East, 182 mentions two heads of MTS *politotdels* arguing for lower plans.

128. North Caucasus, 759–61, n. 147; Moldavia, 310.

129. Western region, 664, n. 70; Kazakhstan, vol. 1, 496–97, 538–39.

130. For information on rural specialists, see Central Volga, 418–19; on 1933 purges of collective farms, see Central Industrial Region, 668; Northwestern region, 410, n. 54; *Iz istorii kollektivizatsii sel'skogo khoziaistva i kolkhoznogo stroitel'stva v Tadzhikskoi SSR* (Dushanbe, 1973), 523; *Istoriia kollektivizatsii sel'skogo khoziaistva Gruzinskoi SSR* (Tbilisi, 1970), 19, 479.

131. Western region, 518; Western Siberia, 264.

132. Georgia, 436, 482.

133. Western Siberia, 280–81, reports the presence of far-off fields and strip farming in the collective farms and claims that many land and plot boundaries remained unchanged since before the revolution. Also reported are cases of private peasants having plots *within* the territory of collective farms.

134. Central Industrial Region, 743; also see *Kollektivizatsiia sel'skogo khoziaistva Iakutskoi ASSR* (Iakutsk, 1978), 192, for reports of negative rumors concerning the new charter.

135. Belorussia, vol. 3, 213–14; Kazakhstan, vol. 2, 483, 500–502; North Caucasus, 703; Central Black Earth Region, 280–81; Iakutiia, 219–22; Central Volga, 27.

136. Western region, 611–13, 615–17, 628; Northwestern region, 338, 413, n. 71.

137. Dagestan, vol. 2, 160–64.

138. Central Volga, 450; Belorussia, vol. 3, 98–99, 120.

139. Central Industrial Region, 646; Tadzhikistan, 635–36; Moldavia, 401.

140. On women's resistance to collectivization, see Central Industrial Region, 258, 443–44; Western region, 183–84, 266–67; North Caucasus, 225, 260, 266–67, 533; Iakutiia, 92–93; Central Volga, 171–74, 632–35; Northwestern region, 102–103. On pay discrimination and/or lack of voting rights for women in collective farms, see Moldavia, 176; Central Industrial Region, 321, 804–805; Saratov (1930–32), 42.

141. North Caucasus, 62–63, 98; Kuban, vol. 1, 102; vol. 2, 23; Far East, 82–84, 95–99.

142. North Caucasus, 6–7, 295–98, 347; Kuban, vol. 1, 116–21; vol. 2, 22, 32, 52–53, 113–15.

143. Western region, 521–34; Western Siberia, 263-64; Central Volga, 375.

144. Especially rich in information is the collection on the Northern region (316–19, 482–88, 600–601, 681–82, n. 43, 682, nn. 44–45). Also see Kazakhstan, vol. 1, 282, 474; Dagestan, vol. 2, 218–19; Western Siberia, 163–64; Turkmenistan, vol. 2, 62–63, 79–83; North Caucasus, 248–52, 258–59, 274–75, 267, 738, n. 60 (information on escapes from exile; bandits; special settlements for deportees, etc.).

Appendix

Istoriia kollektivizatsii sel'skogo khoziaistva SSSR
An Annotated Bibliography

Bor'ba za zavershenie sotsialisticheskoi rekonstruktsii narodnogo khoziaistva v Adzharii: Sbornik dokumentov i materialov, 1933–41 gg. (Batumi, 1986). This volume examines many different topics including industry, agriculture, medicine and health issues, physical culture, retail stores, and homeless children in the mid–1930s. The documents are mostly in Georgian.

Istoriia kollektivizatsii sel'skogo khoziaistva Gruzinskoi SSR (1927–1937 gg.) (Tbilisi, 1970). This volume includes good information on the internal workings of the collective farms and on the developments surrounding the publication of the 1935 collective farm charter. The volume contains three (name, geographical, and subject) helpful indices.

Istoriia kolektivizatsii sil's'kogo gospodarstva Ukrains'koi SSR, 3 vols. (Kiev, 1962–1971). This very extensive collection is almost exclusively in Ukrainian and is arranged both chronologically and thematically.

Istoriia kollektivizatsii sel'skogo khoziaistva Urala (1927–1937 gg.) (Perm, 1983). This volume contains excellent materials on the early collective farm movement and collectivization, but provides scant coverage of the years after 1932.

Istoriia kollektivizatsii sel'skogo khoziaistva v Vostochnoi Sibiri (1927–1937 gg.) (Irkutsk, 1979).

Iz istorii kollektivizatsii sel'skogo khoziaistva Dal'nego Vostoka (1927–1937 gg.) (Khabarovsk, 1979).

Iz istorii kollektivizatsii sel'skogo khoziaistva i kolkhoznogo stroitel'stva v Tadzhikskoi SSR, 1926–1937 gg., vol. 1. (Dushanbe, 1973). This volume is among the least interesting of the collections.

Iz istorii kollektivizatsii sel'skogo khoziaistva Riazanskoi oblasti, 1927–1935 gg. (Riazan, 1962).

Iz istorii sotsialisticheskogo preobrazovaniia sel'skogo khoziaistva na Khersonshchine, 1918–1941 gg., 4 vols. (Kherson and Simferopol, 1957–78).

Kolkhozno-kooperativnoe stroitel'stvo v Kirgizii (1918–1929 gg.) (Frunze, 1969).

Kollektivizatsiia i razvitie sel'skogo khoziaistva na Kubani (1927–1941 gg.) (Kras-

---

*Collections not formally in series.

nodar, 1981). This volume contains some useful information on Cossacks.

Kollektivizatsiia krest'ianskikh khoziaistv Litovskoi SSR (Vilnius, 1977). Deals with postwar period.

Kollektivizatsiia krest'ianskikh khoziaistv v pravoberezhnykh raionakh Moldavskoi SSR (Kishinev, 1969).

Kollektivizatsiia sel'skogo khoziaistva Bashkirskoi ASSR, 1927–1937 (Ufa, 1980).

Kollektivizatsiia sel'skogo khoziaistva Belorusskoi SSR (1927–1941 gg.), 3 vols. (Minsk, 1973–1985). These volumes contain mostly Belorussian language documents.

Kollektivizatsiia sel'skogo khoziaistva Dagestana ASSR, 1927–1940 gg., 2 vols. (Makhachkala, 1976).

Kollektivizatsiia sel'skogo khoziaistva Iakutskoi ASSR (1928–1940 gg.) (Iakutsk, 1978).

Kollektivizatsiia sel'skogo khoziaistva Kazakhstana, 1926- iiun' 1941 gg., 2 vols. (Alma-Ata, 1967). These volumes contain excellent information on livestock and the settling of nomadic tribespeople, as well as hints of the 1932–33 famine and some interesting coverage of post–1937 developments.

**Kollektivizatsiia sel'skogo khoziaistva na Kubani (1918–1927 gg.)* (Krasnodar, 1959).

Kollektivizatsiia sel'skogo khoziaistva na Severnom Kavkaze (1927–1937 gg.) (Krasnodar, 1972). This is one of the very best collections of the series. It is especially strong on wholesale collectivization and dekulakization in late 1929 and early 1930. Information on women, Cossacks, and demobilized soldiers is included in this volume.

Kollektivizatsiia sel'skogo khoziaistva Tatarskoi ASSR, 1927–1937 gg. (Kazan, 1968).

Kollektivizatsiia sel'skogo khoziaistva Tsentral'nogo promyshlennogo raiona (1927–1937 gg.) (Riazan, 1971).

Kollektivizatsiia sel'skogo khoziaistva Turkmenskoi SSR, 2 vols. (Ashkhabad, 1968–72). These volumes contain some interesting information on inter-tribal (or clan) conflict within collective farms. Information on the settling of nomads is included.

Kollektivizatsiia sel'skogo khoziaistva Uzbekistana SSR, 3 vols. (Tashkent, 1961–80). Published under the following titles: *Sotsialisticheskoe pereustroistvo sel'skogo khoziaistva v Uzbekistane (1917–1926 gg.)* (Tashkent, 1962); *Podgotovka uslovii sploshnoi kollektivizatsii sel'skogo khoziaistva Uzbekistana, 1927–1929 gg.* (Tashkent, 1961); *Sploshnaia kollektivizatsiia sel'skogo khoziaistva Uzbekistana (1930–1932 gg.)* (Tashkent, 1980).

Kollektivizatsiia sel'skogo khoziaistva v Azerbaidzhane, 3 vols. (Baku, 1982–). This collection contains some interesting information on migrant agricultural labor and labor conflicts in agriculture before wholesale collectivization.

Kollektivizatsiia sel'skogo khoziaistva v Nizhegorodskom-Gor'kovskom krae, 1927–1937 (Kirov, 1985). This volume contains very strong coverage of the internal workings of the collective farms.

Kollektivizatsiia sel'skogo khoziaistva v Severnom raine, 1927–1937 (Vologda, 1964). This volume is the best in the series for some rare glimpses into the fate of the (exiled) kulaks.

Kollektivizatsiia sel'skogo khoziaistva v Severo-Zapadnom raione (1927–1937 gg.) (Leningrad, 1970).

Kollektivizatsiia sel'skogo khoziaistva v Srednem Povolzh'e, 1927–1937 gg. (Kuibyshev, 1970). This very strong collection contains some useful excerpts from unpublished memoirs by rural leaders at the very end of the book.

Kollektivizatsiia sel'skogo khoziaistva v Tsentral'no-Chernozemnoi oblasti, 1927–1937 gg. (Voronezh, 1978).

Kollektivizatsiia sel'skogo khoziaistva v Zapadnom raione RSFSR (1927–1937 gg.) (Smolensk, 1968).

Kollektivizatsiia sel'skogo khoziaistva Zapadnoi Sibiri (1927–1937 gg.) (Tomsk, 1972).

*Put' trudovykh pobed. Sbornik dokumentov i materialov. Iz istorii vozniknoveniia i razvitiia sel'skokhoziaistvennykh i rybolovetskikh kolkhozov v Astrakhanskom krae (Volgograd, 1967). This unexpectedly superb collection contains over 50 pages of documents from the Astrakhan special commission on the elimination of the kulak as a class, including *protokoly* and circular letters to district organizations. This volume provides an unequaled exploration of dekulakization and its short-term consequences by providing a detailed look into the implementation process and several lengthy discussions of the peasant rebellion in Nachalova.

*Saratovskaia partiinaia organizatsiia v gody bor'by za zavershenie sotsialisticheskoi rekonstruktsii narodnogo khoziaistva (Saratov, 1963). All of the Saratov collections contain information on a variety of subjects including agriculture, industry, and the regional party organization (including the 1920s opposition and the 1930s purges).

*Saratovskaia partiinaia organizatsiia v gody sotsialisticheskoi industrializatsii strany i podgotovki sploshnoi kollektivizatsii sel'skogo khoziaistva, 1926–1929 gg. (Saratov, 1960).

*Saratovskaia partiinaia organizatsiia v period nastupleniia sotsializma po vsemu frontu. Sozdanie kolkhoznogo stroia, 1929–1932 gg. (Saratov, 1961).

Sotsialisticheskoe pereustroistvo sel'skogo khoziaistva Moldavskoi ASSR, 1920–1937 gg. (Kishinev, 1964).

Guide to Document Series on Industrialization

LEWIS H. SIEGELBAUM

Historians of the industrial revolution in England and its later nineteenth century West European and North American analogues could be excused for regarding students of Soviet industrialization with a certain degree of envy. Reflecting the predominantly *ad hoc* and private entrepreneurial character of those earlier transformations, the source base for studying Western industrialization is, perforce, scattered among local parishes and private collections as well as corporate, academic and governmental libraries, museums and archival institutions. By contrast, Soviet industrialization was a state-led process, launched "from above" by the Stalin leadership that was desperate to catch up to and overtake the advanced capitalist countries. Correspondingly, all documentary records of that process were deposited in state institutions under the aegis of the State Archival Fund and its administrative body, the Main Archival Administration (GAU). No less important, the temporal dimensions of the Soviet experience are considerably narrower—a matter of a little more than a decade, rather than several decades at the very least in other cases.

But the potential advantages that historians of Soviet industrialization may derive from these circumstances have been severely limited by certain practices and procedures long governing access to archival sources. As Patricia Grimsted has noted, "The Soviet Union has traditionally viewed archival research, especially by foreigners, not as an unrestricted right, . . . but as a special privilege."[1] So special, one might add, that until fairly recently, no Western scholar had managed to consult archival holdings for the industrialization period. Within the last several years, however, a fortunate few have succeeded in crossing the archival threshold, and it appears likely that the numbers will increase in the immediate future.

In any case, the historian of Soviet industrialization cannot afford to overlook the considerable body of documentary material that has been published. For those who eventually undertake archival research, this material should be an essential part of their preparation. Given the inaccessibility of archival inventories, these published collections of documents can supplement Soviet monographs, articles, and other resources as finding aids. Working through these collections can also maximize the efficiency of time spent in archives, because documents that have been included in them are sometimes found interspersed in archival portfolios with unpublished material.[2] Over and above such benefits, these volumes can sensitize the researcher to the multitude of issues associated with industrialization and the language in which they were expressed.

What follows is a guide to and critical evaluation of published documentary sources on Soviet industrialization. According to Soviet historiography, the period of industrialization is conventionally understood to have begun in 1926 with the completion of the "restoration of the national economy" to its prewar levels of output. The first phase of industrialization, encompassing the last two years of the New Economic Policy (NEP) and the entire First Five-Year Plan (1928/9–1932), is generally referred to as that of "socialist reconstruction," a term that also applies to the collectivization of agriculture. The Second Five-Year Plan (1933–37) was dedicated to laying the technical and material foundations for socialism. This was followed in turn by the "perfecting" of socialist relations of production and the beginning of the transition to communism, objectives which the Eighteenth Party Congress stressed in 1939.

Periodization, geographical scope, and organizational format

The sources to be surveyed here consist of fourteen volumes published between 1956 and the early 1970s that deal primarily with labor activism, and over thirty volumes that were issued between the mid–1960s and the early 1980s, either under the general title of *Istoriia industrializatsii SSSR. 1926–1941 gg. Dokumenty i materialy* or in a format that closely resembles the one used in the series. The collections on labor activism include six that are on a national scale. Two deal with relatively brief periods of two years each; a third contains documents on a single event (the all-Union congress of shock workers in 1929); a fourth concerns the contributions of youth to economic restoration and socialist construction; a fifth is on socialist competition; and there are five volumes devoted to the trade unions from 1917 to the early 1970s.[3] All others pertain to certain cities and regions (Moscow, Leningrad, Kharkov, Saratov, Ivanovo) and/or specific groups (workers, shock workers, youth, Komsomols, Communists).[4] Their temporal scope ranges from four years to the entire period from the October Revolution up to the mid–1960s.

The series on industrialization consists of four volumes covering the entire USSR in the sequence 1926–28, 1929–32, 1933–37, and 1938–41 (hereafter referred to as the core volumes),[5] and twenty-eight volumes with a regional or republic focus. The areas and years covered as well as the place and date of publication of the individual volumes are listed in Table 1. There are also two volumes in the series devoted to the railroad network, one to the period of "restoration" (1921–25) and the other to the entire industrialization period.[6]

Thus, it would appear that the only areas to be covered to make the series complete would be the Central Industrial Region, the Urals and Azerbaidzhan beyond the First Five-Year Plan, and the Armenian and Uzbek SSRs for the entire period of industrialization.[7] In three cases, those of the Ukrainian, Moldavian, and Tadzhik republics, volumes extending beyond 1941 have been published, and this

Table 1

Publications of Regional and Republican Documents on Industrialization

Northwestern Region	1925–28	(Leningrad, 1964)
	1928–32	(Leningrad, 1967)
	1933–41	(Leningrad, 1969)
Western Region	1926–37	(Briansk, 1972)
Northern Region	1926–41	(Arkhangelsk, 1970)
Central Industrial Region	1926–32	(Moscow, 1969)*
Nizhegorod-Gorkii krai	1926–41	(Gorkii, 1968)
Central Black Earth Region	1926–32	(Voronezh, 1970)
	1933–41	(Kursk, 1972)
Central Volga Region	1926–41	(Kuibyshev, 1974)
Lower Volga Region	1926–41	(Volgograd, 1984)
Northern Caucasus	1926–32	(Groznyi, 1971)
	1933–41	(Groznyi, 1973)
Urals	1926–32	(Sverdlovsk, 1967)
Western Siberia	1926–41	(Novosibirsk, 1967)
Belorussia	1926–41	(Minsk, 1975)
Ukraine	1928–32	(Kiev, 1966)*
	1933–37	(Kiev, 1977)*
	1938–41	(Kiev, 1977)*
Tatar Republic	1926–41	(Kazan, 1968)
Georgia	1926–41	(Tbilisi, 1968)
Azerbaidzhan	1926–32	(Baku, 1957)*
Kazakhstan	1926–32	(Alma-Ata, 1967)
	1933–41	(Alma-Ata, 1967)
Turkmenistan	1926–32	(Ashkhabad, 1978)
	1933–41	(Ashkhabad, 1978)
Tadzhikistan	1926–41	(Dushanbe, 1972)
Kirgizia	1926–41	(Frunze, 1972)

*Denotes volumes that are not formally part of *Istoriia industrializatsii SSSR* series but closely follow format used therein.

may be the trend for other areas in the future.[8]

The collections on labor activism vary in terms of organizational format and elaborateness of their bibliographical apparatus. While most present the documents in chronological order, some are arranged thematically, with documents organized chronologically within each rubric. Where documents were reproduced from archives, it is standard practice to provide complete citations, including *fond, opis',
delo* and *list* numbers after each entry. All the collections contain an introduction, explanatory notes, and a table of contents; some also provide lists of abbreviations and of the documents; and a few contain indices of industrial enterprises and institutions cited in the documents.[9]

The entire series on industrialization was organized by an editorial board of nearly twenty members of which Academician M. P. Kim served as chief editor. Each volume in the series also had its editorial collegium or individual editor as well as one or more compilers (*sostavitel'*). Although each of the four core volumes had a different editor, the organization of documents is absolutely uniform. The first part consists of three chapters on the financing of industry, capital construction, and the organization of production. Part two contains two chapters, one on the number and composition of workers and the second on labor activism. Appendices include notes, a chronology of party and state resolutions on industry, a list of abbreviations, an index of industrial enterprises by branch of industry, and a list of sources.

The other collections in the series vary considerably in these respects. Some, such as the volumes on the Kirgiz and Turkmen republics, apparently were produced according to a minimalist interpretation of editorial responsibility. Others are more elaborately organized and contain some very useful appendices. The last three volumes on the Northwestern Region are particularly noteworthy.[10] As in the core volumes, documents are divided between two sections, one on industrial construction and the other on cadres and labor activism. Each in turn is broken down into a number of topical sub-sections with documents arranged chronologically within them. Containing nearly 300 explanatory notes, lengthy lists of industrial enterprises, and chronologies that run from 10 to 33 pages, the volumes easily match the standard set by the core volumes.

Among the more unusual features found in some of the other collections are indices of individuals cited in the documents (Lower Volga, Georgia), a dictionary of ''eastern'' terms (Tadzhikistan), a guide to administrative-territorial changes (Northern Caucasus), an index of place names (Ukraine, Kazakhstan), and lists of documents consulted but not included in the collections (Central Black Earth, Northern Caucasus, Belorussia and Northwestern Region for 1925–1928).

Sources and method of selection of documents

The organization and expansion of labor activism was primarily the responsibility of trade union, Komsomol, and party organs at enterprises and higher levels. Correspondingly, most of the archival documents in the collections devoted to labor activism are derived from the Central Council of Trade Unions (VTsSPS)—*f.* 5451—in the Central State Archive of the October Revolution, Higher Organs of State Power and Organs of State Administration of the USSR (TsGAOR), the central committees of individual unions (also in TsGAOR), the Komsomol, and the party, as well as oblast-level equivalents of these institutions.

Newspapers constituted the other main source. Aside from *Pravda, Izvestiia TsK VKP(b), Trud,* and *Komsomol'skaia pravda* which are readily available in the West, the collections draw upon organs of republic-, oblast-, raion-, and enterprise-level party, Komsomol, and trade union committees.

As suggested by some of their titles, these collections were intended to evoke pride in the accomplishments of workers during the period of industrialization.

Documents were selected accordingly. Their prevailing tone is exhortational and triumphal. Reports of individual and collective labor heroism, challenges from workers to their counterparts at other enterprises to surpass their quotas and reduce costs, surveys of achievements in particular factories, industries, and regions—this is the stuff of these collections.

Three criteria governed the selection of documents for the series on industrialization: a preference for reports on conditions and results rather than policy directives; final drafts containing precise and accurate information as opposed to preliminary drafts and/or estimates; and documents that refer to the peculiarities of particular regions or republics as opposed to comprehensive coverage of industrial activity in them.[11] The main archival repositories from which such documents were selected for the core volumes were *f.* 17—the Central Committee of the All-Union Communist Party—in the Central Party Archive of the Institute of Marxism-Leninism (TsPA IML), TsGAOR (specifically, *f.* 374—People's Commissariat of Workers' and Peasants' Inspection; *f.* 5446—Council of People's Commissars; *f.* 5451—VTsSPS; and *f.* 5515—People's Commissariat of Labor) and the Central State Archive of the National Economy of the USSR (TsGANKh). The most frequently cited *fondy* in the latter were *f.* 4372—State Planning Commission; and *f.* 7733—People's Commissariat of Finance.

Documents in the regional and republic-based volumes were drawn primarily from party and state archives at the corresponding levels. Here again, the collection on the Northwestern Region is the most impressive. The three volumes include documents from 58 *fondy* of the Leningrad State Archive of the October Revolution and Socialist Construction (LGAORSS), 12 from the Institute of Party History of the Leningrad Party Obkom (LPA), 15 from the Central State Archive of the Karelian ASSR, and many others from both central and oblast-level state and party archives. The range of previously published sources is also broad, taking in statistical compendia, collections of resolutions and directives, official state and party journals and newspapers.

Researchers should be under no illusion that these collections encompass the entire range of possible sources on industrialization. Before taking a closer look at what the documents contain and how they may be used, it is worth considering what has been left out. As implied above, the editors' bias was toward official renditions of conditions and the execution of policy, rather than unexpurgated accounts by disinterested observers. Extracts from memoirs and personal papers, stenographic reports of industrial conferences and the proceedings of trials in which industrial executives figured prominently, and positive or neutral references to individuals who ran afoul of the party and police are noticeable by their absence. Nor do the explanatory notes compensate. Thus, to take one example, a note to a reference to the Central Institute of Labor in a resolution by the party's Central Committee indicates when it was founded, its methodological orientation and extent of activity, but not the name of its visionary founder and director, Aleksei Gastev, who was arrested sometime in the late 1930s.[12]

Moreover, certain key events that had a profound impact on the course of industrialization appear only fleetingly or not at all in the documents. The Shakhty Affair of 1928, in which "bourgeois" engineers and other persons associated with the coal-mining industry were alleged to have organized a counterrevolutionary plot to sabotage production, is a case in point. Generally considered by Western historians to have marked the leftward swing of the Stalin group within the party and its assault on "Rightist" opponents of full-scale industrialization, the affair merits but a single document in the collection on the Northern Caucasus, where the Shakhty mines were located.[13] There is no mention in the documents of the trials of the "Industrial Party" (1930) and the Metro-Vickers engineers (1933), and as far as these collections are concerned, the Great Purge of 1936–38, which devastated the upper echelons of the party and industrial administration, might never have happened.

Another kind of omission of which researchers should be aware has to do with the publication of extracts rather than complete versions of many documents. Thus, a document in the collection on the labor exploits of Muscovites, entitled "From the resolution of the Moscow city trade union council presidium on the third anniversary of the beginning of socialist competition," lists only three of at least eight points in the resolution.[14] Generally in the collections on labor activism, ellipses are used to indicate where omissions have been made. This too is often the case in the series on industrialization, but where substantial sections have been deleted, a note at the foot of the page indicates what is missing.

How to use the documents

Notwithstanding the extent of these gaps and shortcomings, the collections surveyed here can serve as a valuable resource for research on industrialization. The number of topics and issues associated with that epochal process is, of course, vast, and many remain to be identified and explored. Below, I offer some of the ways in which the documents contained in these collections have been or could be used to elucidate various aspects of industrialization.

Industrial growth and productivity

Mark Twain's adage about lies, damned lies, and statistics rings true for much of Soviet history, no more so than in the case of official claims about rates of industrial growth and productivity during the period of industrialization. As many scholars have pointed out, aggregates expressed in rubles are particularly suspect in that they generally do not take into account the upward drift in production costs, and those that are indexed to 1926/27 prices can be worse than misleading.[15] Statistical inflation can also enter into aggregates expressed in natural units, though in this case, what Alec Nove has called the "law of equal cheating"—i.e., the existence of countervailing pressures against the exaggeration of output—would tend to diminish the scale.[16] Still, particularly in the case of consumer goods, statistical series showing increases in factory output fail to register the secular decline in artisanal and domestic-made goods.

What then are we to make of the plethora of statistics on output contained in the documents? First, it is important to note who reported what and when. For example, Gosplan's lengthy year-end report for 1931 generally gives lower figures than the Statistical Administration's survey covering the First Five-Year Plan period.[17] For most articles, the differences are not large, and one may assume that the earlier report was preliminary, failing to take into account year-end output. However, it is hard to believe that a difference of 9.8 million pairs of shoes can be explained in this manner.

What we would need—but what the documents do not provide—is the raw data from which these aggregates were compiled. Then again, the quantity of finished goods was not the only way that output was assessed. To stay with shoes for the moment, the Gosplan report indicates that while the annual plan was underfulfilled by 9.1 percent, output of sandals, which required less leather, exceeded the plan by 44.3 percent. It also notes that the quality of the finished product fell in the last quarter, with first-class goods comprising 69.1 percent of output compared to the target of 90 percent.[18] Some enterprises did not come close to the average. At Leningrad's "Proletarian Victory" No. 2, the figure was 27.7 percent, rising to a reported 50 percent in the first quarter of 1932.[19]

In general, the regional and republic-based volumes enable the researcher to get much closer to the ground, or at least enterprise accounting offices, and to appreciate differential rates of industrialization. Several collections contain documents showing the proportion of goods over time produced in particular areas compared to the entire country.[20] There are also data on investments in different branches of industry and particular enterprises, and a table referring to expenditures on and output of reconstructed and newly constructed enterprises.[21]

What is true of industrial output statistics is also the case with respect to productivity. Figures purporting to show significant increases in labor productivity are rarely disaggregated. It is thus almost impossible to make judgments about the relative contributions of new machinery, methods of production, or other innovations. The most misleading type of statistics, though, are those expressed in terms of percentages of output norm fulfillment. These abound in the collections, particularly in documents concerning the Stakhanovite movement. Fortunately, there are also documents that reveal a good deal about the process of norm determination and its arbitrariness. Despite repeated calls from above to base output norms on the technical capacities of machines, the overwhelming proportion of norms were derived from observation and statistical methods. Thus, as of May 1931 only 19.2 percent of norms at the Dzerzhinskii Metallurgical Factory were technically based, and at the Petrovskii and Lenin Factory, the figure was 2.3 percent. Elsewhere, such as in railroad transport and coal mining, the proportion of technically based norms was no higher.[22]

Industrial administration

One of the reasons why technically based norms were rare is that enterprise management was competing for scarce labor resources and could not afford to drive away workers, particularly skilled workers. The issue was just one of many where the particularistic interests of enterprises clashed with centrally mandated policy, and the documents provide source material for examining them.

Dedicated to replacing market forces by a centrally administered command system of price, credit, and other resource allocation, the central authorities constructed an elaborate network of controls to check up on enterprise performance. The Workers' and Peasants' Inspectorate, commissions and regional branches of Vesenkha (the Supreme Council of the National Economy), Gosplan departments, and chief administrations (*glavki*) of the Commissariat of Heavy Industry all filed reports on plan fulfillment and the compliance—or lack thereof—with central directives. Sections of the Commissariat of Labor (Narkomtrud) and VTsSPS did the same with respect to labor policy. Finally, party and Komsomol organs at the enterprise level were charged with mobilizing control from below in the form of inspection brigades, "light cavalry raids" on enterprise offices, and counter-planning brigades.

With such a maze of overlapping bureaucracies, it is not surprising that lines got tangled and responsibility was ducked. Time and again, the deck was reshuffled. In June 1930, the trusts were stripped of their marketing and supply functions, which were turned over to associations (*ob"edineniia*).[23] Less than a year later, the cumbersome associations were dismantled and replaced by *glavki*, the territorial domains of which were frequently altered. Vesenkha was divided into three commissariats, one of which, the Commissariat of Heavy Industry, was subsequently split up into several new ones.

Often, administrative changes remained on paper. In April 1933, the Donbass coal-mining industry was subjected to a thorough overhaul of its administrative structure, as outlined in a joint resolution of Sovnarkom and the party's Central Committee. The resolution also called for a fundamental reorganization of the wage system, the reassignment of officials and engineers from administrative offices to the mines, a redoubling of efforts to combat turnover, and other measures. In the collection on the Ukraine we can follow the series of resolutions that were, in effect, spin-offs of the central directive.[24] Yet, four years later, we find the Fuel-Energy Section of Gosplan asserting that "the instructions of the party and state of 1933 are not being fulfilled" as far as organizational questions are concerned.[25] And, in March 1940, Sovnarkom and the Central Committee were moved to issue another resolution stating that "in the last three years, the well-known decisions . . . of April–May 1933 . . . have been forgotten."[26]

The making of a Soviet working class

Other than the individual testimonies and collectively signed letters of outstanding shock workers and Stakhanovites, the spontaneity of which may be doubted, these documents offer little on the subjective aspects of working class experience. Problems encountered by workers and their reactions are filtered through informational reports by trade union, Komsomol, and party organizations. Consequently, there is virtually nothing on working class family or community life, and crime might never have existed. Workers' resistance to socialist competition, which, as we know from other sources, was fairly widespread in the late 1920s, is rarely mentioned, and then only in passing.[27]

Even with these limitations, there is much useful information to extract about the process of working class formation. Essentially, three kinds of information are presented: statistical information on the composition of the working class; reports on the material condition of workers, including wages; and a multitude of documents concerning socialist competition.

Statistics on workers

For many reasons, the party was vitally concerned about what kind of people were joining the swelling ranks of the industrial work force. Narkomtrud, the Statistical Department of VTsSPS, the Labor and Cadres Sector of Gosplan, and their union republic equivalents were thus kept busy compiling statistics about the ages, educational backgrounds, production experience (*stazh*), skill levels, sexual composition, and party saturation of the working class. Many of the tables contained in the core volumes of the series on industrialization can be found in earlier published compendia.[28] But quite a few, particularly those appearing in memoranda, are from archival sources, and together with the regional and republic-based collections, they offer a wealth of otherwise unavailable data for different parts of the country, branches of industry, and enterprises.

One aspect of working class formation that has escaped the attention of Western scholars was the "indigenization" (*korenizatsiia*) of white-collar positions. The collections on the Central Asia republics contain numerous tables showing the proportion of indigenous peoples enrolled in educational institutions and courses, among the industrial work force and in higher levels of the industrial hierarchy.[29]

Material conditions of workers

The volumes covering the Northwestern region for the years 1929–41 are exceptional in that they contain sections on the material conditions of workers. Housing space, wage levels, and patterns of consumption are the principal concerns addressed in the fifty documents included in these sections. Much of the information is conveyed via tables, some of which are quite detailed and revealing. For example, there is one on the per capita distribution of housing space among workers and all social groups in Leningrad between 1927 and 1935, and another comparing the quantity and cost of food products that a shock worker and an "experienced producer" were permitted to purchase with their ration cards between October 1934 and March 1935.[30]

No less revealing in its own way is the speech delivered by S. M. Kirov in June 1934 to the Leningrad party gorkom on the housing and food situations. The speech is a litany of complaints about the systematic underfulfillment of the plan for housing construction ("our shame"), the disrepair of many schools and other public buildings, the second-class status of food processing workers, cooks and waiters, and the "impassable filth" in enterprise cafeterias.[31] An example of the demagogy of the regional party boss, no doubt, but the complaints ring true, and not only for the mid–1930s!

Socialist competition

The elimination of unemployment and the narrowing of wage differentials during the First Five-Year Plan placed a premium on other kinds of incentives to increase productivity, lower turnover, and raise labor discipline. Mock displays on boards of shame, fines, and demotions recommended by comrades' courts at the enterprise, and administrative measures, up to and including the denial to "labor truants" of rations and living space in enterprise dormitories were just some of the negative incentives employed. Positive inducements mainly took the form of socialist competition, that is, the assumption by workers of certain obligations over and above what was stipulated in their contracts or set as targets in the enterprise plan and challenges to other workers to emulate or surpass their example.

Virtually every collection devotes considerable space to documents on socialist competition and some are about nothing else. The most numerous and, it must be confessed, the least interesting are the letters and telegrams reporting the completion of a task or plan ahead of schedule or some other achievement. Yet even these are potentially useful. Aside from conveying the changing nature of labor activism, many contain references to the ages, occupations, and skill levels of the workers involved. Thus, one cannot help but notice the preponderance of young semi-skilled and skilled production workers among the shock brigades of the late 1920s and the critical role played by the Komsomol in organizing and sustaining competition among them.

From the spring of 1929, when socialist competition began to be organized on a mass scale, the number of participants and shock workers in a particular factory or region became a criterion for judging the activeness of trade union and party organizations. However, at least some of the challenges issued in the name of workers and certain forms of competition were regarded by enterprise management as unwelcome intrusions into its sphere of competence and disruptive of production flows. Not surprisingly, "parading," "phony shock work" (*lzheudarnichestvo*), and padding of numbers often entered into reports. My favorite example of the latter comes from the Petrovskii Metallurgical Factory in Dnepropetrovsk. According to a resolution passed by the party's Central Committee on 7 May 1933, shock workers outnumbered the total work force employed in the forge shop of the factory.[32]

Still, in the surveys of shock workers and Stakhanovites carried out by higher trade union and party organizations one can find relatively reliable sociological data. In seeking to define "Who were the shock workers?" Hiroaki Kuromiya drew upon such data.[33] And in my own attempt to correlate Stakhanovite status with skills levels, data from the Dzerzhinskii Metallurgical Factory combined with aggregate figures compiled by Gosplan, led me to conclude that "in this branch of industry the average skill grade of Stakhanovites was perhaps only slightly higher than that of other workers."[34]

Finally, such documents provide a window onto the variety of forms that competition assumed, the degree to which they were shaped by officially determined priorities, and the kinds of bonuses and other rewards distributed to outstanding workers. They thus comprise an essential source for understanding the officially sanctioned work culture, if not the extent to which that culture took hold among rank and file workers.

Conclusion

To return to a point made at the outset, the state administration of archival holdings in the Soviet Union presents both difficulties and opportunities to Western researchers, both of which are reflected in the collections under review here. It would not do to minimize the problems—even the dangers—associated with using collections of pre-selected documents. Clearly, the extent to which one can generalize from this published material or assume its representativeness is limited by the very process of selectivity. Moreover, one should never lose sight of the fact that these are for the most part official documents, portraying official versions of a complex and often elusive reality.

Yet, if used in conjunction with other sources on industrialization that are available in the Soviet Union as well as in Western countries, these collections can enrich one's understanding of that reality. Not to avail oneself of them because of their limitations would be a grave error indeed.

Notes

1. Patricia Kennedy Grimsted, "Archival Resources for Social History of the 1920s and 1930s: Soviet Archival Developments and Reference Aids for the Social Historian," *Russian History/Histoire russe* 12: 2–4 (1985), 152.

2. For sensible advice about preparation for Soviet archival work, see Lynne Viola's article, "Archival Research in the USSR: A Practical Guide for Historians," in the present volume.

3. The collections are respectively *Politicheskii i trudovoi pod"em rabochego klassa v SSSR (1928–29)* (Moscow, 1956); *Pervye shagi industrializatsii SSSR (1926–1927)* (Moscow, 1959); *Pervyi Vsesoiuznyi s"ezd udarnykh brigad (K tridtsatiletiiu s"ezda). Sbornik dokumentov i materialov* (Moscow, 1959); *Marsh udarnykh brigad. Molodezh' v gody vosstanovleniia narodnogo khoziaistva i sotsialisticheskogo stroitel'stva. 1921–1941 gg. Sbornik dokumentov* (Moscow, 1965); *Sotsialisticheskoe sorevnovanie v SSSR, 1918–1964 gg. Dokumenty i materialy profsoiuzov* (Moscow, 1965); and *Profsoiuzy SSSR. Dokumenty i materialy*, 5 vols. (Moscow, 1963–73).

4. *Dokumenty trudovoi slavy Moskvichei, 1919–1965* (Moscow, 1967); *Kommunisty Leningrada v bor'be za vypolnenie reshenii partii po industrializatsii strany (1926–1932)* (Leningrad, 1960); *Sotsialisticheskoe sorevnovanie na predpriiatiiakh Leningrada v period pervoi piatiletki (1928–1932)* (Leningrad, 1961); *Pokolenie udarnikov. Sbornik dokumentov i materialov o sotsialisticheskom sorevnovanii na predpriiatiiakh Leningrada v 1928–1961 gg.* (Leningrad, 1963); *Bor'ba trudiashchikhsia Khar'kovshchiny za sozdanie fundamenta*

sotsialisticheskoi ekonomiki (1926–1932) (Kharkov, 1960); *Saratovskaia partiinaia organizatsiia v gody sotsialisticheskoi industrializatsii strany i podgotovka sploshnoi kollektivizatsii sel'skogo khoziaistva (1926–1929)* (Saratov, 1960); *Komsomol'tsy i molodezh' Ivanovskoi oblasti v gody stroitel'stva sotsializma (1921–1940 gg). Sbornik dokumentov i materialov* (Ivanovo, 1967).

5. The core volumes are entitled *Industrializatsiia SSSR . . . gg. Dokumenty i materialy.* The entire series appears under the title *Istoriia industrializatsii SSSR 1926–1941 gg. Dokumenty i materialy.*

6. *Zheleznodorozhnyi transport v vosstanovitel'nyi period* (Moscow, 1979) and *Zheleznodorozhnyi transport v gody industrializatsii SSSR* (Moscow, 1970).

7. As of 1969, collections for the Bashkir and Buriat Autonomous Republics and the Far Eastern krai were reported as being in preparation, but to date they have not been published. See Z. K. Zvezdin and V. E. Poletaev, "O seriinom izdanii dokumentov po istorii industrializatsii SSSR," *Arkheograficheskii ezhegodnik za 1967* (Moscow, 1969), 250. Zvezdin served as compiler of the four core volumes, and Poletaev was chief editor of the second volume covering the period 1929–32. Both were members of the editorial board for the entire series.

8. *Promyshlennost' i rabochii klass Ukrainskoi SSR. 1945–1958 gg.* (Kiev, 1984); *Sotsialisticheskaia industrializatsiia i razvitie rabochego klassa sovetskoi Moldavii, 1926–1958 gg. Sbornik dokumentov i materialov* (Kishinev, 1970); *Iz istorii industrial'nogo razvitiia Tadzhikskoi SSR (1941–1958 gg.)* (Dushanbe, 1981). As of 1982, volumes on postwar industrial development in Uzbekistan, Kazakhstan, Armenia, Turkmenia, and Estonia were in preparation. S. S. Khromov, "Podgotovka obshchesoiuznoi serii dokumentov po istorii promyshlennosti i rabochego klassa," *Sovetskie arkhivy* 4 (1982), 15.

9. Geographical indices of industrial enterprises are provided in *Politicheskii i trudovoi pod"em* and *Pervye shagi industrializatsii.*

10. *Zavershenie vosstanovleniia promyshlennosti i nachalo industrializatsii Severo-Zapadnogo raiona (1925–1928 gg.)* (Leningrad, 1964); *Industrializatsiia Severo-Zapadnogo raiona v gody pervoi piatiletki (1929–1932 gg.)* (Leningrad, 1967); and *Industrializatsiia Severo-Zapadnogo raiona v gody vtoroi i tret'ei piatiletok (1933–1941 gg.)* (Leningrad, 1969).

11. Zvezdin and Poletaev, "O seriinom izdanii dokumentov," 250–53. For documentary collections of resolutions and directives relating to industrialization, see *Sbornik vazhneishikh zakonov i postanovlenii o trude* (Moscow, 1958), and the appropriate volumes in *Kommunisticheskaia partiia Sovetskogo Soiuza v rezoliutsiiakh i resheniiakh s"ezdov, konferentsii i plenumov TsK* (various editions); *Direktivy KPSS i sovetskogo pravitel'stva po khoziaistvennym voprosam* (Moscow, 1957); and *Resheniia partii i pravitel'stva po khoziaistvennym voprosam* (Moscow, 1967).

12. See resolution of the Central Committee VKP(b) "On the preparation and instruction of the work force" (11 March 1926), and n. 40 in *Industrializatsiia SSSR, 1926–1928 gg. Dokumenty i materialy* (Moscow, 1969), 341–42, 503. Another example would be I. P. Rumiantsev, whose name is absent from the documents and notes in *Istoriia industrializatsii Zapadnogo raiona, 1926–1937 gg.* (Briansk, 1972), despite the fact that he served as party obkom secretary from 1934 until his arrest in June 1937.

13. "Resolution of the second plenum of the Northern Caucasus kraikom of the VKP(b), 'On the Shakhty affair,' " *Istoriia industrializatsii Severnogo Kavkaza 1926–1932 gg.* (Groznyi, 1971), 200–203. It should be noted, however, that six documents relating to the affair were published in *Politicheskii i trudovoi pod"em*, 46–52. See also "Resolution of general conference at 'Red Profintern' factory with demand for taking strictest measures against participants in the Shakhty affair and strengthening vigilance on the job" (22 March 1928), *Istoriia industrializatsii Zapadnogo raiona, 1926–1937 gg.*, 121–22.

14. *Dokumenty trudovoi slavy Moskvichei*, 137.

15. For discussions of Soviet industrial statistics see E. H. Carr and R. W. Davies, *Foundations of a Planned Economy*, vol. 1 (Harmondsworth: Penguin, 1969), 990–95; Alec

Nove, *An Economic History of the USSR* (London: Allen Lane, 1969), 192–94, 226, 381–88.

16. Alec Nove, *The Soviet Economic System* (London: Allen & Unwin, 1977), 352.

17. "From Gosplan's survey on the fulfillment of the economic plan for 1931," *Industrializatsiia SSSR, 1929–1932 gg. Dokumenty i materialy* (Moscow, 1970), 272–331, and "Information of TsUNKhU SSSR on output of the most important industrial goods for 1928/9–1932," *ibid.*, 342–46.

18. *Industrializatsiia SSSR, 1929–32*, 315.

19. "Statement of the information bulletin 'Leningrad Industry' on the improvement of quality of shoes" (28 April 1932), *Industrializatsiia Severo-Zapadnogo raiona . . . 1929–32*, 166.

20. See "Information of Lenoblplan on the share of Leningrad industry in the industry of the USSR" (21 Nov. 1936), *Industrializatsiia Severo-Zapadnogo raiona . . . 1933–41*, 158–59; "From a memorandum of the Western administration of economic accounting to the regional executive committee on the results of industrial development of the region during the First and Second Five-Year Plans" (24 July 1936), *Istoriia industrializatsii Zapadnogo raiona, 1926–37*, 532; "Information on the share of Kazakhstan in the production of major food products for 1933–1935," *Istoriia industrializatsii Kazakhskoi SSR (1933–iiun' 1941 gg.)* (Alma-Ata, 1967), 106.

21. See, for example, "List of new and reconstructed industrial works in the system of NKTP, entering operations in 1931–1934" (end of 1934), *Promyshlennost' i rabochii klass Ukrainskoi SSR, 1933–1941. Sbornik dokumentov i materialov v dvukh chastiakh*, vol. 1 (Kiev, 1977), 272–82; "List of reconstructed and newly constructed enterprises in the territory of the Western Region for 1929–1934" (April 1935), *Istoriia industrializatsii Zapadnogo raiona, 1926–37*, 483–88.

22. "From a memorandum of Narkomtrud SSSR to Sovnarkom SSSR on the organization of labor and the system of wages" (29 Oct. 1931), *Industrializatsiia SSSR, 1929–32*, 262–63.

23. "Information on the results of the reorganization of state industrial administration by the administrative office of Sovnarkom SSSR" (16 June 1930), *Industrializatsiia SSSR, 1929–32*, 219–21.

24. See documents Nos. 10, 13, 14, 20, 21, 69, 83, and 89 in *Promyshlennost' i rabochii klass Ukrainskoi SSR*, vol. 1.

25. "From a memorandum of the Fuel-Energy Section of Gosplan SSSR on the results of the Second [Five-Year Plan] and plans for the Third Five-Year Plan for fuel" (17 May 1937), *Industrializatsiia SSSR, 1933–1937 gg. Dokumenty i materialy* (Moscow, 1971), 335.

26. "From a resolution of SNK SSSR and TsK VKP(b) 'On work of the coal industry of the Donbass'" (31 March 1940), *Industrializatsiia SSSR, 1938–1941 gg. Dokumenty i materialy* (Moscow, 1973), 110.

27. See, however, *Politicheskii i trudovoi pod"em*, 215, 249; and "Informational report of Kizelov raikom VKP(b) to Verkhne-Kamsk okruzhkom VKP(b) on development of socialist competition" (10 June 1929), *Istoriia industrializatsii Urala, 1926–1932 gg. Sbornik dokumentov* (Sverdlovsk, 1967), 444.

28. See the statistical series published in the 1930s under the titles *Trud v SSSR, Sotsialisticheskoe stroitel'stvo SSSR* and *Statisticheskii spravochnik VTsSPS*.

29. *Istoriia industrializatsii Kazakhskoi SSR (1926–1932 gg.)* (Alma-Ata, 1967), 329–31, 363–64, 383–95; *Istoriia industrializatsii Kazakhskoi SSR (1933–iiun' 1941)*, 150, 198–200; *Istoriia industrializatsii Kirgizskoi SSR (1926–1941 gg.). Dokumenty i materialy* (Frunze, 1972), 251–52, 465; *Istoriia industrializatsii Turkmenskoi SSR, 1926–1941 gg. Dokumenty i materialy* in two volumes (Ashkhabad, 1978), 1: 153–54, 165–66; 2: 25–26.

30. *Industrializatsiia Severo-Zapadnogo raiona . . . 1933–41*, 298, 301.

31. "Speech of secretary of Leningrad obkom and gorkom VKP(b), S. M. Kirov, to plenum of Leningrad gorkom on housing construction and public catering in Leningrad" (11 June 1934), *ibid.*, 189–92.

32. "Resolution of TsK VKP(b) 'On the work of the party organization of the metallurgi-

cal factory named after Petrovskii (Dnepropetrovsk)'" (7 May 1933), *Promyshlennost' i rabochii klass Ukrainskoi SSR, 1933-1937*, 51.

33. Hiroaki Kuromiya, *Stalin's Industrial Revolution. Politics and Workers, 1928-1932* (Cambridge, 1988), 319-23.

34. Lewis H. Siegelbaum, *Stakhanovism and the Politics of Productivity in the USSR, 1935-1941* (Cambridge, 1988), 176-77.

Laws and Administrative Acts
Sources and Finding Aids

PETER H. SOLOMON, Jr.

For many historians of the USSR navigating and understanding the laws of the Soviet state has constituted a hard, if not bewildering task. To a degree this situation was unavoidable. Like other large, federal governments, the government of the USSR issued a wide variety of laws, edicts, and administrative acts. At the same time, though, mastering the laws of the USSR involves special difficulties.

First, the structure of Soviet government and its bureaucracy changed frequently, sometimes in fundamental ways. Consequently, the researcher bent on using legal sources had to know institutional history.[1]

Second, whatever hierarchy of laws and administrative acts existed in theory, the agencies of government often ignored legal constraints. Throughout the 1920s and 1930s local governments issued ordinances that exceeded their powers. Procuracy officials struggled to identify and correct these breaches of higher law.[2] For their part, the central agencies, that is commissariats of the USSR and RSFSR, regularly issued directives and instructions that went beyond the implementation of laws, creating new rules, some of which contradicted legislation. Performing a kind of constitutional review, the Supreme Court of the USSR during the 1920s declared 86 agency directives to be illegal. (The Court gave similar rulings on 11 laws from republican governments.)[3]

Third, the edicts of the party Central Committee and its subordinate bodies came to assume an importance in the practice of public administration, especially in the period of collectivization, higher than most laws. This happened despite the fact that party pronouncements had no status in law.[4]

Finally, the actual implementation of most laws—even without distortions from administrative acts or party resolutions—remained problematic. The officials charged with executing laws and administrative acts often lacked the resources to implement all of them. In addition, they faced pressures that made some laws or directives more important than others. No historian of the USSR can afford to take laws at face value. It is necessary to discover how particular laws and acts were implemented.

Historians of the USSR in the period after World War II face an additional challenge. By 1945 a significant minority of laws and the bulk of administrative acts were no longer being published in forms accessible to the researcher. Fortunately for the historian of the interwar period, almost all of the laws and most administrative acts did receive open publication. Not only the governments of the USSR and the union republics, but also those of most provinces and cities published laws and ordinances in journals or bulletins. Most commissariats published their directives and instructions in journals, bulletins, and collections. Obviously, there were exceptions, such as regulations relating to the military, internal security, and some operations of the Communist Party. Examining the Smolensk Archive gives the historian an appreciation of the extent and limits of secrecy in party documents.[5]

The purpose of this brief survey is to offer assistance to historians of the interwar period in the USSR in locating laws, administrative acts, and party decrees relating to particular topics. The discussion will focus upon primary sources for this material and on aids in finding laws and acts on particular topics.

I. Sources of legislation and administrative acts

A. Legislation of the central government

Like the official Soviet sources in the 1920s and 1930s, we treat as legislation all laws (*dekrety, zakony*) and decrees (*postanovleniia*) issued by the Central Executive Committee (TsIK) or its Presidium and by the All-Russian Central Executive Committee (VTsIK) or its Presidium, and the edicts (*postanovleniia, ukazy*) issued by the Sovnarkom SSSR, Sovnarkom RSFSR, and the Sovet Truda i Oborony (STO).

For the official texts of all legislation so defined see:

(1) for the USSR: *Sobranie zakonov i rasporiazhenii raboche-krest'ianskogo pravitel'stva SSSR* (Moscow, 1924–1938);

(2) for the RSFSR: *Sobranie uzakonenii raboche-krest'ianskogo pravitel'stva RSFSR* (Moscow, 1917–1938).[6]

Both of these publications contain (in addition to the laws and decrees of the top government bodies) a small number of administrative acts issued by commissariats. By virtue of their publication in *SZ* or *SU* these acts assumed the status of government edicts (equivalent to decrees of the corresponding Sovnarkom). It was also customary to publish the texts of many laws in a government newspaper, first and foremost *Izvestiia*, but also in the case of edicts of the Sovet Truda i Oborony in *Ekonomicheskaia gazeta*.

B. Directives of the People's Commissariats of the USSR and RSFSR

During the 1920s and 1930s most commissariats published their directives and instructions in a journal, bulletin, or series of collections. Thus, the Russian Commissariat of Labor (Narkomtrud RSFSR) published its administrative acts in its journal *Voprosy truda* (1920–1933), and the Russian Commissariat of Justice (Narkomiust RSFSR), published its edicts in *Ezhenedel'nik sovetskoi iustitsii* (1922–1930) and its successor *Sovetskaia iustitsiia*[7] (1930–1941). The directives of the Commissariat of Health (Narkomzdrav) appeared for a time as a supplement to the journal *Voprosy zdravookhraneniia* and later as a separate publication, *Ofitsial'nyi sbornik Narkomzdrava*. The Commissariat of Education (Narkompros) published its directives and instructions in its *Ezhenedel'nik*, later *Biulleten'*, and finally in a separate publication (covering the years 1918–1946). The agency responsible for police, prisons, fire departments, and urban development in the RSFSR, Narkomvnudel, published its voluminous output of decrees in *Biulleten' NKVD*.

After the demise of this commissariat at the end of 1930, the new Commissariat of Urban Development (*Narkom kommunal'nogo khoziaistva*) published its own *Sbornik prikazov i instruktsii* on an annual basis (1931–1941).

For full citations to these and other official vehicles for publishing the administrative acts of any particular commissariat, the researcher should consult *Half a Century of Soviet Serials*, a guide that not only lists most of the periodical publications of the agencies but also North American locations.[8]

In addition to their regular outlets, some commissariats issued occasional collections of administrative acts. These collections might cover the totality of an agency's directives in force at a given time or focus upon those relating to a particular subject. Thus, Narkpmiust published *sborniki* in 1926–1927, 1931, 1934, 1940, and 1948. The USSR Procuracy issued collections of its directives in 1936 and in 1938/39. Narkomvnudel RSFSR issued three specialized collections in 1928 and 1929 dealing with prisons, policing, and criminal investigation.[9] Most of these irregular and specialized collections of administrative acts do not appear in *Half a Century* and must be located through the Cyrillic Union Catalogue and the bibliographical aids for finding Soviet books (such as *Ezhenedel'nik knig*).

C. Laws, ordinances, and administrative acts of republican, provincial, and local governments

The governments of the republics other than the RSFSR and of autonomous republics within the RSFSR published bulletins and collections of laws analogous to those of the USSR and RSFSR, although not always on an annual basis and not always in Russian languages editions. For an exhaustive list of these publications, see *Periodicheskaia pechat' SSSR, 1917–1949*.[10]

Many of the laws of the republics also appeared in republican journals on soviets and institution-building (*stroitel'stvo*), but these journals were invariably in the native language and (with the exception of the Ukraine) had only short runs.

The laws, ordinances, and administrative acts from provincial and city governments found an outlet in the journals and bulletins of the provincial and city soviet executive committees (*gubispolkomy, oblispolkomy, kraiispolkomy,* and *gorispolkomy*). Many of these publications were called bulletins even though they published articles as well as laws (e.g., *Biulleten' Voronezhskogo gubernskogo ispolnitel'nogo komiteta*, 1921–1928). Other provincial journals had more descriptive names (e.g.,

Rabota sovetov, published biweekly by the Voronezh oblast soviet executive committee in 1928 and 1930–1933). Other bulletins and collections, published regularly or irregularly, included only laws and administrative acts (e.g., *Sbornik vazhneishikh postanovlenii prezidiuma i sekretariata Voronezhskogo gorodskogo soveta*, 1933–1936 and *Sbornik postanovlenii i rasporiazhenii prezidiuma Zapadno-Sibirskogo kraiispolkoma i ego otdelov i upravlenii*, Novosibirsk, 1931–1937). For a full listing of this genre of publications, see *Periodicheskaia pechat' v SSSR*.[11]

D. Specialized collections of laws and administrative acts

Collections of laws and directives focused upon particular subjects fall into three groups.

First, to help the officials administering laws and regulations, commissariats and agencies often published collections of a narrow profile. These included such areas as social security, housing, family problems, wages, work discipline, and labor safety.[12] Second, for officials whose jobs required information about laws and administrative acts in a variety of areas, it was common for publishers to issue handbooks (*spravochniki*): for example, handbooks for members and employees of local soviets, for factory managers, for officials of the Worker-Peasant Inspectorate (Rabkrin), and for judges and procurators.[13] Finally, there were the retrospective historical collections of laws. Whether to satisfy the needs of scholars or students in higher education, in the post-Stalin period scholars complied collections of legislation in particular fields that covered decades of Soviet history. Such collections dealt with the history of Soviet government in general, criminal law, corrective-labor law, land law, and kolkhoz law.[14] As a rule these historical collections included only legislation and contained no reference to the regulations and directives issued by agencies.

For a complete listing by subject matter of all of these specialized collections, see the invaluable guide by V. V. Antonov, *Sovetskoe zakonodatel'stvo. Spravochnikputevoditel' po osnovnym izdaniiam*.[15]

E. Party decrees

Edicts and instructions from the Central Committee of the Communist (Bolshevik) Party and resolutions of its plenary sessions had no status as law, but as authoritative statements of policy, assumed great normative significance. In the period of the collectivization and industrialization drives, party pronouncements all but replaced the law on the statute books, and after 1936 party decrees still had an importance equal to law. Often, laws were issued to implement the content of party resolutions, and laws of this sort might have greater authority than other laws. To recognize the relative status of particular laws (and the likelihood of their implementation), the researcher should know the party decrees relating to particular laws.

The publication of party decrees in the 1920s and 1930s was entirely separate from that of laws and administrative acts. All party decrees and resolutions (with the exception of those classified as secret) were published first in the journal *Izvestiia TsK VKP(b)* and its successor after 1929, *Partiinoe stroitel'stvo*, under the rubric *"Ofitsial'nyi otdel"* or *"V Tsentral'nyi Komitet VKP(b)."* In addition, the same decrees and resolutions of Central Committee plenums were reprinted in the *Spravochnik partiinogo rabotnika* which appeared on an irregular basis eight times between 1921 and 1936. While in the 1920s most of these decrees related to the internal life of the party itself and its guiding role in the soviets, trade unions, and cooperatives, in the 1930s a substantial proportion of the decrees related to party guidance in the economy. In contrast to the new series of *Spravochnik partiinogo rabotnika* of the 1950s, 1960s, 1970s, and 1980s, which contained many laws and decrees of the Council of Ministers, the spravochniki of the 1920s and 1930s contained exclusively party decrees and resolutions.

The decrees of republican, provincial, and local party committees appeared in the journals of those bodies. To find their names and periods of publication, consult *Periodicheskaia pechat'*.[16]

II. Finding aids

A. Guides and indexes to official publications

Three of the major journals on law and government during the 1920s and 1930s contained guides or indexes to legislation and administrative acts.

(1) *Vlast' sovetov* (1917–1938) published a survey of these materials arranged by subject area (e.g., finance, agriculture, communal economy, education, health, and so on). The title of the survey varied from *"Obzor postanovlenii i rasporiazhenii raboche-krest'ianskogo pravitel'stva i vazhneishikh vedomstvennykh actov SSSR i RSFSR,"* to *"Obzor opublikovannykh zakonov . . . i postanovlenii narkomatov SSSR i RSFSR,"* to *"Obzor zakonodatel'stva SSSR i RSFSR,"* but at all times included administrative acts. The survey gave titles and references to the place of publication (usually *Izvestiia* or *Sobranie zakonov*).

(2) *Sovetskoe stroitel'stvo* (1928–1937) published an index to the legislation not only of the USSR and RSFSR but also of all the union republics. Under the title *"Sistematicheskii perechen' postanovlenii TsIK i SNK SSSR, prezidiuma TsIK SSSR, SNK SSSR i STO, TsIKov i SNK'ov i Presidium TsIK'ov soiuznykh respublik po ofitsial'nym materialam,"* the journal listed laws by subject area (education, health, etc.) and gave references to the texts both in newspapers and official editions, from the center and the republics. Note that this index covers laws only and does not include administrative acts.[17]

(3) *Ezhenedel'nik sovetskoi iustitsii* (1922–29) and its successor *Sovetskaia iustitsiia* (1930–1941). This journal also contained monthly surveys of legislation by subject matter, for the USSR and RSFSR, that included some administrative acts. The stress in these selective surveys is on the economy. References, sometimes including summaries of the laws in question, cite locations in newspapers and

official publications. The heading varies: *"Obzor zakonodatel'stva,"* *"Tekushchee zakonodatel'stvo i narkomatskoe praktika."*

In addition, a number of indexes to legislation were published as books, often in multiple editions. These include two formidable volumes compiled under the direction of A. M. Iodkovskii. Both of these chronological lists of laws contained detailed subject indexes.[18] For references to other indexes and guides, see Antonov, *Sovetskoe zakonodatel'stvo.*[19]

B. Guides to publications of laws and administrative acts

1. V. V. Antonov, *Sovetskoe zakonodatel'stvo. Spravochnik-putevoditel' po osnovnym izdaniiam* (Moscow, 1981). An annotated guide to all publications of laws of the USSR and RSFSR, 1917–1979. Includes an introduction dealing with the types of laws, their hierarchy, and sources. Divides references into general (universal) publications and thematic ones. Also includes bibliographies of scholarly literature on various areas of law. Within each category, the guide lists publications in reverse chronological order. Most items include a brief description of the publication and its coverage. An essential item for any serious library in Soviet studies.

2. *Periodicheskaia pechat' SSSR. 1917–1949. Bibliograficheskii ukazatel'.* 9 volumes (Moscow, 1958). This authoritative publication includes references to the journals and legislative bulletins of commissariats and central agencies and provincial and local governments, as well as party bodies at all levels. Virtually the only guide to the laws and ordinances of governments below the republican level. Lists publications only; does not provide descriptions of their contents.

3. *Half A Century of Soviet Serials, 1917–1968. A Bibliography and Union List of Serials Published in the USSR.* Compiled by Rudolph Smits. 2 volumes (Washington, D.C.: Library of Congress, 1968). Drawing on a variety of Soviet sources, Smits listed not only journals, but also many collections of administrative acts of commissariats, both regular and irregular. The bibliography also reproduced the references to most provincial and local government journals listed in *Periodicheskaia pechat'*. Besides giving bibliographical coverage, *Half a Century* also recorded North American locations known to the compiler.

Notes

1. See A. A. Nelidov, *Istoriia gosudarstvennykh uchrezhdenii SSSR, 1917–1936 g.* (Moscow, 1962); V. A. Tsikulin, *Istoriia gosudarstvennykh uchrezhdenii SSSR, 1936–1965* (Moscow, 1966); and T. P. Korzhikhina, *Istoriia gosudarstvennykh uchrezhdenii SSSR* (Moscow, 1986).

2. Glenn G. Morgan, *Soviet Administrative Legality. The Role of the Attorney General's Office* (Stanford: Stanford Univ. Press, 1962).

3. T. N. Dobrovolskaia, *Verkhovnyi sud SSSR* (Moscow, 1964), 18–32; Peter H. Solomon, Jr., "The USSR Supreme Court: History, Role and Future Prospects," unpublished paper, June 1988.

4. Peter H. Solomon, Jr., "Local Political Power and Soviet Criminal Justice, 1922–41," *Soviet Studies* 37:3 (1985), 305–29.

5. See *The Smolensk Archive* and *Guide to the Records of the Smolensk Oblast of the All-Union Communist Party of the Soviet Union, 1917–41* (Washington, D.C.: National Archives and Records Service, General Services Administration, 1980).

6. Because of the reorganization of Soviet government produced by implementation of the new Constitution of 1936, these publications were replaced in 1938 by *Vedomosti Verkhovnogo Soveta SSSR* (and . . . *RSFSR*) and *Sobranie postanovlenii pravitel'stva SSSR* (and . . . *RSFSR*).

7. From 1936, Narkomiust SSSR also published its edicts in this journal.

8. *Half A Century of Soviet Serials. A Bibliography and Union List of Serials Published in the USSR.* Complied by Rudolph Smits. 2 vols. (Washington, D.C.: Library of Congress, 1968).

9. *Sbornik tsirkuliarov Narkomiusta RSFSR za 1922–1926 gg.* 2 vols. (Moscow, 1926–1927); *Sbornik tsirkuliarov Narodnogo Komissariata Iustitsii RSFSR* (Moscow, 1931); *Sbornik tsirkuliarov i raz'iasnenii Narodnogo Komissariata Iustitsii RSFSR* (Moscow, 1934); *Sbornik prikazov i instruktsii SSSR* (Moscow, 1949).

Sbornik tsirkuliarov i raz'iasnenii prokuratury SSSR deistvuiushchikh na 1 sent. 1936 goda, ed. Solers and Orlov (Moscow, 1936); *Sbornik prikazov prokuratury SSSR deistvuiushchikh na 1 dek. 1938 g.* (Moscow, 1939).

Deistvuiushchie rasporiazheniia po mestam zakliucheniia. Sistematicheskii sbornik s poiasneniiami, ed. B. S. Utevskii (Moscow, 1929); *Deistvuiushchie rasporiazheniia po militsii*, ed. I. F. Kiselev (Moscow, 1928); *Deistvuiushchie rasporiazheniia po ugolovnomu rozysku*, ed. N. A. Nikolaevskii (Moscow, 1928).

10. *Periodicheskaia pechat' SSSR, 1917–1949. Bibliograficheskii ukazatel'*, vyp.1 (Moscow, 1958), 197–208.

11. *Ibid.*, 173–213.

12. See the collections listed by subject heading in V. V. Antonov, *Sovetskoe zakonodatel'stvo. Spravochnik-putevoditel' po osnovnym izdaniiam* (Moscow, 1981), 62–178.

13. *Ibid.*, 173–213.

14. *Ibid.*, 64–69, and items number 373, 399, 561, 579.

15. *Ibid.*

16. A. M. Iodkovskii, *Khronologicheskii perechen' zakonov SSSR za 1923–1933 gody* (Moscow, 1934) and *Khronologicheskii perechen' zakonov RSFSR, deistvuiushchikh na 1 ianvaria 1933 g.* (Moscow, 1933).

17. Note that issue 2 of 1936 of *Sistematicheskii perechen'* contains a list of the official statutes governing the operation of all agencies of the government of the RSFSR: "*Perechen' postanovlenii pravitel'stva RSFSR o tsentral'nykh i mestnykh organakh vlasti i nakhodiashchikh pri nikh uchrezhdeniiakh na 7.1 1935 god.*"

18. *Periodicheskaia pechat' v SSSR*, vol. 1, 9–36.

19. Antonov, *Sovetskoe zakonodatel'stvo*, 34–37.

Statistical Sources for the Study of
Soviet Social History in the Prewar Period

S. G. WHEATCROFT

Statistics have very seldom been collected for purely historical analysis. They have normally been collected to assist in such functions as administration, planning, and levying taxes. The historian by the very nature of his subject is forced to use other people's statistics. He cannot redesign the surveys and questionnaires that were used in the past, he cannot measure things that were not measured or affect the timing and location of those surveys, censuses, investigations, and registrations that were carried out. He has to make the best use of what statistical data and accounts are available to him. However, before he begins using these data he should attempt to discover how the data were collected and calculated, and by whom these operations were carried out. He should attempt to see why specific operations were carried out in the way that they were, and whether there are any reasons for doubting the reliability of these data. Where doubts do arise as to their reliability, he should attempt to make an assessment of the possible scale of the inaccuracy. It is extremely dangerous to accept any figures on trust without understanding their origin and history.

Western historians working on the social history of the USSR in the prewar period are in an unusual position concerning statistical data. On the one hand they have the advantage of dealing with a country that had a well-developed central statistical agency and was gathering and publishing data on all sorts of social phenomena. This was unique for a country of such scale and social backwardness. On the other hand, they have the disadvantage of knowing that there is considerable uncertainty over the reliability of some of these data, and that until recently there had been no possibility of checking the original sources in the archives.[1]

In order to assess the reliability of these statistical data, the Western historian has to resort to available Soviet[2] published materials on the collection and calculation of these statistics, as well as analyzing the statistics themselves in terms of internal consistency and compatibility with other data. In this article, I will begin by giving a brief outline of some of the general sources of data on statistical materials, and a summary of the main developments in the central statistical agencies during this period, before considering the statistical sources available for the main kinds of subjects of interest to social historians. This article is primarily concerned with central state statistics, although a few examples of other statistics are mentioned.

General sources of data on statistical materials

The main source of data on statistical materials are the notes and appendices that accompany the published figures. In the 1920s, the accompanying appendices and notes were often very detailed, especially in the more technical statistical publications such as the Central Statistical Administration's series, *Trudy TsSU*. In later publications, however, and particularly in the late 1930s, these technical notes tended to disappear or become very abbreviated. The professional statistical journals are also a major source of information on how statistics were collected and processed, and also on their comparability with other data. Until 1929, these journals were very lively and outspoken in their criticism of certain procedures and practices. In the 1930s, there still were a surprisingly large number of critical letters and reports printed at different times.

The main central statistical journals are:

Vestnik statistiki, organ of TsSU (Tsentral'noe statisticheskoe upravlenie SSSR), 1919–1929, and 1949 on;[3]

Biulleten' TsSU, organ of TsSU, 1919–1926;

Statisticheskoe obozrenie, organ of TsSU, 1927–1930;

Narodnoe khoziaistvo SSSR, organ of TsUNKhU (Tsentral'noe upravlenie narod-no-khoziaistvennogo ucheta SSSR), 1932 (eight issues);

Plan, organ of TsUNKhU and Gosplan (Gosudarstvennaia planovaia komissiia SSSR), 1933–1937.

Apart from these central journals, there were numerous other journals published by local regional statistical agencies, the most important of which was *Statistika i narodnoe khoziaistvo* (Moscow: TsSU RSFSR, 1926–1930), the journal of the Central Statistical Administration of the Russian Republic. For other local statistical journals, see the bibliography of statistical publications by Mashikhin and Simchera.[4]

Several statistical manuals and detailed histories of different branches of statistics have been published in the USSR. A useful bibliography of works on the history of Soviet statistics for the period 1917–1970 was compiled by M. T. Goltsman and published in 1972.[5] The main modern general histories of Soviet state statistics, published in 1960 and 1969, both have sections on the history of statistics on population, labor, health and social security, education and culture, housing, and family budgets.[6] Earlier and more informative histories are available for statistical data published in the 1920s.[7] There also exist several books and collections of articles on separate branches of statistics.[8]

Apart from these historical works by statisticians and economists, there are also a number of interesting books on sources by Soviet historians.[9] Some of these books on sources are devoted exclusively to statistical materials, while others include articles on statistical sources together with articles on other types of sources.[10]

Summary of major developments
in Soviet central statistical agencies, 1926–1941

Until January 1926, the Central Statistical Administration (TsSU) was still largely under the control of former prerevolutionary zemstvo statisticians. There had been considerable rivalry between these statisticians and those in the State Planning Commission (Gosplan) over the reliability of certain statistics, planning methodology, and the need to carry out an expensive series of mid-term censuses. The pre–1926 TsSU leadership felt that it was necessary to carry out a series of mid-term censuses[11] on many aspects of the economy in order to provide a more accurate statistical basis for the ambitious planning projects that Gosplan wanted to launch. Faced with persistent government hostility over this and other statistical matters, P. I. Popov, the founding director of TsSU, resigned in January 1926.[12]

The new director of TsSU was V. V. Osinskii, an Old Bolshevik with some statistical experience and a great reputation within the party for political independence and Oppositionist activities.[13] Under Osinskii, TsSU was reformed, party control became stricter and there was greater cooperation with the statisticians in Gosplan.[14] The TsSU statisticians were reluctantly forced to give up their plan for a whole series of censuses and accept one national population census (held in December 1926) and a few minor censuses later.[15] The population census was, however, quite elaborate, involving questions on employment, education, and housing. In general, Osinskii appears to have defended the interests and objectivity of the statisticians, and his removal from office in the spring of 1928 was evidently a consequence of his support of the TsSU statisticians' views on agriculture, which were at odds with Stalin's claims on this subject.[16]

Osinskii was replaced by V. P. Miliutin, who appears not to have taken the job very seriously,[17] and was neither effective in controlling the statisticians nor active in defending their interests. Under Miliutin, TsSU was gradually starved of funds and so had to cut back on its publications, its studies of food consumption, and, of course, its ambitious program of censuses.[18] In the course of 1928 and 1929, both central and local statisticians became increasingly outspoken and critical of some of the statistical procedures being carried out.[19] Finally, TsSU's council of experts refused to inflate the figures evaluating the 1929 grain harvest evaluation and were purged.[20] A few months later, it was decided to close down the Central Statistical Administration entirely, abolish its network of voluntary correspondents and transfer most of its functions to the Statistical Economics Sector of Gosplan.[21]

The scale of central statistical work dropped sharply over the next two years. No general statistical handbooks or statistical journals were published. Several prominent statisticians, including V. G. Groman, were arrested and tried.[22] Independent statistical investigations and censuses were largely replaced by simple record-keeping operations, carried out by the separate People's Commissariats under the general supervision of the Gosplan statistics department, which was renamed the "Administration for National Economic Record-Keeping" (UNKhU) of Gosplan. This resulted in what Osinskii later described as "plan-constructivist distortions," which were distortions caused by substituting the plan target figures for target fulfillment regardless of the real state of affairs.[23]

At the end of 1931, it was decided to reverse the earlier policy on central statistics and reinstate a strong central statistical agency which would have some autonomy.[24] The new agency, TsUNKhU, still bore the title "Administration for National Economic Record-Keeping," but it was now a separate central agency, attached to Gosplan (*pri Gosplane*) but no longer a part of it. An equally significant sign of change and greater commitment to statistical objectivity was that Osinskii, known for his independent and critical attitude in the past, was reappointed director.[25] He immediately set about restoring the staff of statisticians and reassuring them of the break with "Plan constructivism."

During the first six months of 1932, several statistical handbooks were published,[26] work on the balance of the national economy was completed and published,[27] and a new monthly statistical journal, *Narodnoe Khoziaistvo SSSR*, was founded. Some erroneous figures on economic production used earlier were corrected,[28] and plans were made to carry out several censuses and to preserve statistical objectivity.[29]

Unfortunately, not all the aspects of this new improved statistical atmosphere survived the pressures of the next few years. A powerful Stalin supporter, Kraval, was appointed deputy to the politically independent Osinskii in January 1933; and in 1935 Kraval took over as director of TsUNKhU.[30] Even before that, however, Osinskii was forced to back down on his revised objective evaluations of agricultural production.[31] The demographic censuses were again postponed and Osinskii's new statistical journal ceased publication after just eight issues. A new statistical journal called *Plan*, edited by Kraval and somewhat more closely tied in with Gosplan, appeared in 1933, and a new series of statistical handbooks under the title *Sotsialisticheskoe stroitel'stvo* began publication in 1934. A national demographic census was eventually carried out under Kraval's leadership in 1937. In strange circumstances that will be discussed in more detail later, Kraval was accused of wrecking the 1937 census and arrested,[32] and the census results were never published. The statistical journal *Plan* and the *Sotsialisticheskoe stroitel'stvo* statistical handbooks ceased publication in the late 1930s, and many (though not all) statistical publications were discontinued as TsUNKhU was engulfed in the purges. It is unclear, however, whether the TsUNKhU purges were directly related to the agency's statistical and census-taking functions. They may have been primary directed against Kraval and other political figures, non-statisticians, who had been brought into TsUNKhU in the early 1930s. Undoubtedly some demographers (for example, Kvitkin) also suffered, but many survived, and there was a surprising resurgence of the old-time professionals within TsUNKhU.[33]

Later, once Voznesenskii took charge of Gosplan in 1938, the position in

TsUNKhU certainly appeared to improve as regards statistical work, although not as regards the publication of the results. The demographic census was finally carried out in 1939, but its results were only published in a most abbreviated form.[34] A general statistical handbook did appear in 1939 but this was far less detailed and informative than the earlier handbooks.[35]

Statistical sources on social-historical topics

Before discussing specific statistical sources for the main branches of social history, it will be useful to list those sources that cover all aspects of social history. The bibliography by Mashikhin and Simchera covers all statistical publications produced by TsSU and TsUNKhU in this period. These are classified under the following headings: population censuses; women, children, and youth; population numbers (registration data) and migration; health care; education and culture; labor and wages; consumption and budgets; housing conditions; and other specific economic branches (industry, agriculture, transport, etc.).[36] It must be emphasized, however, that these cover only the publications of TsSU and TsUNKhU, and that the statistical publications of other government bodies—individual People's Commissariats, Gosplan and the main state commissions—as well as the publications of non-state bodies such as the trade unions, the cooperatives, and the Communist Party are not included.

There are also a number of historical and archival journals and publications that specialize in reproducing rare statistical material with accompanying notes and explanations, some of which may well be of use to social historians working in this period. The main ones are:

Istoricheskie zapiski (Moscow, 1937–)

Materialy po istorii SSSR: Dokumenty po istorii sovetskogo obshchestva, 7 vols. (Moscow, 1955–1959)

Istochnikovedenie istorii sovetskogo obshchestva (Moscow, 1973, 1975–)

Several series of archival materials (including statistical materials) exist for different topics. For instance, the industrialization series *Industrializatsiia SSSR . . . gg. Dokumenty i materialy* (see Lewis Siegelbaum's article ''Guide to Document Series on Industrialization'' in this volume) contains a great deal of data on the working class, its composition (*sostav*), labor training, and participation in socialist competition. A trade union series (*Profsoiuzy SSSR. Dokumenty i materialy*, vol. 2, 1917–1937 [Moscow, 1963] and vol. 3, 1937–1952 [Moscow, 1963]) contains data on trade union membership and activities in these years. Similar volumes exist for different regions and republics. There is also a series of documents on collectivization in different regions of the USSR entitled *Kollektivisatsiia sel'skogo khoziaistva v . . . gg.* (see Lynne Viola's article ''Guide to Document Series on Collectivization'' in this volume).

Let us now turn to a description and analysis of the major types of statistics relevant to social history, namely demographic statistics, employment data, and statistics on class and socioeconomic differentiation.

Demographic statistics

There are basically three different kinds of demographic data: (i) census data, (ii) current registration data, and (iii) survey data.

Census data

Censuses are especially valuable because they cover the entire population and normally provide material on a wide range of topics of interest to social historians. As explained above, a mid-term census was carried out in the USSR in December 1926. Apart from the purely demographic questions of the number, age, and sex structure of the population, the census was also concerned with employment, unemployment, family conditions, place of birth, length of residence, rural/urban and geographical location, nationality, native language, literacy and, for the urban population, housing conditions, family structure, and social class.

The results of the 1926 census were published in very great detail; three preliminary volumes, numbering 121 pages in all, were published in 1927,[37] ten short complex volumes were published between 1927 and 1929, covering 1,013 pages,[38] and the final results were published in 56 volumes between 1928 and 1933, a total of well over 18,000 pages.[39] These materials, which are readily available in the West, provide a uniquely detailed basis for the social analysis of the country before the major social and economic transformations of the 1930s took place. Parts of these data have been analyzed at some length. V. P. Danilov has analyzed the agricultural population,[40] and L. I. Vaskina has analyzed the working class.[41] In the West, a demographer, Lorimer, and an economist, Eason, have also considered these materials in depth.[42]

Unfortunately, the 1926 census was not followed by any other comparable census. As explained above, there was no demographic census in 1930. A so-called "urban census" in 1931 was more of a registration than a real census, and its results were not systematically published.[43] The population census of 1937 was denounced as a product of wrecking, and no results from it were ever published.[44]

Recent searches in the Soviet archives have so far failed to discover any detailed materials from the 1937 census. However, a document that appears to be a draft of a Central Committee report on the 1937 census has been discovered in the personal archives of P. I. Popov.[45] This report was apparently drafted in early 1937 after the arrest of Kvitkin—the head of the TsUNKhU demographic sector—on 25 March 1937 but before the arrest of Kraval in May 1937. It revealed that the 1937 census had provided a total population figure of 162 million, which was not only lower than Gosplan's projection for population growth (180.7 million), and the implicit TsUNKhU population evaluations (which were of the same order of magnitude) but was also lower than the implicit figure based on registration data indications (which was much lower at 169.3 million). For a number of reasons, it was argued that the 1937 census had underestimated reality, but not by as much as might have seemed from Gosplan's projections and the TsUNKhU evaluations. It was estimated that the true level was probably 167–168 million. Although some emphasis was placed on the error of the census in underestimating reality, much more emphasis was placed on criticizing the TsUNKhU leadership for providing extreme overestimates of the current population size, of failing to withstand "plan-constructivist" distortions, and for having accepted a level of population that was more in line with the Gosplan population projections than with registration data indications.

It was claimed that local investigations were indicating that the 1937 census data needed correction coefficients of between 5 and 7 percent. Interestingly enough, the draft report did not recommend abandoning the census and carrying out a recensus; but later in the year, after Kraval's arrest, it was decided to abandon the 1937 census altogether and to carry out a new census in 1939.

The preliminary results of the 1939 census were published in an extremely abbreviated form that took up only two pages in the daily newspaper.[46] The data were presented in very summary form, with breakdowns for urban and rural population, age (in broad categories), sex, literacy and educational level, nationality, and class. It also listed the population of Union republics, and towns with a population of over 50,000. In 1956, a statistical journal stated that in response to demands it would publish the final results of the 1939 census. But the final reworked figures that were published at this time added little to the earlier two pages of results. The final results were only given in a two-page abbreviated form,[47] and the main addition was the inclusion of a table covering the permanent and the on-hand population.[48] Fuller data from the 1939 census finally appeared in the series of volumes devoted to the 1959 population census, when some of the 1939 results were presented by way of comparison with the 1959 figures.[49] These included a breakdown of urban population by size of urban settlement; a more detailed age breakdown; information on marital status, family size, and educational and literacy level; and breakdowns of population by social group, means of subsistence, and employment (by branch of the economy). They also included detailed breakdowns on occupation and profession—sometimes giving comparative figures not only for 1959 and 1939 but also for 1926—that are very important for social historians.

Registration data

Data on the civil registration of births, deaths, marriages, and divorces were published in some detail for the 1923–1926 period in the late 1920s.[50] Apart from providing data with a regional distribution, these sources provide an urban/rural breakdown, monthly data, a breakdown according to age and sex, and, for the main towns only, cause-specified mortality data. Detailed data on abortions and suicides are also available for these years.[51] After 1929, however, no such detailed statistics were ever published. Scattered figures for this period were reported in the press, but some of these are extremely dubious. In recent statistical handbooks, summary data on births, deaths, and child mortality are reported for the years 1926, 1928, and 1937–1940.[52] The draft of the Central Committee report on the 1937 census referred to above provides a very interesting series of figures on total population for each year in the period 1927–1937. The most interesting feature of this series is an absolute decline in population growth by 1.3 million between January 1933 and January 1934—a clear reflection of the magnitude of the famine.

In 1936 and 1937 several statistical handbooks were produced on women and youth[53] in the USSR, providing some marriage and employment data.

None of the above sources cover data on migration or emigration, which were generally not easily available. However, Osinskii, the director of TsSU in the late 1920s, published a very useful volume which provided a survey of the data for the period before 1928.[54]

Survey data

A system of anamnestic surveys[55] was developed in the early 1930s by the demographers Paevskii and Iakhontov to reconstruct past demographic data for primitive groups that were not covered by the standard registration and census data.[56] In the mid–1930s, this method was apparently applied on a larger scale for the population of the USSR, although no results were published at the time.[57] In the 1960s, the veteran demographer R. I. Sifman organized two more anamnestic surveys of women for TsSU in order to reconstruct their past natality patterns. These surveys were carried out in 1960 and 1967–68 on different age cohorts of women. The results, covering natality patterns in the 1920s and 1930s, were reported in detail in a book written by Sifman.[58]

On the general question of the reliability of Soviet demographic data, Lorimer has argued convincingly that the mortality data of the 1920s underestimate the true level of mortality, and that the census also under-records the number of infants.[59] There is considerable uncertainty over the reliability of the 1937 census, but with the likelihood that the correct level is somewhat higher than the recorded census level of 162 million but significantly lower than the implicit registration data figure of 169.3 million. While the 1937 Central Committee commission of enquiry favored 167–68 million, a lower figure of 163–65 million seems equally likely. There is no evidence to support the claims of Antonov Ovseenko and Steven Rosefielde that the population figure given in the 1937 census was 156 million.[60] The position regarding the reliability of the 1939 census is also somewhat unclear. This census may well have involved some double-counting of the labor camp population, but it is unlikely that the scale of this error was more than 2–3 million.[61]

As regards the registration data and inter-census population estimates, it is clear that in the late 1920s and the first half of the 1930s there was a tendency to overestimate the rate of population growth. This was a form of "Plan constructivism" in demography which was heavily reinforced by Stalin's repeated use of population growth indicators as a sign of social well-being.[62] An almost hysterical decree signed by Stalin and Molotov in 1935 demanded increased vigilance in registration offices, which they claimed were being infiltrated by "class enemies (priests, kulaks, former Whites, etc.)" who slipped into these organizations to carry out counter-revolutionary wrecking work (for example, registering deaths several times for the same person, and under-recording births).[63]

In these circumstances the population estimates and registration data that were reported in this inter-census period must be regarded as highly unreliable, and are no longer cited in Soviet sources. The historian V. P. Danilov has discussed the beginnings of the exaggeration in population growth rate in the late 1920s.[64] B. Ts. Urlanis, the leading Soviet demographer, has written that he would estimate the population in 1933 at about 158 million,[65] which is roughly the size estimated by Lorimer, and implies a large correction to the growth rates earlier claimed by Soviet writers.

Sifman's survey on births seems to be reliable although, like the demographic censuses, it suffers from a certain amount of rounding distortions when it comes to recording age structures.

Employment data

Employment data are available from three main sources: (i) censuses, (ii) current employment records and peasant household registers, and (iii) trade union statistical data. These sources will be discussed below, together with a brief mention of (iv) unemployment data, (v) time budget data, and (vi) sources of data on forced labor. In the West the works of Lorimer, Eason, and Redding provide useful surveys of the employment data.[66]

Censuses

The general outline of the 1926, 1931 urban, and 1939 censuses has been described already. In the 1926 census, 17 volumes of the final results covering about 6,500 pages were devoted to employment,[67] and another volume of 144 pages was devoted to unemployment.[68] The employment data were divided into categories of employment, main branches of employment, and individual professions, all of which were themselves divided according to age, sex, urban/rural location, and region. Details on the dependent population were also supplied.

For the urban "census" of 1931 only a very rough employment breakdown is available.[69] The position is somewhat better for the 1939 census. The published preliminary results only provided a very incomplete breakdown by categories of employment and branches of employment, but much more detailed information on professions appeared in the volumes devoted to the 1959 census.[70] There are, however, problems in reconciling the different categories of employment and professional occupation used in 1926 and 1939.[71]

Apart from the population censuses, there were also several censuses on employment and economic production that also provide some interesting data on employment. The most important of these was a 1927 census on professional employment in large-scale industry, published in nine volumes in 1929.[72] Other censuses and statistical counts of employment in separate enterprises were carried out in 1931, 1934, 1935, 1936, and 1939.[73]

The census of small-scale industry that was carried out in 1929 and published in three volumes in 1932 and 1933[74] is of particular interest to social historians. The censuses on metal-working equipment in industry in 1932–34 provide a very useful source of data on labor skill levels.[75] Other censuses, including detailed censuses of state industry for 1938 and 1939, are listed in Mashikhin and Simchera, but do not yet seem to be available in Soviet or Western libraries.[76]

Current employment records and peasant household registers

Apart from the periodic census data discussed above, more regular statistical counts of workers and employees in different branches of the economy appeared in publications specifically concerned with labor. The main labor journals of the period are:

Statistika truda, monthly organ of the Central Bureau of Labor Statistics (TsBST), ed. A. G. Rashin, 1923–1929

Trud v SSSR. Statisticheskii spravochnik. 1926–1930 gg. (Moscow, 1930)

Biulleten' po uchetu truda. Itogi 1931 g. (Moscow, 1932)

Trud v SSSR. Ekonomiko-statisticheskii spravochnik (Moscow, 1932)

Trud v SSSR. Ezhegodnik (Moscow, 1933)

Trud v SSSR. Ezhegodnik (Moscow, 1935)

Trud v SSSR. Statisticheskii spravochnik (Moscow, 1936).

These volumes contain detailed data on the number of persons employed by category and branch of employment; employment conditions (hours worked); wages; worker turnover; and participation in socialist competition.

Even more detailed data are available for a wide range of individual groups of industry for specific dates.[77]

For agriculture, the number of kolkhoz and non-kolkhoz households were reported in the agricultural statistical handbooks of the People's Commissariat of Agriculture and of TsUNKhU.[78] The data on peasant households in the 1920s will be discussed in the section on social class below.

Trade union data

The trade unions kept current statistics on their members based on membership registrations, but they also carried out censuses and sample investigations among their members. Until 1929, data were collected by the Central Bureau of Labor Statistics, under the combined direction of the trade unions, the Central Statistical Administration, and the People's Commissariat of Labor, and were published in *Statistika truda*, the monthly organ of the bureau, and in other general and labor statistical handbooks. The censuses of certain groups of workers which the trade unions conducted in the early 1930s are of particular importance, as they provide data on workers' length of experience in industry (*stazh*), social origins, connections with agriculture, and participation in socialist competition during this very dynamic period.[79] After a break in the publication of current trade union statistical materials in the early 1930s, current data become available again on a quarterly basis in the statistical handbook published by the Central Council of Trade Unions, *Statistiche-*

skii spravochnik (Moscow, 1935–1941). This source contains detailed data on trade union membership, participation in socialist competition, levels of literacy, library facilities, etc. Apart from these sources there are some important statistical materials on the cultural and welfare activities of the trade unions, and on socialist competition, in a series of publications of trade union archive materials.[80]

Unemployment

Before the formal liquidation of unemployment in 1931, unemployment data were available from three major sources: the population censuses, labor exchange registers, and trade union data. In the 1923 urban census, unemployment was just treated as a category of employment. But the 1926 population census devoted a whole volume to employment, and this provides a wealth of data on numbers unemployed, their age, length of unemployment, current regional location, region of origin, type of former work, and so on.[81]

The labor exchange statistics provide a continuous series from 1922 to 1931, but the coverage changed significantly over the period, both with regard to the number of labor exchanges reporting and the regulations as to who was entitled to be registered, and so they must be treated with great caution. These data were published in *Statistika truda* and other handbooks of labor statistics. A Soviet historian, L. S. Rogachevskaia, has written a survey on the data from labor exchanges held in Soviet archives.[82] For a useful survey of all the data on unemployment see the recent note by R. W. Davies and S. G. Wheatcroft.[83]

The trade unions kept a current register of their unemployed members as well as carrying out periodic censuses of them. Censuses were conducted in October 1925 and October–November 1927, and the results were published in detail in *Statistika truda*.[84]

Time-budgets

A considerable number of time budgets were calculated from surveys of time utilization during the 1920s. This was primarily due to the Soviet interest in labor planning and the movement for the scientific organization of labor. Interest in these questions remained during the 1930s, although some far more limited surveys were still carried out. In recent times, there has been a considerable increase in interest in the time-budget studies, and several reviews of this literature have appeared in the USSR and the West.[85]

Forced labor employment

No official figures on the scale of forced labor employment are available, and scholars have tried to assess it using a variety of sources. The most reliable figures are probably based on disenfranchisement data, employment registration, and census residuals and data on rehabilitations. For a recent review of the data, see my articles in *Soviet Studies* and paper at a recent Michigan State University Conference.[86] However, the availability of data on this subject should improve enormously after the current Politburo Commission on Repression completes its own investigations.

Statistical data on class and socioeconomic differentiation

Statistics on the class composition of the population and on socioeconomic differentiation of the peasantry are perhaps the type of statistics that produce the greatest problems for social historians. It is not the distinction between workers, employees, and peasants that causes the problem, because they can be fairly directly calculated from the standard categories of employment listed in the employment data (see above). The problem lies in the use of such terms as "capitalist," "bourgeois," and "petty-bourgeois," as well as in the categorization of peasant households as "kulak," "middle-peasant," and "poor-peasant."

We will consider the peasantry first. There was considerable debate in the 1920s about the degree of socioeconomic differentiation among the peasants and the type of classification that should be used. Much of this debate (which has been discussed in Moshe Lewin's work)[87] was politically motivated. Nemchinov's 1927 sample census of peasant households, recently described by R. W. Davies,[88] provided the most abundant data on socioeconomic differentiation.

Apart from this census, two other important sources of data on the socioeconomic differentiation of the peasantry, namely taxation data and peasant budget studies, have attracted the attention of Soviet historians. Professor Danilov and his colleagues made a detailed recalculation of the data on peasant income from the People's Commissariat of Finance. Both this study and the original data are of great interest.[89] The peasant budget studies for the early 1920s are also available, and have been analyzed in great detail by Iu. P. Bokarev.[90]

For later periods the data are far more scant. But an indication of the number and importance of kulak households at the end of the 1920s can be ascertained from the taxation data, where such households were assessed for taxation purposes separately from other peasant households.[91] In addition, it is possible to make some indirect assessment of the scale of differentiation from livestock censuses and other materials on agriculture.[92]

The most detailed account of the social composition of the entire population of the USSR in the mid-1920s is contained in the published report of the government (Sovnarkom) commission on tax assessment chaired by M. I. Frumkin, deputy People's Commissar for Finance.[93] Some detailed figures for the years 1928–1930 are available in *The Materials to the Balance of the National Economy*.[94] All later figures come from the censuses and other sources of data on employment.

Data on material welfare and health

This section considers data on (i) the consumption of food and other consumer goods, (ii) housing, and (iii) health.

Consumption of food and other consumer goods

There are basically three different sources of data on consumption: sample survey investigations, trade statistics, and calculations of available resources. Food consumption and other budget investigations were carried out on an unprecedented scale in the 1920s under the competent direction of A. E. Lositskii and L. N. Litoshenko. The results of these surveys up to 1927 were published in great detail.[95] The data for these years appear to be very reliable, although great caution is recommended in comparing the socioeconomic categories used in these budgets over time, and especially in comparing them with prerevolutionary data.

As explained above, the scale of food consumption surveys was greatly reduced in the late 1920s and merged with the general budget studies.[96] The surveys ceased in 1930 when the Central Statistical Administration was closed down and the network of voluntary correspondents abolished.

Some budget investigations were resumed in 1931, but these were mainly confined to households of workers and kolkhoz peasants.[97] With the re-emergence of a central statistical agency in 1932, a new system of budget surveys was introduced, which apparently covered over 14,000 workers, employees, and kolkhoz peasants in 1935. In this and the following year, TsUNKhU evidently published detailed results from the surveys, but these volumes are not yet available in Soviet or Western libraries.[98]

Some scattered consumption figures are cited in various Soviet historical works.[99] The reliability of those that cover the country as a whole can be checked against the balances in physical goods, but in many cases no checking is possible, and we must be very sceptical of the representative nature of the results.

Trade statistics for the 1920s and 1930s are relatively abundant, but they usually provide data in current prices, which are very difficult to translate into real terms (for a discussion of this problem see the work of Janet Chapman and Arvind Vyas).[100]

Calculations of the availability of food resources are very complicated because of the lack of agricultural utilization data in the 1930s and the lack of comparability of agricultural production data.[101] For the period 1928–1930 our knowledge is much better due to the publication of much utilization data in the *Materials to the Balance of the National Economy* for those years.[102] For later years no such detailed data are available.

Data on housing and communal services

As explained above, the 1926 population census collected a great deal of data on urban housing. Two whole volumes of the final census publication, covering over 700 pages, were devoted to housing conditions and the ownership and construction of housing.[103] A series of statistical handbooks covering housing and communal services (water supply, sewerage, electricity, and so on) were published in the 1930s but are not readily available in the West.[104] Some figures on housing stock and communal services are available in the general statistical handbooks of the period. For a detailed account of the history of housing statistics, see the article on this subject by the Soviet writer D. L. Bronner.[105]

Data on health

Most of the available Soviet statistical sources on health are concerned with data on doctors, medical equipment, hospitals, numbers of beds, and the like.[106] Special censuses of medical personnel and facilities were taken in 1930 and 1935,[107] and the population censuses of 1926 and 1939 also gave the number of doctors.

Detailed data on morbidity were published in Soviet statistical handbooks in the late 1920s,[108] but not thereafter. Nevertheless, until April 1937 some such data were sent to the Epidemiological Intelligence Unit of the Health Section of the League of Nations and published in its bulletins.[109] These figures, however, are somewhat lower than the general morbidity figures currently accepted by Soviet epidemiologists.[110]

Data on education, culture, and law

There is a great wealth of data available on literacy, education, higher education, libraries, and publications. Very little is available on political culture and the attitudes and aspirations of Soviet citizens. The numerous statistical handbooks on different aspects of education and culture are all listed in Mashikhin and Simchera.[111] Apart from these, all general statistical handbooks have always devoted a large section to this topic.

Literacy

Data on levels of literacy are available from the 1926 census. The first seventeen volumes cover this topic as well as nationality, native language, and age.[112] Some comparative figures from the 1939 census have also been published,[113] and several statistical handbooks are devoted specifically to this topic.[114]

General and professional education

The census of schools carried out on 15 December 1927, provides the most detailed information on general and professional education. The final results were published in 1930 in two volumes with over 1,100 pages.[115] There were separate volumes on general education and vocational training, each with separate sections on institutions, pupils, and teachers. In addition, numerous detailed annual reports on education were published regularly in the 1920s[116] and for a few years in the early 1930s.[117]

Higher education and science

Apart from the relevant sections of the general statistical handbooks and the statistical handbooks on culture, there were two statistical publications in the 1930s specifically concerned with higher education,[118] two that were concerned with science and research institutions,[119] and two that were concerned with both.[120]

Libraries

During this period, there was one census of libraries, held on 1 October 1934, whose results were published in two volumes.[121] The first volume gave summary data on libraries and had an introduction by Nadezhda Krupskaia. The second contained data on librarians, as well as giving a short description of each library. Apart from this census data, information on libraries was included in some of the general cultural statistical handbooks and in the trade-union statistical handbooks.

Publishing and the press

Apart from data on publications in the general statistical handbooks, a specialized statistical handbook on periodical publications and the movement of workers and rural correspondents (*rabkory* and *sel'kory*) was published in 1930. This handbook covers the period between the Fifteenth and Sixteenth Party Congresses, that is, the time of mass collectivization.[122]

In the late 1930s, there were three works specifically concerned with publications[123] and two concerned with publications, art, and political education.[124]

Political culture: attitudes and aspirations

Very little direct statistical information is available on these topics. Statistics on party membership, including recruitment, drop-out rates, and turnover, are available,[125] but they are difficult to interpret. Some very suspect statistics are offered on high election turn-outs, socialist competition, Stakhanovism, and the shock-work movement (*udarnichestvo*). Other far less favorable indirect statistical indicators are the figures on high absentee rates and high employment turnover.[126] We do have the results of two social surveys covering 5,015 young urban workers in 1936 and 5,127 young kolkhoz workers in 1938 and providing information on party membership, membership of sports and other social clubs, reading and other cultural activities.[127] But it is difficult to relate these directly to political culture and attitudes.

Legal statistics

Until 1929, legal statistics concerning the numbers of arrests, sentences, amnesties, etc., were regularly published in Soviet statistical journals. Subsequently there has been an almost total absence of publication of this type of statistics, and the statistical bibliographers Mashikhin and Simchera failed to include a separate heading for this type of statistic. However, various legal statistics were occasionally published in the specialist statistical and legal journals throughout the 1930s. The Dutch legal expert Professor Ger P. Van Den Berg has done much to collect and analyze the limited amount of available Soviet legal statistics.[128] In a few cases he has made quite heroic assumptions in order to construct a complete and consistent series of arrest and sentence data from the partial evidence available.

Conclusions

The amount of available statistical data on matters of concern to social historians of the USSR in the 1920s and 1930s is very large. It is far more complete in the 1920s than in the 1930s, but there is still a considerable amount of very detailed material available on many aspects of social history for most of this period. The main deficiencies are the lack of detailed published data from the 1939 census, the lack of published results of the budget surveys for the 1930s as a whole, the great lack of statistics on political attitudes and aspirations, and doubts over the reliability of all these statistics, especially for purposes of comparison with prerevolutionary data.

All the available data need to be treated extremely carefully, taking into consideration the statistical procedures adopted in the collection and calculation of the data and the possible sources of distortion. A great deal of information is available for the study of the actual statistical procedures and contemporary debates among statisticians over these procedures. Any social historian wishing to use these data is advised to consider the vagaries of the statistical agencies of the time—particularly their tendency to exhibit "Plan constructivism"—and to study the actual statistical procedure adopted for the data he is interested in. No figures should be accepted on faith. If the historian does not know how any specific set of figures were calculated, he should find out. If he cannot find out how they were calculated, he should be most suspicious of the figures.

Notes

1. Until the changes brought about by *perestroika*, the archives of the Central Statistical Agency and of the State Planning Agency were closed to foreigners.

2. There are very few émigré writings on Soviet statistics, and those that exist are fairly contradictory.

3. A consolidated index to the articles in this journal was published in 1971 (see "Bibliograficheskii ukazatel' statei i materialov po statistike i uchetu," in *Zhurnal "Vestnik statistiki" za 50 let [1919-1968 gg.]* [Moscow, 1971]).

4. E. A. Mashikhin and V. M. Simchera, *Statisticheskie publikatsii v SSSR* (Moscow, 1975), 258-268. This bibliography appears to be more or less complete and even to contain several restricted internal materials. It does, however, have some rather serious omissions such as *Plan* and *Statistika i narodnoe khoziaistvo*.

5. "Bibliografiia rabot po istorii statistiki v SSSR (1917-1970)," in *Sovetskaia statistika za polveka* (Moscow, 1972), 306-330. There are specific sections on demographic statistics, labor statistics, budget statistics, housing statistics, sanitary and medical statistics, and education and culture statistics.

6. *Istoriia sovetskoi gosudarstvennoi statistiki* (Moscow, 1960), and the more complete second edition (Moscow, 1969).

7. The best is V. B. Den and B. I. Karpenko, *Khoziaistvennaia statistika SSSR* (Moscow, 1930).

8. See the articles in *Ocherki po istorii statistiki SSSR. Sbornik*, nos. 1–5 (Moscow, 1957–72) and in *Uchenye zapiski po statistike*, especially vols. XVII and XX (Moscow, 1970 and 1972), both entitled *Sovetskaia statistika za polveka (1917–1967 gg.)*.

9. The main book is *Massovye istochniki po sotsial'no-ekonomicheskoi istorii sovet-skogo obshchestva* (Moscow, 1979). This work, which is introduced by V. Z. Drobizhev and Iu. A. Moshkov, has individual chapters on the following relevant topics: sources on population, sources on the history of the Soviet working class and intelligentsia, sources on peasant households in the 1920s, statistical sources on the history of the kolkhoz and the kolkhoz peasantry.

10. See the article by Drobizhev and Moshkov on statistical sources in I. D. Kovalchenko, ed., *Istochnikovedenie istorii SSSR* (Moscow, 1981). The Soviet literature on the study of sources (*istochnikovedenie*) is immense.

11. A series of censuses had been held in 1920 and another was scheduled for 1930 and every subsequent ten years. The TsSU statisticians claimed that there had been so much disruption and change since 1920 that a mid-term census was urgently needed. See *Biulleten' TsSU* 99 (15 May 1925), and S. G. Wheatcroft, "Grain Production and Utilisation in Russia and the USSR before Collectivisation," unpublished Ph.D. thesis, Birmingham University, 1980, 335–36.

12. Apart from the Sovnarkom decision to renege on its earlier decision to press ahead with the censuses at this time, Popov was also in trouble with the party leadership because Kamenev had used some TsSU data on socioeconomic differentiation for his Oppositionist arguments. See S. G. Wheatcroft, "Grain Production," 308–309 and 335–36.

13. N. (or V. V.) Osinskii (V. V. Obolenskii) (1887–1938). His party membership dated from 1907. He worked in the Kharkov gubernia statistical committee for a while just before the war and wrote (as V. V. Obolenskii) *Urozhai khlebov v iuzhnoi Rossii (1899–1912 gg.)* (Kharkov, 1915). He was a "Left Communist" during the negotiations on the Brest peace. In 1920–21 he was an active member (if not the leader) of the Democratic Centralist group, and in 1923 was associated with the Trotskyist Opposition.

14. Groman, Popov's former rival in Gosplan, was brought into a specially created statistical-planning department to assist cooperation. S. G. Wheatcroft, "Grain Production," 310–12.

15. Apart from the demographic census in 1926, a census of employment in large-scale industry and a census of schools were carried out in 1927 and a census of small-scale industry in 1929.

16. The matter appears to have come to a head at a plenary session of the Central Committee in July 1928, several months after Osinskii had been replaced. See E. H. Carr and R. W. Davies, *Foundations of a Planned Economy, 1926–1929* (London: Macmillan, 1969), 76–78.

17. He continued to edit the main agricultural newspaper and do much journalistic work at the same time as being director of TsSU.

18. See note 15 (above).

19. For unrest in the local statistical agencies see S. G. Wheatcroft, "Grain Production," 452–58.

20. See R. W. Davies, *The Socialist Offensive: The Collectivisation of Soviet Agriculture, 1929–1930* (London: Macmillan, 1980), 64–68.

21. See *Ekonomicheskaia zhizn'*, 27 December 1929.

22. For an account of these trials and the most prominent victims among the statisticians, see N. Jasny, *Soviet Economists of the Twenties. Names to be Remembered* (London and New York: Cambridge University Press, 1972).

23. V. V. Osinskii, *Polozhenie i zadachi narodno-khoziaistvennogo ucheta* (Moscow, 1932), 5.

24. *Sobranie zakonov*, 1931 no. 73, art. 488: decree "O sozdanii TsUNKhU" dated 17 December 1931.

25. *Sobranie zakonov*, 1932 (part 2) no. 1, art. 15: decree dated 9 January 1932.

26. *Narodnoe khoziaistvo SSSR* (Moscow, 1932) (669 pages) and *SSSR za 15 let* (Moscow, 1932) (423 pages).

27. *Materialy po balansu narodnogo khoziaistva SSSR za 1928, 1929 i 1930 gg.* (Moscow, 1932). For an English translation see R. W. Davies and S. G. Wheatcroft, eds., *Materials for a Balance of the National Economy of the USSR, 1928-30* (Cambridge: Cambridge University Press, 1985).

28. For grain in particular, but also for other statistics, see S. G. Wheatcroft, "Statistics and Economic Decision-Making in the USSR under Stalin," unpublished paper (CREES, Birmingham University, 1979), 9.

29. A whole network was set up for grain evaluation which was to be independent of local administrative pressure. See S. G. Wheatcroft, "Statistics and Economic Decision-Making," 8-9.

30. *Sobranie zakonov*, 1933 (part 2) no. 2, art. 29: decree dated 21 January 1933, and *Sobranie zakonov*, 1935 (part 2) no. 13, art. 118: decree dated 8 August 1935.

31. See S. G. Wheatcroft, "Statistics and Economic Decision-Making," 8-11.

32. *Sobranie zakonov*, 1937 no. 27, art. 143: decree "O perepisi 1937 goda," dated 23 May 1937.

33. At the TsUNKhU self-criticism session, reported in *Plan* just before it closed down, we see P. I. Popov and other noted figures from the past criticizing some real faults in TsUNKhU that had been developing under Kraval. See *Plan*, 1937 no.8, 34.

34. Six volumes were apparently prepared for publication in 1939, but have remained in the archives ever since. They may be published in the near future, but so far the only published results of the 1939 census have amounted to a couple of pages of tables.

35. *Sotsialisticheskoe stroitel'stvo SSSR (1933-1938 gg.)* (Moscow, 1939) (207 pages). It is not just that the handbook was much shorter than earlier (i.e., 200 pages instead of 500-700 pages) but also that there was far less data on each page. However, it should perhaps be pointed out that several detailed statistical handbooks did appear at this time covering separate branches of statistics, e.g., *Kul'turnoe stroitel'stvo SSSR* (Moscow, 1940).

36. E. A. Mashikhin and V. M. Simchera, *Statisticheskie publikatsii v SSSR* (Moscow, 1975).

37. *Vsesoiuznaia perepis' naseleniia 17 dekabria 1926 g. Predvaritel'nye itogi perepisi*, vyp. 1-3 (Moscow, 1927).

38. *Vsesoiuznaia perepis' naseleniia 17 dekabria 1926 g. Kratkie svodki*, vyp 1-10 (Moscow, 1927-28). These volumes combined different types of information, e.g., employment by age, but did not contain a detailed regional breakdown.

39. *Vsesoiuznaia perepis' naseleniia 17 dekabria 1926 g. Okonchatel'nye itogi*, 56 vols. (Moscow, 1928-33). These volumes were complex (i.e., combined different types of information) and also gave a detailed regional breakdown.

40. V. P. Danilov, "Sel'skoe naselenie SSSR nakanune kollektivizatsii (po dannym obshchenarodnoi perepisi 17 dekabria 1926 g.)," *Istoricheskie zapiski*, vol. 74 (Moscow, 1963), pp. 64-108, and V. P. Danilov, *Sovetskaia dokolkhoznaia derevnia: naselenie, zemlepol'zovanie, khoziaistvo* (Moscow, 1977), 17-70.

41. L. I. Vaskina, "Rabochii klass SSSR po materialam vsesoiuznoi perepisi naseleniia 1926 g.," *Istoricheskie zapiski*, vol. 92 (Moscow, 1973), 7-56, and idem., *Rabochii klass SSSR nakanune sotsialisticheskoi industrializatsii* (Moscow, 1981).

42. F. Lorimer, *The Population of the Soviet Union: History and Prospects* (Geneva: League of Nations, 1946), 44-111, and W. Eason, "Soviet Manpower: The Population and Labor Force of the USSR," unpublished Ph.D. thesis, Columbia, 1959.

43. Some results from this census are available in *Narodnoe khoziaistvo SSSR* (Moscow: TsUNKhU 1932), pp. 401-409, and in several articles, e.g., I. Berlin and Ia. Mebel,

"Strukturnye sdvigi v naselenii i proletariate," *Voprosy truda*, 1932 no. 11/12, 17–23, and B. Smulevich, "Le Probleme de la Population de l'U.R.S.S.," in *Atti del Congresso Internazionale per gli Studi sulla Popolazione* (Roma, 1931), vol. 6 (Rome, 1934), 479–519. Apparently the results for the Ukraine were published more fully. See *Itogi ucheta chislennosti gorodskogo naseleniia SSSR 1931 g.* (Kharkov, 1933).

44. A population estimate published in *Izvestiia*, 15 December 1937, was presumably influenced by the unpublished results of the January 1937 census. It is much larger than the subsequent figures for 1937 that have appeared, which seem to be based on the results of the 1939 census and registration data.

45. "O perepisi naseleniia 6-ogo ianvaria 1937-ogo goda," TsGANKh, *lichnyi fond P. I. Popova, op.* 105, *ed. khr.* 1, *delo* 10, *listy* 20–153. I am grateful to Professor V. P. Danilov for making a copy of this report available to me. It is hoped to publish the full materials of this report in *Voprosy istorii* early in 1989. P. I. Popov was a member of the Central Committee's commission of inquiry into the 1937 census, which was headed by Ia. A. Iakovlev.

46. *Pravda*, 2 July 1939, and *ibid.*, 29 April 1940. They were partially reproduced in *Sotsialisticheskoe stroitel'stvo SSSR (1933–1938 gg.)* (Moscow, 1939), 8–15.

47. *Vestnik statistiki*, 1956 no. 6, 89–90.

48. The permanent population is the population that is normally resident in a given location. The on-hand population is the population that is actually present at the time of the census. Normally censuses are taken at a time of little population movement when the on-hand population will be as high as possible. One of the more valid criticisms of the 1937 census was that its timing—on Christmas Eve (old-style)—was likely to have led to large-scale under-enumeration, since a large part of the permanent population was likely not to be on-hand at the critical census time.

49. *Itogi vsesoiuznoi perepisi naseleniia 1959 goda. SSSR (Svodnyi tom)* (Moscow, 1962). The accompanying fifteen volumes (1962–63) give results of the 1959 census for the separate republics of the USSR.

50. *Estestvennoe dvizhenie naseleniia SSSR, 1923–1925 gg.* (Moscow, 1928), and *Estestvennoe dvizhenie naseleniia SSSR 1926 g.* (Moscow, 1929).

51. *Aborty v 1925 g. Trudy TsSU*, vol. 35, part 2 (Moscow, 1926), *Aborty v 1926 g. Trudy TsSU*, vol. 35, part 3 (Moscow, 1927), *Samoubiistva v SSSR v 1922–1925 gg. Trudy TsSU*, vol. 35, part 1 (Moscow, 1927), and *Samoubiistva v SSSR v 1925 i 1926 gg.* (Moscow, 1929).

52. See, for instance, *Narodnoe khoziaistvo SSSR, 1922–1972* (Moscow, 1972), 40.

53. *Molodezh' SSSR. Statisticheskii sbornik* (Moscow, 1936) (384 pages); *Zhenshchina v SSSR. Statisticheskii sbornik* (Moscow, 1936) (165 pages) and *ibid.* (Moscow, 1937) (190 pages).

54. See V. V. Osinskii, *Mezhdunarodnye i mezhkontinental'nye migratsii v dovoennoi Rossii i SSSR* (Moscow, 1928).

55. Surveys relying on the interviewee's recollection of past experiences.

56. V. V. Paevskii and A. P. Iakhontov, "O primenenii anamnesticheskikh metodov v demografii," *Trudy Demograficheskogo Instituta*, vol. 1 (Leningrad, 1934), 135–210.

57. Strumilin claims that an article of his which includes some summary results from these mid-1930s surveys was written in 1936, although it was not published until 1957. S. G. Strumilin, *Problemy ekonomiki truda* (Moscow, 1964), 137.

58. R. I. Sifman, *Dinamika rozhdaemosti v SSSR (po materialam vyborochnykh obsledovanii)* (Moscow, 1974).

59. See Lorimer, *op. cit.*, 113–20.

60. A. Antonov-Ovseenko, *Portret tirana* (New York, 1980), 225–26; S. Rosefielde "Excess Mortality in the Soviet Union: A Reconsideration of the Demographic Consequences of Forced Industrialization 1926–49," *Soviet Studies*, July 1983, 406, and elsewhere. For criticisms of these claims concerning the 1937 census, see S. G. Wheatcroft, "A Note on Steve Rosefielde's Calculation of Excess Mortality in the USSR, 1929–1949," *Soviet Studies*, April 1984, 277–78.

61. It may well turn out that part of this double-counting is due to the fact that the *kontingent* or data provided to TsUNKhU by the NKVD for individuals in its care was not up-to-date and that many people who were recorded as alive had subsequently died.

62. I. V. Stalin, *Sochiniia*, vol. 13 (Moscow, 1952), 336. See S. G. Wheatcroft, "Statistics and Economic Decision-Making," (1979), 13.

63. *Sobranie zakonov*, 1935, no. 53, art. 432: decree dated 21 September 1935.

64. V. P. Danilov, "Dinamika naseleniia SSSR za 1917–1929 gg.," in *Arkheograficheskii ezhegodnik za 1968* (Moscow, 1970), 248–53.

65. See B. Ts. Urlanis, *Problemy dinamiki naselenia SSSR* (Moscow, 1974), 319.

66. Lorimer, *op. cit.*, Eason, *op. cit.*, and D. Redding, "Non-agricultural employment in the USSR 1928–1955," unpublished Ph.D. thesis, Columbia, 1958. For an attempt to include the more detailed data on the 1939 census made available after the publication of the results of the 1959 census, see S. G. Wheatcroft, "Population and Employment in the USSR, 1926–1939," unpublished paper presented to the Third Conference of the International Work Group on Soviet Inter-War Economic History, Birmingham, 1982.

67. *Vsesoiuznaia perepis' naseleniia 17 dekabria 1926 g. Okonchatel'nye itogi*, vols. 18–34, part 2 ("Zaniatiia") (Moscow, 1929–30).

68. *Ibid.*, vol. 52, part 4 ("Bezrabotitsa") (Moscow, 1932).

69. See note 43 (above).

70. See note 49 (above).

71. See S. G. Wheatcroft, "Population and Employment" (1982).

72. *Professional'nyi sostav personala fabrichno-zavodskoi promyshlennosti SSSR na 1 noiabria 1927 g.*, 9 parts (Moscow, 1929) (380 pages in all).

73. For a list of these, see Mashikhin and Simchera, *op. cit.*, 94–95. Not all of the listed works on these censuses are available in Soviet or Western libraries.

74. *Melkaia promyshlennost' SSSR po dannym Vsesoiuznoi perepisi 1929 g.*, 3 parts (Moscow, 1932–33) (900 pages in all).

75. *Perepis' oborudovaniia promyshlennosti SSSR, 1932–1934 gg.*, 5 parts (Moscow, 1935) (in all about 600 pages). See J. M. Cooper, "Technology and Labour Skills in the Soviet Engineering Industry in the Inter-War Years," unpublished paper presented to the West European Conference on Soviet Industry and Working Class in the Inter-War Years, Birmingham 1981.

76. See Mashikhin and Simchera, *op. cit.*, 100–102.

77. These had an assortment of titles, e.g., *Chislennost' rabochikh i sluzhashchikh i fondy zarabotnoi platy v narodnoi khoziaistve SSSR (Itogy edinovremennogo ucheta za mart 1934 g.)* (Moscow, 1935) and *Chislennost'. . . za mart 1936 g.* (Moscow, 1936). A volume with a similar title (*Itogy edinovremennogo ucheta chislennosti i fonda zarabotnoi platy rabochikh i sluzhashchikh za sentiabr' 1939 g.* [Moscow, 1940] [147 pages]) was apparently produced for September 1939 but does not appear to be available in any Soviet or Western library.

78. Although these were listed as annuals, only three issues are available, two produced by the Commissariat of Agriculture and one by TsUNKhU. *Ezhegodnik po sel'skomu khoziaistvu Sovetskogo Soiuza za 1931 god* (Moscow, 1933), *Sel'skoe khoziaistvo SSSR. Ezhegodnik 1935* (Moscow, 1936), and *Sel'skoe khoziaistvo SSSR. Statisticheskii spravochnik* (Moscow, 1939). Other important TsUNKhU handbooks are *Kolkhozy vo vtoroi stalinskoi piatiletke. Statisticheskii spravochnik* (Moscow, 1939), and the earlier results of the kolkhoz investigations: *Kolkhozy v 1928 g. Itogi obsledovaniia kolkhozov* (Moscow, 1932), *Kolkhozy v 1929 g. Itogi sploshnoi obsledovaniia kolkhozov* (Moscow, 1931); and *Kolkhozy v 1930 g. Itogi raportov kolkhozov XVI s"ezdu VKP(b)* (Moscow, 1931); and *Kolkhozy vesnoi 1931 goda* (Moscow, 1932).

79. See A. G. Rashin, *Sostav fabrichno-zavodskogo proletariata SSSR. Predvaritel'nye itogi perepisi metallistov, gornorabochikh i tekstil'shchikov v 1929 g.* (Moscow, 1930), *Sostav novykh millionov chlenov profsoiuzov* (Moscow, 1933). See also V. Z. Drobizhev and Iu. A. Moshkov, *op. cit.*, 99–106.

80. *Profsoiuzy SSSR. Dokumenty i materialy*, of which volumes 2 and 3 (Moscow, 1963) cover the period under discussion.

81. See *Vsesoiuznaia perepis' naseleniia 17 dekabria 1926 g. Okonchatel'nye itogi*, vol. 52 (Moscow, 1931). For a discussion of these data see L. I. Vaskina, *Rabochii klass SSSR nakanune sotsialisticheskoi industrializatsii* (Moscow, 1981), 162–82.

82. L. S. Rogachevskaia, "Kon"iunkturnye obzory po trudu kak istochnik dlia izucheniia bezrabotitsy i ego likvidatsii v SSSR," in *Arkeograficheskii ezhegodnik, 1966* (Moscow, 1967), 178–88.

83. R. W. Davies and S. G. Wheatcroft, "Note on Unemployment Statistics," in David Lane, ed., *Labour and Employment in the USSR* (Brighton: Wheatsheaf, 1986), 36–49.

84. *Statistika truda*, 1926 no. 3, 1–7; *ibid.*, 1928 nos. 3–4, 1–32; and *ibid.*, 1928 nos. 11–12, 21–39.

85. See the numerous reprints of the earlier works on time budgets by S. G. Strumilin and L. E. Mints and the survey in V. I. Bolgov, *Biudzhet vremeni pri sotsializme* (Moscow, 1973), 33–53, on time budgets in the 1920s and 1930s. In the West, see the work of Jiri Zuzanek, "Time-budget trends in the USSR: 1922–1970," *Soviet Studies*, April 1979, 188–213, and *Work and Leisure in the Soviet Union: A Time Budget Analysis* (New York: Praeger, 1980).

86. S. G. Wheatcroft, "On Assessing the Size of Forced Concentration Camp Labour in the Soviet Union, 1929–56," *Soviet Studies*, April 1981, 265–95; "Towards a Thorough Analysis of Soviet Forced Labour Statistics," *Soviet Studies*, April 1983, 223–37; "Towards Assessing the Scale and Significance of Terror in the USSR in the 1930s," Paper presented to the Conference on State Terrorism, East Lansing, Mich., November 1988.

87. M. Lewin, *Russian Peasants and Soviet Power: A Study of Collectivisation* (London: George Allen & Unwin, 1968), chapters 1 and 2, and Lewin, "Who was the Soviet Kulak?" *Soviet Studies*, October 1966, 189–217.

88. See R. W. Davies, *The Socialist Offensive: The Collectivisation of Soviet Agriculture, 1929–1930* (London: Macmillan, 1980), 24–26. The published results of the census appeared in *Statisticheskii spravochnik 1928* (Moscow, 1929), 88–134 and 144–55, and *Sel'skoe khoziaistvo SSSR 1925–1929 gg.* (Moscow, 1929), 24–141. The principles of classification were explained in V. S. Nemchinov, *Izbrannye proizvedeniia*, vol. 1 (Moscow, 1967), 44–127 (a reprint of articles first published in 1925–1930).

89. *Sel'skoe khoziaistvo SSSR v . . . god po dannym nalogovykh svodok po edinomu sel'-khoznalogu*, for 1923/24 to 1928/29 (Moscow, 1924–1931); V. P. Danilov and T. I. Slavko, *Krest'ianskoe khoziaistvo. Kolkhozy i sovkhozy SSSR v 1924/25–1927/28, po dannym nalogo-vykh svodok Narkomfina SSSR*, vyp. 1–3 (Moscow, 1977).

90. *Krest'ianskie biudzhety 1922/23 g. i 1923/24 g. Trudy TsSU*, vol. 21, parts 1–3 (Moscow, 1926–27); *Krest'ianskie biudzhety 1924–25 g.* (Moscow, 1928); *Krest'ianskie biudzhety 1925/26 g.* (Moscow, 1929); *Denezhnyi balans krest'ianskikh khoziaistv po biud-zhetnym zapisiam za 1926–1927 gg.* (Moscow, 1930); *Denezhnyi oborot v krest'ianskikh khoziaistvakh za 1927 g. po mesiatsam* (Moscow, 1929); and Iu. P. Bokarev, *Biudzhetnye obsledovaniia krest'ianskikh khoziaistv 20-kh godov kak istoricheskii istochnik* (Moscow, 1981).

91. See *Otchet Narodnogo Komissariata Finansov SSSR ob ispolnenii edinogo gosudarst-vennogo biudzheta SSSR za 1928–1929 g.* (Moscow, 1930), and reports for 1929/30, 1931, 1932, 1933, 1934, and 1935.

92. See Mashikhin and Simchera, *op. cit.*, 105–107.

93. See *Tiazhest' oblozheniia v SSSR (sotsial'nyi sostav, dokhody i nalogovye platezhi naseleniia SSSR v 1924/25, 1925/26 i 1926/27 godakh)* (Moscow, 1929). It is interesting to note that Frumkin, in addressing the Politburo in June 1928 on the dangers of letting the policy of attacking the kulak spread to the middle peasant, was speaking with the authority of chairman of the main state commission looking into the question of the socioeconomic differentiation of the peasantry. This makes Stalin's casual dismissal of his views all the more remarkable. For this incident see E. H. Carr and R. W. Davies, *Foundations of a Planned*

Economy, 1926–1929 (London: Macmillan, 1969), 74–75.

94. *Materialy po balansu narodnogo khoziaistva SSSR 1928, 1929 i 1930 gg.* (Moscow, 1932), 170 and 254–57.

95. For food consumption survey results for the urban population see *Sostoianie pitaniia gorodskogo naseleniia SSSR, 1919–1924 gg. Trudy TsSU,* vol. 25, part 5 (Moscow, 1926) and *Sostoianie pitaniia gorodskogo naseleniia SSSR v 1925/26 sel'skokhoziaistvennom godu. Trudy TsSU,* vol. 30, part 5 (Moscow, 1927); and for the rural population see *Sostoianie pitaniia sel'skogo naseleniia SSSR 1920–1924. Trudy TsSU,* vol. 30, part 2 (Moscow, 1927). For peasant budget studies, see note 82 (above). For worker and employee budgets see *Biudzhety rabochikh i sluzhashchikh, parts 1–3* (Moscow, 1929).

96. In 1929, 20,000 peasant households were surveyed by expeditionary methods and over 9,000 by constant budget records collected by the voluntary correspondents. See Bokarev, *op. cit.,* 55.

97. This apparently covered 5,000 worker households in some detail (see *Istoriia sovetskoi gosudarstvennoi statistiki* [Moscow, 1960], 304), and was presumably carried out by the trade unions and the Commissariat of Labor. At the same time, the People's Commissariat of Finance investigated the money incomes balance of a large number of kolkhoz and individual peasants (see Bokarev, *op. cit.,* 56). The results of these surveys have not been published.

98. *Biudzhety rabochikh, kolkhoznikov i inzhenerno-tekhnicheskikh rabotnikov. Aprel' i 1 kvartal 1936 g.* (Moscow, 1936) (338 pages), and *Biudzhety rabochikh i ITR za 1935 g. Tablitsy* (Moscow, 1937) (170 pages).

99. Consumption norms for 1928–1930 were published by Iu. A. Moshkov in his *Zernovaia problema v gody sploshnoi kollektivisatsii* (Moscow, 1966), 136. Some figures for 1932 and 1937 were published in M. A. Vyltsan, *Zavershaiushchii etap sozdaniia kolkhoznogo stroia (1935–1937 gg.)* (Moscow, 1978), 208.

100. Janet G. Chapman, *Real Wages in Soviet Russia since 1928* (Cambridge, Mass.: Harvard University Press, 1963), and Arvind Vyas, *Consumption in a Socialist Economy: The Soviet Industrialisation Experience, 1929–37* (New Delhi: People's Publishing House, 1978).

101. For a discussion of this problem see S. G. Wheatcroft, "A Re-evaluation of Soviet Agricultural Production in the 1920s and 1930s," in R. C. Stuart, ed., *The Soviet Rural Economy* (New Jersey: Rowman and Allenheld, 1983), 36–39.

102. *Materialy po balansu narodnogo khoziaistva SSSR 1928, 1929 i 1930 gg.* (Moscow, 1932), 308–31.

103. *Vsesoiuznaia perepis' naseleniia 17 dekabria 1926 g. Okonachatel'nye itogi,* vol. 53, part 5 ("Vladeniia, stroeniia, zhil'e i nezhilye pomeshcheniia v gorodakh i gorodskikh poseleniiakh SSSR") (Moscow, 1929), and *ibid.,* vol. 54, part 6 ("Zhilishchnye usloviia gorodskogo naseleniia SSSR") (Moscow, 1932).

104. For a list of these, see Mashikhin and Simchera, *op. cit.,* 97–98.

105. D. L. Bronner, "Iz istorii zhilishchnoi statistiki v SSSR (1917–1967)," in *Sovetskaia statistika za polveka (1917–1967 gg.)* (Moscow, 1972), 207–59.

106. *Zdorov'e i zdravookhranenie trudiashchikhsia SSSR. Statisticheskii sbornik* (Moscow, 1936) and (Moscow, 1937), and *Spravochno-statisticheskie materialy po zdravookhraneniiu za 1913, 1932, 1937 i 1940 gg.* (Moscow, 1943).

107. The results of the 1930 census are given in *Narodnoe khoziaistvo SSSR* (Moscow, 1932), 562–67, and in *Vsesoiuznaia perepis' uchrezhdenii zdravookhraneniia i meditsinskikh kadrov* (Moscow, 1932). For the later census see *Perepis' meditsinskikh kadrov v sisteme zdravookhraneniia RSFSR* (Moscow, 1935).

108. See *Statisticheskii spravochnik SSSR 1928* (Moscow, 1929), 912–19.

109. See League of Nations, Health Section, *Annual Epidemiological Intelligence Reports for the Year . . . (1924–1937)* (Geneva: League of Nations, 1924–38), and similar monthly reports. The original materials (Obshchesoiuznoe Biuro Zagranichnoi Sanitarnoi Informatsii, *Biulleten' o dvizhenii zaraznykh zabolevanii* [Moscow, monthly 1929–April

1936]) are available in the League of Nations Archives in Geneva.

110. See the data presented (in graphical form) in O. V. Baroian, *Itogi polvekovoi bor'by s infektsiiami v SSSR* (Moscow, 1968), 49–143. The current Soviet epidemiological series has been compared with the series given to the League of Nations in S. G. Wheatcroft, "Famine and Factors Affecting Mortality in the USSR," (CREES Discussion Papers, Birmingham University, Soviet Industrialization Project Series (SIPS) no. 21), 43–44 (Appendices).

111. Mashikhin and Simchera, *op. cit.*, 89–92. The main general statistical handbooks on culture are: *Kul'turnoe stroitel'stvo SSSR v tsifrakh* (Moscow, 1935) and (Moscow, 1936), and *Kul'turnoe stroitel'stvo SSSR. Statisticheskii sbornik* (Moscow, 1940).

112. *Vsesoiuznaia perepis' naseleniia 17 dekabria 1926 g. Okonchatel'nye itogi*, vols. 1–17, part 1 ("Narodnost'. Rodnoi Iazyk. Vozrast. Gramotnost'.") in each volume (Moscow, 1928–29).

113. *Vestnik statistiki*, 1956 no.6, 90.

114. *Gramotnost' v Rossii* (Moscow, 1922) (55 pages). *Vseobshchee obuchenie. Likvidatsiia negramotnosti. Podgotovka kadrov. Statisticheskii ocherk* (Moscow, 1930) (164 pages).

115. *Vsesoiuznaia shkol'naia perepis' 15 dekabria 1927 g.*, 2 vols. (Moscow, 1930).

116. The volumes for 1921–25 and 1925/26 appeared as *Trudy TsSU*, vol. 28, parts 1–3 (Moscow, 1926–1927). For 1926/27 and 1927/28 they appeared as *Narodnoe prosveshchenie v SSSR, 1926/7 ucheb. g.* (Moscow, 1929) and *Narodnoe prosveshchenie v SSSR* (Moscow, 1929), part 2 for 1927/28.

117. *Massovoe prosveshchenie v SSSR*, parts 1–2 (Moscow, 1932–33), and for vocational training, *Podgotovka kadrov v SSSR, 1927–1931 gg.* (Moscow, 1933).

118. *Vysshie uchebnye zavedeniia SSSR v 1934/35 ucheb. g. (Statisticheskie materialy)* (Moscow, 1935) (94 pages) and *Vysshaia shkola za 10 let* (Moscow, 1938) (27 pages).

119. *Nauchnye kadry i nauchno-issledovatel'skie uchrezhdeniia SSSR* (Moscow, 1930) (103 pages) and *Dopolnitel'naia razrabotka otchetov nauchno-issledovatel'skikh uchrezhdenii po sostoianiiu na 1 ianvaria 1933 g.* (Moscow, 1934).

120. *Nauchno-issledovatel'skie instituty i vysshie uchebnie zavedeniia SSSR v 1932 g.* (Moscow, 1933) (91 pages) and *Itogi kul'turnogo stroitel'stva v tsifrakh*, part 3 (Moscow, 1934) (87 pages).

121. *Vsesoiuznaia bibliotechnaia perepis' 1 oktiabria 1934 g.*, vols. 1–2 (Moscow, 1936) (559 pages in all).

122. *Periodicheskaia pechat' SSSR i rabsel'korovskoe dvizhenie mezdu XV i XVI s"ezdami VKP(b)* (Moscow, 1930) (127 pages).

123. *Pechat' SSSR v 1928, 1933 i 1934 gg.* (Moscow, 1936) (96 pages); *Pechat' v SSSR za 20 let sovetskoi vlasti* (Moscow, 1938) (34 pages); *Itogi kul'turnogo stroitel'stva v tsifrakh*, part 4 (Moscow, 1934) (32 pages).

124. *Predvaritel'nye itogi po politprosvetu, iskusstvu i pechati za 1935 g.* (Moscow, 1936) (34 pages) and *Politprosvet, iskusstvo i pechat' k nachalu 1937 g.* (Moscow, 1937) (48 tables).

125. See Sheila Fitzpatrick, "Sources on the Social History of the 1930s" (in this volume), and Peter Gooderham, "Party Publications and Other Sources on Cadres in the 1930s," *Russian History* 12 (1985, 2–4), 284–87.

126. See above, section on *Employment data*.

127. *Sotsial'nyi oblik rabochei molodezhi po materialam sotsiologicheskikh obsledovanii 1936 i 1972 gg.* (Moscow, 1980), 33–39, and *Sotsial'nyi oblik kolkhoznoi molodezhi po materialam sotsiologicheskikh obsledovanii 1938 i 1969 gg.* (Moscow, 1976), 20–25. In both instances the results for the 1930s have been compared with more recent results.

128. Ger P. Van Den Berg, *The Soviet System of Justice: Figures and Policy*, vol. 29 in the series *Law in Eastern Europe*, edited by F. J. M. Feldbrugge (Dordrecht: Martinus Nijjhoff Publishers, 1985).

Newspapers and Journals

SHEILA FITZPATRICK

Historians who have worked previously on the 1920s will be struck by a change in the balance of their sources as they move into the 1930s, particularly after the first years of the decade. Newspapers become more important as a source, journals less. This means that historians have to adjust their research technique. Working on social issues of the 1920s, it is often possible to orient oneself quickly in a given topic by reading the relevant journals. Working on similar issues of the 1930s, the researcher often has no good journal to rely on and must become used to scanning large numbers of newspaper pages in order to extract a relatively small amount of relevant data.

Newspapers

Newspapers, especially national newspapers, are one of the types of sources that suffer a marked change in style and content and a decline in informational quality as a result of increased censorship at the beginning of the 1930s. They are nevertheless an invaluable source for the Stalin period. Regional (oblast and krai) newspapers are particularly useful sources for social historians. Appendix I (National, Republican and Regional Newspapers) provides basic information on titles and profiles of newspapers published in the 1930s. The most detailed finding aid is the 5-volume *Gazety SSSR, 1917–1960. Bibliograficheskii spravochnik* (Moscow, 1970–1984). For national newspapers, *Letopis' gazetnykh statei* provides an index of articles starting in 1936.

The number of newspapers published and their total circulation both rose sharply in the 1930s. By the end of the decade there were a total of 46 national newspapers, 114 republican, 393 regional (krai, oblast and okrug, plus newspapers of autonomous ethnic republics and oblasts), 3,393 raion and city, and 4,604 enterprise and other lower-level newspapers (excluding mimeographed publications). The circulation of *Izvestiia* had risen from 427,000 in 1928 to 1,600 in 1938, that of *Pravda* from 620,000 to 1,914,000, and that of *Komsomol'-skaia pravda* from 167,000 to 600,000.[1] Over the period 1928–37, the number of newspapers published in the Soviet Union rose from 1,197 to 8,521, and the number of newspapers distributed each day rose from 9.4 million to 36 million.[2]

National newspapers

National newspapers (see list in Appendix I, A) are the most easily accessible, since many of them have been microfilmed and are available in major U.S. libraries. They are also the most authoritative purveyors of government/party policy, but by the same token they tend to be less rewarding than other types of newspapers (notably evening and oblast newspapers) in giving casual insights into the way the society actually functioned, as against the way it was supposed to function. From the end of the 1920s, Soviet national newspapers of the 1930s developed a new style and tone, characterized by heightened propaganda content, a preference for ponderous generalization over specificity, and the exclusion of the news category Marc Ferro calls *"faits divers"* (accidents, fires, murders, natural disasters, human-interest stories).[3]

Although American scholars have sometimes seemed unwilling to look beyond the party organ *Pravda* and the government organ *Izvestiia*, there were a considerable number of national newspapers in the 1930s, and they were uniform neither in content nor (within limits) in point of view. Even in the Stalin period they did not all say the same thing, except on a few issues of particular political moment and delicacy. There were open polemical exchanges between newspapers on specific policy issues, as well as arguments and policy advocacy presented in Aesopian terms.

The newspapers had their own individual profiles, partly determined by their official focus and constituencies (labor, industry, agriculture, youth, the military, and so on) and partly reflecting editorial judgment and the strengths and interests of their journalists. For example, the industrial newspaper *Za industrializatsiiu* covered a broad range of economic and social questions in the 1930s, and—like other industry-related institutions of the period—tended to gather more talent and display more independence and self-confidence than the norm. *Komsomol'skaia pravda*, though less thorough and professionally accomplished than *Za industrializatsiiu*, often had a usefully idiosyncratic perspective and retained a penchant for amateur sociological surveys long after surveys had generally gone out of fashion in the Soviet Union.[4] The labor newspaper, *Trud*, provided good coverage of the trade unions as well as issues of everyday life such as the 1936 abortion debate.[5] It was *Trud*, too, that in 1935 ran an offbeat expose article on fake amateurism in sport and the "stipends" and perks available to promising young sportsmen.[6] On factory conditions and work life, however, *Trud* was often less illuminating than *Za industrializatsiiu*.

In the 1920s, several newspapers were aimed explicitly at a mass popular audience, urban and rural, notably *Rabochaia gazeta* (1922–32), *Bednota* (1918–31), and *Krest'ianskaia pravda* (1923–39). While their success in reaching this audience may be doubted,[7] they contain a great deal of material from local correspondents and about local conditions which is particularly valuable to social historians. There was no newspaper of the 1930s that was intended specifically for a popular working-class audience in the tradition of *Rabochaia gazeta*.[8] *Krest'ianskaia gazeta*, however, continued publication until 1939 as a specifically peasant paper with large type, stories that were shorter and written in simpler language than the norm, and many photographs and drawings. While it was slighter in informational content than the main agricultural newspaper, *Sotsialisticheskoe zemledelie, Krest'ianskaia gazeta* published more letters to the editor, many of them from peasants. These letters are a useful source for social historians, though more heavily censored and edited than those published in the Leningrad paper *Krest'ianskaia pravda* (see below). As we know from the Smolensk Archive,[9] however, *Krest'ianskaia gazeta*'s mail was considerably more interesting than its printed correspondence columns suggest. Historians should bear in mind that the newspaper's archive, if preserved, may constitute a major source of material on peasant life in the 1930s.

An anomaly among national newspapers was *Nasha gazeta*, organ of the Central Committee and Moscow branch of the trade union of Soviet and trading employees in the late 1920s and first half of the 1930s. For a number of years, *Nasha gazeta* (which, despite its national status, was clearly directed primarily toward a Moscow constituency) followed its own idiosyncratic path and concentrated on topics that were evidently of particular interest to its readers—for example, the status problems of white-collar employees; private trade and the black market; purges in the government bureaucracy; and plans for the resettlement of urban Jews in agriculture. *Nasha gazeta* was the only newspaper of the period that consistently reported and editorialized about anti-Semitism.

Evening city newspapers

Evening newspapers became something of a rarity in the 1930s,[10] but those that existed were distinguished by the liveliness and immediacy of their coverage of their city's social, commercial, and cultural life. The best known and most accessible of the evening newspapers is *Vecherniaia Moskva* (available in the Library of Congress), which took the interests of Moscow consumers to heart and provided detailed information on goods in city stores and their prices, as well as publishing vivid, if not necessarily strictly accurate, accounts of the scandals that periodically erupted in Moscow's trading and cultural institutions. *Vecherniaia krasnaia gazeta* (Leningrad) had similar characteristics, as well as reflecting the strong local patriotism of the city's inhabitants. Dnepropetrovsk's *Zvezda* was more serious than the Moscow and Leningrad evening papers. Indeed, it was a very high quality paper by Soviet standards, well-written and with a penchant for investigative reporting.

Regional newspapers

Regional (oblast and krai) newspapers are exceptionally valuable sources for the 1930s. In fact, social historians working primarily or entirely without archives may find that reading a range of regional newspapers from different parts of the country is the best way to get a sense of the real-life significance of central policy pronouncements and their implementation. To date, however, these sources have been comparatively little used by Western scholars, and they are generally cited by Soviet scholars only in regional histories that draw on one or two of the local papers. The basic problems in using them are, first, that the volume of material is so large, and second, that it is necessary to know the newspapers' titles in order to obtain and work on them. To help scholars solve the latter problem, a selected list of oblast and krai newspapers (with title and place) is given in Appendix I, C. A few oblast newspapers are available in the Library of Congress, notably a reasonably good run of the Rostov-on-Don paper, *Molot*, in the 1930s, but generally researchers will have to find them in the Soviet Union.[11] Compared to central newspapers, the regional ones seem to have been less heavily, or at least less systematically, censored, and were more likely to contain items like small advertisements and local announcements on questions like passport renewals and gun permits that may be of particular interest to social historians. Most published frequent reports from city and oblast courtrooms, especially when the cases being heard had political import or were connected with local scandals. Like *Vecherniaia Moskva*, the regional papers were good on consumer affairs: the arrival of a large consignment of goods for sale in the regional capital was likely to be announced triumphantly, often with prices and detailed listing of the new items available.

The dominant concerns of individual regional papers varied widely according to the nature of the region's economy and demographic make-up. Khabarovsk's *Tikhookeanskaia zvezda*, for example, was exceptional in its coverage of banditry, hooliganism, rape, shortage of women, and ethnic tensions in the Far East in the 1930s, giving a picture of Soviet life that is quite startlingly different from the familiar one focused on Moscow, Leningrad, and an idealized Magnitogorsk. Simferopol's *Krasnyi Krym*—generally a high-quality paper in journalistic terms—had something of the city's resort spirit, especially in the summer months when the area was swamped by holiday-makers, for whose entertainment there were gypsy clubs, performances by Yiddish singers, and 3 a.m. closing for one of Simferopol's downtown food (and drink?) stores. A newspaper like Ivanovo's *Rabochii krai* or Iaroslavl's *Severnyi rabochii* tended to be oriented toward industrial issues and workers' concerns, whereas one like *Tambovskaia pravda* had an agricultural focus.

The Smolensk paper, *Rabochii put'*, is of particular interest to Western scholars since it complements the Smolensk Archive. The existence in the West of that Archive also makes it possible to make some judgments about the reliability and thoroughness of an oblast newspaper in covering local events. I have not done this systematically, but can offer some tentative impressions. With regard to the wild collectivization drive of the winter of the 1929–30, for example, the Archive contains some hair-raising reports of excesses. These were not matched in the newspaper coverage, although the tense and occasionally hysterical tone of *Rabochii put'* throughout January 1930 suggested that something was seriously amiss. With regard to the onset of the Great Purges in the Western Oblast in the first half of 1937, both Archive and newspaper are excellent sources, and the historian working on this topic would be at a disadvantage lacking either. During the same period, it should be noted that *Rabochii put'* was giving extensive coverage to an important sociopolitical issue which is scarcely mentioned in the Smolensk Archive files,[12] namely the religious upsurge in the countryside and its impact on the Supreme Soviet election campaign.

The Leningrad oblast newspaper *Krest'ianskaia pravda* (published by the Leningrad obkom and oblispolkom throughout the 1930s) deserves special mention. It is by far the best newspaper source on peasant life of the 1930s, particularly in the years 1935–37, when it was edited first by P. Skrotinin and then by L. Shaumian. Its correspondence columns (*"Signaly s mest"*) were exceptionally frank and circumstantial; and it also had good journalists who managed to maintain relatively high standards of investigative reporting, particularly in the raions of Leningrad oblast. Its detailed reports from district show trials in Leningrad oblast during the fall of 1937 are exceptionally useful as a source on rural officials, peasants, and the relations between them. In addition, the paper often published unusual news items and features on oblast and national affairs: for example, on the expulsion of "social aliens" from the city of Leningrad carried out by the NKVD after Kirov's murder,[13] on regulations relating to frontier zones,[14] and on the 1936 suicide of Khandzhian, secretary of the Armenian Communist Party, who was suffering simultaneously from advanced tuberculosis and the threat of disgrace for his alleged lack of political vigilance.[15] Characteristic of the idiosyncratic style of the paper was a reflective (but unsigned) story filed from a 1935 conference of Stakhanovites on Stalin's public persona and interaction with delegates—in effect, an early attempt at objective analysis of the Stalin cult, albeit not unsympathetic to Stalin and the principle of charismatic leadership.[16] A full run of this newspaper can be found in INION.

Local newspapers at a lower (okrug and raion) level are rarely accessible to Western scholars,[17] although there are (or were) some in the newspaper collection of the Academy of Sciences' Library in Leningrad. Raion newspapers, on my admittedly limited experience with this source, seem disappointing: lacking the resources and journalistic talent available to the oblast level, they tended to contain relatively little local reportage and to lift a large amount of material straight from the central press.

Journals

Overall, the 1930s saw a sharp decline in the quality and quantity of information available in journals. This was partly because of censorship, but partly also because newspapers were taking a larger share of the market, and journals were squeezed out for that reason. Over the period 1928–32, the number of journals and serials published annually in the Soviet Union rose from 2,074 to 2,144, then dropped down to 1,880 by 1937, while their total circulation rose from 303 million in 1928 to 318 million in 1932 and then dropped to 250 million in 1937. Over the same period, newspaper circulation and the total number of newspapers published (see above) increased by a factor of 4.[18]

An invaluable finding aid for journals is the 9-volume *Periodicheskaia pechat' SSSR 1917–1949: Bibliograficheskii ukazatel'* (Moscow, 1955–63). The journals are also indexed from 1933 in *Letopis' periodicheskikh izdanii SSSR*.

Economic, statistical, labor, and agricultural journals

The main economic journals of the 1930s are *Problemy ekonomiki* (1929–41), the more theoretically oriented *Planovoe khoziaistvo* (1923–41), and the TsUNKhU journal *Plan* (1933–37), which is useful for both social and economic historians. As indicated by Wheatcroft (*Statistical Sources*, above), most of the statistical journals that flourished in the 1920s disappeared in the early 1930s: *Vestnik statistiki, Statisticheskoe obozrenie, Statistika truda,* amd *Ekonomicheskoe obozrenie* all ceased publication in the years 1929–31. Another casualty in the economic field was the valuable Vesenkha (later Narkomtiazhprom) journal, *Puti industrializatsii.*

The year that saw the demise of the Commissariat of Labor, 1933, was the last year of publication of no fewer than three labor journals: *Voprosy truda, Na trudovom fronte,* and *Izvestiia Narodnogo Komissariata Truda SSSR.* In addition, a number of journals of individual trade unions ceased publication in the early to mid–1930s, including *Metallist* (1918–31), *Gornorabochii* (1920–31), *Golos kozhevnika* (1917–34), and *Kommunal'nyi rabotnik* (1917–34). In their place came a new journal on general trade-union affairs, *Voprosy profdvizheniia,* later *Profsoiuzy SSSR* (1931–41), which is necessary if pedestrian reading for labor historians, and the journal *Stakhanovets* (1936–41), which focused primarily on Stakhanovite work techniques and technical innovations and seldom strayed into the broader reaches of working-class life, organization, and culture.

The chief agricultural journal of the 1930s was *Sotsialisticheskaia rekonstruktsiia sel'skogo khoziaistva* (1930–38; earlier title, *Puti sel'skogo khoziaistva;* later title, *Sotsialisticheskoe sel'skoe khoziaistvo*). Like most publications of the period, it was production- rather than peasant-oriented, which makes it a disappointing source for social historians. *Na agrarnom fronte,* the journal of the Society of Marxist Agrarians and the Communist Academy, lost its importance as a center of intellectual debate around 1930 and ceased publication in 1934. The journal *Kollektivist* (1925–33) is unique in its focus on peasants and the social and psychological aspects of collectivization. The Narkomzem journal *Sotsialisticheskoe zemleustroistvo* (1930–35) is an important source both on the practical problems of organizing kolkhoz land allocation and on agronomists and surveyors as a professional group.

"Thick" and general-interest journals

Because of the constraints on debate, these are not as valuable to the social historian as their counterparts in the 1920s. But it is still worth checking them for coverage of social issues. Of the "thick" journals of the 1920s, *Pechat' i revoliutsiia* ceased publication in 1930, as did RAPP's polemical *Na literaturnom postu* two years later. The following "thick" journals of the 1920s continued to appear through the 1930s: *Krasnaia nov'* (with fewer controversies and diminished intellectual quality); *Novyi mir*;[19] the Komsomol journal, *Molodaia gvardiia* (without the verve and polemics of the 1920s); *Oktiabr'*; and the Leningrad journal *Zvezda*. Among new "thick" journals were *Literaturnyi kritik*, which in the 1930s took over the challenging role of *Krasnaia nov'* in the 1920s and *Novyi mir* in the post-Stalin period; *Internatsional'naia literatura*, organ of the International Association of Revolutionary Writers, also published in English, French, German and a variety of other languages (1931–43); and two journals dedicated to bland celebration of Soviet achievements and the industrialization drive: *Nashi dostizheniia* (1929–37), which was founded by Gorky, and *SSSR na stroike* (1930–41). The lighter-weight *Prozhektor*, notable for its excellent cartoons and lively social reportage, survived until 1935. The entertainment-oriented *Ogonek* and the satirical weekly *Krokodil* were published uninterruptedly from the early 1920s.

The weekly *Literaturnaia gazeta* published throughout the 1930s, should also be mentioned here, although it was strictly speaking a newspaper and not a journal. The *Literaturnaia gazeta* of the 1930s was more purely literary and cultural in focus than its present-day descendant, and devoted less attention to social issues. Nevertheless, it is one of the most convenient and manageable sources to consult for orientation on any specific controversy, policy, or event affecting the cultural world.

Legal journals

The legal journals of the 1930s (discussed in Peter Solomon's essay Legal Journals and Soviet Social History) are a welcome exception to the rule of declining quality and diminishing returns for the researcher. *Sovetskaia iustitsiia* and *Sotsialisticheskoe zakonodatel'stvo*, the two major law journals published throughout the 1930s, are essential for every type of social history research. No serious social historian can ignore them, whether the subject of his or her research is the peasantry, marriage and family questions, housing, or labor. Their great value (for the social historian) is twofold. First, Soviet legal theory was based on class premises, that is, it assumed that an individual's social class was relevant to an evaluation of his actions and of the way he should be treated in the courts. This meant that officials in the legal system, particularly State Procurators and judges, functioned almost as practicing sociologists—and continued to do so long after academic sociologists had been driven out of business. Second, the legal journals often focused, for instructional or examplary purposes, on specific cases, rather than indulging in the abstract and misleading generalizations about society that are so commonly found elsewhere.

Medical and public health journals

Among the most useful public health journals from the social historian's standpoint is *Sotsial'naia gigiena* (Moscow, 1922–30), continued in the 1930s as *Gigiena i sanitariia*. Other journals of interest to historians include *Meditsinskii rabotnik* (Moscow, 1919–35), organ of the Central Committee of the medical workers' union, and *Fel'dsher i akusherka* (Moscow, 1936–).

Educational/cultural/scientific journals

Kommunisticheskoe prosveshchenie (1931–36) succeeded *Narodnoe prosveshchenie* as the main organ of the Russian Commissariat of Education. *Front nauki i tekhniki* (1928–38) absorbed the journal of the Section of Scientific Workers of the Teachers' Union, *Nauchnyi rabotnik*, in 1930, although it did not play the latter's assertive role as spokesman for professorial interests. The Communist Academy published a journal, *Vestnik Kommunisticheskoi Akademii* (1924–35), which is a valuable source for a variety of debates on economic and social policy, law, the social sciences, and the humanities. A number of educational and cultural journals ceased publication at the end of the 1920s or in the early 1930s: these include *Kul'turnaia revoliutsiia, Revoliutsiia i kul'tura*, the psychologically oriented *Pedogogiia*, the teachers' journal *Rabotnik prosveshcheniia*, and the journal of the Society of Marxist Pedagogues, *Na putiakh k novoi shkole*.

The weekly newspaper *Uchitel'skaia gazeta* played a similar role in the educational field as *Literaturnaia gazeta* in literature. It is particularly valuable as a source on the teaching profession and the primary and secondary school system.

Party journals

Party journals are an important (and relatively easily accessible) source. They not only published party resolutions on social policy but also provided information on problems of implementation, i.e., societal responses. They were issued at national, republican, and regional level.

At the national level, the Central Committee of the Communist Party published the following journals:

Izvestiia TsK (full title, *Izvestiia Tsentral'nogo Komiteta Vsesoiuznoi Kommunisticheskoi partii (b)*) (Moscow, 1919–29), which continued as *Partiinoe stroitel'stvo* (1929–46);

Bol'shevik, theoretical and political journal of the Central Committee of the All-Union Communist Party (Moscow, 1924–), which is often cataloged under its post–1952 title, *Kommunist*;

Spravochnik partiinogo rabotnika, a serial publication appearing irregularly from 1921 to 1939 (and again from 1956), of which volumes 7 (2 parts, 1930), 8 (1934), and 9 (1939) fall into our period.

In addition, the Central Control Commission of the Communist Party (TsKK) published a journal, *Biulleten' Ts[entral'noi] K[ontrol'noi] K[omissii] i N[arodnogo] K[omissariata] R[aboche]-K[rest'ianskoi] I[nspektsii] SSSR i RSFSR* (1924–29), which is exceptionally useful for social historians. The great value of TsKK/Rabkrin material for the social historian is that these bodies conducted investigations and responded to complaints. Unfortunately, TsKK/Rabkrin was dissolved in 1934 and replaced by the Commissions of, respectively, Party and State Control, which did not have any regular press organs.

At the republican level, most party committees published journals, but only some of them were in Russian or had a Russian-language edition. These included:

Partrabotnik, organ of the Central Committee of the Azerbaidzhanian Communist Party (Baku, 1937–38);

Bol'shevik Belorussii (Minsk, 1927–41);

Partiinoe stroitel'stvo, organ of the Georgian Communist Party (Tbilisi, 1933–41);

Bol'shevik Kazakhstana (Alma-Ata, 1931–).

For the years 1925–27 only, the Ukrainian party journal, *Izvestiia Tsentral'nogo Komiteta Kommunisticheskoi Partii [bol'shevikov] Ukrainy*, published in Kharkov (later Kiev), appeared in Russian.

In addition, some republican party control commissions published journals in the 1920s, e.g., the Ukrainian *Biulleten' TsKK KP(b)U—NK RSI USSR*.

A large number of regional (guberniia, oblast, krai, and city) party committees published journals on a monthly or biweekly basis, usually containing articles as well as instructions and regulations. Titles vary. In the 1920s, many regional journals followed the pattern of the central *Izvestiia TsK* (for example, the Siberian kraikom's *Izvestiia Sibirskogo Kraevogo Komiteta Vsesoiuznoi Kommunisticheskoi Partii [bol'shevikov]*, published in Novosibirsk, 1925–30), but others invented their own titles. For example, the Lower Volga kraikom published a biweekly journal called *Kommunisticheskii put'* (Saratov, 1921–30) which was exceptionally lively and accomplished in the 1920s, probably because it drew on the talents of the sizeable contingent of exiled Oppositionist intellectuals resident in Saratov. In the 1930s, the most popular title for regional party journals was *Partrabotnik*,[20] followed by *Na leninskom puti* or *Leninskii put'*.[21] By contrast, Stalin's name was evoked only by one journal, the Saratov obkom's *Stalinets* (1939–41), which may have sought to dissociate itself from the non-conformist tradition of its predecessor, *Kommunisticheskii put'*.

In addition to these journals, some regional party organizations also published monthly bulletins of instructions and resolutions.[22] For complete listings of regional party journals, see *Periodicheskaia pechat'*, vol. 1.

Youth and children's journals

The Komsomol Central Committee published an important "thick" journal, *Molodaia gvardiia*, from 1922 to 1941. It also published a journal for Komsomol activists, *Iunyi bol'shevik* (1918–38), continued as *Molodoi bol'shevik* (1939–41); a journal for students, *Krasnoe studenchestvo* (1925–35);[23] a monthly children's journal, *Pioner* (1924–); a journal for Pioneer leaders, *Vozhatyi* (1924–); and a journal for young schoolchildren, *Murzilka* (1924–).[24] The Leningrad Komsomol organization published *Iunyi proletari* from 1917 to 1936.

Women's journals

Women's journals are excellent social history sources that have been surprisingly little used, except to some extent on women's history themes. The journals are, of course, excellent for that purpose, but it should be emphasized that their potential utility is much broader. Women's journals of the 1930s, like law journals, are much more likely than most sources of the period to deal with living and working conditions, social life and social problems, and indeed individual human beings. They can be used to fill in some of the gaps in documentation that plague social historians of the Stalin period. In the sphere of working-class life, for example, there were no journals called *Rabochii* or *Rabochaia zhizn'* in the 1930s—but there was a journal called *Rabotnitsa*,[25] and labor historians cannot afford to overlook it. The same applies to the sphere of peasant life (the journal *Krest'ianka*),[26] and even to the life of the new Soviet elite (the journal *Obshchestvennitsa,* discussed below).

The Central Committee's department for work among women workers and peasants, commonly known as the *zhenotdel*, published the journal *Kommunistka* from 1920 until the department's dissolution in 1930. The journals *Rabotnitsa* and *Krest'-ianka* appeared throughout the 1930s. *Zhenskii zhurnal*, a more frivolous journal of prerevolutionary antecedents published by *Ogonek* in the years 1926–30, included fashion, romantic short stories, and dressmaking patterns.[27]

The best of the woman's journals of the Stalin period is undoubtedly *Obshchestvennitsa* (Moscow, 1936–41). Indeed, this is one of the best journal sources of any kind for social historians. An anomalous publication, founded under the patronage of Ordzhonikidze and originally published as an organ of the Commissariat of Heavy Industry of the USSR (later, after Narkomtiazhprom was split up in 1937–38, organ of a large number of industrial commissariats), this was the journal of the wives' volunteer movement.[28] *Obshchestvennitsa* was a journal aimed at middleclass readers—primarily wives of Communist officials and professionals, not professional women or (in contrast to the earlier *Kommunistka*) Communist activists.[29]

Newspapers and journals as sources for history "from below"

"Blank spots" are as much a problem in the social history of the 1930s as they are in the political history. What are most often lacking in the sources are the individual human dimension and a grass-roots, popular perspective on events. The public documents of the period strove for a spirit of high seriousness, thereby eliminating much that is grist to the social historian's mill. Newspapers stopped publishing *faits divers* and many types of human interest stories at the beginning of the 1930s. (Even the weather got short shrift, except in the agricultural newspaper *Sotsialisticheskoe zemledelie,* which published a daily weather map of the Soviet Union.) Lightweight entertainment journals disappeared. Many forms of popular culture were officially frowned upon, and therefore existed largely in oral, undocumented form.[30]

Thus, the great challenge for the social historian is to discover sources and types of data that help fill in the missing dimension. The journals of the 1930s are, on the whole, unsatisfactory sources for history "from below." The main exceptions are law journals such as *Sovetskaia iustitsiia* and *Sotsialisticheskaia zakonnost'*, particularly in their reports of court cases and their instructions to local judicial personnel on problems of interpretation and implementation of laws, and women's journals, particularly *Obshchestvennitsa*.

Newspapers are richer sources on everyday life and popular attitudes, if properly used. There is a handful of newspapers that are consistently valuable, notably Leningrad's *Krest'ianskaia pravda*, Moscow's *Vecherniaia Moskva*, Dnepropetrovsk's *Zvezda*, and *Nasha gazeta*. In general, oblast and evening papers tend to be more useful to social historians than the major central newspapers. But all newspapers contain a good deal of useful data under various rubrics. Reports of court cases and satirical feuilletons (*fel'etony*) are always worth scanning. Features about women and women's groups often provide information about consumer affairs and other problems of everyday life. Anti-religious news items and stories, which appeared intermittently in the daily press as well as the Militant Atheists' newspaper *Bezbozhnik*,[31] are also valuable sources for social historians.

The correspondence columns in the daily press cannot be overlooked as a source, although the published letters are usually censored and edited (and sometimes perhaps even written by the newspaper as "*vox populi*" endorsement of policy or justification of impending policy change). These published letters can scarcely be treated as authentic, unmediated expressions of grass-roots opinion. We know, however, that all newspapers received a large amount of genuine correspondence expressing individual complaints, grievances, and criticisms. In planning programs of archival research, social historians should remember that Soviet newspaper archives are likely to contain extremely valuable files of unpublished correspondence illuminating a wide variety of social problems.

Notes

1. Data from *Sotsialisticheskoe stroitel'stvo Soiuza SSR (1933–1938 gg.). Statisticheskii sbornik* (Moscow–Leningrad, 1939), 132.
2. Data from *Kul'turnoe stroitel'stvo SSSR. Statisticheskii sbornik* (Moscow, 1956), 322.
3. For a suggestive discussion of the significance of this exclusion, see M. Ferro, "Faits divers, faits d'histoire. Presentation," *Annales. Economies. Société. Civilisations*, July–August 1983, 821–25. Although Ferro seems to date the exclusion of *faits divers* from 1917, it is probably more accurate to date it from 1929. The newspapers of NEP carried *faits divers* and advertisements, though in lesser quantity than their pre-revolutionary predecessors.
4. See, for example, the survey of 865 young workers of the Stalin Auto Plant (Moscow) conducted by *KP*, in *Komsomol'skaia pravda*, 7 November 1937, p. 4.
5. One of the most interesting collections of opinions from blue- and white-collar workers and professionals, male and female, on the proposal for a law banning abortion appeared in *Trud* over the period 26 May–4 June 1936.
6. N. Burov, "Vrednaia sistema 'verbovki' sportsmenov," *Trud*, 12 December 1935, 4.
7. See Jeffrey Brooks, "Public and Private Values in the Soviet Press, 1921–1928," *Slavic Review* 48:1 (1988), 16–35, for a valuable analysis and discussion of Soviet newspapers aimed at the common reader in the 1920s.
8. Despite its name and its original designation as a paper for Moscow workers (Brooks, *op. cit.*, 18), the oblast newspaper *Rabochaia Moskva*, published by the Moscow Party

Committee, was just a run-of-the-mill party newspaper in the 1930s, giving special coverage to Moscow party affairs. Its name from 1939, *Moskovskii bol'shevik*, more accurately indicated its content. Since 1950, it has appeared as *Moskovskaia pravda*.

9. It was the practice of *Krest'ianskaia gazeta* and other newspapers to forward letters of complaint and criticism to appropriate institutions, often regional or district party committees. The Western obkom, at least, was conscientious in investigating these complaints and trying to rectify abuses disclosed.

10. When the Press Department of the party's Central Committee held a meeting of editors of evening newspapers in the Soviet Union early in 1936, those represented were *Vecherniaia Moskva* (Moscow), *Vecherniaia krasnaia gazeta* (Leningrad), *Bil'shovik* (Kiev, in Ukrainian), *Stalinskii rabochii* (Stalino), *Khar'kovskii rabochii* (Kharkov), *Zvezda* (Dnepropetrovsk), *Gor'kovskii rabochii* (Gorky), *Tiflisskii rabochii* (Tiflis) and *Musha* (Tiflis, in Georgian). *Vecherniaia Moskva*, 3 February 1936, 1.

11. This is not as easy as it sounds. INION has no oblast newspapers (other than those of Moscow and Leningrad). In the first half of the 1980s, the Lenin Library's collection, which is probably the most complete, was essentially inaccessible to foreigners at Khimki, and the Saltykov-Shchedrin newspaper collection in Leningrad was closed. That left the Istoricheskaia biblioteka (GIPB) in Moscow and the Library of the Academy of Sciences (BAN) in Leningrad, but then the GIPB collection became inaccessible in connection with rebuilding, and subsequently it is rumored to have been damaged by water. The BAN collection suffered to a yet undetermined extent in the great fire of 1988. In the summer of 1988, the Lenin Library's collection became accessible to foreigners again, albeit on a limited basis.

12. This is presumably because the Smolensk Archive is a party archive, and the elections were a soviet rather than a party concern.

13. *Krest'ianskaia pravda*, 24 March 1935, 3.

14. *Krest'ianskaia pravda*, 23 May 1935, 4.

15. *Krest'ianskaia pravda*, 12 July 1936, 4.

16. "Komu aplodiroval Stalin," *Krest'ianskaia pravda*, 16 November 1935, 3.

17. But see the interesting discussion on the Ukrainian okrug newspaper *Krasnoe zaporozhe* (later *Chervone Zaporizhzhe*) in Anne Rassweiler, "The Local Press as a Source: Dneprostroi Newspapers, 1927–33," *Russian History/Histoire russe* 12:2–4 (1985), 327–38.

18. Data from *Kul'turnoe stroitel'stvo SSSR. Statisticheskii sbornik* (Moscow, 1956), 322.

19. For the contents of this journal in the early 1930s, see *Bibliographical Index of the Contributions to Novyi Mir, 1925–1934*, compiled and edited by Tamara Miller (Ann Arbor: Ardis, 1983).

20. Used by the Gorky obkom, Gorky (formerly Nizhnyi Novgorod), 1932–41; the Leningrad obkom and gorkom, Leningrad, 1928–32, the Sverdlovsk obkom, Sverdlovsk, 1934–37; and, in the variant *Partiinyi rabotnik*, by the West Siberian obkom, Novosibirsk, 1930–33.

21. *Na leninskom puti* was the title of the journals of the West Siberian kraikom, Novosibirsk, 1927–37, and the Ivanovo obkom, Ivanovo, 1925–34, while *Leninskii put'* was chosen by the Central Black Earth (Voronezh) obkom, Voronezh, 1927–41, and the North Caucasus kraikom, Rostov on Don, 1927–31.

22. For example, *Biulleten' Kazakskogo kraevogo komiteta VKP(b)* (Kzyl-Orda Alma-Ata, 1928–30), *Biulleten' Leningradskogo oblastnogo i gorodskogo komitetov VKP(b)* (Leningrad, 1925–34).

23. Also published under the title *Krasnaia molodezh'* (1924–25) and *Sovetskoe studenchestvo* (1935–41).

24. Felicity Ann O'Dell's *Socialisation through Children's Literature. The Soviet Example* (Cambridge: Cambridge University Press, 1978), which is an analysis of the content of *Murzilka* over a fifty-year period and the changing values it sought to inculcate, gives quite extensive coverage to the 1930s.

25. Published in Moscow by "Pravda" publishing house from 1923.

26. Published in Moscow by "Pravda" publishing house from 1922.

27. For a full listing of women's journals, see *Periodicheskaia pechat'*, vol. 8 (Moscow, 1958), 84–89.

28. On the volunteers' movement and the journal *Obshchestvennitsa*, see Sheila Fitzpatrick, "'Middle-class Values' and Soviet Life in the 1930s," in Terry L. Thompson and Richard Sheldon, ed., *Soviet Society and Culture. Essays in Honor of Vera S. Dunham* (Boulder, Colo.: Westview Press, 1988), 32–34.

29. After the war the place of *Obshchestvennitsa* was taken by a new journal, *Sovetskaia zhenshchina*. This "general-political and literary-artistic journal" first appeared under the auspices of the Anti-Fascist Committee of Soviet Women and the All-Union Central Council of Trade Unions in 1945.

30. The journal *Sovetskaia etnografiia* (1931–34, 1934–37, 1946–) is of some use to historians studying small ethnic minorities of the Soviet Union in the 1930s, but it was not until the early 1950s that it became a really useful source on the Russian peasantry and, to a lesser extent, the Russian urban population. Another ethnographic source of the 1930s worth investigation is the Academy of Sciences serial publication *Sovetskii fol'klor. Stat'i i materialy*, vyp. 1–7 (Leningrad, 1934–41).

31. *Bezbozhnik* (1925–41) was a large-format, illustrated publication, aimed at a mass audience, which included some reporting of contemporary religious observances and practices in the Soviet Union as well as didactic articles exposing priestly fraud, superstition, and links between organized religion and exploitation in every part of the world and throughout human history. The Society of Militant Atheists also published an instructional-informational journal for cadres, *Antireligioznik* (1926–41), which occasionally carried illuminating reports from local activists on popular religious life.

Legal Journals and Soviet Social History

PETER H. SOLOMON, Jr.

The legal journals of almost any country make good sources for the study of social history. By illuminating the substance of the law and the way it is applied, they are bound to provide insights into the nature of social institutions, the relationships among social groups and classes, and the dynamics of change in social structure. The law journals of Stalinist Russia before World War II are no exception to this rule. On the contrary, these journals offer a particularly rich vein of information and analysis relevant to the concerns of the social historian.

One reason is that the development of Soviet law and legal institutions in the years from 1928 to 1941 was intimately connected with the transformation of Russian society. Soon after the First Five-Year Plan was launched, the law was subordinated to the goals of collectivization and industrialization, and the men of the law were mobilized to serve as soldiers on these and other fronts of the great struggle. Local procurators and judges joined in raids of the villages, seeking out hoarders of grain and other opponents of regime policies; while their urban counterparts sought and prosecuted those who could be blamed for accidents and for the production of defective goods. At the same time, justice officials were instructed to ignore the niceties of legal procedure, that is "to simplify," but within a few years official attitudes toward legal forms and procedure made an about-face. By mid-decade Stalin and Vyshinskii were calling for the restoration of law as an instrument of central rule, a new line which facilitated the larger conservative shift in the policies and values sponsored by the regime. In seeking to restore the status of law, the leaders used it both to consolidate the new social order (e.g., strengthen the family, increase the birth rate, discipline workers, and remove troublemakers from the streets) and to legitimate it.[1]

A second reason for the particularly rich coverage of social history in Soviet legal journals before the war lies in the breadth of functions performed by one legal agency, the procuracy. From its beginnings in the early 1920s the procuracy was supposed to have served not only as the prosecutorial arm of the state but also as a body that supervised the observance of legality throughout government. Clearly this supervisory mandate was too broad and sensitive to be executed in full, but it did involve procurators in many spheres of public life, especially at the provincial and local levels. Frequently procurators paid close attention to the behavior of local governments, whose ordinances and actions routinely violated their legal powers; it was common for the officials to investigate complaints from citizens about illegal and unfair activities on the part of all sorts of officials and agencies. In the mid-1930s procurators were expected to deal with complaints made directly to them but also with "signals" provided by the newspapers.[2]

A third and crucial reason why the legal journals of the 1930s constitute an especially good source for the social historian is the character of the journals themselves. With one exception the major legal journals were not academic but rather house organs of government agencies, and as a rule these agencies assigned the tasks of writing and editing to a corps of literate and capable officials. This made sense, for these journals performed important functions. On the one hand, they guided officials throughout the country in the performance of their jobs; on the other hand, the journals also served as a medium of communication among officials at all levels about the nature of law enforcement, judicial and administrative practice. As a result, the journals are packed with information about local practice, from the vantage points both of central officials and of the local officials themselves. On a regular basis officials in the central agencies contributed analyses of the behavior of the police, procuracy, and courts—sometimes on the basis of the reports submitted by provincial and local authorities, other times following personal investigations of particular localities (*kommandirovki*). At the same time, provincial and local officials generously supplied their own letters, notes, and even articles, the publication of which brought them financial reward.[3]

In this essay I shall illustrate in a selective way the abundance of evidence that the major legal journals offer for the study of Soviet social history of the prewar Stalin years, and then characterize briefly these and the other legal journals of the period.

Illustrations

1. *Collectivization and class war in the countryside*

The major legal journals[4] in the years from 1928 to 1935 give a striking portrait of the part played by investigators, procurators, and judges in the procurement of grain and the collectivization of the countryside. Encouraged both by directives from the Commissariat of Justice (Narkomiust) and by pressure from raion-level politicians, legal officials spent long periods of time in the villages, especially during the harvest and other campaigns. While in the countryside, the officials responded to signals from the local *aktivy*, sought out violators of the law, and processed their cases in short order.[5] The legal journals of the time were preoccupied with monitoring and criticizing how legal officials pursued these responsibilities, but the reader can discern what was happening. From the fall of 1930 to the middle of the decade, most of the peasants that judges convicted of hoarding grain or failing to make payments of hard quotas were neither incarcerated nor deported but instead subjected to fines or corrective work. This pattern of sentencing suggests that what one is witnessing is not the brutal coercion directed against a minority of the peasantry supposed to be kulaks but rather the "squeeze" that soon forced the majority of rural inhabitants (including many kulaks) either to flee to the cities or join the kolkhoz. To be sure, this is a partial view of events in the countryside, one that misses out on the activities of the OGPU as revealed in the Smolensk Archive, but is an important view all the same (one that is underrepresented in the Archive). Without more attention to this other face of collectivization our image of the process will remain one-sided.[6]

The legal journals also show how raion authorities tried to use the criminal law to manage rural officialdom. Regularly in 1929–32 the chairmen both of rural soviets and of collective farms were charged with mismanagement or abusing their powers. Sometimes the charges were deserved (as when the chairman in question had been "systematically drunk" and failed to perform his duties) but other times they were frivolous (as when a kolkhoz chairman was charged with criminal negligence for not building a horseshed). By 1934, the lines of conflict had changed as rural-soviet leaders themselves were joining their bosses in the raion agricultural establishment in bringing charges against kolkhoz chairmen for not fulfilling procurements of grain or flax. More often than not, conviction for such misdeeds did not bring a term of imprisonment, but it still constituted grounds for dismissal from office, making the threat of criminal prosecution into a deterrent for rural officials.[7]

A special chapter in the history of collectivization belongs to the artificially induced famine of 1932–33, and the legal journals shed light on this event as well. As peasants in the grain-producing centers were forced to give up the very grain they needed to survive, many turned to theft or deception. Their resistance to starvation as well as to regime policies was, however, met by the application of the new draconian law of 7 August 1932, which made theft from state or public agencies a capital offense and stipulated long terms of imprisonment for relatively minor thefts, including those perpetrated out of need. During the winter of 1933 the hard-pressed officials implementing the new law intensified their attack on the peasantry, and the standards of legal proceedings deteriorated sharply. When in May 1933 Stalin called for a halt to these "excesses," the victims of legal repression had grounds to flood higher courts with appeals, which occupied those courts well into 1935.[8]

Righting the wrongs done by local justice officials was not left entirely to the victims and the legal agencies; from time to time members of the public also played a part. Thus, in the village of Veshensk on the shores of the "quiet Don" did the writer Mikhail Sholokhov make appeals on behalf of peasants he thought to have been wronged. In 1934, G. was accused of theft from a kolkhoz after 15 puds of flour were discovered in his cellar. G. had been growing rye on his own land, but the flour consisted of 10 percent rye and 90 percent wheat! G. insisted that the mill had made a substitution for the 20 puds of rye he had brought in from his plot, but the authorities ignored his explanation, convicted him of theft according to the law of 7 August, and sentenced him to ten years in prison. Then Sholokhov intervened. He came forward and told the authorities: "Look carefully. This man is on our side (*nash chelovek*). His uncle, a communist, was an investigator for a revolutionary tribunal who was shot in 1919 during an uprising. I wrote about this in *Quiet Flows the Don*. . . ." Perhaps Sholokhov's tarnished reputation deserves partial rehabilitation![9]

2. The industrialization drive

From the discussions of the work of procurators and judges on the industrial front one gets a candid and striking picture of the consequences of excessive tempos and distorted priorities associated with the industrialization drive. Both in transport and in factories accidents were rampant, and the quality of industrial production, already low, reportedly declined during the early and mid–1930s. To confront these problems (or at least to explain them), politicians issued new laws and directives and urged legal officials to actively seek out those managers who might be held responsible for accidents and substandard production. The policy of criminalizing mismanagement in industry, though, was difficult to put into effect. To start, the procurators themselves were loathe to intervene in factory affairs and did so only when their agents (members of plant-level "assistance groups") called for help. Those arrested were rarely top-level management, moreover, but as a rule lower technicians and shop foremen. Could the procurators have done otherwise, once (from 1931 on) they had to reconcile the instructions to pursue managers with other directives warning against the harassment of specialists?[10]

During the course of the 1930s procurators and judges were also drawn increasingly into the affairs of the workers—the regulation of work discipline and the protection of shock-workers (*udarniki*) and Stakhanovites. The expansion of industry during the First Five-Year Plan was based upon a new work force recruited from the peasantry, and these fresh recruits had much to learn about the routine and requirements of factory work. Their failings became the subject of a fast-developing labor law, and from 1929 to 1933 comrades courts operated in many factories to help discipline the unruly and the careless.[11] The problem of labor discipline generated criminal cases as well. A whole class of cases involved the accidental "spoiling" of machines by the workers who used them. Since the acts were not intentional and their perpetrators did not hail from so-called alien classes, these unfortunates were not charged with the serious political crime of "wrecking." At least in the Urals in 1930, though, many of these cases were qualified as "petty wrecking" (*melkoe vreditel'stvo*), a category not found in the criminal code![12] Later in the decade, when the demands for a disciplined labor force increased and the labor laws proved inadequate, a broader range of labor infractions became criminal offenses.

Throughout the 1930s ordinary workers resented their fellows who were singled out as models and awarded prizes or privileges. Attacks upon shock-workers were commonplace, and legal officials were urged to pay special attention to them, qualifying the actions as serious offenses. In 1935–37 the journals contain much material on the persecution of Stakhanovites, not only in industry but in the villages as well. Readers will be rewarded with a catalog of ingenious methods used not only by fellow-workers but also by management against these unpopular norm-breakers.

3. Transport and pioneer life

A special and unusual view of the modernization of the USSR is provided by the materials on transport justice. As remote regions of the country were opened up through the extension of railroad and shipping lines, so special networks of courts and procurators were established (in the early 1930s) to handle crimes in this sector and disputes within the communities along the lines. The work of transport justice supplies an appalling picture of the consequences of the pressure to perform quickly without adequate equipment or trained personnel. Catastrophic accidents with multiple fatalities and huge financial losses were commonplace during the first half of the decade, not only in remote places but even in Moscow and Leningrad. In each instance legal officials were expected to punish those responsible for these disasters, or at least to find scapegoats.[13] The procuracies and courts of the railroad and shipping lines also dealt with the everyday crimes and civil disputes involving persons working and living along the lines—hooliganism, assault, family problems, and so on. From this aspect of transport justice one can look into the life of outlying settlements, the pioneer life in parts of the USSR.

4. The conservative shift and the new social relations

The legal journals offer perspectives on many facets of the conservative shift of the mid- and late–1930s and of the new social relations which emerged after the Third Revolution. As would be expected, there is an abundance of material on the law-and-order campaigns (e.g., against hooliganism), on the repression of juvenile crime, and on the laws designed to limit divorces and reduce abortions. In reading this material, one is struck by the reality of the problems prompted by the conservative shift—particularly the extent of family disruption and social disorder engendered by the rapid movement of population from village to city during the Third Revolution. I was also impressed by the serious, though often unsuccessful attempts by officials and scholars to interpret, adjust, and sometimes to work around the harshness of some laws so as to produce feasible ways of confronting these problems.

The journals contain as well a good deal of information about the new civil order, e.g., the laws regulating kolkhoz and rural property; laws on property in general; labor law; and family law. For all of these branches of civil law, one may learn not only about the developments in the law itself but also about new interpretations and practices which appeared in the mid- and late–1930s as civil caseload (after a lapse in the early 1930s) revived and resumed its place in the courts. Soviet judges faced a special challenge in assuring that their civil settlements were actually implemented, for the enforcement mechanisms (the *sudebyne ispolniteli*) left much to be desired. The evidence indicates that they had particular difficulty in enforcing alimony decrees.[14]

5. Society and authority

From the journals' coverage of the work of procurators in handling complaints from citizens one can learn much about the frustrations and grievances of ordinary members of society, about their expectations from local authorities, and about their willingness to resort to mechanisms of appeal and review. One can also learn about the types of grievances to which various authorities managed to respond and how these changed over time.

Of course, no system of appeals could satisfy all of the many persons who felt wronged in these years of turbulent change, and a portion of the dissatisfied took matters into their own hands. In the early 1930s many of the cases of so-called counter-revolutionary activity comprised nothing more than instances of physical attack by ordinary citizens upon representatives of Soviet power. The latter were defined to include not only such venerable dignitaries as raion-level officials, but also village notables, such as the chairmen of the rural soviets, the peasant correspondents for the central and provincial press, and during the height of the collectivization drives the "25,000ers." Not all of the attacks upon these figures, however, were politically motivated. To the distress of the central legal officials reviewing the cases, all too often the peasants who were charged with a state crime had done little more than make the mistake of choosing the chairman of a rural soviet as a drinking partner. The blows delivered in the ensuing arguments were better qualified as hooliganism than as a challenge to Soviet authority, and often higher courts made the change.[15] Later in the decade the analogous requalification had to be made in some cases of attack upon Stakhanovites.

Another common type of conflict in the early 1930s pitted entrenched local authorities against the activists in the villages who pursued the policies of the center, i.e., peasant correspondents and school teachers. In one example from the Black Earth region in the winter of 1930 the activist in question was a teacher who had openly criticized village authorities. The immediate cause of his troubles was his attempt to have electoral rights removed from a kulak previously convicted for bribery. This kulak, though, was himself the drinking partner of the head of the rural soviet, and the latter in turn helped his friend first by convincing the raikom to order the teacher out of the oblast (sic!) and then by prompting the police to launch a prosecution against the teacher for "stealing the protocol of a meeting at which poor peasants had defended him," for careless work, and for "exploiting" two hired hands, the women who cooked his soup and washed his shirts.[16]

6. Society and public life in the republics

The legal journals indicate that during the 1930s the work of government in the outlying republics was weakly managed from the Russian center and tended to reflect traditional political culture. This was clearly the case in the realm of justice. Hardly any legal textbooks had been translated into the local languages and hardly any legal officials could read Russian.[17] With insufficient information about the new norms that the regime wanted to impose, legal officials in Central Asia and the Caucasus could interpret laws in a manner consistent with local custom. The reports on court practice in these and other Asiatic parts of the USSR attest to the continuation of exchange relationships, which to the European eye smack of corruption. When in

1935 the secretary of the obkom of the Kazakh ASSR surveyed the courts in his republic, he had to report that "while we no longer have bribery in all of our courts" (as they apparently did in 1933), the problem remained serious.[18] In the fairy-tale land of Abkhazia, that Georgian backwater made famous by the contemporary writer Fazil Iskander, things were no better. In the mid/later 1930s justice in the Autonomous Republic of Abkhazia was dominated by the chairman of the ispolkom, one N. Lakoba. As a matter of routine, Lakoba had all important cases appealed to him personally and proceeded to resolve them in accordance with his interests, both personal and financial. In one case, a distant cousin of Lakoba was charged with a murder committed out of revenge, no doubt to defend the honor of the clan. After the intervention of the powerful relative, the young man's offense was qualified in a unique way as "privileged murder" (no such term existed in Soviet law); he was declared to be a Stakhanovite; and on these bases he received a modest term in prison, from which he was released after three months on medical grounds.[19]

Material in the legal journals indicates that at least for a time the Soviet government took an interest in encouraging peaceable relations among its national groups. During the late 1920s through 1930 Soviet courts convicted a number of offenders for displaying chauvinist and especially anti-Semitic tendencies, and procurators were encouraged to seek out such cases.[20] In addition, a subset of the journals (those focusing upon public administration in the RSFSR and USSR) deals extensively with the nationality policies of the regime and with their implementation in the various republics (e.g., the policy of *korenizatsiia*).

7. The development of the legal system

The legal journals of the prewar Stalin years cover many aspects of social history, but none more prominently than the development of legal institutions. In so doing, the journals provide extensive documentation on a variety of themes: the attempt to operate a modern legal system using as procurators and judges uneducated workers and peasants; the effect upon legal institutions of the ambivalence toward law on the part of Bolshevik leaders and some legal officials; the leaders' eventual acceptance of law as an instrument of rule and their attempt to promote it and the impact of the Great Purge (and of terror in general) upon the work of law enforcement and criminal justice. In writing a history of Soviet criminal justice during the Stalin years, I am dealing with all of these subjects, and I am planning to touch as well upon many of the other topics discussed in this essay.

The journals

The illustrations of the utility of law journals for inquiry into the social history of the prewar Stalin years were based upon my reading of eight major journals of the era. I shall now describe the contents of these journals and then survey the other legal periodicals published in the USSR during the 1920s and 1930s.

1. Ezhenedel'nik sovetskoi iustitsii

Organ of Narkomiust RSFSR, 1922–41 (later *Sovetskaia iustitsiia*). This was the prototypical agency journal, supplying rich and systematic coverage of the practice of local justice agencies and material relating to most of the themes discussed in this essay. During the 1920s the journal dealt with criminal and civil matters, but at the end of the decade the emphasis shifted decisively toward the criminal. Only in the mid-1930s did civil law issues regain their place of prominence. At the same time, *Sovetskaia iustitsiia* of the mid-1930s devoted less space than before to the procuracy, largely because of the launching of the procuracy's own journal *Za sotsialisticheskuiu zakonnost'*. By the end of the decade *Sovetskaia iustitsiia* took on an even narrower profile and became a journal for judges, devoted in the main to instructing new peoples' judges (*narsudy*). Throughout the 1920s and 1930s the journal published extensive surveys of legislation, most of the circulars of Narkomiust, and selected decisions of the Supreme Courts (except when the latter were presented in separate publications—see below). At all times the journal contained annual indexes arranged by general subject matter ("systematic index").

2. Za sotsialisticheskuiu zakonnost'

Organ of the USSR Procuracy, 1933–present (later *Sotsialisticheskaia zakonnost'*). While covering a broad range of law enforcement topics, this journal focuses especially upon the work of procurators and procuracy investigators. The bulk of its contents concerns either criminal work (including techniques of investigation) or the supervisory functions of the procuracy (including both the flow of complaints and grievances and the official responses to them). The journal has an index, but it offers extensive coverage neither of legislation nor of bibliography. The publication of directives and orders of the procuracy was occasional and irregular.

3. Administrativnyi vestnik

Organ of Narkomvnudel RSFSR, 1925–30. Until its demise late in 1930, the Commissariat of Internal Affairs published this monthly journal dealing with policing and corrections and with the administrative nightmares faced by that agency's officials in attempting to coordinate these functions throughout the RSFSR. The journal contains some unusual material on the early phases of collectivization, including the acting Commissar Shirvindt's condemnation of the initial excesses.[21] For most years, the texts of instructions and directives of the commissariat are to be found in a companion journal, the *Biulleten' Narkomvnudela RSFSR*.

4. Revoliutsiia prava

Journal of the legal section of the Communist Academy and then of its successor, the academy's Institute of Soviet Construction and Law (later, *Sovetskoe gosudarstvo i revoliutsiia prava*, *Sovetskoe gosudarstvo*, and finally *Sovetskoe gosudarstvo i pravo*). As its original title suggests, this academic journal started as a forum for debates over legal theory, but its profile changed markedly. First, in the early 1930s, the emphasis shifted to the theory and practice of public administration in the new Soviet state; then in the last years of the decade the journal abandoned this broad terrain in favor of explorations of the substance and meaning of the law. In the first part of the decade, when public administration dominated its pages, the journal contained articles on federalism, on purges in the apparatus, and on collectivization, and it featured an impressive bibliography on Soviet construction and law (with such headings as "classes and class war," "soviets," "nationality construction," and "finance and economy"). When in the last years before World War II the journal turned back to the law, it also became more academic and as a rule remote from the practice of justice and government more generally.

5. *Vlast' sovetov*

Founded in 1919 as a publication of Narkomvnudel RSFSR, it became the organ of VTsIK in 1923 and remained so until its demise in August 1938. As a broad-gauged journal directed at government officials at all levels within the RSFSR, *Vlast' sovetov* touched upon many of the major political and administrative issues of the day. In the late 1920s it featured articles on nationality policy (e.g., *korenizatsiia*); on women and public life; on the soviets, urban and rural, and their apparatus; on vydvizhenie; and on the economy. Prominent topics in the mid-1930s included schools and mass work, housing and communal economy, railroad construction, labor resources, *sotssovmestitet'stvo* (the use of prize workers as helpers in government work, e.g., as judges) and economic affairs (livestock, harvests, agricultural campaigns). Subject indexes were published at irregular intervals.

6. *Sovetskoe stroitel'stvo*

Journal of TsIK SSSR, 1926–37. Another general journal of public administration, this time directed at officialdom throughout the USSR. The journal listed the laws issued by the union republics, and as a symbolic gesture the title was printed in all of the languages of the republics. Apart from nationality issues, prominent topics included the work of central government agencies (especially Presidium TsIK and its commissions); constitutional and budget issues; female labor; the Academy of Sciences; construction of state farms and so on. During the early 1930s *Sovetskoe stroitel'stvo* published a monthly bibliography of articles on Soviet construction drawn from a wide variety of journals and newspapers (with headings like "nationality policy," "cultural development," "literacy," "women," and so on). Indexed, but not reliably so.

7. Krest'ianskii iurist

Published by Narkomiust RSFSR from 1928 to 1935 (later *Derevenskii iurist*), "to help the countryside learn about Soviet law" and "to provide legal aid to the rural *aktiv*" (e.g., members of rural soviets, people's assessors in courts, rural correspondents, teachers, lower police, and court workers). Designed to compensate in some way for the lack of lawyers in the countryside, this semi-popular journal explained the laws (new and old) and how they should be implemented; reported on selected cases from the Supreme Court; amused its readers with stories about legal affairs; reviewed books; and, most importantly, in a section on legal aid, tried to answer the questions submitted by its readership (for example, the manager of an agricultural artel asked in 1932 whether kolkhoz work-day credits could be used to compensate nannies hired to watch children in kolkhozy which lacked creches). In its first years, the journal was profusely illustrated, containing photographs (e.g., of meetings of rural soviets), drawings and cartoons. From 1932, under the new title, the journal's mandate was to provide legal aid to the collectivized countryside. Its circulation grew dramatically, its content became more weighty and more attention was paid to criminal matters (the murder of an *udarnik*; protecting rural correspondents). Still, the journal maintained its question-and-answer section under a new heading, "kolkhoz consultation." Contains both a subject and a systematic index.

8. Sud idet

Published by the Leningrad oblast court (1924–31), this popular journal which dealt with legal affairs was aimed at a national audience. Half of its contents consisted of quasi-journalistic accounts of major and distinctive criminal cases heard in the courts of Leningrad oblast or in the Supreme Court of the RSFSR. A veritable rogue's gallery appears in these accounts, including swindlers of all kinds, devious kulaks, persecutors of rural correspondents, negligent employees held responsible for accidents, peasants who failed to meet hard quotas, anti-Semites, and local officials who dekulakized too thoroughly. The journal also included a question-and-answer section that dealt primarily with civil matters; accounts of the activities of various Leningrad bodies (meetings of oblast justice workers; juvenile affairs commissions); and extensive, detailed coverage of cases heard in the comrades courts of Leningrad factories during the years 1929–31.

In addition to these eight major legal journals, a variety of other legal periodicals were published in the USSR during the 1920s and 1930s:

1. Republican law journals

Among the national republics only the Ukrainian SSR issued continuing journals on legal affairs. They were *Vestnik sovetskoi iustitsii* (later *Visnik radianskoi iustitsii*), organ of Narkomiust of the Ukraine, 1923–30 (in Russian until 1928); *Chervone pravo*, also an organ of Narkomiust of the Ukraine, 1926–30; and succeeding both, *Revoliutsione pravo*, 1931–41, organ of the Ukrainian Narkomiust, Supreme Court, and Procuracy.

2. Provincial and local journals

Especially during the 1920s, a number of provincial courts, police departments, and soviet executive committees sponsored journals. The most accessible are *Proletarskii sud*, 1922–28, published by the Moscow provincial court; *Rabochii sud*, 1923–30, published by the Leningrad provincial court, and *Sud idet* (described above). Between 1924 and 1926 the Leningrad provincial police put out *Na postu*. Among the journals of soviet executive committees, which should include materials on policing, the most promising are *Na sovetskom postu* (Novosibirsk, 1928–33) and *Put' sovetov* (Rostov on Don, 1925–33). The police and ispolkom journals are available only in Soviet libraries.

3. Provincial and local bulletins

Especially during the 1930s provincial courts and procuracy offices published, usually at irregular intervals, information bulletins directed at raion-level officials. A 1937 review of provincial court bulletins indicated that they often contained little more than circulars and instruction letters, sometimes even reprints of directives from central agencies;[22] the bulletins of the procuracy and provincial court of the Western oblast contained in the Smolensk Archive, however, provide valuable information on trends in legal practice and in crime.[23] Since few court and procuracy bulletins are listed in *Periodicheskaia pechat' SSSR, 1917–49: bibliograficheskaia ukazatel* (e.g., *Biulleten' Kalininskoi oblastnoi prokuratury*, 1935–36), one may surmise that most of them were classified.

4. Academic journals and periodicals

During the 1920s two non-Marxist academic law journals were published in Moscow: *Sovetskoe pravo* (1922–28), organ of the Russian Association of Research Institutes in the Social Sciences, and *Pravo i zhizn'*, privately published by a group of distinguished professors of law. In the 1930s there was no academic law journal other than *Sovetskoe gosudarstvo i pravo*, but the Institute of Criminal Policy (later All-Union Institute of Juridical Sciences) published a series of collections (*sborniki*) first under the title *Problemy ugolovnoi politiki* (1935–37) and then as *Problemy sotsialisticheskogo prava* (1938–40).

5. Reports on court decisions

Throughout most of the 1920s and 1930s, decisions of the RSFSR and USSR Supreme Courts were reported in *Ezhenedel'nik sovetskoi iustitsii* and in its supplement *Sudebnaia praktika* (1928–31). From 1925 to 1929, however, decisions of the USSR Supreme Court are to be found in *Biulleten' Verkhovnogo Suda SSSR i Prokuratury SSSR* (1925–29). The decisions of the state arbitration board of the USSR Sovnarkom—covering disputes between industrial enterprises—were published in a separate journal, *Arbitrazh,* 1931–40.

For further information on small and irregularly published law journals in the republics and localities, the reader should consult *Periodicheskaia pechat' SSSR 1917–49: bibliograficheskaia ukazatel'* (Moscow: 1955–63). For the holdings of Soviet journals in North American libraries and general bibliographic information, see *Half a Century of Soviet Serials, 1917–68. A Bibliography and Union List of Serials Published in the USSR.* Compiled by Rudolph Smits (Washington, D.C.: Library of Congress, 1968), 2 vols.

Notes

1. This analysis is based upon the author's current research, as presented in an April 1983 seminar to the Center for Russian and East European Studies, University of Michigan, entitled "Law as an Instrument of Rule: The Revival of 'Legality' under Stalin," and in an article "Local Political Power and Soviet Justice, 1922–1941," *Soviet Studies* 37:3 (1985), 305–29.
2. For an outline history of the supervisory function of the procuracy, see Glenn G. Morgan, *Soviet Administrative Legality: The Role of the Attorney General's Office* (Stanford: Stanford University Press, 1962).
3. "Pochtovoi iashchik," *Administrativnyi vestnik,* 1930 no. 3, 64; "Ot redaktsii," *Sovetskaia iustitsiia,* 1932 no. 8, 23.
4. The illustrations of the bearing of legal journals on the social history of the prewar Stalin years are based upon a reading of the following journals: *Ezhenedel'nik sovetskoi iustitsii, Za sotsialisticheskuiu zakonnost', Administrativnyi vestnik, Revoliutsiia prava, Vlast' sovetov, Sovetskoe stroitel'stvo, Krest'ianskaia iustitsiia,* and *Sud idet.*
5. In the Central Black Earth region during the largest campaign of 1930/1931, court and procuracy officials reportedly spent 8,409 days in the countryside, surveyed 4,626 organizations, and among other things convicted 7,347 peasants for non-fulfillment of hard quotas, 1,414 of hiding or speculating in grain, and 3,066 of crimes relating to offices. Included in these efforts were 5,682 members of local *aktivy.* Ia. Gurevich, "Organy iustitsii TsCho na khlebzagotovitel'nom fronte," *Sovetskaia iustitsiia,* 1931 no. 19, 22–24.
6. For preliminary treatment of the squeezing of the peasantry see Moshe Lewin, "Taking Grain: Soviet Policies of Agricultural Procurements before the War," in Chimen Abramsky ed., *Essays in Honour of E. H. Carr* (London: Macmillan, 1974), 281–323.
7. "Ob itogakh raboty organov iustitsii po khlebozagotovkam za 1930 god," "Postanovlenie kollegii Narkomiusta, utverzh. tov. Krylenko, 15/II 1931 g.," *Sovetskaia iustitsiia,* 1931 no. 9, 25–26; K. Palkin, "Polozhit' konets neosnovatel'nom privlecheniem predsedatelei kolkhozov," *loc. cit.,* 1935 no. 15, 20.
8. A. Shliapochnikov, "Okhrana obshchestvennoi (sotsialisticheskoi) sobstvennosti," *Za sotsialisticheskuiu zakonnost',* 1935 no. 1, 14–17; M. Kozhevnikov, "Nadzornaia praktika Verkhovnogo suda RSFSR," *Sovetskaia iustitsiia,* 1935 no. 22, 4–5.
9. Lisitsyn, "Po narsudam Severodonskogo okruga," *Sovetskaia iustitsiia,* 1935 no. 24, 4–5.
10. See, for example, "Vzryv na shakhte 'Mariia' na Donbasse," *Sud idet,* no. 17

(1930), 17–18; R. Orlov and L. Chernov, "God zakona 8 dekabriia," *Za sotsialisticheskuiu zakonnost'*, 1935 no. 11, 15–18.

11. On the history of comrades courts under Stalin, see Peter H. Solomon, Jr., "Criminalization and Decriminalization in Soviet Criminal Policy, 1917–1941," *Law and Society Review* 16:1 (1981–82), 9–44. For detailed accounts of meetings of these lay courts see *Sud idet*, 1929–31, *passim*.

12. Vs. Luppov, "Kak rabotaiut organy iustitsii promyshlennykh raionov Urala," *Sovetskaia iustitsiia*, 1930 no. 19, 24–26.

13. See, for example, V. Odintsev, "Kak rabotaiut lineinye zheleznodorozhnye sudy Moskovskogo oblastnogo suda," *Sovetskaia iustitsiia*, 1931 no. 9, 17–20.

14. "Pervoe vsesoiuznoe soveshchanie rabotnikov suda i prokuratury po grazhdanskim delam," *Sotsialisticheskaia zakonnost'*, 1937 no. 2, 87–111; K. Iakunenkov, "Eshche raz o sel'skikh ispolniteliakh," *Vlast' sovetov*, 1937 no. 8, 38–40.

15. "O rassledovanii del o kontr-revoliutsionnykh prestupleniiakh," Instruktivnoe pis'mo vsem kraevym prokuroram . . . , Tsikuliar Narkomiusta no. 61, *Sovetskaia iustitsiia*, 1930 no. 16, 27–30.

16. Rusakov, "Neveriatno, no fakt," *Sovetskaia iustitsiia*, 1930 no. 11, 6–12.

17. V. Chikhvadze, "55-yi Plenum Verkhsuda SSSR o pravovom obrazovanii," *Sotsialistcheskaia zakonnost'*, 1936 no. 10, 52–53.

18. L. Mirzoian, "Ob ocherednykh zadachakh rabotnikov sudebno-prokurorskikh organov," *Za sotsialisticheskuiu zakonnost'*, 1935 no. 10, 22–25.

19. Shoniia, "O nekotorykh itogakh raboty prokuratury Abkhazskoi ASSR za 1937 g., *Sotsialisticheskaia zakonnost'*, 1938 no. 3, 88–90.

20. See, for example, "Topor antisemita (Protsess ubitsii Bolshemennikova)," *Sud idet*, 1929 no. 9, 471–78. The trial of this particular murder on anti-Semitic grounds was made into a movie, "Protsess Trofimova."

21. E. G. Shirvindt, "Zadachi NKVD i ego mestnykh organov v rekonstruktivnom periode," *Administrativnyi vestnik*, 1930 no. 2, 1–5.

22. Naumov, "Informatsionnaia rabota v sudakh," *Sovetskaia iustitsiia*, 1937 no. 6, 28–29.

23. E.g., WKP 525, 199–203; WKP 261, 1–5; 24–37.

Soviet City Directories

J. ARCH GETTY

Students of the bureaucratic or urban history of imperial Russia have used *Vsia Moskva* and other city directories published before 1917. Their colleagues in Soviet history are less familiar with the directories published after the revolution, even though obvious problems of archival access force them to explore various classes of primary material and to tease information from a variety of disparate and sometimes offbeat sources.

Soviet city directories are important volumes which provide scarce and sometimes unique reference information on the early Stalin years. *Vsia Moskva, Ves' Leningrad,* and other directories are considerably more than street guides.[1] They are combination city directories, bureaucratic lists, service guides, and telephone books which provide an informative glimpse at urban life and bureaucratic organization in the first two decades of Soviet power.

Social historians, political scientists, urban geographers and others interested in politics, society, and organization during the twenties and thirties can look up the members of the science faculty of Moscow State University, the chief engineer at the Putilov factory, the number of clinics in Moscow, the department chiefs of Gosplan, or the changing names of streets and neighborhoods. One can look up the name of the deputy commissar of food, Bukharin's telephone number, the seating plan of the Stanislavskii Theater, or the location of all pharmacies in the city. But these directories are also more than simple reference books. With care and proper critical attention to their weaknesses, one can use them as aggregate sources for the study of social, political, and institutional trends.

Vsia Moskva was among the casualties of the storm and stress of the 1917 revolutions and subsequent civil war. It was not until 1923 that it resumed publication under the auspices of the state publishing house (Gosizdat).[2] The 1923 edition included descriptive material on the city of Moscow along with 468 pages of personnel listings. After a hiatus of one year, the Moscow Soviet published *Vsia Moskva* in an expanded 1925 version and continued publication through 1931. A final edition appeared in 1936.[3]

An earlier version of this paper was presented at the 14th Annual Convention of the American Association for the Advancement of Slavic Studies, Washington, D.C., 15 October 1982. The author is grateful to the University of California, Riverside's Academic Senate Committee on Research for its support.

The Leningrad city directory enjoyed a less troubled publication history. Published by a private concern as *Ves' Petersburg, Ves' Petrograd*, and then *Ves' Leningrad*, the directory was taken over by the Executive Committee (Ispolkom) of the City Soviet in 1923. The Leningrad Soviet then published the directory without interruption through 1934.[4]

The 1927 edition of *Vsia Moskva*, a typical example, included over 1,500 pages. It began with an 86-page index of organizations and institutions and a 40-page introduction to Moscow's history and growth, economy, transportation, and architecture. The introductory section also includes descriptions of the various districts, neighborhoods, and suburbs of the city.[5]

The descriptive and personnel lists in both *Vsia Moskva* and *Ves' Leningrad* are particularly useful guides to the structure of government, the provision of social services, and the cultural and economic activities of the city. The sections on city government in both directories offer guides to the myriad departments of the city, neighborhood, and outlying soviets, and give information on the quantity and organization of public services as well as general descriptive information on the technical organization of the city bureaucracy. Sections on health provide the numbers, locations, and personnel of hospitals, neighborhood clinics, and pharmacies, and chapters on educational institutions give the locations, descriptions, and lists of faculties from pre-school to university. Until the end of the 1920s, both *Vsia Moskva* and *Ves' Leningrad* regularly listed the names of all lawyers and doctors in the city. The lists of physicians were subdivided both by specialty and location.

Since Moscow was the center of Moscow province and the capital of both the Russian Republic and the USSR, the scope of *Vsia Moskva* extends beyond the level of city institutions and services. The directory provides detailed party, state, and soviet personnel listings for agencies, commissariats, and organizations at the USSR, RSFSR, Moscow province, city, and district levels. The layout of the listings shows the hierarchical relationships among various departments, sectors, and committees and the personnel lists offer data on staffing and appointments not available in other non-archival sources. The listing for a typical organization includes a description of the agency's competencies, responsibilities, relation to other agencies, address and hours of operation. Next come the names, titles, addresses, and telephone numbers of the agency's leading personnel from chairman/commissar to presidium to department, sub-department and middle-management levels.

Cultural institutions and organizations were also included in both *Vsia Moskva* and *Ves' Leningrad*. The listings cover the theaters, orchestras, ballets, and opera companies in the city, showing the artistic and administrative personnel and even seating plans. Comprehensive sections on the press and literary organizations give descriptions and list the members of the editorial boards for virtually all newspapers and periodicals published in the city.

Both *Vsia Moskva* and *Ves' Leningrad* end with a large section of names, addresses, and telephone numbers. In *Vsia Moskva*, the list was usually an alphabetical index of persons "mentioned in *Vsia Moskva*."[6] It includes "leaders and skilled workers" in agencies, organizations, and enterprises, as well as representatives from trade and industry. Unfortunately, the directory does not specify the precise criteria for inclusion in these categories. The index also includes persons from the "free professions" but notes that only professionals affiliated with societies and associations (which submitted lists to the editors) are included.[7] For each person listed, the entry includes surname, first name, patronymic, profession (if a member of a free profession), street address, telephone number, and place of employment.[8] The corresponding list in *Ves' Leningrad* is even less clearly defined. It is an "Alphabetical Index of the Inhabitants of Leningrad." While the content of individual listings is similar to that in the *Vsia Moskva* list, the Leningrad index provides no criteria for inclusion, and one wonders whether every inhabitant had an equal chance of making the list.

City directories are particularly good sources on economic life. Sections on trade unions, banking and credit institutions, and consumer and production cooperatives include bureaucratic lists of personnel and committees. Indeed, some of the most valuable and interesting sections concern industry and trade.

From 1925 through 1930, editions of *Vsia Moskva* included a great deal of information on the administration of industry and trade as well as on the organization of individual enterprises. A section on state trusts, syndicates, and industrial and trade administrations gave information on the various branches of industry along with lists of leading administrative personnel for each branch. Typically, the listing for a trust or syndicate included the names of its chairman, deputy chairman, board members, and department administrators. Beginning with the 1926 edition, *Vsia Moskva* also listed the numbers of workers employed by each trust or syndicate. Next, there were listings of the various factories and enterprises under the trust or syndicate.

At the level of individual factories, other "productive undertakings," and retail trade outlets, *Vsia Moskva* provided listings of enterprises grouped by product and subdivided by type: state, cooperative, or private. For each establishment, the listing provides the name and address of the concern plus the names of the director, deputy director, and often the chief engineer. For factories and trade outlets, *Vsia Moskva* included the numbers of "employees" and "workers" employed by each enterprise.

Ves' Leningrad also included information on trusts, syndicates, and individual concerns, although its listings were less complete and comprehensive than those in the Moscow directory. While the Leningrad information on trusts and high-level administrations is analogous to that given in *Vsia Moskva*, the Leningrad directory does not list the number of employees in each trust and is less informative on individual enterprises. Listings of productive or trade undertakings are broken down by product or function, but the numbers of employees or workers are not given. The Leningrad listings are not subdivided into state, cooperative, and private categories, although the type of enterprise can often be deduced from its title.

While individual volumes of *Vsia Moskva* and *Ves' Leningrad* are useful for reference purposes, the study of a series of city directories is also rewarding. Perusal of a set of directories in the 1920s and 1930s offers both impressions and hard data and provides a changing panorama of economic, social, and urban life. One can trace the expansions, contractions, and evolution of services and institutions from the height of the NEP through the Stalin Revolution. For example, along with data on urban population the directory lists would allow one to "map" the provision of health and social services across the city over a period of years.

One can also watch the decreasing numbers of advertisements for private businesses and professional services through the late 1920s. Similarly, the names of private defense attorneys were listed in *Vsia Moskva* until the 1929 edition, when they were replaced by an impersonal notice for "Juridical Consultants." Private doctors were listed by medical specialty until the 1930 edition, when the listings disappeared and were replaced by the occasional private advertisement by a physician. These ads disappeared altogether by 1936. Similarly, the names of owners and directors of privately owned factories were listed with decreasing frequency after 1926, and by the 1930 edition the numbers of workers in such enterprises were usually omitted. Numbers of employees in private retail trade were listed until 1929, although private traders continued to be listed in the 1930 edition. The 1936 edition laconically noted that as of press time, the "reorganization of retail trade" resulting from the liquidation of consumer cooperatives was not complete, and thus no listings could be provided.

Since the listings are available over a period of years, statistical and aggregate comparisons are also possible. Using the bureaucratic lists in several editions, one could also easily trace the persistence, turnover, and reorganization of personnel in various institutions through the twenties. One could examine the leadership of a trade union (or group of unions) in a particular year. By tracing their names back through earlier volumes, one could determine career backgrounds and tenure in office. By tracing the names forward in time, one could produce data on future fates and career lines. Large-scale systematic analysis of personnel information allows the researcher to measure multiple office-holding, "interlocking directorates," and even the persistence of bureaucratic constituencies and "family circles." Such series analyses of personnel, cohorts, and structure could be repeated for scores of political, cultural, or social institutions. The research possibilities and approaches to systematic and aggregate analysis are numerous but are limited by the selectivity of the listings and therefore by the sizes of working data sets.[9]

Using city directories as analytical tools requires methodological care and a critical appreciation of their weaknesses as sources. This involves a consideration of the credibility and selectivity of the directory listings. There is little reason to doubt the credibility of particular listings and descriptions. Since the directories were published for contemporary reference use inside and outside of government, there would have been little point in falsifying the lists.

Selectivity presents a greater problem. Some agencies are not listed in any of the editions of *Vsia Moskva*. Agencies with sensitive or security functions such as the secret police, departments of the party's Central Committee, and the Red Army are omitted from most editions. In some cases, positions and offices (particularly in party organizations) are listed without the name of the official holding the post.[10]

If we examine the space devoted to personnel listings in the various editions of

Vsia Moskva, we find that the editors were increasingly selective in their criteria for inclusion. The space devoted to party, soviet and governmental, enterprise, city, and professional listings reached its apogee in the 1925 edition, when 885 pages were allocated to personnel and institutional information. After 1925, however, such listings declined to about 800 pages in 1926–27 and then to around 650 in 1928–29. The last edition (1936) contained only 627 pages devoted to personnel.[11] There was also a tendency from 1925 to 1936 to include fewer specific names and positions on those pages that were published. The size of the party/state bureaucracy grew tremendously in this period as the state took over the activities of the declining private sector. Since the space in *Vsia Moskva* allocated to government listings shrank in the same period, it is clear that the listings became less comprehensive with time.

It is tempting to conclude that political factors associated with the rise of Stalinism were at work in limiting the flow of information in the city directories. Yet while we know little about the criteria for inclusion of various officials in the directory, a careful look at the listings suggests that other editorial factors may have been important.

An analysis of the reporting characteristics for personnel in *Vsia Moskva* shows that for party, soviet, and commissariat-level organizations at the RSFSR and USSR levels, 5,326 names of officials were given in 1927. By 1929, such listings had declined to 3,992 and by 1931 only 2,701 persons were listed in the directory: a decrease of about one quarter every two years.[12] Table 1 gives the numbers of reported positions with names for national (USSR) level posts in state agencies. For each year, the numbers are broken down by rank level across all the USSR agencies.

Clearly, the systematic under-representation of lower-level positions became more pronounced over time. At least at the level of Soviet government state positions, there was a precipitous decline in the reporting of positions at the level of department members and below.[13]

It seems, therefore, that while Stalinist reticence and censorship may have played a role in limiting the contents of later editions, more pedestrian editorial decisions were at least as important. Taking the 1927–1931 reporting information in its entirety, one can see that the pattern of selection involved progressively limiting the inclusion of lower-level state posts rather than more politically sensitive leading positions. Considerations of utility and space probably had as much to do with the declining size of *Vsia Moskva* as did censorship.

Researchers interested in using city directory listings in aggregate form are obliged to evaluate the selectivity criteria in the particular data they intend to use. This allows one to control for selectivity and produce reliable source material. Table 2, for example, is an analysis of turnover/persistence rates in the state and party bureaucracies which controls for the underrepresentation of lower-level positions by including only positions at the levels of department chief and above.

In addition to such systematic, rank-specific hierarchical selectivity (for which one can control in statistical analysis) there also exist apparently random and unpredictable omissions in both *Ves' Leningrad* and *Vsia Moskva*. Researchers with access

Table 1

Soviet Government Positions Reported in *Vsia Moskva* in 1927, 1929, and 1931

		Year	
Rank	1927	1929	1931
Commissar/chairman	86	67	80
Presidium	181	192	282
Department head	127	123	207
Department member	457	281	218
Sub-department head	575	614	370
Sub-department member	913	436	98
Technical specialist	170	192	68
Personal secretary	44	50	27
Total government posts	2,970	2,270	1,439

Source: Vsia Moskva, 1927, 1929, 1931.

Note: Our categorization of rank levels is as follows:

  Commissar/chairman: the executive leadership of the agency: Commissar (or Chairman), Deputy Commissar (Deputy Chairman), Member (i.e., Member of Gosplan), First Secretary (party only), Secretary (party only), Deputy Secretary (party only), Second Secretary (party only).

  Presidium: the members and candidate members of the agency's presidium or collegium.

  Department head: chief or head of a department (defined as the first subdivision of the agency's organization and variously called *otdel, upravlenie*, or less commonly *sektor* or *chast'*).

  Department member: ranks at this level include deputy chief, department assistant, department secretary, department member, department instructor, department consultant.

  Sub-department head: chief or head of a sub-department (a subdivision of a department usually called *sektor, chast', gruppa*, and less commonly *otdel*).

  Sub-department member: ranks similar to those for department member.

  Technical specialist: ranks such as engineer, referent, specialist, controller, bookkeeper, inspector.

  Personal secretaries: clerical officials attached explicitly to a leading official.

to Soviet archives have reported that some junior and even middle-level officials are not listed in the directories. Both the systematic and apparently random omissions mean that certain instances of lateral or downward movement could put an official out of the directory. Like archives, memoirs, newspapers, and other sources, the city directory personnel listings are incomplete. Statistical generalizations based solely on directory listings must therefore be made with care and are subject to the same problems and errors as those based on, say, census data or sampling techniques.

The turnover (or renewal) rate was extremely high for all agencies in the group, including even relatively stable agencies such as the highly specialized Commissariat of Foreign Affairs. Some agencies were almost completely restaffed in two years or less. Gosplan, Vesenkha, and the Commissariats of Labor and Finance (all of them economic agencies) were virtually recreated with new personnel.

Since the purpose of this essay is to describe city directories and to suggest possibilities for their use, it is outside our scope to provide a detailed discussion of

Table 2

Sources of Recruitment of Upper-level Officials in Selected State and Party Agencies, 1931

Agency	Top-level staffers in 1931	In same agency in 1929		Not in same agency in 1929	
		no.	%	no.	%
(a) State					
Ts.I.K.	82	33	40.2	49	59.8
Sovnarkom	36	11	30.6	25	69.4
Gosplan	28	4	14.3	24	85.7
Comm. of Foreign Affairs	35	20	57.1	15	42.9
Comm. of Transportation	55	9	16.4	46	83.6
Comm. of Posts and Telegraphs	17	4	23.5	13	76.5
Comm. of Labor	30	1	3.3	29	96.7
Comm. of Finance	42	6	14.3	36	85.7
Rabkrin	25	11	44.0	14	56.0
Vesenkha	105	12	11.4	93	88.6
mean			25.5		74.5
(b) Party					
Politburo	16	12	75.0	4	25.0
Central Committee	137	102	74.5	35	25.0
Secretariat	6	4	66.7	2	33.3
Orgburo	15	6	40.0	9	60.0
Central Control Commission	191	75	39.3	116	60.7
Moscow Party	114	4	3.5	110	96.5
mean			49.8		50.2

Source: Data from the Soviet Data Bank Project. J. Arch Getty, William Chase, and Charles Wetherell, "Patterns of State and Party Officeholding in the Soviet Bureaucracy, 1929–1931," unpublished paper presented to the Third National Seminar for Russian Social History, Philadelphia, Pa., January 1983.

Note: Difference of means tests (t) indicate that the differences between state and party persistence (column 3) and state and party turnover (column 5) are significant at the 0.05 level.

mobility and turnover in the 1929–1931 period. The imperatives of collectivization and industrialization dictated an expanding bureaucracy to deal with new tasks. Given greatly increased demand for competent officials and a corresponding shortage of skilled bureaucratic talent, it would not be surprising to find a situation in which functionaries were shifted from place to place with little tenure in any one post. Whatever the underlying reasons for this turnover, procedural and administrative chaos must have been extraordinary when most responsible officials were new to their jobs.

Aside from the magnitude of bureaucratic turnover, city directory data allow us to compare internal promotions with recruitment from outside. Were new personnel in Agency "A" typically recruited from Agencies "B" or "C"? For example, if we look at the newly formed USSR Commissariat of Agriculture in 1931, we find that members of the top staff, collegium, and department heads were largely recruited from the Workers' and Peasants' Inspection (Rabkrin), Gosplan, and the RSFSR Commissariat of Agriculture. If we take the Supreme Council of National Economy (Vesenkha) in 1931 and look back to the members' 1929 positions, we find that significant numbers of top staff, collegium, and department heads had backgrounds in Rabkrin, the Commissariat of Finance, and the Central Committee, with Rabkrin comprising the largest group.[14]

Finally, perusing a city directory rewards the reader with unsystematic but valuable impressions of the texture and color of the times. Thumbing through the 1927 directory one finds the young Andrei Vyshinskii as Rector of Moscow State University. One finds that Avel Enukidze's office was three doors down from Kalinin's, and that Vesenkha occupied five floors of a building on Ploshchad' Nogina. Corresponding commissariats at the RSFSR and USSR levels usually shared the same building and sometimes the same office space. Advertisements for everything from soap to steamship tickets are scattered through the pages. Whether used as reference books or data sources, the city directories are an untapped source which can give us tidbits of information, larger quantities of hard data, and indicators of areas for future study.

Notes

1. See Appendix B (below) for bibliographic information on city directories. This essay concentrates on *Vsia Moskva* and *Ves' Leningrad*. In addition to covering the two largest cities, these directories are available for spans of years in the twenties and thirties.

2. *Vsia Moskva; adresnaia i spravochnaia kniga* (Moscow, 1923). The introduction (LXXIII) to the 1923 edition hints that a 1918 edition was published. Attempts to verify and locate a 1918 edition in American, European, and Soviet libraries have not been successful.

3. It is not known why the directory did not appear in 1924, 1932–35, or after 1936.

4. From 1928 on, *Ves' Leningrad* was renamed *Ves' Leningrad i Leningradskaia Oblast'*. The first part (*chast'*) was the usual Leningrad directory. The second part included a collection of mini-directories for cities and towns such as Novgorod and Pskov in Leningrad oblast.

5. See Appendix I for a detailed contents summary of this edition. *Ves' Leningrad* for the same year included largely similar sections in its 1,068 pages.

6. The alphabetical index appeared in *Vsia Moskva* from 1925 to 1931. The 1923 edition contained a list of names and addresses of "Permanent Residents" of Moscow and the 1936 edition contained no list at all.

7. The preface to the lists in *Vsia Moskva* contained an appeal to unaffiliated writers, artists, doctors, engineers, and other free professionals asking them to provide address and telephone information on themselves for future editions.

8. The index warned that the home addresses of some high ranking party and state officials may not be included.

9. The Soviet Data Bank Project, under the direction of William Chase and the author, has completed the first stage of computerizing *Vsia Moskva* office-holding data on party and state bureaucrats in the twenties and thirties. Supported by grants from the National Endow-

ment for the Humanities and the National Council for Soviet and East European Research, the project aims at creating a publicly available, machine-readable data bank on leading political and economic figures.

10. Such was the case for Communist Party positions in *Ves' Leningrad*. Some other directories (*Vsia Zapadnaia oblast'*, for example) included much information on the size, activities, and even work forces of various enterprises, farms, and organizations but listed practically no names of officials.

11. The exact page allocations are: 468 (1923), 885 (1925), 796 (1926), 797 (1927), 646 (1928), 666 (1929), 583 (1930), 627 (1936).

12. Reporting of party officials did not decrease as quickly as did that for state office-holders. Reported party positions in the three editions were 505, 342, 416. State position reports were 4821, 3650, 2285.

13. Practically identical reporting characteristics were observed in analysis of RSFSR state positions for the same years.

14. For a history of the organization and reorganizations of Soviet state institutions in this period, see A. A. Nelidov, *Istoriia gosudarstvennykh uchrezhdenii SSSR, 1917–1936 gg.: uchebnoe posobie* (Moscow, 1962).

Appendix A

Vsia Moskva, 1927
Outline of Contents

What follows is a schematic outline of the contents of one of the more complete editions of *Vsia Moskva*. Page ranges roughly indicate the number of listings.

197–201   Party Organizations
                    Comintern
                    Communist Party (Moscow city and region)
                    Control Commission (Moscow city and region)
                    Komsomol (Moscow city and region)
                    for each of above: personnel and department lists
201–220   Trade Unions
                    listings for all national unions from national level
                    to local branches
                    for each: members of central committee, department,
                    staffs, commissions
221–247   Societies
                    rural societies
                    medical institutes
                    writers' associations and unions
                    music and art societies
                    Proletkult
                    sports clubs
                    other clubs and societies
248–260   Scientific and Pedagogical Institutes
                    personnel staffs, departments, addresses
261–276   Museums
                    personnel staffs, departments, addresses
277–290   Libraries
                    personnel staffs, departments, addresses
291–342   Education
                    personnel staffs, departments, addresses
                    MGU
                    Institute of Red Professors
                    VTUZy higher technical schools
                    rabfaks
                    technicum
                    secondary schools by raion
                    preschools and child care by raion
343–377   Press
                    descriptions of newspapers, periodicals
                    editorial boards, staff lists
                    departments
382–414   Theater
                    descriptions, artists, ticket information, seating plans
                    theaters
                    operas
                    ballet companies
                    orchestras

415–540	Health and Medical
	Staffs, descriptions, addresses:
	hospitals
	clinics (by district)
	veterinarians
	pharmacies (by district)
	doctors (by specialty and district)
541–559	Banks
	lists of banks and personnel (public and private)
	lists of credit unions
560–656	Industry
	Descriptions, personnel, addresses:
	industrial banks
	industrial councils
	lists of factories (by industry)
	artels
	advertisements for private firms
657–795	Trade
	Lists of businesses and enterprises with descriptions, staffs, etc.:
	state
	private
	cooperative
	mixed
1*–188*	City Streets
	list of streets and locations
	street list
	old names/new names reference
	trolley and bus maps
189*–707*	List of Names
	list of officials, professionals, and others mentioned in the directory
End	Fold-out street map of Moscow

Appendix B

Availability of Soviet Directories

This is a list of some of the known editions of Soviet city and similar directories with notations on their locations.

Abbreviations

HC = Harvard College Libraries (Widener Library)
HO = Hoover Institution Library, Stanford University
LC = Library of Congress
LL = Lenin Library, Moscow
NYP = New York Public Library

Ves' Dal'nii Vostok; spravochnik (Khabarovsk, 1925) [LC]
Ves' Kazakhstan; spravochnaia kniga na 1931 g. (Alma-Ata, 1931) [LC]
Ves' Kharbin'; spravochnaia kniga na 1923 g. (Kharbin, 1923) [LC]
Ves' Kuibyshev; spravochnik-putivoditel' (Kuibyshev, 1936) [LC]
Ves' Leningrad; adresnaia i spravochnaia kniga (Leningrad, 1894–1934) [Note: directory appeared as *Ves' Peterburg* (1894–1914), *Ves' Petrograd* (1915–1923), *Ves' Leningrad* (1923–1927), and *Ves' Leningrad i Leningradskaia Oblast'* (1928–1934)] [HC, LC, NYP]
Ves' Tashkent; adresnaia i spravochnaia kniga (Tashkent: n.d.) [LC]
Vsia Belorussia; spravochnaia kniga (Minsk, 1925–1927) [LC]
Vsia Donskaia oblast' i Severnyi Kavkaz (Rostov, n.d.) [LC]
Vsia Moskva; adresnaia i spravochnaia kniga (Moscow, 1896–1907, 1912, 1923 [LC], 1925 [LL], 1926 [HO], 1927 [LC], 1928 [LC, NYP], 1929 [HC, LC], 1930 [LL, NYP], 1931 [HC, NYP], 1936 [HC, LC])
Vsia Odessa (Odessa, n.d.) [LC]
Vsia Sibir'; spravochnaia i adresnaia kniga (Leningrad, 1924) [LC]
Vsia Srednaia Aziia; spravochnaia kniga na 1926 g. (Tashkent, 1926) [LC]
Vsia Zapadnaia oblast' RSFSR; spravochnik (Moscow, 1932) [LC]

Perestroika and the Study of Sources
on Soviet Social History

V. Z. DROBIZHEV, E. I. PIVOVAR, A. K. SOKOLOV

The present is a time of great responsibility for Soviet historians. Society is making new demands of the historian as scholar and citizen, requiring both a reevaluation of the Soviet past in general and the filling in of particular "blank spots" (*belye piatna*) in the story. With the active participation of the general public, intense debates are in progress on every topic, especially on the 1920s and 1930s and the meaning of the historical experience of the Soviet people as a whole. In their internal professional discussions, as well as in their radio and television contributions to the broad public debate, Soviet historians are arguing about the achievements and shortcomings of industrialization and collectivization, the existing but unrealized models for the building of socialism, the structural factors inhibiting Soviet development, the Stalin cult, the causes of the political mistakes and miscalculations made on the eve of and during the Second World War, and many other questions.

Without wishing in any sense to diminish the significance of what has already been accomplished in recent years, we must note one peculiarity of the historical upheaval—a peculiarity testifying to the fact that in this field of *perestroika*, as in others, rhetoric has sometimes taken precedence over substance. The impassioned debates have given birth to new research topics and new approaches, and unjustly forgotten names have been resurrected from the past. Even the archives are feeling the impact of *perestroika*, both with respect to the accessibility of a whole series of archival *fondy*, and with respect to the formulation of new legal guidelines for the functioning of archival institutions. Yet at the same time the question of historical professionalism—justification of conclusions by proper presentation of evidence, awareness of the importance of improving the historian's professional tools and techniques for understanding the past—has somehow been relegated to a secondary position in recent discussions.

In our present situation, it might seem that questions of professionalism and improvement of the methods of historical analysis would not simply become more pressing than before, but would even acquire cardinal importance. If *perestroika*, democratization, and *glasnost'* create enormous opportunities for the creative scien-

---

This essay was translated and edited by Sheila Fitzpatrick.

tific work of historians, they also make increasing demands on the quality and intensification of historical research. These demands can be met only by refining the methods of analysis and expanding the repertoire of research techniques and tools, so that historical scholarship can free itself from the traditions of vulgarization and simplistic illustration of received truths (*illiustrativnost'*), and avoid sensationalism and political time-serving. After all, a truly scientific study of historical experience, which must be the foundation of *perestroika* in history, is quite incompatible with attempts to "fortify" some contemporary cause or "justify" or indict aspects of the past in the eyes of a later generation, whether this is done by the use of selective "historical examples" or by offering even the boldest and most original hypotheses without adequate supporting evidence and serious research investigation. Otherwise, historians will once again be giving their readers a cloudy and unfocused projection of the present instead of a real and vivid picture of the past.

Many archival *fondy* have now been opened for researchers. As it turns out, however, documents that historians particularly need are not there. In the *fond* of the Central Statistical Administration (TsGANKh, *f*. 1562: TsSU), for example, there are no traces of the population census of 1937. When the senior officials responsible for the census were arrested, evidently the actual census documents were also removed from the TsSU archive. Thus, the historian is faced with the task of reconstructing the source. That requires a major investigative effort involving study of the materials in local archives and the collection and processing of scattered data.

The archives contain very few personal documents such as letters, memoirs, and diaries. This reflects shortcomings in the work of Glavarkhiv USSR, which over many years oriented archivists to attach only secondary significance to personal documents. As a result, historians are left without the sources that would characterize the social psychology, attitudes, and everyday life of individual people. There is no way of replacing these missing sources. What is required, it appears, is an organized effort on a national scale to collect memoirs and record oral history.

In our opinion, a simple expansion of the source base of historical research will not be a sufficient or even a basic remedy for the outmoded illness of "*illiustrativnost'*" and the condition that reduced history, as publicists still often remark, to a mere "handmaid of propaganda." The crucial factor, in our opinion, is that historians should energetically utilize scientific methods, that is, methods that are amenable to verification and duplication, allow disclosure of the latent information content of the sources, facilitate the modeling of various historical processes, introduce a comparative dimension into historical analysis, and involve the processing of large quantities of data.

In this connection, the question of the use of computers and the creation of computerized data banks must undoubtedly be recognized as one of the most important practical issues facing the historical profession.

In recent years, an active process of computerization has been going on in all spheres of life. History has not stood apart from this process, as witness the numerous articles in the press by Academician I. D. Koval'chenko, in his time a pioneer of the application of quantitative methods in history, and his disciples. With regard to

Soviet social history, however, the necessity of taking a major initiative in the use of computers in historical research is particularly clear, for it is in this area above all that we have an accumulation of unsolved problems and unresearched themes and topics.

In the first period of Soviet computer use, there was much rapturous enthusiasm and expectation that computers in themselves would provide the "open Sesame" that would enable all complicated and controversial historical questions to be solved. The first attempts to use computers and quantitative methods were little more than apprentice exercises. It took years of trial and error, of tireless searches and intensive effort, before the best ways of using computers and quantitative methods were found. Unfortunately, the unrealistic radicalism of inexperience (*"detskaia" bolezn'*) tends to repeat itself as each new generation of researchers comes to grips with computerization.

The use of computers in the field of Soviet social history began with the processing of large-scale data sources compiled with the purpose of characterizing the balance of forces (class, social, and political) in the country at the moment of the decisive revolutionary transformations. One source was found which had been preserved in the archives for many years but never subjected to scientific analysis. This was the professional census of 1918 (see Appendix, C.2), whose scope covered more than a million workers of Soviet Russia. Computer processing of the census materials disclosed some important characteristics of the Soviet working class.

Traditionally, the main emphasis in analysis of the Russian working class was on social origin. In those terms, a stratum of hereditary (*potomstvennye*) workers was identified within the proletariat, and allocated the leading role. The term "pure" (*chistokrovnyi*) proletarian was even coined to describe it. Workers who came from the village were considered not completely "pure." And God forbid that they left something behind in the village—the right to land, a plot cultivated by relatives, a house, family—for in that case they were immediately relegated to the category of semi-worker/semi-peasant.

On the basis of complex analysis of the materials of the 1918 professional census, we managed to establish that hereditary (second- or third-generation) membership of the working class, as against peasant background (first-generation membership) was not in itself an adequate criterion for evaluating the internal homogeneity of the proletariat. The social structure of the working class could only be correctly understood when the interaction of many factors including historical, economic, and political characteristics was taken into account—that is, with the aid of multivariable analysis.

The chief factor determining the development of the working class turned out to be the character of labor. This factor was a combination of a whole series of indices including the sophistication of the production process itself, the environment in which the workers lived, their job training, and their level of skill. The length of the workers' experience in industry and their membership in workers' organizations, education, and level of consciousness played a major role. Using these criteria, it was possible to distinguish advanced (*peredovye*), middle, and lower strata within the working class.

The large-scale statistical studies of white-collar employees in the state bureaucracy in 1918 and 1922 (see Appendix, C.1 and 6) are first-class sources for social history amenable to computer analysis. Almost 250,000 white-collar employees of Moscow were investigated in the course of these censuses. As a practical matter, it would have been impossible to analyze the materials effectively by the historian's traditional methods. Moreover, bearing in mind the so-called latent information contained in these large-scale data sources, the project could not have been carried out at all by the traditional manual methods of source analysis.

As a result of many years' work by dozens of faculty members and graduate students and hundreds of undergraduates in the history departments of Moscow State University and the Moscow State Historical-Archival Institute, machine-readable data bases have been created which incorporate information from hundreds of thousands of archival files.

Personal questionnaires (*ankety*) filled in by delegates to the All-Russian and All-Union Congresses of Soviets (see *Appendix*, A.1–16) and deputies of the Supreme Soviet of the USSR (see Appendix, A.17–19) were among the sources used for the data bases on Soviet social history. Important types of documents as the personal dossiers (*lichnye dela*) of employees in the state bureaucracy and the registration forms (*uchetnye kartochki*) of workers in factories, state farms, and the like also fall within our scope. We have already made plans and begun work on the computer processing of important sources such as the 1927 All-Union census of Communist Party membership, the 1919 census of exploiting classes in Russia (see Appendix, C.4), the protocols of Vesenkha and Gosplan, and so on.

There is another important aspect of the application of computers to the study of society. The scientific-technical revolution has led to the introduction of computers in the sphere of production and administration. As a rule, the annual reports of enterprises on their workforce and production record now exist as machine-readable documents. Such historical documents cannot be analyzed without using computers and mastering the methodology of computerized analysis.

The logic of research leads us further. New researchers and additional collectives of scholars have to be involved in computer work, experience must be exchanged, and a network of general teaching and methodological centers must be created. Our research team at the Moscow Historical-Archival Institute is no longer alone in the field. There is the Sverdlovsk (formerly Novosibirsk) group of V. V. Alekseev and T. I. Slavko, V. E. Poletaev's group at the Academy of Sciences' Institute of History of the USSR, and a whole series of others. Analogous research teams are being set up in Dnepropetrovsk, Ivanovo, and at the Higher Komsomol School under the Komsomol Central Committee.

The nature of the tasks to be performed determines the choice of methodology for the computer processing of sources. The historical profession is now going through a stormy process of mastering methodology. Often individual researchers are inclined to absolutize their achievements. But these are growing pains which the creation of data bases will help us to overcome.

Soviet historians were arguably among the first in the world to begin to use computers and mathematical methods in historical investigations. However, we must recognize that historians in the United States—and, indeed, not only there—are now far ahead of us in the creation of informational-search systems in archives and scholarly centers, in the organization of data bases and archives of machine-readable documents, and in the development of joint programs, uniting historians and other specialists. Almost every professional historian in the United States has a personal computer, which not only enables him to rationalize his scientific research work, but also encourages and accustoms him in the use of quantitative methods. The spectrum of these methods is quite broad—from elementary calculations up to the use of very complicated mathematical models. A substantially greater number of historians are using such methods in the United States than in the Soviet Union.

As a revolutionary leap forward in the development of Soviet society, *perestroika* requires new approaches, new ways of thinking, and the broadening of international contacts among historians, including contacts in the field of computerization. Of course, some groundwork has already been laid for new approaches to international contacts in the historical profession. One example is the positive experience of Soviet and American historians using quantitative methods and computers in their research. This collaboration has already been in operation for more than ten years, and has been expressed in the holding of joint symposia and through the simulta- neous publication in the USSR and the United States of books summarizing the investigations of Soviet and American historians. The preface to the Soviet publica- tion, which came out under the title *Kolichestvennye metody v sovetskoi i amerikan- skoi istoriografii*, justly emphasized that "the publication of this collection is con- vincing proof of the possibility of fruitful and mutually beneficial scientific collaboration between social scientists of the USSR and the USA, despite the difference of world-views and political beliefs" [Moscow: Nauka, 1983—Eds.].

For the time being, more extensive use of computers in historical research in the Soviet Union is being inhibited for various practical and organizational reasons. Soviet historians are still extremely inadequately equipped with computer hardware and software. Despite the creation of special laboratories for the use of computers and quantitative methods in a number of institutions, we have to admit that in practice not one of these has a computer bought on its own budget. In the best case, for example, at the Moscow State Historical-Archival Institute, the laboratory has temporary use of a computer. In other cases, historians have only very restricted access to a general computer center.

In our time, when the Soviet public is showing an ever deepening interest in history, the solution of these purely organizational problems acquires particular resonance. After all, it is absolutely clear that without a cardinal improvement in the material-technical base of historical research, accomplished with the aid of quantita- tive methods and computers, we cannot expect any basic improvement in the level of research or, as a consequence, any serious increase in our understanding of the past.

Appendix

Soviet Computerized Data Bases

Editor's note: Professor Drobizhev's group, earlier working at Moscow State University and now centered in the Moscow State Historical-Archival Institute and its Laboratory for the Application of Mathematical Methods and Computers in Historical Research, has been working for a number of years on a major project involving the creation of computerized data bases on Soviet social history. A number of these data bases are already on-line, and there are plans to make them accessible to Western users on a commercial basis via international computer networks in the relatively near future. This Appendix contains brief descriptions of 34 data bases which were on-line or close to completion as of January 1989. It is the first detailed information on the data bases to appear in print either in the West or in the Soviet Union.

Western scholars wishing to use the data bases may apply to Moskovskii Istoriko-Arkhivnyi Institut, kafedra istorii SSSR sovetskogo perioda, ul. 25 Oktiabria, d. 15, Moscow K–12, USSR 103642.—S.F.

A. Congresses of soviets

1. Third All-Russian Congress of Peasant Deputies (January 1918)

Questionnaires from 422 delegates have been entered on the computer tape under such headings as attitude to Soviet power and its decrees; attitude to the Constituent Assembly and its dissolution; attitude to the war and the peace negotiations; evaluation of the army's capacity to fight; information on desertion and the process of army demobilization; the role of land committees in the countryside, their inter-relationship with the soviets and their dissemination in the countryside; attitude to the dividing up of noble estates and the correctness of the land distribution; data on stocks of agricultural equipment, food procurements, the existence of food reserves and consumption norms; information on agitational-propaganda work, the publication of newspapers, nationality relations, the organization of medical services and homes for invalids and orphans. In addition, there are general data on delegates' sex, age, education, [Communist] party membership (*partiinost'*), length of time in the party, nationality, and basic profession, on representation of gubernias and different organizations, and so on. A total of 77 variables.

2. Third All-Russian Congress of Workers' and Soldiers' Deputies (January 1918)

The computer tape contains data on 708 delegates broken down by 52 variables, including territorial representation; representation of various types of soviet bodies; sex; age; family position; basic profession; social estate (*soslovie*); nationality; education; party membership (*partiinost'*) and length of time as a party member; participation in the work of party, soviet, trade-union organs in 1905 and 1917; participation in the revolutionary struggle before 1917; publicist and literary work in soviet organs; experience of prison, hard labor and exile before the revolution, and so on.

3. Fourth Extraordinary Congress of Soviets of the RSFSR (March 1918)

Data from 1,226 delegates' questionnaires, analyzed in terms of 27 variables: sex; age; nationality; family position; education; profession; party membership; length of time as a party member; territorial representation. There is a block of data about the soviets that sent delegates to the congress: level of delegation (oblast, gubernia, uezd, volost, and so on); number of voters; party composition of local government organs. Also, data on the participation of delegates in the work of various leading organs; and data on pre-revolutionary political persecution experienced by delegates.

4. Fifth All-Russian Congress of Soviets (July 1918)

1,361 questionnaires, with 20 variables used in the coding system: sex; nationality; family position; education; party membership; length of time as a party member; age; participation in work of leading party organs; political persecution before the Revolution; participation in previous congresses of soviets. Information about the soviets that sent their representatives to the congress: where the delegate came from; which soviet he represents; the number of electors and the party breakdown of the soviet.

5. Sixth All-Russian Congress of Soviets (November 1918)

Data about 1,224 delegates are entered on the tape under the following headings: sex; age; territorial representation; nationality; family position; education; party membership; duration of the delegate's party membership; participation in the work of party organs; profession; level of delegation and number of electors who sent the delegate to the congress. There is a block of information about the Committees of the Poor (whether they exist in a given locality; what is the attitude of soviet organs toward them), and data about delegates' pre-revolutionary persecution for political reasons and their participation in previous congresses of soviets.

6. Seventh All-Russian Congress of Soviets
(December 1919)

Data from 1,306 questionnaires broken down by the following variables: status as a delegate; sex; age; nationality to which he belongs; territorial representation; address; family position; composition of the delegate's family; his education; basic profession; party membership; length of time as a party member; participation in work of leading party organs. There is a block of data on the electoral system: level of delegation; number of electors; how the elections were conducted (at a congress of soviets, in the soviet, or in the ispolkom, the revkom or the division, and so on); and whether elections were conducted according to the Constitution of the RSFSR. There are data about delegates' pre-revolutionary political persecutions and about their participation in previous congresses of soviets of the RSFSR.

7. Eighth All-Russian Congress of Soviets
(December 1920)

The machine-readable data archive contains information from 2,532 questionnaires of delegates analyzed according to 20 variables: status; sex; age; nationality; party membership; length of time as a party member; territorial representation; delegates' participation in leading party and soviet work and in previous congresses of soviets; and political persecution suffered earlier by delegates. [There is] information on the soviets that sent their representatives to the congress: level of delegation; how the delegate was elected (at a congress of soviets, in the soviet, in the ispolkom and so on); number of electors and size of the population that the delegate represents.

8. Ninth All-Russian Congress of Soviets
(December 1921)

Data from 1,993 delegates' questionnaires entered under 33 headings: status; age; sex; nationality; territorial representation; social position; party membership; length of time as a party member; education; place of work at the time of the congress. [Also], changes in profession and job (party, soviet, trade-union, and other) over the period since before the war (up to 1914, during the war, February and October 1917, Civil War, and up to the convocation of the congress). [There is] a series of data on the election procedure for the congress and on participation of delegates in the work of previous congresses of soviets.

9. Tenth Congress of Soviets of the RSFSR—
First Congress of Soviets of the USSR
(December 1922)

Data on 2,241 delegates under 51 headings: status; sex; age; nationality; territorial representation; social position; party membership; length of time as a party member; the delegate's ties with the land; education; place of work and employment at the time of the congress. A block of data on delegates' changes in occupations (professional, party, soviet, trade-union, Komsomol, and so on) up to 1914, during the war, between February and October, in the period of the Civil War, and at the time of the congress. A few headings deal with the electoral system for the highest organ of state power at the time of the creation of the USSR [i.e., 1922] and the participation of delegates in previous All-Russian congresses.

10. Second Congress of Soviets of the USSR
(January–February 1924)

2,138 delegates' questionnaires, with information entered according to 26 variables: sex; age; nationality; social position; party membership; length of time as a party member; profession; basic occupation before the October Revolution; participation in the work of political and social [obshchestvennykh] organizations before the October Revolution; work at the time of convocation of the congress; place of residence; education; territorial representation.

11. Third Congress of Soviets of the USSR
(May 1925)

2,368 questionnaires, with data entered under 17 headings, among them: sex; age; nationality; representation of territorial units and representation of organizations; social position; party membership; length of delegate's party membership; his basic profession; chief occupations before the October Revolution and during the session of the Congress; education; place of permanent employment.

12. Fourth Congress of Soviets of the USSR
(April 1927)

2,355 questionnaires, with data entered under 15 headings: sex; age; representation of delegations (by territorial units and organizations); nationality; occupations in the past and at the time of the session of the Congress; place of permanent employment; party membership; length of time as a party member; education; participation in congresses; proxy powers (polnomochiia) at this Congress.

13. Fifth Congress of Soviets of the USSR
(May 1929)

2,397 questionnaires, with data entered under 16 headings: sex; age; nationality; territorial representation; education; party membership; length of time as a party member; social position; place of residence (urban/rural); occupational category; participation in previous congresses of soviets.

14. Sixth Congress of Soviets of the USSR
(March 1931)

2,218 questionnaires, with data entered under 15 headings: representation by territory and organizations; sex; age; nationality; education; party membership; length of time as a party member; address; social position of delegate; name of enterprise or institution in which he works; occupational category; participation in previous congresses of soviets; participation of delegates in socialist competition.

15. Seventh Congress of Soviets of the USSR
(January–February 1935)

The machine-readable data base of this congress (2,646 questionnaires) is made up of several separate blocks of data: data on the delegates from union republics (1,554 questionnaires), which include information on the delegates' status, territorial representation, age, sex, nationality, place of residence and education; [data on] organizations represented at the congress; [data on] social position, party membership, length of time as a party member, sphere of activity and concrete occupations, shock-work, and participation in previous All-Union congresses of soviets (a total of 16 variables). The questionnaires of members of VTsIK (XVI convocation) and the TsIK SSSR (VII convocation), numbering 1,092, make it possible to extract data on another 9 variables: chamber (*palata*) (for members of TsIK USSR), educational specialization, educational institution completed, basic profession, date of entry to job held at the time of the Congress, nature of delegate's previous work, other changes [of job] by the delegate and when they occurred (for the period up to and including 1937), and participation in previous convocations of TsIK.

16. Eighth Congress of Soviets of the USSR
(November–December 1936)

2,217 questionnaires, with data entered under 27 variables: status; sex; age; nationality; education; educational level completed; representation by territory and organizations; party membership; length of time as a party member; social position and social origin; sphere of activity; job and place of work; salary; participation in the Stakhanovite movement; work norms achieved. For the military, there are data on the branch of the armed forces and on military education received. There is information on soviet work carried out by delegates, decorations conferred on them, and when the enterprises at which the delegates work were established. Participation of delegates in previous congresses of soviets of the USSR is also entered.

17. First Convocation of the Supreme Soviet of the USSR (1937–1946)

1,515 deputies' questionnaires, entered under 39 headings: chamber [of the Supreme Soviet]; electoral districts (distinguishing All-Union and autonomous republics, krais, oblasts, autonomous oblasts, national districts); sex; age; nationality; deputy's education (including college degree); party membership; length of time as a party member; length of time as a member of the Komsomol; social position; sphere of activity and job; titles, awards, and decorations; information on other work in higher and local soviet organs, and also data on year of election to the Supreme Soviet; job transfers while serving in the Supreme Soviet; the date and reasons for leaving the Supreme Soviet.

18. Sixth Convocation of the Supreme Soviet of the USSR (March 1962–June 1966)

Biographical data on 1,441 deputies are entered in the machine-readable data archive under 38 headings: territorial representation; where the deputy was elected (urban or rural location); age; social origin; nationality; education (including college graduation); party membership and length of time in the party; work in Commissions of the Supreme Soviet; participation in previous convocations of the Supreme Soviet; awards and titles. There is a block of data on the career paths of the deputies: in what sphere and in what job working life was begun; where the deputy is currently employed; whether he holds more than one job; number of job transfers; war service; record of public work.

19. Eleventh Convocation of the Supreme Soviet of the USSR (March 1984–1989)

Information on deputies taken from the biographical publication [presumably *Deputaty Verkhovnogo Soveta*.—Trans.], with data entered under 43 headings: chamber; territorial representation (republic, krai, oblast, etc.); electoral district (city or other); sex; age; nationality; education; college graduation; party membership and length of time in the party; sphere of activity and job, both at the beginning of the deputy's working life and currently; number of professional and job changes; membership in Commissions of the [All-]Union Soviet and the Soviet of Nationalities; service in the Great Patriotic War; awards; prizes; membership in the Presidium of the Supreme Soviet; work in higher party organs; higher [academic] degrees.

B. Congresses of trade unions

1. First All-Russian Congress of Trade Unions (January 1918)

123 questionnaires. Data entered according to 36 variables, among them the delegate's status (voting or non-voting); sex; which trade union or organization sent the delegate to the congress; the place from which he was sent; personal address and the address of his trade union; education; age; profession (occupational category), both before the Revolution and after the Revolution; what enterprise the delegate was working in at the time of the congress; duration of his trade union membership; official position in the trade union; paid job in the trade union; salary earned in that position; number of hours devoted to union work each day by the delegate; other salaried occupations and the salary received; other work in institutions and organizations and length of service in those positions; participation in congresses (not just trade-union) in 1917; political/social work and membership of political parties before the Revolution; total length of trade-union membership; [Communist] party membership and its duration at the time of the congress; political persecution before the Revolution; whether the delegate has been abroad and, if so, where.

2. Seventh Congress of Trade Unions of the USSR (1926)

1,274 delegates, data from questionnaires entered under 28 headings: territorial representation; institution represented by the delegate (specific trade union, territorial and industrial trade-union branch); sex; age; delegate's education and nationality; his basic profession; social position; membership in a specific trade union; work carried out in the trade union and its character (whether released [for full-time trade-union work] or not); participation in work of other elective organs; year of entry into the trade union and duration of work in trade-union organs; participation in previous congresses of All-Union Central Council of Trade Unions and other trade-union forums; [Communist] party membership and length of time in the party; previous membership in other parties; status of delegate.

3. Eighth Congress of Trade Unions of the USSR (1928)

1,290 questionnaires, with information under 32 headings: sex; age; nationality; education; social position; delegate's party membership and length of time as a party member; where he came from; what trade union organization sent him as a delegate; his basic profession and current paid employment in state institutions and state enterprises; trade-union work performed; membership in a specific trade union; character of work and concrete obligations in the trade union; work in other elective organs; year of entry into the trade union; duration of active work in the trade union; participation in previous congresses of VTsSPS; participation in other trade-union forums.

4. Ninth Congress of Trade Unions of the USSR (1932)

1,292 questionnaires, with data broken down by 38 variables: sex; age; nationality; membership of [Communist] party (including former membership); education; social position; delegate status; whether he has decorations; decorations; which trade-union organization sent him as a delegate; where he came from; which trade union he belongs to; year of entry into the trade union; basic profession and work at the time of the congress; the delegate's specific work in the trade union; length of total work experience; length of time working at a particular enterprise; whether the delegate is a shockworker or a member of a cost-accounting brigade; whether he performs other public service in elected organs; how long he has been involved in active trade-union work; whether he participated in previous congresses of VTsSPS or in other trade-union forums.

C. Censuses and other bodies of data on blue- and white-collar workers and other social groups

1. 1918 census of employees in Soviet institutions of the city of Moscow

The census covered 231,000 white-collar employees, and processing of the data is still in progress. The data from personal questionnaires have been entered into the machine-readable data archive under 29 headings: sex; employment characteristics (institution, institutional division [*glavk*], department, sub-department); position (*dolzhnost'*); length of service in the given institution; service in any institution merged with the present one, with the name of that institution; previous employment, indicating the sphere of activity and specific job or profession; questions of family position and make-up of family (number of children and other dependents); salary; additional earnings and their extent; child payments (*posobiia*); state of health of person filling in questionnaire; data on job satisfaction, whether [institutionally provided] meals and so on are taken, and degree of satisfaction with them; cultural opportunities (books, theater) and degree of satisfaction with them; recommending institution and organization and person writing reference; party membership and length of time in the party.

2. 1918 professional census of the working class

A selective sample (4–5 percent of the personal dossiers of workers in representative industrial geographical regions—Iaroslavl, Petrograd, Ivanovo-Voznesensk, Penza, and Vitebsk gubernias) of about 11,000 personal dossiers has been taken from the enormous collection of original returns in the machine-readable data archive. The variables chosen were those that are relevant for the analysis of social structure of the working class, among them information on the work environment of workers; type of settlement (*poselenie*); branch of industry; large, medium, or small enterprise; profession and skills; wage; length of time in industry; length of time in profession; whether parents worked in factories; age of starting work; previous occupation; ties with the land before the Revolution; living conditions; family's place of residence; location of home; seasonality of labor and employment during breaks in production; participation in field work; place of birth; nationality; sex; age; family position; organizational memberships (trade-union, cooperative, sickness fund); public activity; also—in small quantities—information on payments in kind, expenditures, living conditions, conditions of labor, and so on.

3. Industrial census of 1918, Petrograd and Moscow

The machine-readable data archive contains information on 701 Petrograd enterprises under 166 headings, among them general information on the enterprise (location, branch of industry, owner, year of establishment, type of production) and its work (has the enterprise closed and why, when it renewed its activity, information on the condition of equipment and on the seasonality of work of the enterprise); data on the system of management at the enterprise (administrative, technical, commercial, involving workers' control, factory committees, a factory directorate or other bodies); extensive data on various groups of persons employed over the period 1913–18 and their wages; on the sex and age breakdown of workers over the years 1913–18; on the average pay in the enterprise over the period 1913–18; on other payments and remunerations; on provision of social security at the enterprise, and so on.

4. Registration materials on representatives of former exploiting classes (September–December 1919)

There was no single program of investigation: the representatives of exploiting classes gave information about themselves in the form of statements and certificates or filled in questionnaires worked out by local soviet organs. Accordingly, the machine-readable data archive takes the data of Petrograd gubernia, which had its own questionnaire. At our disposal are data from 394 returns, entered under 29 headings: sex; age; size of family; address; information on work career (employment on the eve of the February Revolution; number, dates, and reasons for job changes in life; information on holding of senior administrative positions in stock companies; employment at the time the survey was conducted; date and manner of entry into Soviet employment; duration of that employment); information on property-owning (ownership of shares and immovable property and its extent and location; existence of unearned income), also whether guarantees of loyalty to Soviet power were extracted from the respondent.

5. VTsIK Commission for Investigation of People's Commissariats of the RSFSR (March 1920): The Commissariat of Education

2,693 questionnaires from employees, with data broken down according to the following variables: age of the respondent; his education (including the type of school from which he graduated and the number of classes he finished); data on make-up of family; age, place of employment or work of each member of the family; profession of respondent; the position he holds and his length of service in it; information on how he obtained his present position (recommendations and so on); date of entrance into Soviet employment; place of work. Also, employment and reasons for leaving jobs in the following periods: from 1914 to February 1917, between February and October, and from October 1917 to the present; information about whether the respondent was in government employment [under the old regime] and at what rank; what awards and decorations had he received, and for what; what were his means of subsistence, if he was not in government employment and did not work for wages (had he an estate, and if so, what and where); liability to military service; party membership and length of time as a party member; Civil War participation and its nature; place of employment and official position of father before the February Revolution; whether father owned immovable property; type of employment and occupations of parents at the present time.

6. 1922 census of employees of Soviet institutions of the city of Moscow

The data base consists of a selective sample comprising 6,500 questionnaires of employees of People's Commissariats. The data have been entered in the machine-readable data archive under 22 headings: party membership; sex; age; education (separate entries for completion of short-term courses); geographical location of schools (geografiia obrazovaniia); official position (including whether it was a regular [shtatnyi] or temporary appointment, and whether this job was held in combination with others); year of first employment in a People's Commissariat; salary level; year of appointment to current position; previous position; place of residence before starting work in a People's Commissariat; sphere of activity before joining the staff of a People's Commissariat; pre-revolutionary activity; number of additional jobs held; how they are remunerated; living conditions; number of dependents; income (distinguishing money earnings and payments in kind).

7. Workers' budgets of the 1920s

The collection includes 35 budgets for 1924 and a set of budgets for 1929. The machine-readable data archive contains the following data: general information on the family (sex, age, and ethnic composition, relationship of members, and so on); information on income and expenses of the family (by the month); current information on the family (arrivals and departures, change of apartment and job, firings, deaths, divorces, births, what they read, visits to cinema, theaters, lectures and exhibitions, interesting events in the home and at work, etc.). [There is] information (by the month) on accommodation and attitude to religion of the head of the family and family members; information on vacations of head of family and family members; family reading; attendance at cultural events and the system of upbringing of children; and some information on the career paths of the head of family and family members.

8. Budgetary investigations of white-collar employees of the 1920s

74 budgetary investigations for 1922 and 50 for 1923 have been coded. The investigations covered budgets of families of employees in Moscow and Leningrad. We have at our disposal information under the following headings: general information on the family (its sex and age breakdown, cultural-educational level, party membership of members of the family, membership in trade unions, the Komsomol, and so on); information on family incomes (of each member) and how they are constituted (from salary, trade, participation in mutual-aid funds, and so on); information on expenditure (food, clothing, various purchases, utilities payments, taxes, and so on).

9. All-Union investigation of small and artisan/craft industry of 1925 (Form 3: Selective investigation of small enterprises and artisan businesses)

The investigation—the first attempt at government registration of small enterprises—was conducted on four forms. The data from Form 3 (78,227 enterprises with 126,998 employees) have been entered in the machine-readable data archive under 118 headings, which cover branch of industry and geographical location of the enterprise; owner; his family position; relation to the cooperative movement; use of rented means of production; date of establishment of the enterprise; data on premises, fuel base, use of hired labor, seasonal continuity of work, and average degree of employment (*zaniatost'*) of workers; supply sources and volume of finished and raw materials used; volume and cost of different lines of production; their distribution; production expenses and taxes. There are data on the class make-up and demographic characteristics of persons working at the enterprise.

10. Personal dossiers of employees of the People's Commissariat of Heavy Industry and its divisions [glavki] (1932–1937)

The data base has been compiled from the inventory of personal dossiers of personnel of the Department of Hiring and Firing of the Business Division (*upravlenie delami*) of the Sector of Fuel Supply and the inventory of personal dossiers of senior personnel (*rukovodiashchie rabotniki*) of the Division for the Metallurgical Industry. The data are entered under 73 headings, among them: general information on personnel (sex, nationality, basic occupation of parents); information on their political activity (which party they first joined and when, duration of membership in that party; previous [sic] party membership, time of joining that party and duration of membership; [Communist] party membership and its duration at the time when the Cadres Registration Form was filled out); trade-union membership and duration of membership in a trade union; information on education (general and specialized education, with dates; courses completed, if any, with particulars of type and dates; party-political and military-political education, if any, with dates).

[There are also] data on work history: basic productive activity before the Revolution; total length of working life before the Revolution; total work experience since October 1917, with separate entries on types and duration of activity from October 1917 until the commencement of work in the administrative apparatus; last employment before entering the administrative apparatus and its duration; work experience, if any, before 1933 and 1936; total work experience; year of first employment in the administrative apparatus; year of leaving agriculture or leaving production as a blue-collar worker*; total length of service in the Soviet administrative apparatus; the industrial administrative apparatus; the military; the NKVD, Vecheka, and OGPU; in the sphere of transport, trade, finances, statistics, adult education (*proveshchenie*), school education (*obrazovanie*), medicine, art, culture, agriculture, supply and procurements; in the legal sphere; and in party and government bodies.

[There is a range of data on employment at various levels of industrial administration, namely]: the apparatus of Vesenkha and the industrial People's Commissariats, with duration of service and specific dates of employment in these jobs; industrial divisions (*promglavki*), with duration, positions, and specific years of employment; industrial associations (*promob'edineniia*), with similar particulars; the productive-administrative apparatus (*proizvodstvenno-upravlencheskii apparat*), with similar particulars; current position; previous and subsequent [sic] positions.

[There is also] some additional information on participation in elections and in the revolutionary movement; service in the old [Imperial] Army, the Red Guards, and the Red Army; service in the Civil War; service in White governments; awards and material incentives (*pooshchreniia*); the individual's record in party purge investigations and party reprimands, if any; data on previous positions; and the People's Commissariat and division in which the individual was currently employed.

---

*This is a paraphrase of one of the standard questions on personnel forms of the 1930s whose purpose was to identify *vydvizhentsy*, i.e., persons who had been upwardly mobile from the peasantry or the urban working class during the Soviet period.—S.F.

11. All-Union census of socialist industry on 1 January 1940 (Forms on Small Enterprises —1918 Definition [Tsenz])

The census was one in a series conducted by TsUNKhU in the period 1932–39. The data base was compiled from materials of local archives and information from the general census form (when that was lacking, the data were supplemented with information from other forms). The machine-readable data archive contains information on 127 enterprises from the North-East of the country (Magadan and Kamchatka oblasts, Koriak and Chukotka autonomous oblasts) which have been entered under 51 headings: oblast and administrative region of the enterprises; branch of industry; socioeconomic group; administrative jurisdiction (People's Commissariat, public [obshchestvennye] organizations, cooperatives, and so on); location (urban or rural); production information (year of commencement of work, how many days in the year the enterprise worked, whether or not it operated without a subsidy [samostoiatel'nyi ili net balans]).

[There is also] information on the labor collective (number of workers at the end of the reporting year, average number of workers during the year, sum of wages and salaries paid; similar data on ITR [engineering-technical personnel], white-collar employees, apprentices, and MOP [junior service personnel]; the total workforce of the enterprise and the total number of hired personnel [naemnye rabotniki]); information on productive capacity (engines, buildings, and structures owned at the end of the reporting year and at the end of the previous year); similar information on other means of production owned, on total means of production owned, on non-productive property, on productive and non-productive means of production leased; information on turnover tax.

Soviet Memoirs as a Historical Source

HIROAKI KUROMIYA

Historians turn to memoirs for a variety of reasons: they are an indispensable source for biographies; they may be factually informative and useful for illustrative purposes. The need to bridge gaps in the official record makes it difficult for Western historians of Soviet society to do without memoirs; and there is an enormous body of Soviet memoirs. However, unlike historians dealing with West European countries and the United States, where politicians' memoirs have established themselves as a solid historical source, historians dealing with Soviet society under Stalin have almost no memoirs or personal correspondence by such important political figures as Stalin, Molotov, or Kaganovich.

Historians are well aware of the "subjectivity" inherent in memoirs. Western historians of Soviet society have treated Soviet memoirs with considerable caution, and for good reason: as is discussed below, Soviet memoirs contain particular problems rare in Western memoirs. Western historians, distrustful of Soviet memoirs, tend to draw heavily on memoirs published in the West to augment official documents. There are a substantial number of these memoirs written by émigrés, Westerners, or Soviet dissidents.[1] It is true that they provide us with much factual information otherwise unobtainable, as well as an idea of the atmosphere of the Stalin years. Western scholars, however, do not seem to treat them with the same degree of caution that they apply to Soviet memoirs.[2] Yet the heavily political and moral nature of memoirs dealing with the Stalin years appear to give little compelling reason to believe that the memoirs published in the West are more "objective" than Soviet memoirs.

This is not to downplay the utility of the memoirs published in the West, but to point out the difficulties involved in memoirs as a historical source pertaining to the Stalin years. Historians are not free from the temptation to draw on memoirs (as well as documents) that fit their hypotheses or biases and to exclude those that do not. This temptation appears to be particularly strong in Soviet history, and its potential danger looms all the greater.

With few exceptions,[3] Western scholars have yet to address directly the value of Soviet memoirs as historical sources. It is this issue that the present essay discusses. First, the collection and publication of Soviet memoirs will be discussed briefly. Then, textual problems peculiar to Soviet memoirs will be analyzed. Third, the use of Soviet memoirs will be examined through the example of one of the most enigmatic periods of the Stalin era, the purge years. Fourth and finally, the issue of authorship will be discussed.

The collection and publication of memoirs

In the Soviet Union, history has been and still is manipulated for political purposes. Memoir literature is deemed a particularly useful tool to add credibility to the official account of history. In the 1930s the politics of memoir literature was aimed at the legitimation and glorification of the rule of Stalin. Naturally the publication of memoirs focused on what were regarded as major achievements of the regime: rapid industrialization and, to a much lesser degree, the collectivization of agriculture.[4] In the mid-1930s a vast number of memoirs on the "heroic period of socialist construction" were written and collected. However, only parts of them were actually published: in the midst of the Great Purge, many were lost or left to oblivion and still remain to be unearthed.[5] Instead, a number of success stories were published in the late 1930s. Of special importance are memoirs written by national heroes such as Stakhanovites.[6] These were people of "humble" origin turned Soviet heroes; and interestingly enough, many of them belong to the generation of Leonid Brezhnev (1906–1982) who experienced the October Revolution and the Civil War in their teens and Stalin's "revolution from above" in their twenties.[7] These memoirs exemplify the political use of memoirs and must be read with this fact in mind. As will be discussed below, however, today these seemingly uninteresting memoirs prove to be very useful historical sources.

Soviet memoirs, like other Soviet publications, have treated certain topics with candor and enthusiasm and have avoided other topics almost completely, depending upon changing political circumstances. The political relaxation that followed Stalin's death in 1953 and the official criticism of his rule in 1956 unleashed a phenomenal torrent of memoirs concerning the Stalin era. Stalin's successors, hard pressed by an enormous popular hunger for "facts" and their explanations, deemed it politically useful to expose "facts" in some detail in order to de-mythify Stalin's infallibility and to highlight the overall achievement and legitimacy of the regime; from their point of view it was politically less risky to expose "facts" in memoirs than it was in official documents. Camp survivors and families and relatives of the victims of Stalin's rule often turned to memoir writing in order to press for their political rehabilitation. For writers such as Ilya Ehrenburg to write memoirs was a means both of personal reflection upon the painful era and of alleviating the guilt of having "kept silent" during the period.[8]

Historians, too, were enthusiastic about memoirs. Post-Stalin Soviet historians concur that under Stalin, when the orthodox history of the party and society had been imposed and the use of "objective" official documents dictated, historians were discouraged from using memoirs as a source because of their "subjective" biases. In 1962, at the height of "de-Stalinization," I. M. Maiskii, an Academician and a former diplomat who himself was a memoirist, declared to an all-Union conference of historians:

> Why does the question of memoir literature now gain great significance? There exists a widespread opinion, among historians as well, that a full-fledged history can be written on the basis of nothing but official documents. This is not quite true. Even if the documents are reliable (and we know from experience during the period of the cult of personality of Stalin that not all documents are reliable), they for the most part relate certain activities or events, and rarely shed much light upon the (individual and collective) motives for the actions of people. . . . The period of the cult of personality simply killed this genre of literature. . . . [Even now] a number of publications and periodicals treat memoirs as if they were, I would say, a hot potato.[9]

Maiskii's complaint certainly reflected an upsurge of intellectual interest among Soviet historians in memoirs as historical sources.

Finally, there were pressures on the part of the military, which had "suffered most from the subordination of historical research on World War II to narrow propagandistic and ideological schemes." In the decade 1957–1967 alone, war memoirs amounted to "over 150 full-length books and several hundred articles."[10] Thus, the enthusiasm for memoir writing and the flood of memoirs during the decade or so of "de-Stalinization" were a result of the confluence of various forces which sought to use memoirs for their own particular political, military, intellectual, or personal purposes.

The publication of Soviet memoirs, however, was subjected to the change in political climate that occurred after Brezhnev took over in 1964. The case of the journal *Novyi mir* illustrates this issue. During the 1960s the chief editor of the journal, A. T. Tvardovskii, had made a conscious effort to utilize memoirs and autobiographical accounts as a way of approaching difficult questions concerning the Stalin era. Tvardovskii went to considerable lengths to publish memoirs and stories by writers like Ehrenburg, camp survivors like Solzhenitsyn and A. V. Gorbatov, diplomats like Maiskii, and industrial experts like V. S. Emelianov, who often quite frankly discussed the Great Purge, the foreign policy and the war conduct of Stalin, and other difficult issues of Stalin's rule.[11] With the immediate purposes of "de-Stalinization" achieved, however, the new political authorities under Brezhnev attacked and, in 1970, forced Tvardovskii out of the editorship of the journal. The case of *Novyi mir* illustrated the degree of candor with which Soviet memoirists were allowed to discuss the Stalin question.

Having examined Soviet war memoirs, however, Seweryn Bialer has concluded that "an evolution has taken place in the post-Khrushchev period toward a more accurate description of the Second World War . . . with the explicit reservation for some aspects of Stalin's policy which were treated with greater candor and honesty under Khrushchev, in particular, the Great Purge."[12] This appraisal seems to apply to other categories of Soviet memoirs as well.

Despite the multitude of problems plaguing Soviet historians of the Stalin era, the collection of memoirs, too, appears to be making progress. In the late 1950s and early 1960s, Soviet historians started to collect memoirs by participants in and witnesses of socialist construction in the late 1920s and 1930s and to conduct extensive interviews with them.[13] In the late 1960s and early 1970s, this effort became more systematic and organized.[14] Clearly, Soviet historians put serious effort into this sphere of work, because according to one historian, "time and tide waits for no man" and many unrecorded experiences are being lost forever with the passing away of people who lived in the Stalin era.[15]

The *glasnost'* campaign Mikhail S. Gorbachev launched in the mid-1980s has enormously facilitated the publication of memoirs on the Stalin years. Evidently Gorbachev and his advisers deem it necessary for the *perestroika* of Soviet society to fill in the "blank spots" of history. This officially endorsed historical mini-renaissance has almost freed the discussion of the Stalin years from strict state censorship, with the result that, at the time of writing this essay (August 1988), an unprecedented torrent of publications, including memoirs, on those years is deluging the Soviet press.[16] This welcome phenomenon, however long it may last, will undoubtedly stimulate and facilitate the study of the Stalin years.

Of the various categories of Soviet memoirs, politicians' memoirs are the most important, but their publications are very few, and these, moreover, tend to leave the Stalin era out.[17] Yet there are a number of important biographies of politicians, which are partially based on unpublished memoirs by those who were close to them.[18] Of particular value are some very recent memoirs by old party members, Komsomol leaders, and Kremlin guards which shed much new light on higher politics.[19] It is also noteworthy that surviving wives and other family members often play an active role in consolidating their man's reputatation by writing memoirs or biographies.[20] (The rehabilitation of victims of the Stalinist terror by the *glasnost'* campaign will undoubtedly generate more memoirs of this kind.) Moreover, many industrialists (*khoziaistvenniki*), engineers, People's Commissars, and local party leaders have written memoirs, which provide a good deal of information on bureaucratic political processes and even high politics.[21] Because official documents concerning high politics became progressively scarcer as the 1930s wore on, these memoirs are of particular value. Memoirs by military leaders and diplomats are also insightful and suggestive of new perspectives on high politics.[22]

Journalists' accounts constitute another important category of Soviet memoirs: they not only are eyewitness accounts but also often draw on otherwise unavailable archival and statistical material, so they are especially rich in factual information ranging from high politics to the detailed operation of factories.[23] Memoirs by intellectuals such as writers, scientists, and scholars are also valuable in revealing their intellectual and personal reflections upon the Stalin era.[24] Memoirs by workers and peasants are also important.[25] Those of former Stakhanovites are particularly interesting.[26] And now many memoirs on labor camps are being published amid the *glasnost'* campaign.[27]

Unfortunately, no comprehensive bibliography of the memoir literature concerning the Stalin era is available. The only general bibliography of memoirs of the Soviet period, *Istoriia sovetskogo obshchestva v vospominaniiakh sovremennikov, 1917–1957* (Moscow, 1957), and chast' 2, vyp. 2 (Moscow, 1967), is far from comprehensive, and bibliographic information on unpublished memoirs is even more limited.[28] A projected six-volume bibliography of Soviet memoirs, *Sovetskoe obshchestvo v vospominaniiakh i dnevnikakh. Annotirovannyi bibliograficheskii ukazatel' knig, publikatsii v sbornikakh i zhurnalakh*, edited by V. Z. Drobizhev, the first volume of which was published in 1987 by Nauka, Moscow, is expected to fill in the gap considerably, as far as published literature is concerned. Yet scholars will need to consult the specialized bibliographies, monographs, and articles which provide valuable information on memoirs in particular fields: industrialization;[29] the working class;[30] the history of factories;[31] agriculture;[32] World War II;[33] the party;[34] the Komsomol;[35] and diplomacy.[36] It is also helpful to keep up with various current newspapers and periodicals such as *Voprosy istorii, Istoriia SSSR, Voprosy istorii KPSS, Sovetskie arkhivy, Molodaia gvardiia, Zvezda, Novyi mir, Oktiabr', Znamia, Literaturnaia gazeta, Moskovskie novosti, Ogonek, Iunost'*, and *Istochnikovedenie istorii sovetskogo obshchestva*. Some of these publish memoir literature on a regular or semi-regular basis, and some of these provide bibliographical information on memoir literature. Flagships of *glasnost'* such as *Ogonek, Moskovskie novosti*, and *Argumenty i fakty* carry numerous letters from readers containing fascinating autobiographical and biographical data.

The text

Memoir literature has intrinsic problems which concern historians, namely factual errors, distortions, falsifications, and self-censorship. Although these problems are of course not confined to Soviet memoirs, Western historians are well aware of the need to take special care in dealing with Soviet memoirs. However, they have not examined in earnest the most fundamental issue here, the text. Certainly, this is an extremely difficult task: many errors, distortions, and falsifications may not be detected at all. Before we discuss the utility of Soviet memoirs, it is necessary to discuss the textual problem and thereby illustrate the degree of care to be taken in using Soviet memoirs.

There are at least two aspects to this problem: distortions and falsifications through self-glorification and self-justification on the part of the memoirist, and distortions and falsifications on the part of editors and censors. In a country where conformity to the official policy and official interpretation of history is emphasized, the room for individuals' self-glorification and self-justification may be relatively small. In fact, we have little reason to believe that Leon Trotsky's memoirs, for instance, are freer of this problem than are Soviet memoirs. But clearly we need to be extremely careful. Let us take a somewhat comical example. This is not related to the Stalin era, but it is highly indicative of the issue we are faced with. M. K. Ter-Arutiuniants, who in October 1917 was a commissar of the Kromverskii arsenal at the Fortress of Peter and Paul in Leningrad, contributed his reminiscences to the collection of memoirs by participants in the October Revolution, *Velikaia Oktiabr'-skaia sotsialisticheskaia revoliutsiia. Sbornik vospominanii uchastnikov revoliutsii v Petrograde i Moskve* (Moscow, 1957). Bent on showing himself as a great leader at the Fortress in the October days, Ter-Arutiuniants made a number of unjustifiable assertions, most of which were corrected by the compiler, the Institute of Marxism and Leninism affiliated to the Central Committee of the Communist Party of the Soviet Union. Yet bending to his self-aggrandizing pressure, the Institute made a correction in the errata attached to the book: instead of being a mere commissar of the arsenal, Ter-Artutiuniants was a much more important person—one of the commissars of the Fortress itself.[37] Although this is a rather minor falsification, which was fortunately discovered, it is certainly indicative of the pitfalls of which we ought to beware.

The second issue, namely distortions and falsifications on the part of editors and censors, has rightly concerned and still concerns Western historians. This concern is shared by Soviet historians as well.[38] The issue of outside intervention can be vividly illustrated by the example of the memoirs by I. P. Bardin, who was the chief engineer of Kuznetskstroi in the early 1930s and became an Academician in 1932. Bardin's memoirs, *Zhizn' inzhenera*, published in Moscow in 1938, underwent several stages of editing. First, apparently in 1935, Bardin narrated his reminiscences to the writer, I. P. Zaslavskii, who then extensively edited the transcript. Furthermore, the published version as we see it is not identical with the edited version. This suggests that the memoirs were further edited by someone else.[39] We can see how Bardin's reminiscences were distorted in the process. For instance, concerning the behavior of the so-called "Iukhnovtsy" (who allegedly had been organizing a strike for wage hikes) at the time of a flood in the spring of 1930, Bardin stated:

> I was amazed at the calmness people maintained. There was no unnecessary muddle or rushing around. It should be said that this favorably influenced the whole situation. Iukhnovtsy, too, took part in this [struggle against the flood], but they swore at and quarreled with each other.[40]

Zaslavskii edited this passage:

> People were flooded out of their lodgings. At first they lost their heads. But then they dashed hard and passionately into the struggle against the flood. These were masons and navvies [i.e., Iukhnovtsy], who only yesterday, fuming [at their bosses] and demanding higher wages from the construction project, would not work. Yet today the same people rushed to defend the project, risking their lives.[41]

Although neither Bardin's nor Zaslavskii's passage is available in its entirety, clearly Bardin's reminiscence is distorted by Zaslavskii. In the published edition, this passage reads:

Masons and navvies lost their heads at first. But the Communists and worker cadres did not. They . . . incessantly displayed courage and heroism, and mobilized and organized people for the struggle with the disaster. They dashed fiercely and passionately into the struggle against the flood. Among them were masons and navvies, who only yesterday, fuming [at their bosses] and demanding a little higher wages from the construction project, would not work.

Yet today the same people rushed to defend the project, risking their lives.[42]

It is hard to know from the published version what Bardin actually meant. Exactly what happened is not clear, although it may be revealed in the contemporary press and other memoirs.[43]

This case may not be a serious problem, because we have at least several accounts. A more perplexing case is also found in Bardin's memoirs. Working for a while (1910–1911) in the United States, Bardin went back to Russia rather disillusioned (according to the published version). In the original transcript, Bardin stated:

Although I had hung around there for about a year and half, my knowledge of American technology was meager.[44]

Zaslavskii edited this passage as well:

Now I had known Americans . . . I had already had an idea of American industry and now in real earnest learnt the most advanced metallurgy in the world.[45]

In the published version, it is stated that:

Later I understood that in the United States I had familiarized myself with large-scale mechanized metallurgical production, new open-hearth steel, rolling shops, and observed there a totally new mechanized metallurgical process. America had widened my technological horizon.[46]

This is a good example of sheer distortion and one that is otherwise almost impossible to detect. Having examined these variants, the Soviet historian Iu. A. Ivanov declared that if someone really wants to know Bardin, *Zhizn' inzhenera* will not give an accurate impression of him.[47]

Yet another example of editorial interventions can be illustrated by the collection of memoirs *Byli gory Vysokoi* by a collective of authors who worked at the iron mine, Vysokogorskii, in Nizhnii Tagil in the Urals. Two editions were published in 1935,[48] and the third edition in 1960; the first two editions have been available to the author, but the third has not. However, to see how they were edited, one can draw on an interesting Soviet work which has examined several variants of manuscripts in the archives.[49]

In the autumn of 1932, a collective of authors was formed; "Almost all of them were illiterate or semi-illiterate." (It was alleged later that among them there had been former "contractors, White guards, and class aliens," whose real names were cited in the collection.)[50] Individual and group conversations, questionnaires, and dictations were conducted for the projected book. By 1934, the manuscripts had been composed. The compilers, however, rather freely tampered with them, dissecting and combining stories by several authors into a set of memoirs arranged thematically. This created a number of inconsistencies. Further, M. Gorkii made some three hundred editorial corrections. In the last analysis, it is said that these tamperings cast doubt on the authenticity of the memoirs.[51] The third edition published at the time of "de-Stalinization" was also subjected to numerous arbitrary distortions. According to a Soviet historian, the result was a "falsification of events."[52]

As this last case suggests, we have to be as careful of publications at the time of "de-Stalinization," because they, too, may have been tampered with for political purposes. Unless we have access to the original, textual criticism is almost impossible. A comparison of the two editions, published in 1970 and 1974, of *Sud'ba rabochego* by the former Stakhanovite, Ivan Gudov, reveals numerous differences between the two. For instance, in the 1970 edition Gudov stated that in mid-1936 Ordzhonikidze, then People's Commissar of Heavy Industry, "thoroughly cleansed [*prochistil*]" the Gorkii Motor Plant of its leaders upon hearing Stakhanovites' complaint about disorder in its forge workshop.[53] Yet in the 1974 edition, the phrase "*prochistil*" is replaced by "*propesochival*," a word not associated with the political purge of the 1930s.[54] The latter phrase may be Gudov's correction, but it is not unlikely that it is an editorial correction. Such cases as this are numerous in Soviet memoirs.

Both self- and official censorship affect profoundly the text and the contents of memoirs. This state of affairs is certainly unfavorable for historians. One cannot rely solely upon the published version of *Zhizn' inzhenera* to study Bardin or for that matter *Sud'ba rabochego* to study Gudov. Certainly the cases examined above may be rather extreme; the majority of published memoirs may be much more authentic. At any rate, these cases do illustrate the need for us to keep in mind that published memoirs may be heavily distorted.

The use of memoirs

Here we shall focus upon a topic that has been traditionally avoided in Soviet memoirs, the purges in the second half of the 1930s, both to attempt a content analysis, if not textual criticism, of Soviet memoirs and to illustrate their utility as a historical source.[55] This focus is taken deliberately. Although secrecy still veils the history of the purge years (particularly 1937–1938), some memoirs published in the 1930s, especially by Stakhanovites, contain vivid accounts of the purge phenomenon as witnessed "from below." Their retrospective accounts, moreover, are also available. This enables us to compare both contemporary and retrospective accounts by the same individuals.

The 1930s were a politically tense era in internal and international terms. Nearly everything, no matter how trivial, was politicized. Recalling the era almost fifty years later, Leonid Brezhnev remarked:

> In the thirties the task of instructing and educating, of tempering the ideology of personnel, first and foremost of the intelligentsia engaged in scientific and techno-logical work, was a particularly important one. And I therefore felt that the work offered me in 1933 was very crucial: as a third-year student, I was appointed head of the *rabfak* [the workers' faculty] and then Director of the Dneprodzerzhinsk Metallurgical Technical College. I worked with a will. I wanted to do more for my comrades. The instruction manual for those years has been preserved. I looked with a smile through the old, and what now must seem in some ways, naive directions, but that was politics then. We considered it our duty to fight for every student, persuaded the factory children to study, strove to help them with trade union grants and simply to feed them well in our canteen.[56]

This passage eloquently reveals that in the 1930s young Brezhnev took "naive" matters for quite serious politics. His was not an isolated case at all. "It is laughable to remember," a former worker at the "Krasnyi Proletarii" plant in Moscow recalled in the early 1970s, "that [in the late 1920s and early 1930s] the engineers and other specialists were considered representatives and hirelings of the bour-geoisie."[57] In other words, at that time it was not laughable at all for workers to regard the engineers and other specialists as "representatives and hirelings of the bourgeoisie."

The case of Aleksei Stakhanov, after whom the famous Stakhanovite movement was named, is also interesting. When asked in the early 1970s what his principal duty to society now was, he remarked:

> For us, who got hardened in the course of victorious socialist construction and who came out of the crucible of severe class combat [*skhvatki*], there is no task more important than to help our boys and girls to cultivate a proper world outlook and *class approach* to life. This is our duty, the party's assignment, and, if you will, our historical mission.[58]

This remark may be a simple cliché. Yet it is also likely that whatever he meant by "class approach" he still thought in the vocabulary of the Stalin era and lived the life of "class approach" if not "class struggle."

The vocabulary used by the workers was clearly a reflection of that of their leaders. For instance, Ordzhonikidze, who is usually regarded in the Western litera-ture as a moderate, frequently used such strong words as "saboteurs" in relation to industrial managers, particularly after 1935 when the Stakhanovite movement got underway. According to Semen Gershberg, a *Pravda* correspondent in the 1930s, Ordzhonikidze remarked in December 1935:

> The Stakhanovite movement was born from below in the Donbass against the trust leaders (*trestoviki*) and without them. Now some of them want to wreak revenge

on us and slow the Stakhanovite movement down. It started without us, they say, nothing will come out of it. These are rotten people. We need to forewarn that we will replace them with Stakhanovites.[59]

The Stakhanovite movement made the industrial managers very vulnerable to attack both from above and from below. In his conversation in November 1935 with Konstantin Petrov, the party organizer of the mine Tsentral'naia-Irmino in the Donbass, the birth place of the Stakhanovite movement, Stalin revealed why he was so interested in the movement. Confirming the fact that Stakhanov's wife initially opposed the undertaking of her husband,[60] Stalin reportedly remarked:

These facts [of opposition to the movement] mean this, comrade Petrov. The birth of the Stakhanovite movement immediately gave birth to its opponents, its enemies. That is how it always is. The old always stands in the way of the new. The new can win only in a struggle with the old. This is why I am so interested in the Stakhanovite movement. Who are they? What measures of help [for the Stakhanovites] should be taken?[61]

In their speeches and articles, party leaders frequently used highly politicized concepts such as "saboteurs," "enemies," and "opponents."

Upon perusing their memoirs, one comes away with the impression that workers like the Stakhanovites took these political concepts quite seriously and concretely. They appear to have perceived that enemies were actually active in the factories. Throughout his memoirs, *Rasskaz o moei zhizn'* (1938), Stakhanov branded his bosses—who had apparently been put on trial or arrested—as "saboteurs," "wreckers," "enemies," and so on. Similar accusations against bosses are also found in memoirs by other Stakhanovites such as Gudov, *Put' stakhanovtsa* (1938) and Busygin, *Zhizn' moia i moikh druzei* (1939). Moreover, these Stakhanovites openly declared that the Old Bolsheviks put on trial in 1936–38 were actually "wreckers," "Fascist spies," etc. Boasting that it was the NKVD and Stakhanovites who had "unmasked" these "traitors,"[62] Stakhanov remarked:

If these reptiles [Piatakov and others] had fallen into our hands, each of us would have torn them into pieces. But the old rascal Trotsky is still alive. I think that his time is also coming, and we will settle accounts with him properly. . . . [When the trial of Piatakov and others started] we immediately demanded that they be shot. This was an opinion of all of our miners and, generally, our whole population. . . . We have to be able to catch sight of the enemy, seize them by the hand, and liquidate them.[63]

We need to wonder, however, if this was indeed Stakhanov's own perception. Is the original heavily distorted like Bardin's? The answer is not clear, although we do know that according to Busygin, Stakhanov seriously believed that Piatakov and others were "enemies of the people."[64] Or was Stakhanov under irresistible political pressures at that time? Certainly there were people who wanted to show events in the manner described. Yet there is evidence to show that Stakhanov rather sincerely believed in the purges: in his memoirs published in 1975, Stakhanov still named his erstwhile bosses as "saboteurs,"[65] although he was reticent about the "reptiles." Certainly his account is softened in this later edition. Yet its substance is not very different from his 1938 memoirs.

Stakhanov was far from an isolated believer. For example, Petro Grigorenko, the only Soviet general ever exiled, believed at the time of the Great Purge that "most of those arrested were actual 'enemies.'"[66] In a similar vein, Lev Kopelev, a former Trotskyite turned a "true believer" of Stalinism and now an émigré, believed that "Zinoviev's men had directed Kirov's assassination."[67] Many memoirs currently being published owing to the *glasnost'* campaign reveal the same popular belief.[68]

To be sure, many Soviet memoirs now demonstrate that political labels such as "enemy of the people" were extensively applied to people for reasons of expediency. For instance, in 1937 I. M. Danishevskii, then director of an aviation plant in Siberia, waged a "war" with the chief construction engineer, B. D. Dlugach, concerning technical issues. Some thirty years later, Danishevskii related that Dlugach was an "excellent" engineer but was "obstinate." Danishevskii found it impossible to work with him; at the request of Danishevskii, Dlugach was removed from his post. Apparently Dlugach was arrested, because in his memoirs Danishevskii admitted, expressing some anguish, that this "most honest man, principled and genuinely devoted to the Soviet state" had been taken by him "for, in the terminology of that time, an 'enemy of the people.'"[69] We also know that in the 1970s former Stakhanovites like Gudov and Busygin, who had accused their bosses of being "enemies of the people" in the 1930s, recanted the accusations: Gudov says that at that time he became very suspicious and imagined that his bosses' "malicious intention" was responsible for ordinary production defects.[70] In a similar vein, Busygin recalls: "Only now, looking back into the past, do I think that the blame for everything lay in my impatience about defects in the factory and my screaming around about them."[71]

Similar retrospective accounts are also given by individuals who had held responsible positions but survived the purge years. At the February–March 1937 plenum of the Central Committee of the Communist Party, which appears to have triggered the wave of purges in the industrial sector, Molotov accused, among others, V. Iakovlev, then construction director of the Cheliabinsk electrometallurgical complex, of "wrecking" and cited his "confession" to that effect.[72] One of his colleagues, V. Emelianov, then technical director of the Cheliabinsk ferro-alloying plant, recalled in the 1960s that at that time he "could not but believe Molotov, could not but believe that he indeed cited the testimony of Iakovlev himself."[73]

We should not preclude the possibility of these retrospective accounts being tampered with. We also have to consider the possibility that the former Stakhanovites may have been under pressure because of the rehabilitation of their erstwhile bosses. But a comparison of their contemporary and retrospective accounts suggests that Gudov, Busygin, and others had come to recognize the idiosyncrasies of that time from the vantage point of two decades later, when political concepts such as "class enemy" and "enemy of the people" were either discarded or depoliticized. Following Brezhnev, these memoirists may well say that such political concepts may seem "naive in some ways," but that "that was politics then."

We must not, however, extrapolate these retrospective accounts back into the Stalin era. Even at the height of "de-Stalinization" under Khrushchev, there were people who still believed that their former bosses had actually been "enemies of the people." Recalling the 1930s in his memoirs written in 1961, I. Ia. Vasilev, a steelworker at the Kuznetsk metallurgical complex, "painted a black picture of almost all people around him and in particular his [former] bosses." He presented them as having been "enemies of the people" and "friends of the wreckers." The apparent reason for this indiscriminate accusation was that in the 1930s he had been demoted for lack of knowledge and discipline.[74] It is hard to believe that Vasilev complied in his writing with the dominant political climate, which in 1961 was at variance with his assertions.[75] In the 1930s, people like Vasilev may have simply revenged themselves on their bosses by branding them as "enemies of the people." It seems likely that people like Vasilev could not comprehend their own manipulations and abuses as such. Whatever the case, at the very least this story shows that political concepts like "enemies of the people" were manipulated and abused not only from above but from below as well. As Ivanov, having examined Vasilev's memoirs, points out, this kind of obsession was a reflection of the political and socio-psychological climate of that era, or of the "atmosphere of mutual distrust and suspiciousness."[76]

Firmly believing in the Moscow party leadership, those Communists who rose to local party leadership in the aftermath of the Purge drew interesting political conclusions from these "abuses from below." N. S. Patolichev, for example, who in early 1939 became the first secretary of the Iaroslavl obkom, went to considerable lengths to contain the lingering local purges, and warned at the XVIII party congress (March 1939) against the "enormous harm" caused by the "over-vigilant." He cited a case in which the secretary of the Rostov raikom (in Iaroslavl), K. V. Stepanova, was accused at a Iaroslavl conference of her "linkage" with the "enemy of the people": after her mother died, her father remarried another woman only to die shortly after; her stepmother then remarried a man who subsequently turned out to be an "enemy of the people."[77] In his memoirs Patolichev tells of a similar incident in which the "hard-working, modest, and authoritative" third secretary of the Iaroslavl city committee, Lazarev, failed to be re-elected a member of the committee. During the discussion of candidates at a committee conference (held probably in early 1939), one delegate asked Lazarev which village he was from, and he himself answered his own question. (Apparently this delegate sought in a subtle way to lead the other delegates to suspect that Lazarev was of questionable, i.e., kulak origin.) Lazarev, confused though he was by an unexpected question, confirmed the answer. All present were puzzled; when the chairman of the conference asked the delegate what he meant, he answered again puzzlingly: "Oh, never mind." Lazarev was not elected, because "some" delegates voted against him. Patolichev was to remember this incident again and again, especially when "some comrades" demanded multi-candidate ballots in the name of party democracy. This incident made Patolichev undeviatingly believe that such a democracy, i.e., Western-style pluralistic ballots, could in reality be reversed and used against the best candidates such as Lazarev.[78] Patolichev's memoirs indicate that the purge experience may have contributed to the consolidation of a peculiar Soviet political culture, which Gorbachev now seeks to dismantle.

The authorship of Soviet memoirs

A large majority of Soviet memoirists belong to the beneficiaries of the Stalin era. To be sure, some of its victims and sufferers have written stories of their own, but their publication in the Soviet Union has until recently been very limited. Yet the issue of partisan authorship is not simple at all.

In the Soviet Union, as in other societies, upwardly mobile individuals, especially those turned heroes, take special pride in their achievements and often are given to writing about their lives; the political authorities never fail to take advantage of success stories to add legitimacy to the regime. Soviet memoir literature is particularly important in illuminating the ethos of those upwardly mobile individuals.[79] However partisan their memoirs may be, they should not be ignored or dismissed. The contemporary Soviet memoir literature of the Stalin era reveals the *collective* perception of the era by upwardly mobile individuals such as Stakhanovites. Some memoirs are extensively edited to suit the official account, as is the case with Bardin's memoirs. As far as those of Stakhanovites are concerned, as discussed above, there appears to have been little contradiction between the collective and the individual accounts of the Stalin era. However naive or absurd they may appear today, such political concepts as "class enemy" and "enemy of the people," which framed the political thinking of that time, were at once comprehensible and quite meaningful for the Stakhanovites. The authorship of their memoirs appears to be of little significance, because their experiences were almost interchangeable. Only when the political climate altered and those concepts formerly deemed self-evident became problematic was the collective perception of the era individualized. Post-Stalin Soviet memoirs thus reveal varied accounts: we see diehards such as Stakhanov and Vasilev on the one hand and somewhat "repentant" Stakhanovites such as Gudov and Busygin on the other hand.

It would be a wrong assumption, then, that a single official account is dictated to Soviet memoirists. Memoirs by educated people often describe the purges of the 1930s as having appeared "inexplicable."[80] By contrast, neither contemporary nor retrospective accounts by the Stakhanovites indicate that the purges appeared to them to be "inexplicable," although some like Gudov and Busygin do repent of their behavior in retrospect.

The reflection of intellectuals upon the purge phenomenon, moreover, is not uniform at all. Ehrenburg, for example, recalled in the mid–1960s that people had been quite aware of the terror, but that they had "kept silent or whispered" because of fear.[81] The Soviet political and literary authorities, however, attacked Ehrenburg's memoirs as a self-serving afterthought. Writing in 1966 in *Oktiabr'*, an archenemy of *Novyi mir* which had published Ehrenburg's memoirs, K. Bukovskii (who had participated in the grain seizures in the 1920s and 1930s), argued against Ehrenburg:

> My optimism—let alone realism—concerning that time [the Stalin era] lies in the fact that in those years we had no doubts about anything and were still less aware of anything. We saw only what we wanted to see. Whether this was "hypnosis" or simply our romantic notion (based on belief and conviction) about the surroundings, I do not know; but rather it was still our conviction. . . . We had no doubts whatsoever. . . .[82]

Certainly one should not take this partisan account at its face value. Yet it is important to note that Bukovskii is far from an isolated believer of Stalin's rule, and the belief is not confined to Soviet memoirs. Recalling the purge years in his memoirs published in the West, *The Education of a True Believer* (the Russian original is *I sotvoril sebe kumira*), Kopelev stated:

> I had known that they [his arrested friends] were true believers in the party, in Soviet power. . . . And still I had put the distance between myself and them out of fear and calculation: Don't help them, it's too dangerous.
> However, at the time I could not permit myself to explain it all so simply—"fear and calculation." No, I had to convince even my closest friends, from whom I hid nothing, that this was decided by a higher necessity.[83]

Whatever his private feelings, this passage clearly indicates that Kopelev was ideologically integrated into Stalin's regime. When the ideology of the regime lost momentum, private feelings came to the fore in people like Ehrenburg and Kopelev, whereas in others like Bukovskii the old ideology was still dominant.

This phenomenon of individualized retrospections is not peculiar to post-Stalin Soviet intellectuals, but common among intellectuals in other postwar societies such as Germany and Japan who had undergone somewhat comparable political experiences. This phenomenon, however, poses an important question concerning the collective mentality of the intelligentsia. Certainly Ehrenburg has repeatedly emphasized the individuality of his memoirs:

> I should like to stress once again that the book is the story of my life, of the searchings, errors and discoveries of one man. It is therefore extremely subjective and I have never claimed to be writing a history of the epoch.[84]

This contrasts sharply with Bukovskii's use of "we." Brezhnev's insistence on the collective nature of his life is worth quoting:

> I feel that my biography is a part of the biography of the entire Soviet people. . . .
> It was only Soviet power that enabled me, the son of a worker, who began life as an
> ordinary worker, to rise to the leadership of a glorious many-millions-strong party
> and of history's first socialist state.[85]

Yet Ehrenburg's claim to subjectivity has reflected his effort to challenge the official
account of history in a subtle way. He has quite consciously sought to touch on
sensitive topics and thus to fulfill the role of the intelligentsia as conscience of the
society.

Not all Soviet memoirists are partisan; neither do they invariably insist on the
collective nature of their experience. Some Soviet memoirs do reflect the collective
mentality of people like Stakhanov and Brezhnev who embodied the upward social
mobility associated with Stalin's revolution from above. Yet others reveal quite
different mentalities and experiences. Many memoirs of the *glasnost'* campaign
even reveal pent-up anger toward the sacrifices imposed and the terror that struck in
the Stalin years.

Conclusions

Soviet memoirs pertaining to the Stalin years constitute an impressive body of
literature. Their authors range widely from workers to intellectuals, journalists, war
veterans, industrial managers, and politicians; the topics covered are diverse,
though they vary according to the current political climate. The value of Soviet
memoirs as a historical source is accordingly immense: otherwise unavailable archival and statistical data, glimpses of unpublished memoirs and records by and about
Soviet politicians, and numerous episodes unrecorded in the contemporary press and
official documents provide an enormous amount of factual information and an
empirical sense of politics and society.

In dealing with Soviet memoirs, one has to take utmost care and compare different editions of the same memoirs, different accounts made by different persons
involved, and different accounts written under different political climates. One also
has to check them with official documents, the contemporary press, émigré memoirs, and so on. In this way those intrinsic problems of memoir literature in general—
factual errors, distortions, and falsifications—can be minimized; and one can use
Soviet memoirs in a meaningful way.

One also has to be careful of the authorship of Soviet memoirs. As far as the
contemporary Soviet memoirs of the Stalin era are concerned, this issue may be of
little significance, not merely because a single official account was dictated, but also
because their authors—predominantly upwardly mobile achievers and heroes—had
experienced the era in similar and therefore interchangeable ways. Post-Stalin Soviet
memoirs are individualized not merely because a single official account is no longer
strictly dictated, but also because the ideology of the Stalin regime, having lost
momentum, is no longer capable of subsuming the private feelings of the memoirists. Soviet memoirs reveal both the contemporary collective perception of the Stalin

era as accounted by upwardly mobile individuals and retrospective individual (therefore varied) reflections upon that era. This dual characteristic of Soviet memoir literature helps us to reconstruct the cast of mind of Stalin's contemporaries, the dominant political climate and socio-psychological idiosyncrasies of the era, and probably even their changes within its span, and thus to investigate difficult questions of the Stalin era from a perspective rather new to Western historians.

Notes

1. See the following chapter.

2. In this article, Soviet memoirs mean those published in the Soviet Union. The following notes are intended not to be a complete bibliography but merely a sample.

3. See, for instance, Seweryn Bialer, ed., *Stalin and his Generals. Soviet Military Memoirs of World War II* (New York: Pegasus, 1969).

4. *Liudi Stalingradskogo traktornogo* (Moscow, 1933; 2nd ed., 1934); *Kuznetskstroi. Istoriia Kuznetskstroia v vospominaniiakh* (Novosibirsk, 1934); *Belomorsko-Baltiiskii kanal im. Stalina. Istoriia stroitel'stva* (Moscow, 1934); *Liudi i stal'. Rasskazy znatnykh liudei Krasnogo Oktiabria* (Stalingrad, 1935); *Byli gory Vysokoi. Rasskazy rabochikh Vysokogorskogo zheleznogo rudnika o staroi i novoi zhizni* (Moscow, 1935; 2nd ed., 1935); *Kak my stroili metro. Istoriia metro im. L. M. Kaganovicha* (Moscow, 1935); *Istoriia metro Moskvy. Rasskazy stroitelei metro* (Moscow, 1935) (there are at least two different editions of the same title—both published in 1935); *Rasskazy o sotsialisticheskom masterstve* (Moscow, 1936); *Vek nyneshnii i vek minuvshii* (Moscow, 1937); N. Izotov, *Moia zhizn' i moia rabota* (Kharkov, 1934); S. M. Frankfurt, *Rozhdenie stali i cheloveka* (Moscow, 1935); I. P. Bardin, *Zhizn' inzhenera* (Moscow, 1938); Ia. Gugel, "Vospominaniia o Magnitke," in *God vosemnadtsatyi. Al'manakh shestoi* (Moscow, 1935), etc. Note also the memoirs of workers who participated in the collectivization drive such as S. Zamiatin, *Burnyi god. Opyt raboty piatitysiachnika v Rudnianskom raione na Niznei Volge* (Moscow, 1931). For a comprehensive bibliography of memoirs by the 25,000ers who participated in the collectivization drive, see Lynne Viola, *The Best Sons of the Fatherland. Workers in the Vanguard of Soviet Collectivization* (New York: Oxford University Press, 1987).

5. Note particularly the projected but aborted *Dve piatiletki*, only parts of which were published: V. Bogushevskii, "Kanun piatiletki," in *God vosemnadtsatyi. Al'manakh vos'moi* (Moscow, 1935); and V. Bogushevskii and A. Khavin, "God velikogo pereloma," in *God deviatnadtsatyi. Al'manakh deviatyi* (Moscow, 1936). Note also that in the mid-1930s many prominent industrialists published memoirs in newspapers. For example, S. Birman, a veteran of the Hungarian Revolution and subsequently a forthright Soviet industrial manager who provoked a number of bitter conflicts with the political authorities in the 1920s and 1930s, was an inveterate memoir writer; apparently he wrote book-length memoirs on the 1920s and the First Five-Year Plan, only fragments of which were published in *Za industrializatsiiu*, 24 March, 18 June, 20 July 1935, and 8 March 1936.

6. Note particularly A. Stakhanov, *Rasskaz o moei zhizni* (Moscow, 1938); I. Gudov, *Put' stakhanovtsa. Rasskaz o moei zhizni* (Moscow, 1938); *idem.*, *Besedy o kul'ture na proizvodstve* (Moscow, 1941); A. Busygin, *Zhizn' moia i moikh druzei* (Moscow, 1939).

7. Note the birth years of prominent Stakhanovites: A. Stakhanov (1905), I. Gudov (1907), A. Busygin (1907), etc.

8. See Ilya Ehrenburg, *Post-War Years: 1945-1954*, tr. by Tatiana Shebunina in collaboration with Yvonne Kapp (Cleveland and New York: World Publishing Company, 1967), 321 and 333.

9. *Vsesoiuznoe soveshchanie o merakh uluchsheniia podgotovki nauchno-pedagogicheskikh kadrov po istoricheskim naukam, 18-21 dek. 1962 g.* (Moscow, 1964), 148. For emphasis on the importance of memoirs, see also *ibid.*, 67, 341, 374, 498-99.

10. Bialer, *Stalin and His Generals*, 16 and 20.

11. For a good discussion of this issue and bibliographic information, see Dina R. Spechler, *Permitted Dissent in the USSR. Novyi mir and the Soviet Regime* (New York: Praeger, 1982).

12. Bialer, *Stalin and His Generals*, 34.

13. See, for example. M. Iu. Khazina, "Istochniki po formirovaniiu kadrov Kuznetskogo metallurgicheskogo kombinata v 1929–1937 godakh," in *Iz istorii rabochego klassa v Kuzbasse*, vyp. II (Kemerovo, 1966).

14. G. G. Khaiulin and I. S. Kirillova, "Neopublikovannye vospominanii starykh spetsialistov, kak istochnik po istorii tekhnicheskoi intelligentsii," *ibid.*, vyp. IV (Kemerovo, 1972); T. N. Ostashko, "Iz opyta sbora vospominanii po istorii sibirskoi intelligentsii," in *Iz istorii sovetskoi intelligentsii* (Novosibirsk, 1974).

15. Ostashko, "Iz opyta," 67.

16. See, for example, S. G. Wheatcroft, "Unleashing the Energy of History, Mentioning the Unmentionable and Reconstructing Soviet Historical Awareness: Moscow, 1987," *Australian Slavonic and East European Studies* 1:1 (1988); R. W. Davies, "Soviet History in the Gorbachev Revolution," *Socialist Register*, 1988 (London: Merlin Press, 1988), and Hiroaki Kuromiya, "The Stalin Years in the Light of Glasnost'," forthcoming in *Interrogations et Orientations—Annales du Monde Soviétique et de l'Europe Centrale et Orientale.*

17. Note, however, L. I. Brezhnev, *Memoirs*, tr. by Penny Dale, (Oxford: Pergamon, 1982). The Russian original is *Vospominaniia. Zhizn' po zavodskomu gudku. Chuvstvo rodiny* (Moscow, 1981). See also A. A. Andreev, *Vospominaniia, pis'ma* (Moscow, 1985), and A. I. Mikoian, "V pervyi raz bez Lenina," *Ogonek*, 1987 no. 50 (December), 5–7. Note also that anniversary articles often include memoir elements. See for example A. I. Mikoian, "Iz vospominanii o Sergo Ordzhonikidze," *Iunost'*, October 1966, and his "Tovarishch Sergo," *Pravda*, 27 October 1966.

18. Note particularly the series *Zhizn' zamechatel'nykh liudei* (see *40 let ZhZL. Katalog 1935–1973* [Moscow, 1974]), which includes I. M. Dubinskii-Mukhadze, *Ordzhonikidze* (Moscow, 1963; 2nd ed., 1967); *idem.*, *Kuibyshev* (Moscow, 1971); S. S. Sinelnikov, *Kirov* (Moscow, 1964); G. A. Moriagin, *Postyshev* (Moscow, 1965); V. Kardashov, *Voroshilov* (Moscow, 1976); V.P.Kartsev, *Krzhizhanovskii* (Moscow, 1980). Note that *Oktiabr'* has announced the publication of D. Volkogonov's biography of Stalin, *Triumf i tragediia*, parts of which are already published in *Literaturnaia gazeta*, 9 December 1987, and elsewhere.

19. See, for example, Vladimir Glotov, "Bilet do Leningrada" (interview with an old party member, Z. Nemtsova), *Ogonek*, 1988 no. 27; A. Milchakov, "Pisat' vse tak nado!," *Smena*, 1988 no. 12; A. T. Rybin, "Riadom s I. V. Stalinym," *Sotsiologicheskie issledovaniia*, 1988 no. 3. Note also Iurii Idashkin, "Znakomyii po portretam. Davnee interv'iu s V. M. Molotovym," *Literaturnaia Rossiia*, 1988 no. 29.

20. For example, S. Dzerzhinskaia, *V gody velikikh boev* (Moscow, 1964); N. Lunacharskaia-Rozenel, *Pamiat' serdtsa. Vospominaniia* (Moscow, 1965); G. V. Kuibysheva et al, *Valerian Vladimirovich Kuibyshev: biografiia* (Moscow, 1966). Note some very recent ones: E. N. Tukhachevskaia, "V teni monumenta," *Ogonek*, 1988 no. 17; "On khotel peredelat' zhizn', potomu chto ee liubil" (interview with Bukharin's widow, A. M. Larina, *ibid.*, 1987 no. 48; Aleksandr Rusov, "Pis'mo," (on A. P. Serebrovskii), *Znamia*, 1987 no. 9; "Mikhail Tomskii—kakim on byl?" (interview with Tomskii's son, Iu. Tomskii), *Trud*, 20 April 1988; Aleksei Adzhubei, "Te desiat' let" (on Khrushchev), *Znamia*, 1988 nos. 6 and 7; and A. M. Larina, "Nezabyvaemye," *Znamia*, 1988 nos. 10–12.

21. *O Sergo Ordzhonikidze. Vospominaniia, ocherki, stat'i sovremennikov* (Moscow, 1981); *O Viacheslave Menzhinskom. Vospominaniia, ocherki, stat'i* (Moscow, 1985); S. G. Ginzburg (former Commissar of Construction), *O proshlom —dlia budushchego* (Moscow, 1983); A. G. Zverev (former Commissar of Finance), *Zapiski ministra* (Moscow, 1974); *idem.*, "O nekotorykh storonakh istorii sovetskoi finansovoi sistemy," *Voprosy istorii*, 1969 no. 2; B. L. Vannikov (former Commissar of Armaments), "Oboronnaia promyshlennost'

SSSR nakanune voiny (Iz zapisok narkoma)," *ibid.*, 1968 no. 10 and 1969 no. 1; *idem.*, "Iz zapisok narkoma vooruzheniia," *Voenno-istoricheskii zhurnal*, 1962 no. 2; A. I. Shakhurin (former Commissar of the Aviation Industry), "Aviatsionnaia promyshlennost' nakanune Velikoi Otechestvennoi Voiny (Iz vospominanii narkoma)," *Voprosy istorii*, 1974 no. 2; N. S. Patolichev (former Iaroslavl obkom secretary), *Ispytanie na zrelost'* (Moscow, 1977); A. Chuianov (former Stalingrad obkom secretary), *Na stremnine veka. Zapiski sekretaria obkoma* (Moscow, 1976); *Direktor. I. A. Likhachev v vospominaniiakh sovremennikov. I. A. Likhachev o zavode i o sebe* (Moscow, 1971); A. Sulimov, "Nachalo Magnitogorska," *Novyi mir*, 1970 no. 3; A. Iakovlev, *Tsel' zhizni. Zapiski aviakonstruktora* (Moscow, 1960; 2nd ed., 1968); V. S. Emelianov, *O vremeni, o tovarishchakh, o sebe* (Moscow, 1968); *idem.*, *Na poroge voiny* (Moscow, 1971) (these two books by Emelianov were republished in one volume in 1974 under the former's title); *idem.*, "U istokov atomnoi promyshlennosti," *Voprosy istorii*, 1975 no. 5; *idem.*, "O nauke i zhizni," *Nauka i zhizn'*, 1963 nos. 4, 5, 7, 9 and 12; 1964 nos. 3, 5, 6, 10 and 11; 1965 nos. 4, 5, 9, 11 and 12; I. V. Paramonov, *Puti proidennye* (Moscow, 1966; 2nd ed., 1970); *idem.*, *Uchit'sia upravliat'. Mysl' i opyt starogo khoziaistvennika* (Moscow, 1967; 2nd ed., 1970); A. M. Terpigorev, *Vospominaniia gornogo inzhenera* (Moscow, 1956); *Byli industrial'nye. Ocherki i vospominaniia* (Moscow, 1970; 2nd ed., 1973); I. V. Komzin, *Ia veriu v mechtu. Vospominaniia i zapiski* (Moscow, 1973); *Kak my rabotali v Rabkrine* (Kharkov, 1963).

22. See Bialer, *Stalin and His Generals*. Note also that the journal *Voenno-istoricheskii zhurnal* published a number of interesting memoirs in the early 1960s. (See for example I. Bagramian, "Dushevnyi chelovek i talantlivyi voennachal'nik," 1963 no. 12; G. Isserson, "Zapiski sovremmenika o M. N. Tukhachevskom," 1963 no. 4; I. Rachkov, "Iz vospominanii o Ia. B. Gamarnike," 1964 no. 5; N. Kuznetsov, "Flagman flota 2 ranga," 1964 no. 8. Recent publications include V. L. Vannikov, "Zapiski narkoma," *Znamia*, 1988 nos. 1 and 2, and K. M. Simonov, "Zametki k biografii G. K. Zhukova," *Voenno-istoricheskii zhurnal*, 1987 nos. 6, 7, 9, 10, and 12.) For memoirs of diplomats, see for example I. M. Maiskii, *Vospominaniia sovetskogo posla*, 2 vols. (Moscow, 1964); V. I. Berezhkov, *S diplomaticheskoi missiei v Berline, 1940–1941 gg.* (Moscow, 1960); and Jonathan Haslam, *The Soviet Union and the Struggle for Collective Security in Europe, 1933–1939* (New York: St. Martin's Press, 1984), 291–92.

23. Iu. Zhukov, *Liudi 30-kh godov* (Moscow, 1968); *idem.*, *Krutye stupeni. Zapiski zhurnalista* (Moscow, 1983); A. E. Khavin, *U rulia industrii* (Moscow, 1968); *idem.*, *Shagi industrii. Zapiski zhurnalista* (Moscow, 1957). Khavin, a correspondent for *Za industrializatsiiu* in the 1930s, wrote a number of memoirs and semi-memoirs in the form of scholarly studies: *Kratkii ocherk istorii industrializatsii SSSR* (Moscow, 1962); *idem.*, "Razvitie tiazheloi promyshlennosti v tret'ei piatiletke (1938–iiun' 1941 gg.)," *Istoriia SSSR*, 1959 no. 1.; *idem.*, "Ot VSNKh k sovnarkhozam nashikh dnei," *ibid.*, 1960 no. 5; *idem.*, "Iz istorii promyshlennogo stroitel'stva na Vostoke SSSR," *Voprosy istorii*, 1960 no. 5; *idem.*, "Kapitany sovetskoi industrii, 1926–1940 gg.," *ibid.*, 1966 no. 5; *idem.*, "Odin iz organizatorov bol'shoi industrii, I. F. Tevosian," *ibid.*, 1967 no. 7. See also A. Magid, *Pamiatnye vstrechi. Zapiski starogo rabkora* (Vladimir, 1960); I. Peshkin, "O Sergo Ordzhonikidze. Iz starykh bloknotov," *Novyi mir*, 1958 no. 6; *idem.*, "Na zare industrializatsii," *Zvezda*, 1978 nos. 6 and 7; Semen Gershberg, *Rabota u nas takaia. Zapiski zhurnalista-pravdista tridtsatykh godov* (Moscow, 1971), etc.

24. The most noteworthy are Ehrenburg, *Post-War Years* and his *Memoirs: 1921–1941*, tr. by Tatiana Shebunina in collaboration with Yvonne Kapp (Cleveland: World Publishing Company, 1964). For scientists' memoirs, see, for example, Emelianov's memoirs listed above, note 21; P. K. Oshchepkov, *Zhizn' i mechta. Zapiski inzhenera-izobretatelia, konstruktora i uchenogo* (Moscow, 1965); E. O. Paton, *Vospominaniia* (Moscow, 1958); K. I. Skriabin, *Moia zhizn' v nauke* (Moscow, 1969); N. M. Druzhinin, *Vospominaniia i mysl' istorika* (Moscow, 1967; 2nd ed., 1979); *Nikolai Ivanovich Vavilov. Ocherki, vospominaniia, materialy* (Moscow, 1987).

25. See, for example, *Govoriat stroiteli sotsializma. Vospominaniia uchastnikov sotsialisticheskogo stroitel'stva v SSSR* (Moscow, 1959); *Idushchie vperedi* (Moscow, 1961); *Klass sozidatelei* (Moscow, 1967); *Neizvedannymi putiami. Vospominaniia uchastnikov sotsialisticheskogo stroitel'stva* (Leningrad, 1967); *V budniakh velikikh stroek. Vospominaniia stroitelei sotsializma* (Perm, 1969); *Revoliutsionnyi derzhite shag*, vols. 1–9 (Moscow, 1968–1981); V. Seminskii, *Zapiski rabochego* (Moscow, 1957); V. Karasev, *Stranitsy zhizni* (Moscow, 1967); V. V. Ermilov, *Schast'e trudnykh dorog* (Moscow, 1972); S. A. Antonov, *Svet ne v okne* (Moscow, 1977); *Po zovu partii. Sbornik vospominanii i statei leningradtsev-dvadtsatipiatitysiachnikov i tridtsatitysiachnikov* (Leningrad, 1961); *Slavnye traditsii. Sbornik dokumentov, ocherkov, vospominanii* (Moscow, 1958; 2nd ed., 1960); "V bor'be za industrializatsiiu SSSR. Govoriat uchastniki sobytii," *Voprosy istorii*, 1968 no. 11; *V budniakh velikikh stroek. Zhenshchiny-kommunistki, geroini pervikh piatiletok* (Moscow, 1986); *Nezabyvaemye 30-e. Vospominaniia veteranov partii—Moskvichei* (Moscow, 1986); D. I. Ortenberg, *Te pamiatnye gody* (Moscow, 1986); Ivan Tvardovskii, "Stranitsy perezhitogo," *Iunost'*, 1988 no. 3.

26. A. Stakhanov, *Rodnik rabochikh talantov* (Moscow, 1973); *idem.*, *Zhizn' shakhterskaia* (Kiev, 1975); *idem.*, "Trud—rodine," *Voprosy istorii*, 1971 no. 3; Ivan Gudov, *Sud'ba rabochego* (Moscow, 1970; 2nd ed., 1974); A. Busygin, *Sversheniia* (Moscow, 1972); M. I. Vinogradova, *Riadom s legendoi* (Moscow, 1981); Konstantin Borin, "A time to reap," *Moskovskie novosti*, 1988 no. 12; P. F. Krivonos, *Magistrali zhizni* (Moscow, 1986).

27. See, for example, S. A. Shved, "Vospominaniia," *Ural*, 1988 no. 2; "Ia chestnyi grazhdanin . . . Pis'ma Symona Baranovykh," *Neman*, 1988 no. 4; L. Razgon, "Nepridumannoe. Povest' v rasskazakh," *Iunost'*, 1988 no. 5.

28. See, for example, G. V. Strelskii, *Memuary kak istochnik Velikogo Oktiabria na Ukraine* (Kiev, 1978), 135; M. N. Chernomorskii, "Memuary kak istochnik po istorii sovetskogo obshchestva," *Voprosy istorii*, 1960 no. 12, 70.

29. *Sotsialisticheskaia industrializatsiia SSSR. Ukazatel' sovetskoi literatury, izdannoi v 1928–1970 gg.* (Moscow, 1972). This bibliography, as well as those cited in notes 30, 31, and 32 below, is a small-edition (*malotirazhnoe*) publication of the Academy of Sciences' Institute of History of the USSR, which is to be found only in Soviet libraries and a few major Western research libraries.

30. V. N. Zemskov (comp.), *Rabochii klass SSSR. 1917–1977 gg. Ukazatel' sovetskoi literatury, izdannoi v 1971–1977 gg.*, 4 parts (Moscow, 1976).

31. *Istoriia predpriiatii SSSR. Ukazatel' sovetskoi literatury, izdannoi v 1917–1978 gg.*, 3 parts, (Moscow, 1978).

32. *Istoriia sovetskoi derevni, 1917–1967. Ukazatel' literatury. 1945–1967 gg.*, 4 parts, (Moscow, 1975).

33. *O voine, o tovarishchakh, o sebe. Velikaia Otechestvennaia voina v vospominaniiakh uchastnikov boevykh deistvii. Annotirovannyi ukazatel' voenno-memuarnoi literarury. 1941–1975 gg.* (Moscow, 1977). See also Bialer, *Stalin and his Generals*, 641–44.

34. See M. N. Chernomorskii, *Rabota s memuarami pri izuchenii istorii KPSS* (Moscow, 1961).

35. A. V. Kholodkov, "Memuary kak istochnik razrabotki istorii VLKSM," *Pozyvnye istorii*, vyp. 4 (Moscow, 1975).

36. A. E. Ioffe, "Memuary sovetskikh diplomatov—tsennyi istoricheskii istochnik," *Istoriia SSSR*, 1974 no. 3.

37. See p. 173 and the errata. This episode is discussed in A. Lukashev, S. Shauman, and S. Shcheprov, "Memuarnaia literatura i istoricheskaia pravda," *Kommunist*, 1959 no. 11, 110–11.

38. See, for example, Golubtsov, *Memuary*, 17, 104–105, 110–12 and Chernomorskii, "Memuary," 68–70.

39. Bardin's shorthand record and the edited version are held in TsGAOR SSSR f. 7952, op. 5. These are quoted in Iu. A. Ivanov, "Voprosy istochnikovedcheskoi kritiki vospomi-

nanii rabotnikov sovetskoi promyshlennosti,'' in *Iz istorii rabochego klass v Kuzbasse*, vyp. 2 (Kemerovo, 1966). The published version is I. P. Bardin, *Zhizn' inzhenera* (Moscow, 1938), which does not say anything about Zaslavskii's editing.

40. Ivanov, "Voprosy istochnikovedskoi kritiki," 121.

41. *Ibid.*

42. Bardin, *Zhizn' inzhenera*, 155.

43. See, for example, Lupinin, "Otpor stikhii," *Kuznetskstroi*, 70–72 and M. A. Pavliushin, "Kto vy, rabochie ili net?," in *ibid.*, 73–74. According to these stories, some 1,000 "Iukhnovtsy, class aliens, were lured from the village Vyshnee of the Kaluga guberniia to the construction site by "deceptive" terms offered by recruiters; upon coming to the site, they were offered much lower wages than expected, so they threatened to walk out. It was at this time that the flood crisis took place; some participated in the struggle, others did not. After the crisis was over, the "Iukhnovtsy" walked out for the same reason and threatened to leave the site. When the party committee of the construction project "announced an inquiry into the ringleaders' backgrounds" (i.e., suggested that they might be kulaks), 300 of the "Iukhnovtsy" left the site. Among the ringleaders, however, were party and trade union members, some of whom were expelled from the party and the union for this incident.

44. Ivanov, "Voprosy istochnikovedcheskoi kritiki," 121.

45. *Ibid.*

46. Bardin, *Zhizn' inzhenera*, 28. See also p.187. Apparently, V. Mezentsev's biography, *Bardin* (Moscow, 1970), 42, follows this published account.

47. Ivanov, "Voprosy istochnikovedcheskoi kritiki," 122.

48. See note 4, above.

49. R. Ia. Okuneva, "Kak sozdalis' 'Byli gory Vysokoi.' Istochniki i priemy raboty," *Maloissledovannye istochiniki po istorii SSSR XIX-XX vv. Istochnikovedcheskii analiz* (Moscow, 1964), 3–32. See also the accounts of the compiler of the collection, Iu. Zlygostev, "O 'Byliakh gory Vysokoi.' Iz opyta raboty nad knigoi," *Literaturnaia ucheba*, 1936 no. 2, 144–62, and *idem.*, "Byli gory Vysokoi," *Istoriia zavodov. Sbornik*, nos. 3–4 (1934), 121–27.

50. See Okuneva, "Kak sozdalis'," 13 and the two 1935 editions.

51. *Ibid.*, 15.

52. *Ibid.*, 31.

53. Gudov, *Sud'ba rabochego* (1970), 97.

54. Gudov, *Sud'ba rabochego* (1974), 96.

55. For stimulating interpretations of the Great Purge based largely on official documents, the Smolensk Archive, and the contemporary press see J. Arch Getty, *Origins of the Great Purges. The Soviet Communist Party Reconsidered* (Cambridge and New York: Cambridge University Press, 1985); and G. T. Rittersporn's articles, especially "L'État en lutte contre lui-même: Tensions sociales et conflits politiques en URSS, 1936–1938," *Libre*, 1978 no. 4; "Staline en 1938: apogée du verbe et defaite politique," *ibid.*, 1979 no. 6; *ibid.*, 1979 no. 6; "Société et appareile d'État soviétique (1936–1938): Contradictions et interférences," *Annales E.S.C.*, vol. 34 no. 4 (July–August 1979).

56. Brezhnev, *Memoirs*, 30. (The Russian original is *Vospominaniia*, 35.)

57. Ermilov, *Schast'e trudnykh dorog*, 132. Born in 1909, Ermilov belongs to the Brezhnev-Stakhanov generation.

58. V. Diunin and V. Proskura, *Shagni pervym* (Moscow, 1972), 136. Italics added.

59. Gershberg, *Rabota u nas takaia*, 377. The exact date of this speech is not known. It may have been given in mid-1936.

60. This is reported in Stakhanov, *Rasskaz o moei zhizni*, 26.

61. See Gershberg, *Rabota u nas takaia*, 371, and Stakhanov, *Zhizn' shakhterskaia*, 117. According to Gershberg this was adopted in a novel by B. Gorbatov, *Donbass*. (See his *Sobranie sochinenii*, vol. 3 [Moscow, 1955], 401.) Apparently this episode first appeared in the novel and then in the memoirs by Gershberg and Stakhanov.

62. Stakhanov, *Rasskaz o moei zhizni*, 179.

63. *Ibid.*, 147–49. For a similar passage, see Gudov, *Put' stakhanovtsa,* 132.

64. Busygin, *Zhizn' moia i moikh druzei,* 46.

65. Stakhanov, *Zhizn' shakhterskaia,* 77–78.

66. Petro Grigorenko, *Memoirs,* tr. by Thomas P. Whitney, (New York and London: Norton, 1972), 76.

67. Lev Kopelev, *The Education of a True Believer,* tr. by Gary Karn (New York: Harper & Row, 1980), 300. It is also noteworthy that at the time of the so-called "Industrial Party" trial in late 1930 the Trotskyites accepted all the charges against the defendants. A Trotskyite in Moscow wrote on the trial that factory workers demanded death sentences, and, when the death sentences were commuted (to ten years of deprivation of freedom), they simply could not understand the "pardon." Impressed by workers' reaction, this Oppositionist reported that "in the working class as a whole there still is genuine revolutionary enthusiasm." See *Biulleten' Oppozitsii* (Paris), no. 19 (March 1931), 18.

68. See Kuromiya, "The Stalin Years in the Light of *Glasnost'*."

69. *Byli industrial'nye,* 100, or 2d ed., 101–102. For a similar case in 1933 at the factory "Serp i Molot" in Moscow, see G. M. Il'in, "Moia zhizn'," *Novyi mir,* 1938 no. 6, 208. For a case in which a manager managed to defend himself in 1937–38 against accusations of "wrecking," see I. V. Paramonov, then manager of the trust Karagandashakhtstroi, *Puti proidennye,* 235–44, or 2d ed., 365–75.

70. Gudov, *Sud'ba rabochego* (1970), 152, or (1974), 150.

71. Busygin, *Sversheniia,* 80–81.

72. See *Pravda,* 21 April 1937.

73. V. Emelianov, "O vremeni, o tovarishchakh, o sebe," *Novyi mir,* 1967 no. 1, 79. The whole discussion on Iakovlev is omitted from his book with the same title published shortly thereafter. See above, note 21.

74. Ivanov, "Voprosy istochnikovedcheskoi kritiki," 125. This was not an isolated case. For similar cases, see Khazina, "Istochniki po formirovaniiu kadrov," 152. For instances in which personal rancor or vindictiveness because of demotion led workers to believe that their bosses were "enemies of the people," see S. N. Zarkhidze, *Zapiski mastera* (Moscow-Leningrad, 1939), 9.

75. For the same phenomenon in the Gorbachev era, see Kuromiya, "The Stalin Years in the Light of *Glasnost'*."

76. Ivanov, "Voprosy istochnikovedcheskoi kritiki," 126. Note also the memoirs of A. Ia. Vedenin (a military commissar stationed in Central Asia at the time of the Great Purge) in which he recalls the plenipotentiary of a division who declared to him: "I see an enemy of the people in everybody." A. Ia. Vedenin, *Gody i liudi. Vospominaniia* (Moscow, 1964), 56.

77. *XVIII s"ezd VKP(b), mart 1939 g. Stenograficheskii otchet* (Moscow, 1939), 584. The name and the title of this person were not mentioned at the congress, but were revealed in Patolichev's memoirs. See Patolichev, *Ispytanie na zrelost',* 91.

78. *Ibid.,* 90.

79. For a similar theme in Soviet fiction in the postwar period, see Vera S. Dunham, *In Stalin's Time. Middleclass Values in Soviet Fiction* (Cambridge and New York: Cambridge University Press, 1976).

80. See, for example, Zhukov, *Liudi tridtsatykh godov,* 311. Zhukov was a correspondent for *Komsomol'skaia pravda* in the 1930s.

81. Ehrenburg, *Post-War Years: 1945–1954,* 321 and 333.

82. K. Bukovskii, "Otvet na lestnitse," *Oktiabr',* 1966 no. 9, 199. From a totally different political perspective, Nadezhda Mandelstam has written of Ehrenburg's view as an apologia of the "victors" (Nadezhda Mandelstam, *Hope Abandoned,* tr. by Max Hayward [New York: Atheneum, 1974], 480). Characteristically, Ehrenburg has suggested that ideology had survived all those human sufferings: "The blow [of the Great Purge] was not dealt to the *idea.* It was dealt to the people of my generation." (Ehrenburg, *Memoirs: 1921–1941,* 430. Emphasis in the original.)

83. Kopelev, *The Education of a True Believer*, 313. See also his *To be Preserved Forever*, tr. by Anthony Austin (Philadelphia and New York: J. B. Lippincott, 1977), 11.

84. Ehrenburg, *Post-War Years: 1945–1954*, 341.

85. See Brezhnev's foreword to *L. I. Brezhnev. Pages from His Life* (New York: Simon and Schuster, 1978), 9.

Guide to Émigré and Dissident Memoir Literature

HIROAKI KUROMIYA

Émigré and dissident memoir literature has long established itself in Western studies of Soviet history. Indeed, memoirs written by those who broke politically with the Soviet Union and published outside the country often prove to be the only available sources for many so-called "blank spots" of Soviet history. The value of these memoirs appears evident to anyone who works in the field.

Like Soviet memoir literature, however, émigré and dissident memoir literature has to be used with caution by historians. If Soviet memoirs are generally censored by the state, émigré and dissident memoirs are usually subjected to the market forces of the Western publishing industry. Émigré and dissident memoirs are published for Western consumption, and large gaps left by Soviet publications create profitable markets for quite unscholarly sensationalism.

Yet the value of some of these memoirs might be confirmed by new developments in the Soviet Union: some memoirs are currently being published in the country thanks to the *glasnost'* campaign.[1] These new developments might also threaten, to some degree, the market for émigré and dissident publications in the West, and blur the distinction between Soviet and émigré and dissident memoirs. Yet the existing émigré and dissident memoirs still make a large and valuable contribution.

This chapter does not discuss the intrinsic problems of memoir literature in general—factual errors, distortions, and falsifications—which are examined in the previous chapter in relation to Soviet memoir literature, and are equally applicable to émigré and dissident memoir literature.[2] Rather, it begins with a brief bibliographical guide, and proceeds to discuss, first, problems peculiar to émigré and dissident memoir literature, and, second, its utility as a historical source.

Bibliography

Unfortunately, no comprehensive bibliography of émigré and dissident memoirs is available, but *Bibliography of Russian Émigré Literature: 1918–1968*, 2 vols., ed. by L. A. Fosteer (Boston: G. K. Hall, 1970), which extensively covers émigré memoir literature, is perhaps the most important and useful guide. Also useful are *Soviet Unofficial Literature* (Durham, N.C.: Duke University Center for International Studies, 1978) and its updated version, *Soviet Dissident Literature. A Critical Guide* (Boston: G. K. Hall, 1983), both edited by Josephine Woll. They include numerous entries of memoirs on the Stalin Era. Z. Vatnikova-Prizel, *O russkoi memuarnoi literature: Kriticheskie analizy i bibliografiia* (East Lansing, Mich.: Russian Language Journal, 1978), which covers émigré as well as Soviet memoir literature, is also valuable. To keep up with current periodical publications, *Abstracts of Soviet and East European Émigré Periodical Literature* is indispensable. (The supplement to this publication, *Review of Russian Émigré Books,* is also useful.)

As is the case with Soviet memoir literature, many émigré and dissident memoirs remain unpublished. The following guides are indispensable references for locating unpublished memoirs: *The Russian Empire and Soviet Union: A Guide to Manuscripts and Archival Materials in the United States,* ed. by Stephen A. Grant and John H. Brown (Boston: G. K. Hall, 1981) and *Guide to Documents and Manuscripts in the United Kingdom Relating to Russian and the Soviet Union,* ed. by Janet M. Hartley (London and New York: Massel Pub. Ltd., 1987).

Another important category of literature is the interviews with war refugees, many of whom were former workers and peasants. Their importance is evident considering that the majority of émigré and dissident memoirists, like other writers, belong to the educated strata of society. The famous Harvard Project on the Soviet Social System, which conducted extensive interviews with Soviet war refugees in the early 1950s, produced a series of publications and unpublished research reports. The bibliography of this project is in Raymond A. Bauer, Alex Inkeles, and Clyde Kluckhohn, *How the Soviet System Works. Cultural, Psychological, and Social Themes* (Cambridge, Mass.: Harvard University Press, 1959), 252–58. The original transcripts of these interviews and answers to questionnaires, which deal mainly with the 1930s, are available at the Widener Library and the Russian Research Center of Harvard University.

Memoirs and eyewitness accounts by foreign residents and visitors may not belong to émigré and dissident literature, but are important historical documents. Peter G. Filene, *Americans and the Soviet Experiment, 1917–1933* (Cambridge, Mass.: Harvard University Press, 1967), Sylvia R. Margulies, *The Pilgrimage to Russia. The Soviet Union and the Treatment of Foreigners, 1924–1937* (Madison-Milwaukee-London: The University of Wisconsin Press, 1968), and Fred Kupferman, *Au Pays des Soviets. Le Voyage français en Union Soviétique, 1917–1939* (Paris: Gallimard/Julliard, 1979) contain extensive bibliographies of this kind of literature. Harry W. Nerhood's *To Russia and Return. An Annotated Bibliography of Travelers' English-Language Accounts of Russia from the Ninth Century to the Present* (n. p.: Ohio State University Press, 1968), has about 300 entries on the period 1925–1941, arranged chronologically by date of travel, with useful short comments on the authors and what they saw. *Books on Soviet Russia, 1917–1942,* ed. by P. Grierson (London: Methuen, 1943) and *Books in English on the Soviet Union, 1917–1973. A Bibliography,* ed. by David Jones (New York: Garland, 1975) also provide useful bibliographical information. As for unpublished memoirs, the aforementioned guides by Grant and Brown and Hartley are again indispensable.

Authorship

Authors of émigré and dissident memoirs generally share a common attitude toward the Soviet regime: they reject the idea of living with it on its own terms. At one point of their lives some broke politically with the regime. Others made the decision to emigrate to the West, or, in the case of war refugees, to remain in the West. Still others, regarded as harmful to the regime, were forced to live in the West. This common experience consequently colors their retrospective accounts, which often touch on subjects avoided by Soviet memoirists and paint dark pictures of the country's history. Some writers and memoirists like Aleksandr Solzhenitsyn and Varlam Shalamov seek quite deliberately to speak in their works for millions of people who perished under Stalin and had no chance to record their experiences, thoughts, and emotions.[3] In this sense, émigré and dissident memoirs possess strongly collective characteristics.

These memoirs, however, also provide so diverse and conflicting views of the Stalin years that Western historians could find evidence in them to support almost any interpretation they like. Lev Kopelev's autobiography,[4] for example, is a fascinating history of a true believer in the Stalinist regime; Anton Ciliga's memoir,[5] by contrast, gives an example of a consistent political fighter against the regime; and Nadezhda Mandelstam's writing[6] provides an absorbing account of a life under Stalin that had never accepted the ideology of the regime but had to live within it. The diverse characteristics of memoirs often furnish a battleground where historians passionately confront each other with their own favorite "evidences."[7]

If this diversity itself is not a problem, secondhand accounts in many émigré and dissident memoirs do present serious problems to historians. The control of the state over information often forced Soviet citizens to rely on rumor, hearsay, and gossip to understand the world in which they lived. Memoir literature proves to be a valuable historical source which helps us to understand what people thought and how they acted. Yet secondhand information in the literature cannot be taken at face value. Western historians do not necessarily take due caution and discretion in this respect. In his recent work on the Great Purges, J. Arch Getty has remarked:

> For no other period or topic have historians been so eager to write and accept history-by-anecdote. Grand analytical generalizations have come from secondhand bits of overheard corridor gossip. Prison camps stories ("My friend met Bukharin's wife in a camp and she said") have become primary sources on central political decision making. The need to generalize from isolated and unverified particulars has transformed rumors into sources and has equated repetition of stories with confirmation.

Getty singles out as a notorious example the leading Western expert on the Great Purges, Robert Conquest, who has written that "truth can thus only percolate in the form of hearsay" and that on political matters "basically the best, though not infallible, source is rumor at a high political or police level."[8]

Conquest offers remedies to the problems of hearsay memoirs as historical sources: "Good rough criteria are whether an author is an authenticable figure, or a mere name on a book (like some writers who have had unexplained success in scholarly circles in the West); and whether the information checks against other— and particularly later—reports, and is itself consonant with the political and general atmosphere."[9] The first remedy is flawed, because authenticable figures do not necessarily write authentic accounts. The second remedy too is at least partially faulty, because, as Getty points out, it is sound only if rumors were not repeated and if memoirists did not read each others's works.[10] These remedies are necessary steps to be taken by historians, but do not guarantee the reliability of information.

Some memoirs are rank forgeries. How vulnerable historians can be to this pitfall can be illustrated by the case of the "Litvinov Diary," which involved one of the foremost Western historians of the Soviet Union, the late E. H. Carr. "Sometime in 1952 or early 1953, Gregory Bessedovsky, former Soviet diplomat resident in Paris, approached officials of various governments and publishing houses, with the manuscript of a diary of the recently deceased Maxim Litvinov (died 1951). At the suggestion of a high official of the British Foreign Office, the English publisher, Andre Deutsch, enlisted the services of Edward Hallet Carr to investigate the manuscript's authenticity. After reading the Russian typescript, Professor Carr encouraged Deutsch to go ahead with the book, and undertook to go to Paris for further checking."[11] Carr had not been able to confirm the authenticity of the manuscript, and suspected that "at least two hands have been at work on the document." Further checking, however, led Carr to the conclusion that the manuscript (which covered the period from 1926 to 1939) "contains a substratum of genuine material emanating in some form or other from Litvinov himself," and that it "has a prima facie claim to be regarded as authentic, and a serious historical document."[12] The manuscript thus was published in 1955 as Maxim Litvinov, *Notes for a Journal*, with an introduction by Carr. As a conscientious historian, Carr regarded the author of the manuscript as an "authenticable figure," checked it against "other—and particularly later—reports," and considered it "consonant with the political and general atmosphere."

Other historians, however, through the same procedures, reached the opposite conclusion: "This book adds to our understanding of Soviet affairs and of Litvinov's personality about as much as a forged banknote adds to our wealth."[13] The diary proved to be a forgery,[14] probably produced by an émigré writer or writers for commercial purposes. The Litvinov Diary case may have been a fortunate case, because, according to Carr, it was "the most sensational work of its kind yet published,"[15] so that it was closely examined by many experts who knew at least something about Litvinov and the political and general atmosphere in which he lived. Social historians, who deal with much less known ordinary people and their lives, would have to take extra caution in using memoir literature.

Another important issue related to authorship is editorial intervention. This is of course not peculiar to émigré and dissident memoir literature, but it would be useful to point out what kind of problems lie here. The famous case of Victor Kravchenko,

I Chose Freedom. The Personal and Political Life of a Soviet Official (New York: Charles Scribner's Sons, 1946) is a good example. Kravchenko's autobiography is an absorbing account of his life from the year of his birth in the Ukraine, 1915, to 1944, when he defected in Washington, D.C. It is extraordinarily rich in information on what he thought and how he acted at various junctions of his life, which like those of many other contemporaries, was intimately related to the history of the whole country. His memoir therefore has been widely drawn on by Western historians.[16]

Kravchenko's book, like many others by émigrés, is passionately anti-Soviet and anti-Stalinist. It unflinchingly discusses the terror, brutality, and injustice of the Stalinist regime. The autobiography was published in New York in 1946 at the beginning of the cold war, and a French edition, *J'ai choisi la liberté! La vie publique et privée d'un haut-fonctionnaire soviétique*, appeared in Paris in 1948 in the midst of the war. The publication of the memoir provoked much anger in leftist circles in the West (not to mention the Soviet Union), particularly in France, where the yet vivid memory of the resistance to Nazism had left a relatively favorable view of the Soviet Union as an ally. To some, political attacks against the Soviet Union appeared to compromise the glorious past of the United Front against Nazism. *Les Léttres Françaises,* originally published by *Le Comité national des écrivains français adhérent au front national,* savagely attacked Kravchenko for his book, contending that it was anti-Soviet propaganda, written by a ghostwriter, with little historical substance in it: "The truth is that Kravchenko is a puppet whose clumsy strings are 'made in U.S.A.' Yes, Kravchenko is nothing but a pawn in an outmoded game." Formerly, the journal claimed, such pawns came from Germany, but "today they are imported from America." "Whether they be inspired by Hitler or Truman, so long as men like Kravchenko exist, so also will there be free men to answer them."[17] Thereupon Kravchenko filed a libel suit against the authors of the accusatory articles.

The suit, which lasted in Paris from 24 January to 4 April 1949, summoned many witnesses—both Kravchenko's fellow émigrés and Soviet citizens, including his former wife. Its transcripts, which contain numerous testimonies to events in Soviet history, make interesting reading for social historians.[18] From the point of view of this article, what is interesting is the discussion that took place in the court on the authorship and the text of the memoir in question. The defendants admitted that much material in the book might have actually been provided by Kravchenko himself, but that the book, tendentiously selective of topics and dramatized to the extreme, "belongs in the domain of fiction."[19] They sought to show that at least two hands had been at work on the book. One witness maintained that "When one is familiar with Russian and American literature, one can see that this book resembles far more an American literary production than anything written in Russian." As an example, he quoted a number of passages that appeared to him to be unlikely for a writer who knows no English:

> On page 133, English edition, there is the phrase "It was a Roman holiday." This has become a proverbial English phrase and is taken from one of Byron's verses.

On page 173, the sentence: "The knowledge that she was a secret police agent was ever a *ghost at the banquet of our affections*" is plainly inspired by Banquo's ghost at Macbeth's banquet. On page 52, English edition, an old man, incapable of understanding the glorious new society, refers to the "brave new world." This is a phrase from Shakespeare's *The Tempest* which Huxley brought into vogue some years ago by using it as a title for one of his books.[20]

Both parties admitted that the book contained much dramatization, but that did not justify the accusations of the defendants. The suit ended in Kravchenko's complete victory.

For historians, however, his victory in the court does not imply that the book is reliable or can be used without caution. One has to assume that there was considerable editorial intervention (which was not the bone of legal contention), and examine carefully the accuracy of the information in the book. Kravchenko's memoir may appear to be more or less "consonant with the political and general atmosphere" of the period. Yet our notion of "the political and general atmosphere" of the Stalin years has been formed to a considerable degree by émigré literature, among others, memoirs like Kravchenko's. Therefore, "being consonant" does not necessarily guarantee the reliability of memoirs as sources of information. Conversely, those memoirs that seem to be quite dissonant with "the political and general atmosphere" should not be dismissed lightly as being exceptional, falsified, or distorted.

Émigré and dissident memoirs are generally written by those whom the regime had failed to satisfy. This experience accords some common outlooks to their writings, just as the common life experiences of beneficiaries of the Stalinist regime tend to deprive their memoirs of individual authorship. In the absence of pressure for political conformity, however, émigré and dissident memoirs are far more diverse than post-Stalin Soviet memoirs. Instead of political pressures, market forces may influence the publication of émigré and dissident memoirs. In using them, one has to be keenly aware of the problems they pose: forgery aimed at profit and sensationalism; secondhand information in the guise of authentic evidence; and editorial intervention which may significantly affect not only the text but also the content.

Utility

With all these problems just discussed, émigré and dissident memoir literature is nonetheless an indispensable historical source. Its particular values lie precisely where Soviet memoir literature is weak: the treatment of the "blank spots" of Soviet history. Forced labor is an obvious one. There are many moving memoirs like Evgenia Ginzburg, *Krutoi marshrut,* in two volumes,[21] and a very useful bibliography is available of this kind of literature: Libushe Zorin, *Soviet Prisons and Concentration Camps. An Annotated Bibliography, 1917–1980* (Newtonville, Mass.: Oriental Research Partners, 1980), which includes publications not only in Russian and English but in other Western and Eastern European languages.[22]

Another obvious strength of émigré and dissident literature concerns the treatment of the secret police. Nearly all memoirs touch in one way or another on the terror of the police, including the Great Purges of 1936–1938.[23] The most notable are memoirs by Alexander Orlov and W. G. Krivitsky, both of whom had worked for GPU (later NKVD) and had an intimate knowledge of it.[24] This category of literature may be found in Raymond G. Rocca and John J. Dziak, with the staff of the Consortium for the Study of Intelligence, *Bibliography on Soviet Intelligence and Security Services* (Boulder-London: Westview, 1985).[25] There seem to be fewer similar memoirs on the Soviet military in the Stalin era, but Petro G. Grigorenko, *Memoirs,* tr. by Thomas P. Whitney (New York-London: W. W. Norton, 1982) is important.[26] Among memoirs by former diplomats, Alexander Barmine, *One Who Survived. The Life Story of a Russian under the Soviets,* with an introduction by Max Eastman (New York: G. P. Putnam's sons, 1945) is outstanding.

The famine of 1932–33 is also well represented in memoir literature. Even though the Soviet press has begun to discuss this tragedy owing to the *glasnost'* campaign, émigré and dissident memoir literature still remains the best source. The aforementioned memoirs by Kopelev and Kravchenko are good examples. Émigrés from the Ukraine, which was hardest hit by the famine, have compiled many eyewitness accounts, the best of which is the two volume series, *The Black Deeds of the Kremlin: A White Book,* ed. by S. O. Pidhany, vol. 1: *Book of Testimonies* (Toronto: The Ukrainian Association of Victims of Russian Communist Terror, 1953), vol. 2: *The Great Famine in Ukraine in 1932–1933* (Detroit: The Democratic Organization of Ukrainians Formerly Persecuted by the Soviet Regime in U.S.A. 1955), a serious publication with absorbing accounts. Much of the émigré and dissident literature on the famine is included in the very useful bibliography, *Famine in the Soviet Ukraine 1932–1933. A Memorial Exhibition,* Widener Library, Harvard University, prepared by Oksana Prucyk, Lenid Heretz, and James E. Mace (Cambridge, Mass.: Harvard University Press, 1986). These memoirs on the famine also provide much information about collectivization and dekulakization.

Émigré and dissident memoir literature, moreover, sheds important light on everyday life in the Stalin years: material and religious life under very hard conditions; moral degeneration in the atmosphere of mutual distrust and suspicion; complex social relations in the factories, offices, and collective farms.[27] Some émigré and dissident memoirs also provide valuable, albeit fragmentary, information on the criminal underworld, subcultures, countercultures, and informal social relations and associations.

Very few memoirs by Soviet political leaders are available. (This has much to do with the fact that few have left their memoirs in the first place.) Virtually the only memoir of this category is N. S. Khrushchev's.[28] Both the tape records and transcripts of his dictations[29] are available at Columbia University's W. Averell Harriman Institute for Advanced Study of the Soviet Union. Parts of his memoir were published in *Khrushchev Remembers,* with an introduction, commentary and notes by Edward Crankshaw, tr. and ed. by Strobe Talbott (Boston: Little Brown, 1970), and *Khrushchev Remembers. The Last Testament,* tr. and ed. by Strobe and Talbott, with a foreword by Edward Crankshaw and an introduction by Jerrald L. Schecter

(Boston-Toronto: Little Brown, 1974). (N. S. Khrushchev, *Vospominaniia. Izbran-nye otryvki,* 2 vols. [New York: Chalidze Publications, 1979–1981] contains portions not included in the English edition.) Meager though the memoirs by Soviet leaders are, there are interesting memoirs about them, notably Svetlana Allilueva (Stalin's daughter), *Twenty Letters to a Friend,* tr. by Priscilla Johnson McMillan (New York: Harper and Row, 1967), and *Only One Year,* tr. by P. Chavchavadze (London: Hutchinson, 1969).[30]

Finally, émigré and dissident memoir literature shows how some Soviet citizens came to refuse to live within the regime on its own terms. To be sure, the émigrés and dissidents are a minority, and their retrospective accounts are often heavily influenced by their exposure to Western politics and culture. Yet belief is rarely absolute, and even the decision by former true believers to break with the political regime has had something to do with what they had experienced in the Stalin years, e.g., social injustice, political terror, and hard material life. Their memoirs often reveal what alienated them from the Soviet political regime.

These are just a few topics on which émigré and dissident memoir literature may provide particularly vital information. Its utility as a historical source is far greater than is suggested here. Certainly, the information is often selective and partial. In the age of *glasnost'*, however, when Soviet memoirists are being allowed to fill in "blank spots," the utility of émigré and dissident memoir literature is perhaps greater than ever before, because it now is becoming possible to check it against Soviet memoir literature and other documents.

Conclusion

Émigré and dissident memoirs constitute an important literature. It has long been, and will be, a valuable (and sometimes only) source for many "blank spots" of Soviet history. Some of these "blank spots" are being (and more will be) filled in by Soviet publications, and some émigré and dissident memoirs are being published in the Soviet Union. (Many more will follow if the *glasnost'* campaign continues.) The publication in the Soviet Union of memoirs hitherto unpublished there, however, does not necessarily imply that they are reliable historical sources. The diversity of émigré and dissident memoirs provides amply grounds for partisan scholarship. Historians have to subject them, just like Soviet memoirs, to close scrutiny in order to use them as historical sources.

Notes

1. For example, the first 24 chapters of Nadezhda Mandelstam, *Vospominaniia* (New York: Chekhow, 1970; English ed.: *Hope against Hope,* tr. by Max Hayward [New York: Atheneum, 1970]) were published in *Iunost'*, 1988, no. 8; parts of Evgenii Gnedin (who had worked for the People's Commissariat of Foreign Affairs in the 1930s), *Katastrofa i vtoroe rozhdenie. Memuarnye zapiski* (Amsterdam: Fond im. Gertsena, 1977), and *idem., Vykhod iz Iabirinta* (New York: Chalidze Publications, 1982), in *Novyi mir*, 1988, no. 7. From Arthur Koestler's autobiography, *The Invisible Writing* (London: Hamish Hamilton, 1954), a chapter on his famous book *Darkness at Noon* was published in *Literaturnaia gazeta*, 3 August 1988.

The chapteer includes a long quotation from the equally famous memoir by a former NKVD official W. G. Krivitsky, *I Was Stalin's Agent* (London: Hamish Hamilton, 1939), which describes how the confessions of Old bolsheviks were extracted to stage the Moscow show trials.

2. A recent good example of discussion of these problems is Leo Van Rossum, "A. Antonov-Ovseenko on Stalin: Is it Reliable? A Note," *Soviet Studies*, 36:3 (July 1984), which examines A. Antonov-Ovseenko, *Portret tirana* (New York: Khronika, 1980) and its English edition, *The Time of Stalin. Portrait of a Tyranny*, tr. by George Saunders with an introduction by Stephen F. Cohen (New York: Harper & Row, 1981). See also M. Dovner, "Lubok vmesto istorii," *Pamiat'. Istoricheskii sbornik*, no. 4 (Paris: YMCA Press, 1981). The conclusions of their examinations are clear: Antonov-Ovseenko's memoir is very unreliable as a historical source.

3. Aleksandr Solzhenitsyn, *Arkhipelag Gulag*, 1918–1956, vols. 1–7 (Paris: YMCA Press, 1974–1975; English ed.: *The Gulag Archipelago*, parts 1–7, tr. by Thomas P. Whitney [New York–London: Harper & Row, 1974–1976]); Varlam Shalamov, *Kolymskie rasskazy* (London: Overseas Pubs. Ltd., 1978). Parts of the latter have recently been published in the Soviet journals *Novyi mir*, 1988 no. 6, and *Iunost'*, 1988 no. 10.

4. Lev Kopelev, *I sotvoril seve kumira* (Ann Arbor, Mich.: Ardis, 1978; English ed: *The Education of a True Believer*, tr. by Gary Kern [New York: Harper & Row, 1980]), *Khranit' vechno* (Ann Arbor, Mich.: Ardis, 1975; partial English tr.: *To be Preserved Forever*, tr. by Anthony Austin [Philadelphia–New York: Lippincott, 1977]), and *Utoli Moia pechal'* (Ann Arbor, Mich.: Ardis, 1981; English ed.: *East My Sorrows. A Memoir*, tr. by Antonina W. Bouis [New York: Random House, 1983]).

5. Anton Ciliga, *The Russian Enigma* (London: Routledge, 1938).

6. Nadezhda Mandelstam, *Vospominaniia*, and *Vtoraia Kniga* (Paris: YMCA Press, 1972; English ed. *Hope Abandoned*, tr. by Max Hayward [New York: Atheneum, 1974]), and *Kniga tret'ia* (Paris: YMCA Press, 1987).

7. See for a recent example: Robert W. Thurston, "Fear and Belief in the USSR's Great Terror; Response to Arrest, 1935–1939," Robert Conquest's response, and Thurston's rejoinder, in *Slavic Review*, 45:2 (Summer 1986).

8. J. Arch Getty, *Origins of the Great Purges. The Soviet Communist Party Reconsidered*, 1933–1938 (Cambridge–New York: Cambridge University Press, 1985), 5; and Robert Conquest, *The Great Terror. Stalin's Purge of the Thirties* (New York: Macmillan, 1968), 754. The recent publication, N. Romano-Petrovna, *Stalin's Doctor, Stalin's Nurse. A Memoir by N. Romano-Petrovna* (Princeton, N.J.: The Kingston Press, 1984), is a good example of hearsay writing. It claims to be based on notes given to the author by Dr. D. D. Pletnev, who was a private doctor of Stalin and subsequently was tried along with Bukharin and others. This secondhand story, with numerous absurd contentions, seems utterly unreliable.

9. Conquest, *The Great Terror*, 755.

10. Getty, *Origins*, 222.

11. Bertram D. Wolfe, "The Case of the Litvinov Diary. A True Literary Detective Story," *Encounter*, January 1956, 39.

12. *Ibid.*, and Maxim Litvinov, *Notes from a Journal*, with an introduction by E. H. Carr (London: Andre Deutsch, 1955), 12.

13. *The Times Literary Supplement*, 9 September 1955, 527, (unsigned). See also Wolfe, "Case," and Rudolf Schlesinger, "Litvinov's Ghost," *Soviet Studies*, 7:4 (April 1956).

14. See Carr's bibliography in *Essays in Honour of E. H. Carr*, ed. by C. Abramsky (London: Macmillan, 1974), 368. Similarly, the authenticity of *Testimony. The Memoirs of Dmitri Shostakovich as Related to and Edited by Solomon Volkov*, tr. from the Russian by Antonina W. Bouis (London: Hamish Hamilton, 1974) is contested. See Laurel Fay, "Shostakovich versus Volkov: Whose Testimony?" *The Russian Review*, October 1980.

15. Litvinov, *Notes from a Journal*, 7.

16. See, for a recent example, Kendall E. Bailes, *Technology and Society under Lenin and*

Stalin. Origins of the Soviet Technical Intelligentsia, 1917–1941 (Princeton, N.J.: Princeton University Press, 1978).

17. Quoted in *Kravchenko versus Moscow. The Report of the Famous Paris Case*, with an introduction by the Rt. Hon. Sir Travers Humphreys, P.C. (London–New York: Wingate, [1949?]), 15.

18. *Le Procés Kravchenko. Compte rendu sténografique*, 2 vols. (Paris: Editions albin Michel, 1949). there is an abridged English edition: *Kravchenko versus Moscow* (see note 17). Kravchenko subsequently wrote an account of this suit: *I Chose Justice* (London: Robert Hale, 1951).

19. *Kravchenko versus Moscow*, 63.

20. Ibid., 185–86. Emphasis in the original.

21. Evgenia Ginzburg, *Krutoi marshrut*, 2 vols. (Milan: Mondadori, 1967–1979; English eds. *Journey into the Whirlwind*, tr. by P. Stevenson and M. Hayward [New York: Harcourt, Brace and World, 1967] and *Within the Whirlwind*, tr. by Ian Boland [New York: Harcourt Brace Jovanovich, 1981]). Parts of these accounts have recently been published in *Iunost'*, 1988, no. 9.

22. Note also Mikh. Rozanov, *Solovetskii Kontslager' v monastyre. 1922–1939 gody. Fakty, domysly, "parashi." Obzor vospominanii solovchan solovchanami*, 3 vols. (Frankfurt a/m., 1979–1987). Recent publications include Oleg Volkov, *Pogruzhenie vo t'mu* (Paris: Atheneum, 1987), and Karlo Štajner, *Seven Thousand Days in Siberia* (New York: Farrar, Straus and Giroux, 1988), originally published as *7000 dana u Sibiri* (Zagreb: Globus, 1971).

23. For this, see Marshall S. Shatz, "Soviet Society and the Great Purges of the Thirties in the Mirror of Memoir Literature," *Canadian-American Slavic Studies*, 7:2 (Summer 1973), which discusses, among others, Mandelstam, Ginzburg; *The Memoirs of Ivanov-Razumnik*, tr. by P. S. Squire (London, 1965), Marie Avinov, *Pilgrimage Through Hell. An Autobiography Told by Paul Chavchavadze* (Englewood Cliffs, N.J.: Prentice-Hall, 1968); and Vladimir Petrov, *It Happens in Russia. Seven Years of Forced Labour in the Siberian Goldfields* (London: Eyre Spottiswoode, 1951).

24. Alexander Orlov, *The Secret History of Stalin's Crimes* (New York: Random House, 1953) and W. G. Krivitsky, *I Was Stalin's Agent* (London: Hamish Hamilton, 1939).

25. For memoirs dealing with the secret police from the victims' side, see, for example, A. Weissberg, *The Accused* (New York: Simon and Schuster, 1951. The British title is *Conspiracy of Silence* [1952]). Note also F. Beck and W. Godin, *Russian Purge and Extraction of Confessions*, tr. from the German by E. Mosbacher and D. Porter (New York: Viking, 1951), which is a sort of memoir-cum-monograph.

26. Note also I. Akhmedov, *In and Out of Stalin's GRU: Escape from Red Army Intelligence* (Frederick, Md.: University Publications of America, 1984).

27. The most important sources are the interviews with war refugees (see Section "Bibliography"). Publications based on them include Raymond A. Bauer, *The New Man in Soviet Psychology* (1952); *idem., Nine Soviet Portraits* (1955); George Fischer, *Soviet Opposition to Stalin. A Case Study in World War II* (1952); Joseph S. Berliner, *Factory and Manager in the USSR* (1957); and Alex Inkeles and Raymond Bauer, *The Soviet Citizen. Daily Life in a Totalitarian Society* (1959); all by Harvard University Press. *Komsomol. Sbornik statei. (Vospominaniia byvshikh komsomol'tsev)* (Munich: TsOPE, 1960; English ed. *Soviet Youth. Twelve Komsomol Histories*, ed. by N. K. Kovak–Decker [Munich: Institute for the Study of the USSR, 1959]), and *Thirteen Who Fled*, ed. by Louis Fischer (New York: Harper & Brothers, 1949) are collections of stories by war refugees. Other interesting recent publications include Valentina A. Bogdan, *Studenty pervoi piatiletki* (Buenos Aires: Nasha Strana, 1973), *idem., Mimikriia v SSSR. Vospominaniia inzhenera, 1935–1942 gody, Rostov na Donu (n.p., n.d.); Black on Red. My 44 Years Inside the Soviet Union (An Autobiography by Black American Robert Robinson with Jonathan Slevin)* (Washington, D.C.: Acropolis Books, 1988); and Suzanne Rosenberg, *A Soviet Odyssey* (Toronto–New York: Oxford University Press, 1988).

28. L. Trotsky's famous memoir, *My Life* (New York: Pathfinder, 1971), ends in 1929 when he was exiled abroad.

29. For an account of them by Nina Petrovna Khrushcheva, Khrushchev's widow, see Aleksei Adzhubei, "To desiat' let," *Znamia*, 1988, no. 7, 132–33.

30. Note also Boris Bazhanov, *Vospominaniia byvshego sekretaria Stalina* (Paris: Tret'ia Volna, 1980); Lidiia Shatunovskaia, *Zhizn' v Kremle* (New York: Chalidze Publications, 1982).

A Note on Military Sources

MARK von HAGEN

Two sets of fundamental problems confront the historian who turns to military sources for the history of the Soviet Union in the 1930s. First, at least until recently, the political elite behaved in accord with a virtual obsession regarding very broadly defined issues of national security. That obsession, which the leadership shared with a large part of Soviet society, continues to obstruct those who seek access to most materials on the military, foreign relations, or the security police. Archivists have been especially reluctant to admit foreign as well as Soviet scholars to those parts of their collections that contain materials related to military matters, though this is a phenomenon far from unique to the Soviet Union. Even large sections of general library collections and consultations with Soviet specialists in the field are often inaccessible.

The second set of difficulties that a historian of the Soviet armed forces faces can be characterized more readily as intellectual problems than political or administrative ones. First, the Civil War and Second World War, or Great Patriotic War, continue to play important roles in the legitimizing ideology of the Soviet leadership. In part because the victories in those two conflicts have proved useful in vindicating the leadership and the socialist system, but also because military historians have generally preferred to write about armies at war rather than during peacetime, Soviet bibliographers and military historians have turned nearly all their attention in recent years to these two wars and have left the intervening period of relative peace virtually unexamined. Again in part out of similar motivations and proclivities, Western historians, as a rule, have largely ignored the Civil War and focused even more narrowly on the Second World War. In particular, the wartime alliance and major contribution of the Red Army to the allied war effort have attracted several Western historians to the study of the Second World War. Finally, both Western and Soviet historians have focused on the army; they have devoted considerably less attention to other service branches, such as the Soviet navy and air force. Standard Soviet histories of the period examine the growth of the army from half a million troops in 1926 to 1,300,000 in 1939; the technological restructuring of the military during the prewar Five-Year Plans; and the victories of the Red Army over the "Chinese militarists" in the dispute over the Chinese Eastern Railway and over the "Japanese militarists" at Lake Khasan and Khalkhin-Gol. Soviet historians barely mention other important military actions, particularly the involvement of Soviet officers and advisors in the Spanish Civil War, the Soviet-Finnish War, and the occupation of territories in Eastern Poland, Rumania, and the Baltic states. Significantly, the painful subject of the purge of the Red Army received great attention during the Khrushchev years, disappeared from the pages of historians' works during the Brezhnev years, and has returned to the center of attention only since 1987. In general, the interwar years have been relegated a decidedly inferior position in the history of the armed forces. As a result, Soviet bibliographers have compiled important guides to the wars, but nothing equivalent is available for the history of the armed forces in the 1920s or 1930s.[1]

The center of historical writing on the armed forces is the Institute of Military History under the jurisdiction of the Ministry of Defense and the Academy of Sciences; its current director is Dmitrii Volkogonov. Military historians also work at the Lenin Military Party Academy in Moscow and at regional military and higher party schools.[2] To a far greater extent than is true in the West, nearly all histories of the armed forces are written by military officers. The central journal of military historians is *Voenno-istoricheskii zhurnal*, followed by *Kommunist vooruzhennykh sil*, and the major civilian historical journals.[3] For surveys of Soviet historiography, the standard work is *Ocherki sovetskoi voennoi istoriografii*, edited by P. A. Zhilin.[4] The official history of the armed forces is *150 let vooruzhennykh sil SSSR* (Moscow, 1968), which has been supplemented by *Sovetskie vooruzhennye sily* (Moscow, 1978). A good work covering only the interwar years is N. F. Kuzmin's *Na strazhe mirnogo truda, 1921-1940* (Moscow, 1959).[5] In addition to the general surveys, each service branch and supporting force (ground forces, artillery, border troops, communication, engineering, rocket forces, navy, air force, civil defense, etc.) has its own official history,[6] as does each military district.[7] Depending on the year of publication and authors' collective, these more specialized works can contain a great deal more information than the general overviews do. Another useful source of information on the military, particularly in regard to biographies and histories of smaller units, are several military encyclopedias. The most comprehensive reference work is the *Sovetskaia voennaia entsiklopediia* (1976–1980), in eight volumes and currently scheduled to be superseded by a larger and more revealing edition. Also useful is a one-volume military encyclopedic dictionary, *Voennyi entsiklopedicheskii slovar'* (Moscow, 1983). Especially good for biographical data, details of battles, unit histories, and maps are two encyclopedias devoted to the Civil War and Great Patriotic War.[8] One area of particularly intensive investigations by Soviet historians has been Party activities in the armed services, including the work of commissars and political officers, the Political Administration, and Party-military relations. In addition to some good monographs,[9] military historians have published several annotated collections of documents from the archives.[10] Finally, Soviet reference materials must be supplemented by the ample bibliographies and bibliographic essays in the works of John Erickson, Michael Parrish, and Myron J. Smith, Jr.,[11] and the available volumes of an English-language encyclopedia of Russian and Soviet military and naval affairs.[12]

In addition to official published sources and histories, some mention should be made of military and related archives. The Central State Archives of the Soviet Army (TsGASA) and Soviet Navy (TsGAVMF) contain materials from the prewar period. All later materials are housed in the Central Archive of the Ministry of Defense. Materials on the armed forces can also be found in several other central and local archives, especially the Central State Archives of the October Revolution (TsGAOR), of the National Economy (TsGANKh), of Film and Photographic Documents (TsGAKFD), and the archives of the Ministry of Foreign Affairs and the Academy of Sciences.[13] Until recently these holdings have been off limits to Western historians. Lately, however, the Main Archival Administration has announced that some of its holdings on World War II may be declassified;[14] moreover, in connection with the announced plans to build a memorial to the victims of Stalin, historians and publicists have proposed opening access to the records of victims of the purge trials as well. Whether or not these announcements indeed signal a new era for historians of the military will depend in large measure on the willingness of archivists to open their holdings and on budgetary measures to insure adequate numbers of personnel to handle the increase in researchers. Other primary materials are located in national and regional military museums.[15] From time to time, archival materials have been published in journals such as *Istoricheskii arkhiv* and *Sovetskie arkhivy*. Outside the Soviet Union, other archives hold valuable materials for historians. The most easily accessible collection remains the records of the Smolensk party organization.[16] As the national archives of major Western nations declassify their prewar and wartime holdings, many new sources are becoming available for the study of the interwar Soviet military. Recently, the British and American foreign intelligence and diplomatic reports have been declassified.[17] Western historians also have turned to the archives of France and Italy for information on diplomatic and military affairs.[18] For much of the 1930s, the best-informed intelligence service was the German, whose collection of biographical data on the Soviet officer corps is exceptionally rich.

The military press is an invaluable source, particularly for social historians of the military. Throughout the 1930s, *Krasnaia zvezda* was the central daily military newspaper. The other national newspapers were *Na strazhe*, *Boevaia podgotovka* and *Krasnyi flot*. The central officers' journal was *Voennyi vestnik*; the soldiers' popular journal was *Krasnoarmeets*. Each military district published its own newspapers and journals, often targeted for specific audiences. For example, nearly every district had a mass journal or newspaper for soldiers, one each for junior and senior officers, and another for political workers. By 1941 military districts and fleets were publishing 21 journals.[19]

Memoirs and biographies of individual commanders, even after passing the strict censors of the military publishing houses, provide many details of the everyday life of military men and women. Again, the overwhelming majority of memoirs and biographies published by Voenizdat, Politizdat, and Molodaia gvardiia (in its series *Zhizn' zamechatel'nykh liudei*) center on the Second World War, but frequently the authors devote several chapters to the prewar years. Unfortunately, no one has systematically reviewed this immense literature, but some early attempts give an idea of the riches that can be found here.[20]

Several émigrés and refugees have published their memoirs, a few as books but most in émigré newspapers and journals, which often treat military service experience. The most notable recent memoir is Petro Grigorenko's.[21] Most of the refugees leaving the Soviet Union in the past fifteen years were too young to have served in the Red Army during the 1930s. Nonetheless, any available data should be available from the Soviet Interview Project, headed by James Millar, which conducted oral history work among this group of émigrés.[22] By contrast, those refugees interviewed by the remarkable team of social scientists affiliated with the Harvard émigré project after World War II often did have recent military experience. The voluminous interview records for the Harvard project are housed in the Russian Research Center at Harvard.[23] Nearly a million Soviet soldiers were captured as prisoners-of-war and later served in the German Army. The largest group formed the Russian Army of Liberation under a former Major General in the Soviet Army, Andrei Vlasov. Several of the participants have written memoirs or published articles in émigré newspapers and journals. In addition, German Wehrmacht staff officials who played key roles in organizing the Vlasov Army and other Germans of Baltic descent have written scholarly accounts of the movement. Although the participants in the Vlasov movement were branded as traitors to the Soviet state and published anti-Soviet materials in emigration, their prewar service in the Red Army is often reflected in their attitudes toward Stalin, the Soviet state and military life.[24]

An unexpected and rich source for the social history of the Army are the letters from home, diaries, and official documents collected from the bodies of fallen Soviet soldiers during the Soviet-Finnish War of 1939–40. The former Socialist-Revolutionary V. Zenzinov discusses the value of this collection in his *Vstrecha s Rossiei: Kak i chem zhivut v Sovetskom Soiuze. Pis'ma v Krasnuiu Armiiu*, 1939–1940, which includes the texts of many letters.[25] Finally, Vera Dunham offers suggestive ideas on the use of fictional literature, in her "Troublemakers in Uniform."[26] Although Professor Dunham's paper focuses on wartime and postwar fiction, she hints that similar insights can be derived from careful readings of earlier fiction and discussions of short stories and novels in letters to the editor and in reviews in the Soviet press.

Notes

1. Some welcome exceptions to this generalization are the works of Z. P. Levashova, *Bibliografiia sovetskoi voennoi bibliografii. Sistematizirovannyi ukazatel' osnovnykh bibliograficheskikh ukazanii za 1938–1947 gg.* (Moscow, 1948); Z. P. Levashova and K. V. Sinitsyna, *Bibliografiia sovetskoi voennoi bibliografii. Sistematizirovannyi ukazatel' osnovnykh bibliograficheskikh ukazanii za 1948–1957 gg.* (Moscow, 1959); and I. V. Efebovskii, "Sovetskaia voennaia bibliografiia a 40 let," *Sovetskaia bibliografiia* 49 (1958): 3–12.

2. Many valuable dissertations are available at the Lenin Library Dissertation Division in the former Pashkov mansion.

3. See also an article on the value of professional military theoretical and scientific journals by Ivan A. Korotkov, "Voenno-nauchnye zhurnaly kak istoricheskii istochnik, *Voenno-istoricheskii zhurnal*, 1970 no. 1, 83–91.

4. (Moscow, 1974), especially chapters 1, 5, and 6.

5. For surveys of historiography, see the following articles: I. Rostunov, "Sovetskaia voennaia istoriografiia v mezhvoennyi period," *Voenno-istoricheskii zhurnal*, 1967 no. 11, 86–93; A. Grylev, "Sovetskaia voennaia istoriografiia v gody Velikoi Otechestvennoi voiny i v poslevoennyi period," *Voenno-istoricheskii zhurnal*, 1968 no. 1, 90–100; and A. Zilberman, "Na sluzhbe Sovetskikh Vooruzhennykh Sil. K 50-letiiu sovetskoi voennoi bibliografii," *Voenno-istoricheskii zhurnal*, 1967 no. 9, 102–111.

6. See, for example, *Inzhenernye voiska sovetskoi armii, 1918–1945* (Moscow, 1985).

7. Currently the Soviet Union is divided into sixteen military districts, four groups of forces abroad, and four fleets. See, for example, *Istoriia ordena Lenina Leningradskogo voennogo okruga* (Moscow, 1974); *Krasnoznamennyi Prikarpatskii* (Moscow, 1982); *Kievskii krasnoznamennyi* (Moscow, 1974).

8. *Grazhdanskaia voina i voennaia interventsiia v SSSR* (Moscow, 1983); *Velikaia otechestvennaia voina: 1941–1945* (Moscow, 1985).

9. See, for example, the works of Iu. Petrov, especially *Partiinoe stroitel'stvo v sovetskoi armii i flote (1918–1961)* (Moscow, 1964); *Stroitel'stvo politorganov, partiinykh i komsomol'skikh organizatsii armii i flota (1918–1968)* (Moscow, 1968).

10. *KPSS o vooruzhennykh silakh Sovetskogo Soiuza* (two editions, Moscow, 1958, 1969); *Partiino-politicheskaia rabota v Krasnoi Armii. Dokumenty, iiul' 1929 g.–mai 1941 g.* (Moscow, 1985); and *Vsearmeiskie soveshchaniia politrabotnikov, 1918–1940* (Moscow, 1984). The collections also include lists of documents listed in other sources or titles that indicate the contents of documents that have not made their way into any collection.

11. See "Source Materials and Bibliography," 809–48, in *The Soviet High Command: A Military-Political History, 1918–1941* (Boulder, Colo.: Westview Press, 1984), especially Erickson's discussion of the German War Documents Project, film collections, French and British documents; also "Sources and References," in *The Road to Stalingrad* (Boulder, Colo.: Westview Press, 1984); and "References and Sources," in *The Road to Berlin* (Boulder, Colo.: Westview Press, 1983); Michael Parrish, *Soviet Armed Forces. Books in English, 1950–1967* (Stanford, Cal.: Hoover Institution Press, 1970); also *The USSR in World War II. An Annotated Bibliography of Books Published in the Soviet Union, 1945–1975*, with an addendum for the years 1975–1980, intro. by John Erickson (New York: Garland Press, 1981); Myron J. Smith, Jr., *The Soviet Army, 1939–1980. A Guide to Sources in English* (Santa Barbara, Cal. and Oxford, England: ABC-Clio, Inc., 1982), especially 1–34; and the companion volumes, *The Soviet Air and Strategic Rocket Forces, 1939–1980; The Soviet Navy, 1941–78* (both published in Santa Barbara, Cal. and Oxford, England: ABC-Clio, Inc., 1980 and 1981, respectively).

12. David R. Jones, ed., *Military-Naval Encyclopedia of Russia and the Soviet Union*, planned 50 vols. (Gulf Breeze, Fla.: Academic International Press, 1978–). To date three volumes have appeared.

13. See section in Patricia Kennedy Grimsted, *Archives and Manuscript Repositories in the USSR: Moscow and Leningrad* (Princeton, 1972); and a recent article by M. V. Stegantsev, "Arkhivnye dokumenty o vooruzhennykh silakh SSSR," *Sovetskie arkhivy*, 1988 no. 1, 24–30.

14. See the announcement in *Izvestiia*, 17 July 1987.

15. A guide was prepared for the Central Museum, *Tsentral'nyi muzei vooruzhennykh sil SSSR. Putevoditel'* (Moscow, 1965).

16. The Smolensk oblast was located in the Belorussian Military District; many records in the archives pertain to military matters. See Smolensk Archives. *Records of the Smolensk Oblast of the All-Union Communist Party of the Soviet Union. 1917–1941* (Washington, D.C.: National Archives and Records Service, 1980).

17. In November 1987, the reports of the U.S. military attaches in Riga, Moscow, Tallin, and Warsaw were declassified. See also *British Documents on Foreign Affairs. Reports and Papers from the Foreign Officer Confidential Print* (available from University Publications of

America, Frederick, Md.); *British Foreign Office Files (Russian, 1883–1948)*, and *U.S. Department of State Official Records. Correspondence of the Military Intelligence Division Relating to General, Political, Economic, and Military Conditions in Russia/the Soviet Union, 1918–1941*, available from National Archives microfilm (both British and American collections distributed by Scholarly Resources, Inc., Wilmington, Del.).

18. See, for example, the two volumes by Jonathan Haslam, *Soviet Foreign Policy, 1930–1933* (London, 1983); and *The Soviet Union and the Struggle for Collective Security in Europe, 1933–39* (London, 1984); and the recent dissertation by Joseph Calvitt Clarke III on Soviet-Italian relations in the 1930s, "Italy and Russia Against Germany: The Fascist-Bolshevik Rapprochement of 1933 and 1934" (University of Maryland, 1988).

19. The best guide to the military press is I. A. Portniankin, *Sovetskaia voennaia pechat'* (Moscow, 1960), especially chapters two and three on the prewar period. See also the articles in *Sovetskaia voennaia entsiklopediia*, vol. 2, 454–56 (on newspapers) and vol. 3, 350–52 (on journals); and T. V. Sokolova, *Sovetskaia voennaia periodika. Ukazatel' zhurnalov* (Moscow, 1977).

20. Especially revealing is the collection of military memoirs edited and introduced by Seweryn Bialer, in his *Stalin and His Generals: Soviet Military Memoirs of World War II* (Boulder, Colo.: Westview Press, 1984), 15–52, 641–44. See also the section devoted to the interwar years in *Istoriia sovetskogo obshchestva v vospominaniiakh, 1917–1957* (Moscow, 1958), 235–60 and *passim*; and the Erickson works cited earlier.

21. Petro Grigorenko, *Memoirs* (New York: W. W. Norton, 1982).

22. See *Politics, Work, and Daily Life in the USSR: A Survey of Former Soviet Citizens*, edited by James Millar (New York: Cambridge University Press, 1987).

23. For more on the project, see Alex Inkeles and Raymond Bauer, *The Soviet Citizen* (New York: Atheneum, 1968), esp. 3–20.

24. The best study of the Vlasov movement in English is by George Fischer, *Soviet Opposition to Stalin: A Case Study in World War II* (Cambridge, Mass.: Harvard University Press, 1952; reprinted by Greenwood Press, 1970). Fischer's monograph is based on primary sources, newspapers, and oral testimony, all listed in a helpful bibliography. Several volumes of memoirs and testimony of participants were published by the Arkhiv Russkoi Osvoboditel'-noi Armii and Vseslavianskoe izdatel'stvo; see the works of M. V. Shatov, A. Aldan, M. Kitaev, and V. Osokin. Among the German studies, the best are: Wilfried Strik-Strikfeldt, *Against Stalin and Hitler. Memoir of the Russian Liberation Movement, 1941–1945*, translated by David Footman (New York: The John Day Company, 1970); Sven Steenberg, *Vlasov*, translated by Abe Farbstein (New York: Alfred A. Knopf, 1970; original German edition, Cologne, 1968); Juergen Thorwald, *The Illusion. Soviet Soldiers in Hitler's Armies*, translated by Richard and Clara Winston (New York and London: Harcourt Brace Jovanovich, 1975; German edition, 1974).

25. (New York, 1944). Copies of about 500 letters are in the Zenzinov papers located in the Bakhmeteff Archive at Columbia University.

26. Paper no. 22, Kennan Institute for Advanced Russian Studies, Woodrow Wilson International Center for Scholars. See also her *In Stalin's Time: Middleclass Values in Soviet Fiction* (London and New York: Cambridge University Press, 1976).

Appendix I
National, Republican, and Regional Newspapers

Compiled by
ANNE RASSWEILER and SHEILA FITZPATRICK

A. Major national newspapers

Bednota. Moscow: TsK VKP (b), 1918–1931. Agricultural newspaper. Merged with *Sotsialisticheskoe zemledelie* (see below) in February 1931.

Bezbozhnik. Moscow: Tsentr. soveta Soiuza voinstvuiushchikh bezbozhnikov SSSR, 1922–1934, 1938–1941. Organ of the Council of the Society of the Godless.

Ekonomicheskaia zhizn'. Moscow: TsK VKP (b), 1918–1941. Continuing. (Organ of publication varies. 1927–1930: STO SSSR and Ekon. sovet RSFSR; 1930 [March–November]: Nar. komissariaty SSSR—vneshn. i vnutr. torgovli, putei soobshcheniia i finansov; 1930–1931 [February]: Nar. komissariaty SSSR—snabzheniie, vneshn. torgovli, putei soobshcheniia i finansov; 1931–1932 [December]: Gosplan and Narkomfin SSSR; 1932–1941: Narkomfin SSSR, Gosbank SSSR, Prombank, Sotszembank, Tsekobank, Vsekobank, TsK Soiuza fin.-bankovskie rabotniki, etc.). From 1937–1941, title is *Finansovaia gazeta*. Main financial and banking organ.

Gudok. Moscow: Narkom putei soobshcheniia SSSR and TsK Profsoiuza rabochikh zh.-d. transporta, 1917–. Organs of publication vary slightly, including at times water transportation union, drivers' union, local transport, etc., but basically the organ of the railroads.

Izvestiia sovetov deputatov trudiashchikhsia SSSR. Moscow: TsIK and VTsIK, 1917–. The official organ of the government.

Komsomol'skaia pravda. Moscow: TsK VLKSM, 1925–. Published by the central committee of the Komsomol.

Krasnaia zvezda. Moscow: Narkom oborony SSSR (organ of publication varies: 1930–1934—Revvoensovet SSSR), 1924–1960. This is the central newspaper of the military.

Krest'ianskaia gazeta. Moscow: TsK VKP (b), 1923–1939. The official peasant newspaper. Equivalent in coverage to *Rabochaia gazeta*.

Literaturnaia gazeta. Moscow: Pravlenie Soiuza pisatelei SSSR, 1929–.

Nasha gazeta. Moscow: TsK i MGO profsoiuza Sovtorgsluzhashchikh SSSR, 1926–34. Organ of white-collar employees' trade union.

Pravda. Moscow: Tsk VKP (b)/KPSS, 1917–. Main organ of the Communist Party of the Soviet Union. Largest circulation of all newspapers in the USSR.

Rabochaia gazeta. Moscow: TsK VKP (b), 1922–1932. Official workers' newspaper, includes worker-correspondents' reports, coverage of regional and local news, and factory news. Relatively colorful and detailed.

Sotsialisticheskoe zemledelie. Moscow: Narkomzem RSFSR, Narkomzem SSSR, Kolkhoztsentr, etc. (slight variations in organ of publication), 1929–. Published under the title *Sel'skokhoziaistvennaia gazeta* (1929–Jan. 1930), *Sotsialisticheskoe zemledelie* (1930–1953). Merged with *Bednota* (above) in February 1931. Superior reporting on the countryside.

Sovetskaia torgovlia. Moscow: TsK Profsoiuza rabotnikov gos. torgovli i potreb. kooperatsii, 1926–1941, 1953–1960. Issuing institution varies. Title also varies: *Kooperativnaia zhizn'* (1926–February 1931); *Snabzhenie, kooperatsiia i torgovlia* (1931–1934).

Sovetskii sport. Moscow: Tsentr. sovet Soiuza sportivnykh obshchestv i organizatsii SSSR i VTsSPS (organ of publication varies), 1933–. Title varies: *Krasnyi sport* (1933–1946).

Stroitel'naia gazeta. Moscow: Vsesoiuz. profsoiuz stroitel. rabochikh (organ of publication varies in accordance with variations in union's title), 1924–1941, 1954–. Title varies: *Postroika* (1924–1937); *Stroitel'nyi rabochii* (1937–1939). Organ of the construction workers' trade union.

Trud. Moscow: VTsSPS, 1921–. The newspaper of the Central Council of Trade Unions. Reports on union issues, labor, industry, etc.

Uchitel'skaia gazeta. Moscow: Narkompros soiuznykh respublik and TsK profsoiuzov rabotnikov nach. i sred. shkoly RSFSR, USSR, BSSR, etc., 1924–. Slight variations in organs of publication. Title varies: *Za kommunisticheskoe prosveshchenie* (1930–1937). Coverage of education and the teaching profession.

Za industrializatsiiu. Moscow: VSNKh SSSR i RSFSR (to 1932); Narkom tiazheloi promyshlennosti (from 1932), 1921–41. Title varies: *Torgovo-promyshlennaia gazeta* (1922–December 1929); *Industriia* (1937–1940). Main industrial newspaper.

Note: See I. V. Kuznetsov and E. M. Fingerit, *Gazetnyi mir Sovetskogo Soiuza*, vol. 1 (Moscow, 1972), for a more complete listing of central newspapers. For less concise, but more complete information, see *Gazety SSSR, 1917–1960. Bibliograficheskii spravochnik*, vol. 1 (Moscow, 1970).

B. Major republican newspapers (in Russian)

Russia (RSFSR)

(see central and oblast/krai newspapers)

Ukraine

Sovetskaia Ukraina. Kiev: TsK KP (b) Ukrainy i Kievskii Kom. KP (b) Ukrainy, January 1938–. From 1938, title becomes *Pravda Ukrainy* and issuing institution varies. For more complete coverage of the prewar period, readers must rely on the Ukrainian-language newspaper, *Komunist* (published in Kiev by the TsK KP (b) Ukrainy and other Ukrainian party committees, 1918–1943).

Belorussia

Rabochii (after 1937, *Sovetskaia Belorussiia*). Minsk: TsK KP (b) Belorussii, 1927–.

Uzbekistan

Pravda Vostoka. Tashkent: Sredneaz. biuro TsK VKP (b) (to 1934), TsK KP (b) Uzbekistana, and other organs, 1917–.

Kazakhstan

Kazakhstanskaia pravda. Alma-Ata: TsK KP (b) Kazakhstana and other organs, 1923–. (*Sovetskaia step'* is title to 1932).

Georgia

Zaria Vostoka. Tbilisi: Zakavkaz. kraikom VKP (b) i TsIK ZSFSR (to 1937); TsK and Tbil. kom. KP (b) Gruzii and other organs (after 1937), 1922–.

Azerbaidzhan

Bakinskii rabochii. Baku: TsK i Bakin. kom. KP (b) Azerbaidzhana and other organs, 1917–1918, 1920–.

Kirgizia

Sovetskaia Kirgiziia. Frunze: TsK KP (b) Kirgizii i TsIK Kirg. and other organs, 1925–.

Tadzhikistan

Kommunist Tadzhikistana. Stalinabad/Dushanbe: TsK KP (b) Tadzhikistana i TsIK sovetov Tadzh. SSR and other organs, 1925–. From 1925 to 1930, title is *Sovetskii Tadzhikistan*.

Armenia

Kommunist. Erevan: TsK KP (b) Armenii, 1934–.

Turkmenia (Turkmenistan)

Turkmenskaia iskra. Ashkhabad: TsK KP (b) Turkmenistana i TsIK Turk. SSR and other organs, 1924–.

Note: See I. V. Kuznetsov and E. M. Fingerit, *Gazetnyi mir Sovetskogo Soiuza*, vol. 2 (Moscow, 1976), for further information on these newspapers and for the native language press of the union republics. For less concise, but more complete information, see *Gazety SSSR*, volume 1.

C. Selected krai and oblast newspapers (1930s titles)

Astrakhan	*Kommunist*
Barnaul	*Krasnyi Altai*
Blagoveshchensk	*Amurskaia pravda*
Briansk	*Brianskii rabochii*
Cheliabinsk	*Cheliabinskii rabochii*
Dnepropetrovsk	*Dneprovskaia pravda*
Gorkii (previously	*Gor'kovskaia kommuna*
Nizhnyi Novogorod)	(earlier, *Nizhegorodskaia kommuna*)
Iaroslavl	*Severnyi rabochii*
Irkutsk	*Vlast' truda* (later, *Vostochno-Sibirskaia pravda*)
Ivanovo	*Rabochii krai*
Kalinin (previously Tver)	*Proletarskaia pravda* (earlier, *Tverskaia pravda*)
Kazan	*Krasnaia Tatariia*
Kemerovo	*Kuzbass*
Khabarovsk	*Tikhookeanskaia zvezda*
Kirov (previously Viatka)	*Kirovskaia pravda* (earlier, *Viatskaia pravda*)
Krasnodar	*Krasnoe znamia* (later, *Bol'shevik*)
Krasnoiarsk	*Krasnoiarskii rabochii*
Kuibyshev	
(previously Samara)	*Volzhskaia kommuna* (earlier, *Kommuna*)
Kursk	*Kurskaia pravda*
Leningrad	*Krest'ianskaia pravda*
	Leningradskaia pravda
Lugansk	*Luganskaia pravda*
Makhachkala	*Krasnyi Dagestan* (later, *Dagestanskaia pravda*)
Moscow	*Rabochaia Moskva* (later, *Moskovskii bol'shevik*)
Murmansk	*Poliarnaia pravda*
Novosibirsk	*Sovetskaia sibir'*
Odessa	*Odesskaia pravda*
Omsk	*Omskaia pravda* (earlier, *Rabochii put'*)

Orel	*Orlovskaia pravda*
Penza	*Trudovaia pravda* (later, *Rabochaia Penza,* *Stalininskoe znamia*)
Perm	*Zvezda*
Petrozavodsk	*Krasnaia Kareliia*
Piatigorsk	*Severo-kavkazskii bol'shevik*
Pskov	*Pskovskaia pravda*
Rostov-on-Don	*Molot*
Saratov	*Kommunist* (later, *Saratovskii rabochii*)
Simferopol	*Krasnyi Krym*
Smolensk	*Rabochii put'*
Stalingrad	*Stalingradskaia pravda* (earlier, *Bor'ba*)
Stalino (previously	*Diktatura truda*
Iuzovka, Donetsk)	*Sotsialisticheskii Donbass*
Sverdlovsk	*Ural'skii rabochii*
Taganrog	*Krasnoe znamia*
Tambov	*Tambovskaia pravda*
Tomsk	*Krasnoe znamia*
Tula	*Kommunar*
Ufa	*Krasnaia Bashkiriia*
Vladivostok	*Krasnoe znamia*
Vologda	*Krasnyi sever*
Voronezh	*Kommuna*
Zaporozhe	*Krasnoe Zaporozh'e*

Note: See Kuznetsov and Fingerit, *Gazetnyi mir*, vol. 2, for other oblast, krai, and okrug newspapers, as well as newspapers published by other organs. See *Gazety SSSR* for complete reference information.

D. Reference works on newspapers

(i) General works

Gazety SSSR, 1917–1960. Bibliograficheskii spravochnik (Moscow, 1970–1984), 5 volumes

Volume 1 contains listings of central (All-Union, Moscow, Leningrad) and republican (capitals) newspapers. Volumes 2–4 contain listings of krai, guberniia, oblast, okrug, uezd, raion, and city level newspapers. Also included in this collection are transport and military newspapers. The following types of newspapers are not included: *mnogotirazhki* publications (e.g., factory, kolkhoz, MTS newspapers, and other "house publications"), wall newspapers, and newspapers that were printed within the pages of other newspapers and never became independent publications. This is the best guide to Soviet newspapers and relatively easy to use. Each entry in the collections gives information on newspaper titles (over time), organs of publication (over time), language of publication, and information on newspaper mergers. Entries are listed according to city of publication and cross-references are provided in case of mergers and title changes. Volume 5 contains indices of newspapers according to place of publication, non-Russian languages, and topics, as well as a very extensive bibliography of reference sources on newspapers.

Letopis' periodicheskikh izdanii SSSR (Moscow, 1933–)

An annual (and then irregularly issued serial) covering newspapers (national, republican, krai, oblast, raion, and city levels), as well as other types of serial publications. From 1954, title varies with separate issues for newspapers, journals, and scholarly serials (e.g., *Uchenye zapiski, Biulleteni, Trudy*).

Letopis' gazetnykh statei (Moscow, 1936–)

A weekly serial listing newspaper articles by subject and containing an index of authors.

Katalog gazet na russkom iazyke, khraniashchikhsia v fonde GPIB (1801–1972 gg.) (Moscow, 1972)

Section 2 contains Soviet period newspapers, giving library's holdings by years. This is a particularly important source because the GPIB is the only Moscow library where foreign scholars can obtain oblast newspapers (albeit not complete runs) without problems. In 1986, however, extensive reconstruction of the GPIB began and oblast newspapers (except current ones) became inaccessible to researchers. GPIB is not expected to resume normal operation for a number of years. INION also has some regional level newspapers, but they are limited to Moscow and Leningrad. In Leningrad, BAN is probably the best library for oblast and krai level newspapers and, in terms of coverage, perhaps superior to the GPIB. For the time being, however, the newspaper collection may be inaccessible to researchers because of the 1988 fire at the BAN library; the extent of the damage to the collection is not yet clear.

N. N. Bessonova and O. N. Nizheva, *Krupneishie gazetnye fondy nauchnykh biblio-tek strany. Annotirovannyi ukazatel'* (Moscow, 1984)

I. V. Kuznetsov and E. M. Fingerit, *Gazetnyi mir Sovetskogo Soiuza*, 2 vols. (Moscow, 1972–1976)

Volume 1 is a gem of a book, covering central newspapers from 1917–1970. Descriptions are given of each newspaper and include information on dates of publication, organs of publication, size of edition (*tirazh*), titles of different columns and regular sections, major contributors, and editorial staff. This work is written in a readable form, with index of names and index of newspapers. Volume 2 provides similar information for republic, krai, oblast, and okrug newspapers. This work is the easiest to read of all Soviet reference guides to newspapers.

(ii) Specialized works

B. P. Beliaev et al., *Leningradskaia pressa* (Leningrad, 1984)

G. V. Bulatskii, *Pechat' Belorussii v period zaversheniia sotsialisticheskoi rekonstruktsiia, 1933–1937* (Minsk, 1960)

A. P. Khomskii and P. S. Chekhovskoi, *Gazety i zhurnaly SSSR. Spravochnik na 1929 g. o vsekh periodicheskikh izdaniiakh vykhodiashchikh v SSSR* (Moscow, 1929)

A. P. Kupaigorodskaia, "Mnogotirazhnye fabrichno-zavodskie gazety kak istochnik po istorii rabochego klassa. (Na materialakh Leningradskoi pechati)," *Istoriia rabochego klassa Leningrada. Sbornik statei*, vyp. 1 (Leningrad, 1962). Contains information on factory newspapers: titles, numbers of issues per year, content description.

I. V. Kuznetsov and A. Shumokov, *Partiino-sovetskaia pechat' Moskvy (1917–1945)* (Moscow, 1980)

B. Muravych, *Gazety zavodiv y borot'bi za tekhniku* (Kharkov, 1932). General descriptions with excerpts from certain newspapers.

Pechat' Chuvashkoi ASSR (Cheboksary, 1957)

Pechat' sovetskogo Uzbekistana (Tashkent, 1967)

Pechat' Tadzhikskoi SSR, 1928–1958 (Stalinabad, 1959)

Pechat' Turkmenskoi SSR, 1927–1956 (Ashkhabad, 1957)

L. S. Popov, *Pechat' na industrial'nom fronte* (Cheliabinsk, 1975). Historical account of the local press, featuring documents concerning the goals and use of local newspapers. Two other collections of documents on the press, although general in content, are also worth noting: O partiinoi i sovetskoi pechati. Sbornik dokumentov (Moscow, 1954); and *O partiinoi i sovetskoi pechati, radioveshchanii i televidenii. Sbornik dokumentov* (Moscow, 1972).

Anton S. Romanov, *Pechat' Kalmykii 20-kh godov* (Elista, 1971)

M. D. Slanskaia, "K istorii vozniknoveniia mnogotirazhnykh gazet na zavodakh i stroikakh sovetskoi strany (1922–1932)," *Vestnik MGU*, Seriia 11: Zhurnalistika. No. 5 (1971). Lists titles of factory and *stroika* newspapers, size of editions, history of their publication.

G. V. Zhirkov, *Sovetskaia krest'ianskaia pechat'—odin iz tipov sotsialisticheskoi pressy* (Leningrad, 1984). Excellent history and guide to central, regional, and local rural press.

Z. K. Zvezdin, "Periodicheskaia pechat' kak istochnik po istorii trudovogo pod"ema rabochego klassa SSSR 1926–1929 godov," *Problemy istochnikovedeniia*, vyp. VIII (Moscow, 1959). Useful analysis of the press as a source of labor history. Information on factory level newspapers is included.

Note: The Union Republics generally publish their own guides to the press and to newspaper articles. These are titled: *Letopis' pechati* . . . and *Letopis' gazetnykh statei* . . . , followed by the name of the republic.

E. Locations of newspaper holdings

(i) US locations

P. Horecky, *Russian, Ukrainian, and Belorussian Newspapers, 1917–1953. A Union List* (Washington, D.C.: Library of Congress, 1953). Incomplete, dated, but still useful.

Harold M. Leich, *Checklist of Slavic and East European Newspapers. University of Illinois Library*, typewritten ms. (Urbana, Ill.: University of Illinois, 1978). This book includes few titles for the prewar Stalin period but it is worth checking with the library as it is constantly acquiring new material.

K. Maichel, *Soviet and Russian Newspapers at the Hoover Institution. A Catolog* (Stanford: Hoover Institution, 1966)

K. Maichel and M. Schatoff, *A List of Russian Newspapers in the Columbia University Libraries* (New York: Columbia University Libraries, 1959)

Newspapers on Microfilm (Washington, D.C.: Library of Congress, continuing publication)

(ii) British and European locations

P. Bruhn, *Gesamtverzeichnis russischer und sowjetischer Periodika und Serienwerke in Bibliotheken der Bundesrepublik Deutschland und West-Berlins*, 4 vols. (Wiesbaden: Harrassowitz, 1962–1976)

Catalogue collectif des périodiques conservés dans les bibliothèques de Paris et dans les bibliothèques universitaires de France: périodiques slaves en caractères cyrilliques. Etats des collections en 1950, 2 volumes and supplements (Paris: Bibliothèque Nationale, 1956)

Russian Periodicals in the Helsinki Library (Washington, D.C.: Library of Congress, 1958). Also records holdings of Library of Congress, New York Public Library, and Harvard College Library. Note, however, that the holdings of this collection are generally the strongest in the pre–1917 period.

Russian Serials and Newspapers Held in Helsinki University Library (New York: New York Public Library, 1986)

J. D. Stewart, *British Union Catalogue of Periodicals. A Record of the Periodicals of the World from the Seventeenth Century to the Present Day in British Libraries* (London: Butterworth, 1955–1962). Annual supplements, 1968–.

Appendix II

Stenographic Reports of
Party, Soviet, and Other Meetings
(Congresses, Conferences, Plenums, *Soveshchaniia*)

Compiled by SHEILA FITZPATRICK

A. Party congresses, conferences, and plenums

1. Central congresses (complete list, 1927–1941)

XV s"ezd Vsesoiuznoi Kommunisticheskoi Partii (bol'shevikov). Stenograficheskii otchet (Moscow, 2nd ed., 1928)

XVI konferentsiia Vsesoiuznoi Kommunisticheskoi Partii (bol'shevikov). Stenograficheskii otchet (Moscow, 1929)

XVI s"ezd Vsesoiuznoi Kommunisticheskoi Partii (bol'shevikov). Stenograficheskii otchet (Moscow, 2nd ed., 1931). Later edition: *XVI s"ezd VKP(b). 26 iiunia–13 iiulia 1930 g. Stenograficheskii otchet*, 2 parts (Moscow, 1935).

XVII konferentsiia Vsesoiuznoi Kommunisticheskoi Partii (bol'shevikov). Stenograficheskii otchet (Moscow, 1932)

XVII s"ezd Vsesoiuznoi Kommunisticheskoi Partii (bol'shevikov), 26 ianv.–10 fev. 1934 g. Stenograficheskii otchet (Moscow, 1934)

XVIII s"ezd Vsesoiuznoi Kommunisticheskoi Partii (bol'shevikov), 10–21 marta 1939 g. Stenograficheskii otchet (Leningrad, 1939)

XVIII konferentsiia VKP(b), 15—20 fevralia 1941 g. No stenographic report was published in book form. However, a large part of the proceedings appeared in the form of verbatim reports in *Pravda*, 18–24 February 1941.

Note: In the early 1960s, the Institut Marksizma-Leninizma pri TsK KPSS began republication of all protocols and stenographic reports of party congresses and conferences, but this project was not completed. For the period 1927–41, the only volumes published were:

Piatnadtsatyi s"ezd VKP(b), dekabr' 1927 g. Stenograficheskii otchet, 2 vols. (Moscow, 1961–62)

Shestnadtsataia konferentsiia VKP(b), aprel' 1929 g. Stenograficheskii otchet
(Moscow, 1962)

2. Republican congresses

Ukraine

*Desiatii z"izd komunistichnoi partii (bil'shovikiv) Ukraini 20–29 listopada 1927
r. Stenograficheskii zvit* (Kharkov, 1928). Despite Ukrainian title, most speeches are
published in Russian.
*XI z"izd komunistichnoi partii (bil'shovikiv) Ukraini (5–15 chervnia 1930 roku).
Stenograficheskii zvit* (Kharkov, 1930). Many but not all speeches in Russian.
*XII z"izd Komunistichnoi partii (bil'shovikiv) Ukraini 18–23 sichnia 1934 r.
Stenografichnii zvit* (Kharkov, 1934). In Ukrainian.

Transcaucasus/Georgia

VII s"ezd kommunisticheskikh organizatsii Zakavkaz'ia. Stenograficheskii otchet
(Tiflis, 1934). In Russian.
*IX s"ezd Kommunisticheskoi Partii (b) Gruzii, 10 ianvaria–14 ianvaria 1934 g.
Stenograficheskii otchet* (Tiflis, 1935). In Russian.
*XI s"ezd Kommunisticheskaia Partiia (bol'shevikov) Gruzii. Stenograficheskii
otchet* (Tbilisi, 1938). In Russian.

3. Conferences of regional (krai and oblast) party committees and control commissions

Far East

*IX Dal'ne-vostochnaia kraevaia partiinaia konferentsiia. Stenograficheskii ot-
chet. 22 fevralia–1 marta* (Khabarovsk, 1929)

Kalinin oblast

Pervaia Kalininskaia oblastnaia konferentsiia VKP(b) [1935]. *Stenograficheskii
otchet* (Kalinin, 1936)

Kazakhstan

*6-aia Vsekazakskaia konferentsiia VKP(b), 15–23 noiabria 1927 g.
Stenograficheskii otchet* (Kzyl-Orda, 1927)
*Shestoi plenum Kazakskogo kraevogo komiteta VKP(b), 10–16 iiulia 1933 goda.
Stenograficheskii otchet* (Alma-Ata-Moscow, 1936)
*VIII Kazakhstanskaia kraevaia konferentsiia VKP(b), 8–16 ianvaria 1934 g.
Stenograficheskii otchet* (Alma-Ata, 1935)

Leningrad oblast (gubernia)

XXIV-aia Leningradskaia gubernskaia konferentsiia VKP(b). Stenograficheskii otchet i rezoliutsii (Leningrad, 1927)

Stenograficheskii otchet pervoi Leningradskoi oblastnoi konferentsii VKP(b), 15–19 noiabria 1927 g. (Leningrad, 1927)

Tret'ia Leningradskaia oblastnaia konferentsiia VKP(b). 5 iiunia–12 iiunia 1930 g. (Leningrad, 1930)

Biulleten' ob"edinennoi V oblastnoi i III gorodskoi Leningradskoi konferentsii VKP(b) (Leningrad, 1934)

Moscow oblast (gubernia)

XVI Moskovskaia gubernskaia konferentsiia VKP(b). Stenograficheskii otchet. 20–28 noiabria [1927] (Moscow, 1928). *Note:* Available at Library of Congress.

Vtoroi plenum M[oskovskogo K[omiteta] VKP(b) 31 ianvaria–2 fevralia. Doklady i rezoliutsii (Moscow, 1928). *Note:* This is a numbered edition, marked "Tol'ko dlia chlenov VKP(b)." Available at INION.

Pervaia Moskovskaia oblastnaia konferentsiia Vsesoiuznoi Kommunisticheskoi Partii (bol'shevikov). Stenograficheskii otchet (Moscow, September 1929). *Note:* Marked "Tol'ko dlia chlenov VKP(b)." Available at INION.

Ianvarskii ob"edinennyi plenum M[oskovskogo] K[omiteta] i M[oskovskoi] K[ontrol'noi] K[omissii], 6–10 ianvaria 1930 g. (Moscow, 1930). *Note:* Numbered copy, marked "Sekretno." Available in INION.

III-ia Moskovskaia oblastnaia i II-ia gorodskaia konferentsiia VKP(b). Biulleteni 1–13 (Moscow, 1932)

Chetvertaia Moskovskaia oblastnaia konferentsiia Vsesoiuznoi Kommunisticheskoi Partii (bol'shevikov) (Moscow, 1934)

Northern krai

Pervaia severnaia kraevaia partiinaia konferentsiia. Stenograficheskii otchet. 14–19 avgusta 1929 g. (Arkhangelsk, 1929)

Siberia

III Sibirskaia kraevaia partiinaia konferentsiia 25–30 marta 1927 goda. Stenograficheskii otchet (Novosibirsk, 1927)

Plenum Sibirskogo Kraevogo Komiteta VKP(b), 3–7 marta 1928 goda. Stenograficheskii otchet (Novosibirsk, 1928). *Note:* Marked "Khranit' na pravakh rukopisi." Only Vyp. 1 available at INION.

Chetvertaia Sibirskaia kraevaia konferentsiia Vsesoiuznoi Kommunisticheskoi Partii (bol'shevikov). Stenograficheskii otchet (Novosibirsk, 1929). *Note:* Marked "Tol'ko dlia chlenov VKP(b)." Only Vyp. 2 available at INION.

Chetvertaia Sibirskaia kraevaia konferentsiia V.K.P. (b.). Stenograficheskii otchet (Novosibirsk, 1929)

Pervaia Vostochno-Sibirskoi kraevoi konferentsiia, Irkutsk, 1931. Stenograficheskii otchet (Irkutsk, 1931)

Tataria

Oblastnoi Komitet VKP(b) A[vtonomnoi] T[atarskoi] SSR. Stenograficheskii otchet XV oblastnoi partiinoi konferentsii (5–15 iiunia 1930 g.) (Kazan, 1930)

XVI Tatarskaia oblastnaia konferentsiia. Stenograficheskii otchet (Kazan, 1932)

Ob"edinennyi plenum [Tatarskogo] OK i OKK VKP(b) (19–23 fevralia 1933 g.) Stenograficheskii otchet (Kazan, 1933)

Tiflis

Pervaia Tiflisskaia obshchegorodskaia konferentsiia nizovykh partzven'ev. Stenograficheskii otchet (Tiflis, 1932)

Transcaucasus

III plenum zakavkazskoi kraevoi kontrol'noi komissii VKP(b), 30 sent.–1 okt. 1926 g. Stenograficheskii otchet (Tiflis, 1926)

Urals

Ural'skii oblastnoi komitet VKP(b). Stenograficheskii otchet VIII oblastnoi partiinoi konferentsii (Sverdlovsk, 1927)

IX Ural'skaia oblastnaia partiinaia konferentsiia: Biulleteni 1–6 (Sverdlovsk, 1929). *Note:* Marked "Ne podlezhit oglasheniiu. Tol'ko dlia chlenov partii." Available at INION.

X Ural'skaia oblastnaia konferentsiia Vsesoiuznoi Kommunisticheskoi Partii (bol'shevikov). Biulleteni 1–21 (Sverdlovsk, 1930). *Note:* Marked "Tol'ko dlia chlenov VKP(b)." Available at INION.

XI Ural'skaia oblastnaia konferentsiia VKP(b). Stenograficheskii otchet 23–30 ianvaria 1932 g. (Sverdlovsk-Moscow, 1932)

Voronezh

Vtoraia Voronezhskaia gorodskaia konferentsiia. Stenograficheskii otchet (Voronezh, 1934)

Western oblast

Stenograficheskii otchet 2-oi oblastnoi partkonferentsii [Zapadnoi oblasti], 5–12 iiulia 1930 g. (Smolensk, 1931)

B. Soviet congresses and sessions of soviet executive committees

1. Central

i. All-Union Congresses of Soviets (complete list, 1929–39)

V [Vsesoiuznyi] s"ezd sovetov. 20–28 maia 1929 g. Stenograficheskii otchet (Moscow, 1929)

VI [Vsesoiuznyi] s"ezd sovetov. Stenograficheskii otchet (Moscow, 1931). 8–17 March 1931.

VII [Vsesoiuznyi] s"ezd sovetov. Stenograficheskii otchet (Moscow, 1935). 28 January–6 February 1935.

Chrezvychainyi VIII s"ezd sovetov. Stenograficheskii otchet (Moscow, 1937). November 1936.

ii. Sessions of the Central Executive Committee (TsIK) of the USSR/Supreme Soviet of the USSR

Pervaia sessiia Tsentral'nogo Ispolnitel'nogo Komiteta Soiuza SSR 5 sozyva. [19 maia 1929 g.] Stenograficheskii otchet i postanovleniia (Moscow, 1929)

Tret'ia sessiia Tsentral'nogo Ispolnitel'nogo Komiteta Soiuza SSR 5-go sozyva. [4–12 ianvaria 1931 g.] Stenograficheskii otchet (Moscow 1931)

[Vtoraia] Sessiia TsIK Soiuza SSR 6 sozyva. Stenograficheskii otchet i postanovleniia 22–28 dekabria 1931 g. (Moscow, 1931)

Tret'ia sessiia Tsentel'nogo Ispolnitel'nogo Komiteta Soiuza SSR 6-go sozyva. Stenograficheskii otchet, 23–30 ianvaria 1933 g. (Moscow, 1933)

Chetvertaia sessiia Tsentral'nogo Ispolnitel'nogo Komiteta Soiuza SSR 6 sozyva. Stenograficheskii otchet, 28 dekabria 1933 g.–4 ianvaria 1934 g. (Moscow, 1934)

Vtoraia sessiia Tsentral'nogo Ispolnitel'nogo Komiteta Soiuza SSR 7 sozyva. Stenograficheskii otchet [10–17 ianvaria 1936 g.] (Moscow, 1936)

Pervaia sessiia Verkhovnogo Soveta 12–19 ianvaria 1938 g. Stenograficheskii otchet ([Moscow], 1938)

Vtoraia sessiia Verkhovnogo Soveta SSSR. 12–21 avgusta 1938 g. Stenograficheskii otchet (Moscow, 1938)

Tret'ia sessiia Verkhovnogo Soveta Soiuza. 25–31 maia 1939 g. Stenograficheskii otchet (Moscow, 1939)

Vneocherednaia chetvertaia sessiia Verkhovnogo Soveta 28 avgusta–1 sentiabria 1939 g. Stenograficheskii otchet ([Moscow], 1939)

2. Republican (RSFSR)

XIV Vserossiiskii s"ezd sovetov. Stenograficheskii otchet (Moscow, 1929)

XV Vserossiiskii s"ezdov sovetov. Stenograficheskii otchet (Moscow, 1931)

XVI Vserossiiskii s"ezd sovetov. Stenograficheskii otchet (Moscow, 1935)
Chrezvychainyi XVII s"ezd sovetov (Moscow, 1937)

Note: A similar series of stenographic reports of congresses of Ukrainian soviets
was published in Ukrainian. For details on the congresses of the Ukraine, as well as
those of other republics and autonomous republics, krais, oblasts, and autonomous
oblasts, see *S"ezdy Sovetov Soiuza SSR, soiuznykh i avtonomnykh sovetskikh
sotsialisticheskikh respublik. Sbornik dokumentov*, 7 vols. (Moscow, 1959–65).

C. Other congresses, conferences, and meetings

1. Komsomol

VIII Vsesoiuznyi s"ezd VLKSM, 5–16 maia 1928 g. Stenograficheskii otchet
(Moscow, 1928)
*VI Vsesoiuznaia konferentsiia VLKSM. 17–24 iiunia 1929 goda. Stenografiche-
skii otchet* (Moscow, 1929)
IX Vsesoiuznyi s"ezd VLKSM. Ianvar' 1931 g. Stenograficheskii otchet (Moscow,
1931)
*VII Vsesoiuznaia konferentsiia VLKSM. Stenograficheskii otchet 1–8 iiulia 1932
g.* (Moscow, 1933)
*Desiatyi s"ezd Vsesoiuznogo Leninskogo Kommunisticheskogo Soiuza Molo-
dezhi. 11–21 aprelia 1936 goda. Stenograficheskii otchet, 2 vols.* (Moscow, 1936)

Note: For detailed reports of proceedings of plenums of the Komsomol Central
Committee throughout the 1930s, see *Komsomol'skaia pravda*.

2. Trade unions

*Vos'moi [vsesoiuznyi] s"ezd professional'nykh soiuzov SSSR. 10–24 dekabria
1928 g. Polnyi stenograficheskii otchet* (Moscow, 1929)
Deviatyi Vsesoiuznyi s'ezd profsoiuzov SSSR. Stenograficheskii otchet (Moscow,
1933)

Note: No central congresses of trade unions were held in the years 1933–41. For
detailed reports of plenums of the Central Council of Trade Unions (VTsSPS), see
Trud.

3. Administrators and managers

*Vtoroi Vserossiiskii s"ezd administrativnykh rabotnikov 23–30 aprelia 1928
goda. Sokrashchennaia stenogramma* (Moscow, 1929). [Officials from NKVD penal system.]
1-aia Vsesoiuznaia konferentsiia rabotnikov sotsialisticheskoi promyshlennosti.

Stenograficheskii otchet s 30 ianvaria po 5 fevralia 1931 g. (Moscow-Leningrad, 1931)

Soveshchanie khoziaistvennikov, inzhenerov, tekhnikov, partiinykh i profsoiuznykh rabotnikov tiazheloi promyshlennosti 20–22 sentiabria 1934 g. Stenograficheskii otchet (Moscow-Leningrad, 1935)

Soveshchanie po voprosam stroitel'stva v TsK VKP(b) ([Moscow], 1936)

Soveshchanie khoziaistvennykh rabotnikov sistemy Glavsel'morputi pri SNK SSSR. 13–15 ianvaria 1936 g. Stenograficheskii otchet (Leningrad, 1936)

Sovet pri Narodnym Komissare Tiazheloi Promyshlennosti SSSR, 25–29 iiunia 1936 g. Stenograficheskii otchet (Moscow, 1936)

4. Workers and Stakhanovites

Vsesoiuznoe soveshchanie rabochikh i rabotnits stakhanovtsev promyshlennosti i transporta. [14–17 noiabria 1935 g.] Stenograficheskii otchet (Moscow, 1935)

Pervyi vsedonetskii slet stakhanovtsev-materov uglia 7–10 ianvaria 1936 g. Stalino. Stenograficheskii otchet (Kiev, 1936)

Soveshchanie peredovikov po l'nu i konople s rukovoditeliami partii i pravitel'stva (Moscow, 1936)

Soveshchanie molodykh stakhanovtsev v TsK VLKSM, 4–7 ianv. 1938 g. (Moscow, 1938)

5. Kolkhoz cadres and kolkhozniki

Kolkhozy. Pervyi Vsesoiuznyi s"ezd kolkhozov (1–6 iiunia 1928 g.) (Moscow, 1929)

Pervyi Vsesoiuznyi s"ezd kolkhoznikov-udarnikov peredovykh kolkhozov, 15–19 fevralia 1933 goda. Stenograficheskii otchet (Moscow, 1933)

Vtoroi Vsesoiuznyi s"ezd kolkhoznikov-udarnikov, 11–17 fevralia 1935 g.: Stenograficheskii otchet (Moscow, 1935)

6. Cultural and professional groups

B. Olkhovyi, ed., *Zadachi agitatsii, propagandy i kul'turnogo stroitel'stva. Materialy agitpropsoveshchaniia pri TsK VKP(b) mai–iiun' 1928 g.* (Moscow-Leningrad, 1928). Stenographic report, resolutions, theses.

Sistema narodnogo obrazovaniia v rekonstruktivyi period. Soveshchanie Obshchestvo pedagogov-marksistov 7/II–16/III [1930 g.] (Moscow, 1930)

Trudy pervoi vsesoiuznoi konferentsii agrarnikov-marksistov, vol. 1 (Moscow, 1930)

Vtoroe vsesoiuznoe partiinoe soveshchanie po narodnomu obrazovaniiu (aprel' 1930 g.). Stenograficheskii otchet (Moscow, 1931)

Pervyi Vsesoiuznyi s"ezd sovetskikh pisatelei, 1934. Stenograficheskii otchet (Moscow, 1934)

Rezhisser v sovetskom teatre: Materialy pervoi Vsesoiuznoi konferentsii (Moscow-Leningrad, 1940). Abridged stenographic report.

7. Women's groups

Zhenshchina i byt. Materialy po rabote sredi zhenshchin v klube, krasnom ugolke, obshchezhittii, zhenkruzhke i pr. (Moscow, 1926)

Vsesoiuznyi s"ezd rabotnits i krest'ianok, chlenov sel'skikh i gorodskikh sovetov i volostnykh (raionnykh) ispolnitel'nykh komitetov, 10–16 oktiabria 1927 g. Stenograficheskii otchet (Moscow, 1927)

Vsesoiuznoe soveshchanie otvetstvennykh sekretarei komissii uluchsheniiu truda i byta zhenshchin. Oktiabr' 1929 g. (Moscow, 1930)

Zhenshchina v kolkhozakh—bol'shaia sila. Oblastnoi s"ezd kolkhoznits-udarnits TsChO 6–12 dek. 1933 g. (Voronezh, 1934)

Vsesoiuznoe soveshchanie zhen khoziaistvennikov i inzhenerno-tekhnicheskikh rabotnikov tiazheloi promyshlennosti. Stenograficheskii otchet (Moscow, 1936)

Vsesoiuznoe soveshchaniie zhen komandnogo i nachal'stvuiushchego sostava RKKA. 20–23 dekabria 1936 g. Stenograficheskii otchet (Moscow, 1937)

Index

Agriculture, 85, 155, 157, 164, 234, 237

Archeographic Commission of the Academy of Sciences, 42

Archival arrangement, 33
  delo, 35, 67, n79
  edinitsa khraneniia, n79
  fond, 34, 67, n79
  list, 35, n79
  opis', 35, 67, n79

Archival directory (*spravochnik*), 36, 67, 149–150

Archival documents
  accounting records, 72
  administrative acts, 146–147, 150–151
  administrative or directional documentation, 71
  appraisal of, 31, 121
  control or verification documents, 72
  diplomatic correspondence, 71
  organizational documentation, 70
  planning documents, 72
  reporting/accounting material, 72
  routine correspondence, 71
  statistical documents, 73

Archival guide (*putevoditel'*), 38, 67, 132

Archives
  access
    city directories, 202
    Communist Party archives, 5, 52–53
    difficulties in, 5, 18, 65–66, 70, 78–79, n187
    easing of restrictions, n168
    industrialization material, 132
    inventories, 36
    military sources, 266
    state archives, 47–48
  AF KPSS (Archival Fond of the Communist Party), 28

Archives (*continued*)
  Central Council of Trade Unions, Central Archive, 45
  GAF (*Gosudarstvennyi arkhivnyi fond*), 27–29
  Glavarkhiv (*Glavnoe arkhivnoe upravlenie*), 28–33, 36–38, 40–43, 49, 66, 74, 105, 132, 216
  LOGAV (*Leningradskii oblastnoi gosudarstvennyi arkhiv v g. Vyborge*), 51
  Tsentral'nyi Arkhiv VLKSM (Central Archive of the Komsomol), 53
  TsGA RSFSR (*Tsentral'nyi gosudarstvennyi arkhiv RSFSR*), 37, 44, 46, 48–49
  TsGAKFD SSSR (*Tsentral'nyi gosudarstvennyi arkhiv kinofotodokumentov SSSR*), 47, 268
  TsGAKFFD g. Moskvy (*Tsentral'nyi gosudarstvennyi arkhiv kinofotofonodokumentov g. Moskvy*), 50
  TsGAKFFDL (*Tsentral'nyi gosudarstvennyi arkhiv kinofotofonodokumentov Leningrada*), 52
  TsGALI SSSR (*Tsentral'nyi gosudarstvennyi arkhiv literatury i iskusstva SSSR*), 48
  TsGALIL (*Tsentral'nyi gosudarstvennyi arkhiv literatury i iskusstva Leningrada*), 51
  TsGAMO (*Tsentral'nyi gosudarstvennyi arkhiv Moskovskoi oblasti*), 49
  TsGANKh SSSR (*Tsentral'nyi gosudarstvennyi arkhiv narodnogo khoziaistva SSSR*), 20, 43–47, 97, 136, 216, 268
  TsGANTDL (*Tsentral'nyi gosudarstvennyi arkhiv nauchno-tekhnicheskii dokumentatsii Leningrada*), 46, 52
  TsGAOR g. Moskvy (*Tsentral'nyi gosu-*

Notes on the Contributors

A. B. BEZBORODOV is a *dotsent* at the Moscow State Archival-Historical Institute. He is a specialist on Soviet social history.

VLADIMIR ZINOVEVICH DROBIZHEV, a Doctor of Historical Sciences and a specialist on Soviet social history, held the chair in Soviet history at the Moscow State Historical-Archival Institute until his death in the summer of 1989.

SHEILA FITZPATRICK is Radkey Professor of History at the University of Texas at Austin. Her books include *Education and Social Mobility in the Soviet Union, 1921–1934* (Cambridge and New York, 1979) and *The Russian Revolution* (Oxford and New York, 1983). She is currently working on a book on the peasantry in the 1930s.

J. ARCH GETTY is Associate Professor of History at the University of California at Riverside and Co-Director with William J. Chase of the Soviet Data Bank project. He is the author of *The Origins of the Great Purges: The Soviet Communist Party Reconsidered, 1933–1938* (Cambridge, 1985), and is currently working with co-author Gabor Rittersporn on a book on politics and society in the 1930s.

PATRICIA KENNEDY GRIMSTED is a Fellow at the Ukrainian Research Center at Harvard. She is the author of a number of books on Soviet archives including *A Handbook for Archival Research in the USSR* (Washington, D.C., 1989).

MARK VON HAGEN is Assistant Professor of History at Columbia University. He is the author of the forthcoming book *Soldiers in the Proletarian Dictatorship: The Red Army and the Soviet Socialist State, 1917–1930*.

HIROAKI KUROMIYA is a Junior Fellow at King's College, Cambridge. He is the author of *Stalin's Industrial Revolution: Politics and Workers, 1928–1932* (New York and Cambridge, 1988).

EFIM IOSIFOVICH PIVOVAR is a professor of Soviet history at the Moscow State Historical-Archival Institute and a Doctor of Historical Sciences. His field is Soviet social history.

ANNE RASSWEILER is the author of *The Generation of Power: The History of Dneprostroi* (New York and Oxford, 1988). She is currently engaged in research on women in Soviet Siberia.

LEWIS SIEGELBAUM is Associate Professor of History at Michigan State University. His most recent book is *Stakhanovism and the Politics of Productivity in the USSR, 1935–1941* (New York and Cambridge, 1988).

ANDREI KONSTANTINOVICH SOKOLOV is a professor and department chairman at the Institute of History of the USSR of the Academy of Sciences, and a Doctor of Historical Sciences. He specializes in the study of sources on Soviet social history.

PETER H. SOLOMON, Jr., is Professor of Political Economy at the University of Toronto. He is author of *Soviet Criminologists and Criminal Policy: Specialists in Policy-Making* (New York, 1978), and is currently working on a book on the administration of Soviet justice in the 1930s.

LYNNE VIOLA is Associate Professor of History at the University of Toronto and author of *The Best Sons of the Fatherland: Workers in the Vanguard of Soviet Collectivization* (New York and Oxford, 1987). She is currently working on a book on peasant resistance to the state in the 1920s and 1930s.

S. G. WHEATCROFT is Senior Lecturer in History at the University of Melbourne, Australia. He is the author of many studies of Soviet demographic and economic history in the 1920s and 1930s.